CONSUMER BANKRUPTCY IN GLOBAL PERSPECTIVE

Consumer Bankruptcy and over-indebtedness is an emerging field throughout the world. This book provides a comparative appraisal of global developments in this area. It is one of the first book length publications focusing on comparative consumer bankruptcy and over-indebtedness. It combines theoretical and empirical studies of bankruptcy regimes and consumer credit in civilian and common law jurisdictions as well as exploring current reform trends. The book will be of interest to academics, policymakers and law reformers as well as to practitioners.

Consumer Bankruptcy in Global Perspective

Edited by
JOHANNA NIEMI-KIESILÄINEN,
IAIN RAMSAY
and
WILLIAM WHITFORD

·HART·
PUBLISHING
OXFORD AND PORTLAND, OREGON
2003

Published in North America (US and Canada) by
Hart Publishing
c/o International Specialized Book Services
5804 NE Hassalo Street
Portland, Oregon
97213–3644
USA

Hart Publishing is a specialist legal publisher based in Oxford, England. To order further copies of this book or to request a list of other publications please write to:

Hart Publishing, Salters Boatyard, Folly Bridge, Abingdon Rd, Oxford, OX1 4LB Telephone: +44 (0)1865 245533 Fax: +44 (0) 1865 794882
email: mail@hartpub.co.uk
WEBSITE: http//:www.hartpub.co.uk

British Library Cataloguing in Publication Data
Data Available
ISBN 1–84113–358–2 (hardback)

Typeset by Hope Services, Abingdon Ltd
Printed and bound in Great Britain by
Biddles Ltd, *www.biddles.co.uk*

Contents

Acknowledgments

The editors would like to thank the Law and Society Association which through its Collaborative Research Network programme facilitated the intellectual exchanges that resulted in this book. We are grateful for the financial support provided through this programme as well as for the stimulating intellectual and collegial environment of Law and Society Association meetings. The editors would also like to thank Merel Veldhuis and Amanda Benchimol (Osgoode Hall Law School, 2004) for excellent assistance in editing the essays and Hart Publishing for their efficient production. Iain Ramsay thanks the Social Sciences and Humanities Research Council of Canada for financial support of his comparative research on consumer bankruptcy which aided in the production of this book.

Johanna Niemi-Kiesiläinen
Iain Ramsay
William C Whitford
Helsinki, Toronto and Madison July 2003

List of Contributors

Charles D Booth Associate Professor, Faculty of Law, University of Hong Kong; Director of the Asian Institute of International Financial Law

Jean Braucher Roger Henderson Professor of Law, University of Arizona, James E Rogers College of Law

John Duns Associate Professor, Faculty of Law, Monash University, Melbourne

Rafael Efrat Assistant Professor of Business Law, California State University, Northridge

Catarina Frade Assistant Professor, Faculty of Economics, University of Coimbra

Karen Gross Professor of Law, New York Law School

Nick Huls Professor of Socio-Legal Studies, Erasmus University Rotterdam and University of Leyden

Melissa B Jacoby Associate Professor of Law, Temple University School of Law, Philadelphia, Pennsylvania

Nadja Jungmann PhD candidate, Socio-Legal Studies, University of Leyden

Maria Manuel Leitão Marques Professor, Faculty of Economics, University of Coimbra and Faculty of Law, New University of Lisbon

José Reinaldo de Lima Lopes Professor of Law, Universidade de São Paulo, São Paulo

Rosalind Mason Associate Professor of Commercial Law, University of Southern Queensland, Toowoomba

Bert Niemeijer Head, Research and Documentation Centre, Ministry of Justice of the Netherlands; criminologist at the Free University of Amsterdam

Johanna Niemi-Kiesiläinen LLD, Researcher, Helsinki Collegium for Advanced Studies, University of Helsinki

Iain Ramsay Professor of Law, Osgoode Hall Law School, York University, Toronto

Udo Reifner Professor of Commercial Law, Hamburg University of Economics and Politics, Director of the Institute for Financial Services, Hamburg

Saul Schwartz Associate Professor, School of Public Policy and Administration, Carleton University, Ottawa

Teresa A Sullivan Professor of Sociology, University of Texas at Austin, Executive Vice Chancellor for Academic Affairs, University of Texas System

Thomas GW Telfer Associate Professor of Law and Director of the Area of Concentration in Business Law, University of Western Ontario

Elizabeth Warren Leo Gottlieb Professor of Law, Harvard University

Jay Lawrence Westbrook Benno C Schmidt Chair of Business Law, University of Texas School of Law

William C Whitford Emeritus Professor of Law, School of Law, University of Wisconsin-Madison

Xian-Chu Zhang Associate Professor, Faculty of Law, University of Hong Kong

Introduction

JOHANNA NIEMI-KIESILÄINEN, IAIN RAMSAY,
WILLIAM C WHITFORD*

CONSUMER CREDIT HAS a long history,[1] but for most of the world consumer bankruptcy has not. Twenty years ago an academic book about consumer bankruptcy systems around the world would not have been possible. Most countries did not have a consumer bankruptcy system, and few if any legal academics or practitioners identified as a specialisation consumer bankruptcy and/or other remedies for over-indebtedness[2] by consumers.

Since then, however, there has been rapid growth in consumer credit, nearly everywhere, as well as in problems of over-indebtedness and consumer bankruptcy. This book is the first major effort in history to look at consumer bankruptcy in all parts of the world from a comparative perspective.[3] The book grew out of a series of academic meetings that has illustrated growing interest in this topic. The first was a 1996 panel on comparative consumer bankruptcy held in Glasgow, Scotland, resulting in the publication of a symposium issue on the topic by the *Journal of Consumer Policy*.[4] There was a subsequent 1998

* Except for this introduction, wherever in this book reference is made to another chapter in the book, the phrase 'in this volume' is added to the author's name. In the introduction that phrase has not been added; all references are made simply by the author's name, whether within a textual parenthesis or a footnote. The chapter can be located by use of the Table of Contents.

[1] See eg L Calder, *Financing the American Dream* (Princeton, Princeton University Press, 1999); RM Gelpi and F Julien-Labruyère, *The History of Consumer Credit: Doctrines and Practices* (translated by ML Gavin) (New York, St Martin's Press, 2000).

[2] We will use the term 'over-indebted' or 'over-indebtedness' repeatedly in this introduction, without offering a formal definition. The term is used repeatedly in the contributions in this book, with the different authors perhaps using slightly different meanings. The basic idea is that an individual's indebtedness is substantial enough in relation to income and other resources to cause some of the problems of indebtedness described subsequently in the text.

A recent study conducted for the European Commission concluded that, given the difficulties in determining objectively when a level of debt become critical for a consumer, a useful measure of over-indebtedness is when a consumer 'considers that he or she has difficulties in repaying debts . . .We consider that when consumers say that they are facing difficulties or serious difficulties in repaying loans, then this is generally the situation.' Based on this criterion, 18% of the total population over 18 in the European Union were over-indebted. See OCR Macro *Study of the Problem of Consumer Indebtedness: Statistical Aspects Final Report* (London, ORC Macro, 2001) at 2.

[3] See also J Ziegel, *Comparative Consumer Insolvency Regimes–A Canadian Perspective* (Oxford, Hart Publishing, 2003).

[4] See J Niemi-Kiesiläinen and I Ramsay (eds), 'Special Issue: Changing Directions in Consumer Bankruptcy Law and Practice in Europe and North America' (1997) 20 *Journal of Consumer Policy*

meeting in Toronto, leading to the publication of a symposium issue of the *Osgoode Hall Law Journal*.[5] The papers in this book were first presented in five separate panels conducted as part of academic meetings in 2001 in Budapest, Hungary.[6]

In this introduction we first outline the context in which this developing interest occurred—the phenomenon of the democratisation of consumer credit. We then turn to the comparative study of consumer bankruptcy and over-indebtedness and sketch some emerging themes arising from the contributions included in this book and issues for future research. These are: prevention versus treatment of over-indebtedness; the role of payment plans, discharge and relief from enforcement as treatment modes; administrative versus judicialised systems for implementing laws; the role of the US as a model of consumer bankruptcy in this era of legal transplants.

I. THE DEMOCRATISATION OF CONSUMER CREDIT

During the past two decades there has been rapid growth in consumer credit, nearly everywhere.[7] More importantly for our topic, the groups in society to whom unsecured credit is available has also expanded. Today in an increasing number of countries around the world unsecured credit is much more available to working class families, and we are surrounded by credit advertising that encourages them to take advantage of these opportunities. This development is sometimes called the democratisation of credit. These changes are reported upon in most of the studies included in this book.

There are many causes for this growth and expansion in credit availability. On the supply side the deregulation of consumer credit markets[8] has included both a reduction in direct controls by central banks over levels of consumer credit and the abolition of interest rate ceilings in many countries. The growth of credit scoring technology and credit bureaux have facilitated the management of the risk of large numbers of small loans to consumers. These factors have fuelled the extensive marketing of credit cards in many countries in the

133–287 [Special Issue]. The panel was part of the joint meeting of the Law & Society Association and the Research Committee on the Sociology of Law of the International Sociological Association. Such joint meetings are held once every 5 years.

[5] J Ziegel (ed), 'Symposium: Consumer Bankruptcies in a Comparative Context' (1999) 37(1&2) *Osgoode Hall Law Journal*. The contributions to this volume were mostly from the common law systems.

[6] Once again, the occasion was the joint meeting of the Law & Society Association and the Research Committee on the Sociology of Law of the International Sociological Association.

[7] Growth in credit requires not only availability but also a willingness to consume credit, and that willingness is not universal. Zhang's contribution to this book discusses the difficulties China has had in encouraging consumers to take loans in order to expand consumer spending, due in part to cultural traditions emphasising the virtue of saving.

[8] Several chapters discuss deregulation and its relation to the growth of consumer credit. See eg Reifner, Lopes, Marques and Frade, Ramsay.

world.[9] Credit cards have become an important centre for bank profits and have been marketed extensively to many segments of the consumer credit market, playing a leading role in the democratisation of consumer credit.

The second major cause of the growth in consumer credit has come from the demand side. With the contraction of the welfare state that is occurring across much of the world, consumers are expected to pay for more of their medical care and education. Income support when unemployment strikes is less available. When medical emergencies or unemployment arises, incurring debt is often the only practical course for consumers who would otherwise prefer a lesser debt burden.

As consumer credit has expanded over so much of the world, over-indebtedness has increased as well. Over-indebtedness may result from unforeseen causes or through miscalculations or mismanagement by a consumer. The increasingly influential literature on behavioural law and economics suggests that consumers might be more prone to accept risk than they should be, if they were acting 'rationally'. Saul Schwartz, in his contribution, draws out the implications of behavioural law and economics for a number of issues in consumer bankruptcy law.

The democratisation of credit has enhanced the incidence and persistence of over-indebtedness, since the riskiness of credit extension to working class families is generally greater, and such families are less likely to find ways quickly to resolve an over-indebtedness situation. The extent of over-indebtedness has also been aggravated by a switch in the form of consumer credit. Credit cards differ in important respects from the forms of consumer credit that formerly prevailed. Much credit historically, and still, is secured credit—especially the important forms of credit that enable consumers to purchase homes and motor vehicles. When secured credit is in default, the creditor normally has available reasonably efficient means to repossess or foreclose upon the collateral, and this action commonly marks the end of the creditor's effort to collect upon the debt. Credit card debt is unsecured and so unpaid indebtedness and the problems associated with it cannot be so easily resolved. Continued indebtedness is likely even after a creditor initiates a formal collection action, since it is not likely that the entire indebtedness will be resolved in a single legal action. Credit card debt is also open ended, meaning that there is not a proscribed repayment schedule and no fixed date when, barring default, the debt will be extinguished. In these respects credit card debt differs from instalment debt, the predominant form of consumer indebtedness before the introduction of credit cards and from many other forms of consumer credit, including mortgages over property. A lack of debtor discipline in paying debts is psychologically easier with open end credit, with its minimal required monthly payments. As a result creditors of open end credit are less likely to get an early warning when a debtor is becoming unable

[9] Ramsay's chapter on the Consumer Credit Society in this book develops these points in greater depth.

to manage his indebtedness, an early warning that might enable these creditors to take steps to prevent the emerging problems from becoming more difficult.

The problems associated with consumer over-indebtedness are many and vary from country to country. But three kinds of problems are present in virtually all circumstances, with varying degrees of seriousness. One problem concerns the perverse incentives facing an over-indebted consumer. To the extent such a debtor cannot foresee solvency for a period of years, there is less incentive to earn extra income or to undertake entrepreneurial risk, for any gains will redound to the benefit of creditors without removing the burdens of indebtedness. Such a debtor has reduced incentives to remain a productive member of society and may resort to the underground economy to avoid her creditors.

A second problem is hardship. An over-indebted consumer may begin with enough income to satisfy the necessities of life, but as a consequence of the indebtedness, that consumer is unlikely to be able to devote all that income to such purposes. Creditors will seek to use the various legal powers open to them to seize assets, including income,[10] and often to such an extent that the debtor becomes impoverished. Further, the frequent interactions between creditors seeking payment and debtors in default can be psychologically harassing and cause a dramatic decline in the quality of life.

A third problem concerns economic insecurity. The democratisation of credit has become a vehicle for the privatisation of social insurance, in the form of credit availability, in societies where the public insurance provided by the welfare state has been reduced. However, an over-indebted consumer has reduced, and perhaps no, access to additional credit. If an unforeseen eventuality occurs, such as illness or unemployment, hardship will result and the consumer may have no place to turn for help. Even if an unforeseen event does not occur, there is enhanced insecurity for the over-indebted, precisely because they know that they lack access to additional credit, and this insecurity lowers the quality of life.

When such social problems emerge in a society, law reform is not likely to be far behind. Predictably, following the democratisation of credit around the world, has come legislation dealing with the problems of over-indebtedness. That legislation has commonly, though not always, concerned consumer bankruptcy.

II. THE COMPARATIVE STUDY OF CONSUMER BANKRUPTCY

Consumer bankruptcy, and other legal responses to the problems created by consumer over-indebtedness, is fertile territory for comparative research. As described in the previous section of this Introduction, the expansion of

[10] Sometimes the sanctions available to creditors are more extreme. Efrat discusses how, until recently, creditors in Israel routinely arranged for the imprisonment of over-indebted consumers until somebody, usually relatives, arranged for payment of some or all of their debts.

consumer credit is nearly universal, leading inevitably to increased over-indebtedness. This creates a commonality in different countries that make the differences that do emerge especially interesting. The problems associated with over-indebtedness vary somewhat from country to country—because the existence of problems is dependent in part on the kinds of social insurance systems in place, the kinds of remedies available to unpaid creditors and the like.

The even greater variety is in the types of legal responses to those problems. This provides a rich terrain for persons interested in comparative law. On the one hand, there is the possibility of insights into what produces differences in legal rules and institutions in different legal systems. Because legal change has either happened or is being debated in virtually all the legal systems discussed in this book, there is plenty of material available to study the reasons different problems and different legal approaches emerge in different countries. On the other hand, there is also an opportunity to explore the practical effects of different legal responses to common problems—perhaps making possible conclusions about which responses better serve particular goals.

In the same vein, a central topic in contemporary comparative law is the extent to which globalisation results in convergence or divergence in legal regimes. It is possible to explore in this area whether the different legal systems are gradually moving towards a common approach to common problems, or on the contrary, are continuing to maintain significant institutional and practical distinctions. Understanding the reasons for continuing differences is important given the increasing appeal to comparative models in the reform of consumer bankruptcy.[11]

Only a few of the chapters in this volume are truly comparative, in the sense that they directly comment on the legal and/or commercial situations in several countries (Ramsay, Consumer Credit Society; Niemi-Kiesiläinen). One chapter is best described as exploring economic theory, but it is economic theory thought to be applicable in all market-based economies and thus has potential applicability to all systems (Schwartz). The vast majority of the chapters discuss the policy debate in different countries, with a considerable emphasis on the law as applied and the social problems to which it is addressed. These are not simple statements of the formal law of the countries concerned. Altogether 11 different legal systems are covered. From east to west, they are New Zealand (Telfer), China (Zhang), Hong Kong (Booth), Australia (Mason and Dun), Israel (Efrat), Germany (Reifner), The Netherlands (Huls, Jungmann, and Niemeijer), United Kingdom (Ramsay), Portugal (Marques and Frade), Brazil (Lopes), and the United States (four papers—Jacoby; Braucher; Gross; Sullivan, Warren, and Westbrook). We hope that this book will be the beginning of a fruitful conversation among scholars, law reformers and practitioners.

[11] For further discussion of these themes, see eg G Teubner, 'Legal Irritants: Good Faith in British law' (1998) 66 *Modern Law Review* 11.

A. Issues for Future Research

Change is occurring in virtually all the countries covered by this book. And there are many countries not explicitly covered in this book with consumer bankruptcy systems and/or having contemporary debates about how to deal with the problems of over-indebtedness. Therefore, conclusions drawn at this point may be premature or subject to revision upon further evidence. Nonetheless, based on our years of thinking about comparative consumer bankruptcy and the contributions to this book, we will now offer some tentative hypotheses, as well as suggest some issues for further comparative work. Our discussion will be organised under four headings: (1) Prevention versus treatment of over-indebtedness; (2) Payment plans, discharge and relief from enforcement as treatment modes; (3) Administrative versus judicialised systems for implementing law; and (4) Whether the United States will remain an outlier, or become a world model, with its approach to consumer bankruptcy.

1. Prevention Versus Treatment of Over-indebtedness

Borrowing on a medical metaphor, all systems can be analysed as struggling for an appropriate balance between prevention and treatment of consumer over-indebtedness, but systems also differ, sometimes very radically, in the balance they draw. By treatment, we mean amelioration of the problems that over-indebtedness creates for the consumer.

Discharge of indebtedness is generally understood as the most complete or radical form of treatment. But as Saul Schwartz in particular emphasises, with the theme repeated in many other chapters as well, there is what the economists call a moral hazard problem in making discharge available. If discharge is too readily available, there will not be sufficient incentive for consumers to take steps to avoid indebtedness in the first place. So one approach to prevention is simply not to treat the disease (here over-indebtedness), so that the problems created by the disease serve as a deterrence. As Rafi Efrat reports, Israel, until recently, went one step further and imprisoned the over-indebted, an approach that certainly emphasises deterrence and was once widely adopted in many legal systems, though now largely discarded.

Deterrence of debtors is not the only approach to prevention, however. A society can attempt to limit over-indebtedness by deterring credit granters from extending consumer credit improvidently. Historically many countries have regulated credit extension in the name of protecting the financial solidity of financial institutions, and this regulation has often had the effect of limiting the availability of unsecured consumer credit—widely seen as a riskier form of credit than business lending or consumer lending secured by real estate. In this era of deregulation, such regulations have been abandoned or relaxed in virtually all countries, but some efforts remain, often in the form of self-regulation (Huls, Jungmann, and Niemeijer; Marques and Frade). However, many scholars think that the high level of consumer lending and lax controls in granting such credit are significant causes of over-indebtedness. Somewhat ironically, a liberal provision for bankruptcy discharge can also be seen as a prevention effort in this vein. By imposing costs back on creditors when they have granted credit to someone who is unable to pay, a discharge gives creditors an extra incentive to avoid improvident credit extensions.

Another preventive approach is to judge particular credit extensions invalid, perhaps under some generalised contract law principle, when the terms are deemed too one-sided—most likely, the interest rate is too high—or because the debtor is deemed particularly unsuitable for further indebtedness (Reifner; Lopes). There is always the question whether such judgments merely impact upon the particular case or set a standard to which creditors will later adapt their behaviour. Efforts to improve the effectiveness of systems designed to provide creditors with accurate information about the creditworthiness of prospective borrowers might also be seen as having a prevention goal, since the hope is to discourage further credit extension to those already overextended (Zhang).

Still another approach to prevention is debtor education and counselling, in an effort to persuade debtors that their self-interest is best served by exercising restraint when obtaining credit. Debtor education can take place at any time, and inclusion of this in the curriculum is commonly advocated. The three contributions to this book discussing debtor education and counselling focus, however, on efforts at the time of bankruptcy (Huls, Jungmann, and Niemeijer; Braucher; and Gross). Bankruptcy is normally a stressful moment in a debtor's life, and can provide an educational moment, when the consumer's interest in the subject matter is heightened (Gross). Furthermore, in most countries persons who have once filed for bankruptcy are more likely than the population as a whole to face future over-indebtedness, and perhaps a repeat bankruptcy, in their future. Seeking to help bankrupt debtors avoid this future is the preventive aspect to providing debtor education at the time of bankruptcy (Gross).

Debtor education and counselling can also have a treatment goal, however, by focusing on strategies for dealing with the debtor's particular circumstance. The goal can be to help debtors get through the bankruptcy process, in a manner that repays creditors either as much[12] or as little[13] as is feasible. Many education and counselling programmes have treatment in this sense as essentially their sole focus, paying little attention to generalised financial education issues that might help prevent a subsequent over-indebtedness. The nature and scope of counselling remains controversial in common law countries where only Canada has taken the step of making counselling a mandatory part of the bankruptcy process. In continental Europe, debt counselling is an integral part of state welfare assistance to over-indebted persons as part of a process of social reintegration.

[12] See Braucher on debtor education in the US in the context of Chapter 13 proceedings.

[13] See Huls, Jungmann, and Niemeijer on counselling and efforts to negotiate informal settlements with creditors in The Netherlands.

2. Payment Plans, Discharge, and Relief from Enforcement as Treatment Modes

Few scholars today think that prevention should be the only strategy for addressing the problems associated with over-indebtedness. There will always be bankruptcies resulting from unforeseen or unavoidable hardships. As the welfare state shrinks, the number of bankruptcies primarily caused by such hardships can be expected to increase, as there become fewer alternatives to bankruptcy for providing aid to the victims of hardship. In a number of countries there is already good evidence of significant increases in hardship bankruptcies (Mason & Duns on Australia; Jacoby on the United States). The need is for some way to relieve the problems associated with over-indebtedness in such situations, which is what we call treatment.

Not all legal systems have yet adopted a procedure labelled 'bankruptcy' to redress the hardships associated with over-indebtedness. Yet even the systems without a procedure called bankruptcy are likely to offer some protection to over-indebted consumers from ordinary collection procedures. At a minimum there will be exemption laws, protecting some necessaries from judicial seizure at the initiative of the unsecured creditor.[14] Many legal systems today also offer some legal procedure by which debtors can gain protection from all judicial seizure for a period of time, often upon some condition such as a commitment to make payments to creditors from future income.[15] It is hard to overemphasise the importance of some scheme to protect over-indebted consumers from the hardships that can be wrought by creditor use of legal collection remedies. In virtually all societies with bankruptcy schemes, the desire for relief from these hardships is most often the immediate motive for debtors to initiate a bankruptcy procedure. To continue the medical metaphor, it is the presenting symptom.

Beyond immediate relief from enforcement measures by creditors, it is usual to divide consumer bankruptcy systems into two categories—payment plans and discharge of indebtedness. These are alternative strategies for dealing with the longer term problems presented by over-indebtedness, with the ultimate goal of returning the debtor to solvency.[16] Payment plans generally provide for payment of the indebtedness according to a schedule, with the debtor protected from the rigours of legal collection procedures during the payment period, and perhaps restricted from taking on additional debt during the payment period. Discharge systems terminate legal liability on indebtedness existing at the time of filing, restoring solvency unconditionally in a relatively short period after

[14] For example, Lopes describes the list of 'unattachable' property in Brazil, a country that has no procedure for consumers that would be labelled 'bankruptcy.'

[15] Marques and Frade discuss competing proposals to implement some kind of payment plan in Portugal, another country without a legal procedure labelled 'bankruptcy.'

[16] Restoration of solvency restores the debtor's incentive to be entrepreneurial, maximise income and the like.

initiation of bankruptcy. Discharge systems are ordinarily associated with common law countries, and payment plan systems with legal systems in the civil law tradition.

There is not, however, a simple dichotomy between payment plans and discharge systems. Most countries have some kind of hybrid system. Payment plans may offer discharge in the event of hardship, or after the debtor has made a good faith effort to repay over a fixed period of years.[17] Discharge systems may be conditioned on payment of income in excess of an exempt amount that is received for some period after filing, rendering these systems essentially payment systems followed by discharge. There is a wide range of time periods utilised in these systems before discharge can be obtained, ranging from a few months to several years.[18] Moreover, in all discharge systems some debts are excepted from discharge so that the 'fresh start' widely attributed to a discharge is not truly a wholly new start. These exceptions from discharge include all or virtually all secured debt, and in many systems, especially the United States, an increasing number of unsecured claims as well. The United States also allows debtors to 'reaffirm' debts after discharge, thereby renewing the legal validity of a debt that would otherwise be discharged, and such reaffirmations are quite common.[19]

Countries offering consumer debtors a discharge increasingly also offer debtors the choice of a payment plan as an alternative bankruptcy scheme. Perhaps the oldest of these is the English administration order introduced as the 'poor person's bankruptcy' in 1883. Since the 1930s the United States has had such a system, with a choice offered between 'Chapter 13'—a payment plan, followed by a discharge—and 'Chapter 7,' which offers a relatively quick discharge. In many systems that offer a choice, extra incentives or sometimes not so subtle pressures have been devised to induce debtors to select a payment plan, but in most countries these efforts have not been notably successful.[20]

Because of the prevalence of what we have called hybrid systems, it is tempting to conclude that the world's consumer bankruptcy systems are converging to a common model. Before drawing such a conclusion, systems must be examined in context. There is an emphasis in each of the reports in this book on how each country's system operates in practice—on any difference between the law-in-the-books and the law-in-action. Viewed from this perspective, there may be much greater divergence in consumer bankruptcy systems than first appears.

[17] Reifner describes both the French and German systems. The discharge at the end of a payment plan is discretionary with a court.

[18] In Canada, discharge ordinarily occurs after 9 months. In Australia discharge can occur after 6 months (Mason and Duns), and in England after 12 months (Ramsay—England). In Hong Kong, discharge does not occur until 4 to 8 years after filing (Booth).

[19] See W Whitford, *Changing Definitions of Fresh Start in U.S. Bankruptcy Law*, in Special Issue, above n 4, at 179.

[20] Sullivan, Warren, and Westbrook discuss these efforts in the United States, and their limited success, in considerable detail. Booth discusses the lack of success of a similar effort in Hong Kong. Telfer discusses the limited use of Part XVI plans in New Zealand.

Repayment plans, for example, function very differently depending on the institutional context and role of the professionals and officials administering them. In the United States the vast majority of Chapter 13 payment plans fail and the debtor is denied a discharge altogether. A case can be made that the poorly informed debtors are encouraged, sometimes even forced, to choose payment plans when the election of the Chapter 7 discharge option is much more in the debtor's interest.[21] In Canada and Australia where repayment plans are administered by private sector professionals a substantial minority of plans fail. In other countries, however, there is better counselling and education available to the over-indebted consumer, and conclusion of a voluntary payment plan is seen as very much in the debtor's interest. Completion of the plan and a return to solvency is a likely outcome, during which time the debtor's reputation for creditworthiness may be restored and the debtor may acquire needed learning and good habits about personal financial management.[22]

Johanna Niemi-Kiesiläinen, in her contribution to this book, finds these divergences when systems are examined in context so great that she refuses to call them by the same name. She refers to systems in common law countries as consumer bankruptcy, while using consumer debt adjustment to describe continental European systems. She goes on to suggest that the differences are greater than even an empirical description of the law-in-action can reveal. Underlying the differences is a politically dominant social construction of the relationship between citizen and state. One vision emphasises the role of the citizen as a market actor, who enhances collective welfare by acting energetically in an economically maximising way. Such a vision is attracted to the goal of restoration of a debtor to solvency (ie, a fresh start), so as to avoid the perverse economic incentives facing the over-indebted. Another vision emphasises both the state's obligation to enhance the quality of life of each citizen in all its aspects and each citizen's responsibility not to cause unnecessary harm to others. Such a vision seeks to avoid the discharge of debts irresponsibly incurred and to provide assurance that when a debtor does receive a discharge, it will be part of a bundle of efforts to insure that the debtor's life experiences will improve.[23]

All of this counsels that, as treatment and prevention approaches to over-indebtedness are compared and contrasted, it is not sufficient simply to examine each system's formal characteristics. Examining how the law is applied in practice is important, but so is considering how consumer bankruptcy relates both to other legal rules and institutions and to deeper conceptions of the responsibilities of a legal system.

[21] See W Whitford, 'The Ideal of Individualized Justice: Consumer Bankruptcy as Consumer Protection, and Consumer Protection in Consumer Bankruptcy' (1994) 68 *American Bankruptcy Law Journal* 397.

[22] See Huls, Jungmann, and Niemeijer on the advantages of involuntary settlement with creditors in The Netherlands.

[23] See also I Ramsay, *Models of Consumer Bankruptcy: Implications for Research and Policy*, in Special Issue, above n 4, at 269.

3. Administrative Versus Judicialised Systems for Implementing Law

Consumer bankruptcy is generally a small stakes game. While the amount of indebtedness in a particular bankruptcy may be substantial, the true measure of the stakes in any given proceeding is the difference between what the creditors could collect absent bankruptcy and what they are able to collect through bankruptcy, either under a payment plan or because of exceptions to discharge. The latter amount will always be smaller than total indebtedness, usually much smaller. As a consequence, it is often not economically sensible for either a debtor or the creditors to hire a lawyer to deal with the bankruptcy. No doubt largely for this reason most countries in the world have established a public office with substantial responsibilities for administering consumer bankruptcies. In many countries it is this public administrator, and not courts, who make virtually all the important decisions and establish the detailed interpretations of statutory rules.[24]

The United States represents the other end of the continuum. The public administrator, the United States Trustee, plays an inconsequential role in virtually all Chapter 7 proceedings. Rather the debtor hires a lawyer to guide him or her through the process,[25] with judges making important decisions in the event of conflict. The important precedents that provide the detailed interpretations of statutory rules—that set the 'local legal culture', as it is called in the US literature[26]—are usually made by the judge, and in the US there is a specialised system of bankruptcy courts for reaching such judgments.

There are a number of systems that lie somewhere between these extremes. The Chapter 13 system in the United States is one example. In these cases the standing Chapter 13 trustee plays an important role, one that is almost always far more important than the judge. The Chapter 13 trustee is for all practical purposes a publicly appointed administrative officer (though paid from fees paid in the bankruptcy proceeding, and not from the public purse). Very often his or her decisions are more important than judicial decisions in establishing local legal culture.[27] Another interesting hybrid system, not covered explicitly in this book, is Canada. There a private professional, called a trustee in bankruptcy, plays multiple roles, including acting as an adviser to the debtor and also impartial representative of the interests of creditors. The work of the trustee is monitored by a government agency, the Office of the Superintendent of Bankruptcy.[28] The counsellor in the Dutch system, described in the contribution

[24] See Efrat's description of the Israeli system for an excellent example of this model.

[25] Creditors are free to retain their own lawyers as well, and sometimes do so. In addition a lawyer, called a Chapter 7 panel trustee, is appointed to represent creditor interests.

[26] See Sullivan, Warren, and Westbrook.

[27] J Braucher, 'Lawyers and Consumer Protection: One Code, Many Cultures', (1993) 67 *American Bankruptcy Law Journal* 501–83.

[28] See I Ramsay, 'Market Imperatives, Professional Discretion and the Role of Intermediaries in Consumer Bankruptcy: A Comparative Study of the Canadian Trustee in Bankruptcy' (2000) 74 *American Bankruptcy Law Journal* 399.

to this book by Nick Huls, Nadja Jungmann, and Bert Niemeijer, plays a role similar in some ways to the Canadian trustee. While ostensibly loyal to debtors, the counsellor must establish credibility with creditors with whom she or he regularly deals, in order to be able to broker voluntary settlements. So there is a dual loyalty of a key professional in both systems.

Future comparative research can both attempt to explain why different systems for implementing law have emerged in different countries, and try to draw judgements about whether an administrative or a judicialised system for making key decisions, or some hybrid, is most efficacious. Of course, consistent with admonitions made in the previous part of this introduction, such work must be based on a contextualised description of the systems for implementing consumer bankruptcy. No part of a justice system operates in isolation, and consideration must be given to other parts of each country's legal system.

Future work should also consider how the method chosen for implementing consumer bankruptcy law affects future law reform. The contributions to this book are replete with examples of how the professionals who implement the law play a prominent, and perhaps dominant role, in debates about change. These include Jean Braucher's discussion of the important role of Chapter 13 trustees in the US in initiating financial counselling and debtor education, Iain Ramsay's discussion of the role of the Citizens Advice Bureaux in recent legal reform in England and Wales, and the discussion by Huls, Jungmann and Niemeijer about the conflict between debt advice agencies and judges in The Netherlands. It should not be surprising that persons who come to depend for a living on implementing law should seek to influence future legal changes, if for no other reason then to protect their particular place in the world, but it is an aspect of legal change that is all too often ignored by analysts.[29]

4. *US Consumer Bankruptcy Law: Outlier, or Model for the Future?*

We do not think that in any comparative research one should examine the influence of the United States, simply because it is the only remaining superpower. However, in the area of consumer credit and consumer bankruptcy the importance of the United States is clear. The US has probably led the world in the use of the credit card to democratise credit, and per capita credit card indebtedness remains higher in the US than virtually anywhere else. Furthermore, in the US discharge for individual debtors is more easily available than in almost any other country, and the volume of consumer bankruptcies in the US far surpasses that of any other system, both absolutely and on a per capita basis.[30]

[29] See D Skeel, *Debt's Dominion* (Princeton, 2001), for an historical account of US bankruptcy law that emphasises the role of professionals in influencing legislative change.

[30] In 1999 the US bankruptcy rate was 4.8 per 1000 population. This compares with Canada (2.72), Australia (1.44), and England and Wales (0.55). See *International Consumer Insolvency Statistics* (Ottawa, Office of the Superintendent of Bankruptcy, 2001).

At first glance it may seem incongruous that a country whose commercial law is commonly considered accommodating of merchant interests should adopt a system premised on the availability of an unconditional discharge upon demand and then have that system widely used. But if one believes that the broad vision underlying commercial law in the US emphasises the benefits to society, in terms of economic wealth and growth, of unregulated market capitalism and risk taking, then it is not surprising that there is an emphasis on avoiding the perverse incentives on hard work and entrepreneurial activity that afflict an over-indebted consumer. And since the clear trend in other countries is to adopt consumer bankruptcy systems and to make the availability of a discharge part of that system, it is easy to see how one could characterise the US as a model for the world in this area.

We have already said enough above to indicate our caveat against any quick endorsement of such a conclusion, based as it would be on simplistic comparisons without considering all the contexts in which legal developments are embedded. For one thing, as implemented, the discharge in the US is not nearly as available or unconditional as it first appears. It is undeniable, however, that the US is the leader in consumer bankruptcy volume. We should ask why so many consumers seek this form of treatment for the problems associated with over-indebtedness. Since a majority of consumer bankruptcies in the US are caused in significant part by the financial stresses resulting from illness, unemployment, and other misfortunes,[31] it may be that the US should be viewed as an outlier in having no system other than consumer bankruptcy for treating these problems. If the US is an outlier in this respect, it should probably not become a model for the rest of the world.

Another reason for the high incidence of consumer bankruptcy in the US is its system of access. Debtors normally initiate consumer bankruptcies in the US with the help of a lawyer, partly because successful initiation of a proceeding requires the filing of much detailed information on mandated forms. The volume of consumer bankruptcies is such that many attorneys specialise in representing debtors seeking bankruptcy relief and make an adequate living doing so. Few other countries can claim a specialised bar of this nature. One consequence of having these lawyer-specialists is that they compete for business, and in doing so they advertise to consumers the benefits of bankruptcy rather than continuing to endure the problems of over-indebtedness. Future researchers should consider whether this unique feature of the US system should serve as a model for other countries. There are certainly alternative ways to educate and inform consumers about the possibility of bankruptcy relief, and debtor attorneys are hardly disinterested educators as they are interested in being retained as a bankruptcy attorney, but some education may be better than

[31] The contributions to this book by both Jacoby and Sullivan, Warren, and Westbrook offer documentation for this conclusion.

none at all. And there is little doubt today that in the US lawyers for debtors are the primary educators.[32]

There is one additional topic to consider in this limited discussion of the outlier-model controversy with respect to the United States. As we write, an ongoing political struggle continues in the US about whether to significantly restrict debtor access to an unconditional discharge.[33] The struggle originated in concern that the rapid increase in consumer bankruptcy filings in the US evidenced debtor abuse of the system. Other countries have experienced similar political pressures,[34] yet many other countries are responding to increased over-indebtedness by making bankruptcy and discharge more available than it has been previously. It may be that in the future the US will be seen as an outlier because it will be the one country that restricts access to its primary method for treatment for the problems of indebtedness, in the face of a considerable increase in the existence of such problems. In that respect it may be that the US should remain an outlier and not serve as a model.

[32] Both Braucher and Gross, in their contributions to this book, describe attempts in the US to provide, in other ways, education about bankruptcy and the use of consumer credit.

[33] Jacoby offers some description of this 8 year struggle in her contribution to this book.

[34] Both Telfer on New Zealand and Mason and Duns on Australia describe similar pressures to restrict access to bankruptcy, as a response to increased filings.

Part I:

Theoretical Perspectives on Consumer Bankruptcy

1

Consumer Credit Society and Consumer Bankruptcy: Reflections on Credit Cards and Bankruptcy in the Informational Economy

IAIN RAMSAY*

I. INTRODUCTION

CREDIT CARDS ARE for many commentators the symbol of the consumer credit society or even a 'global credit card society.'[1] They have stimulated sharply conflicting views on this society with some arguing that credit cards represent the 'democratisation of credit'[2] while others worry about the potentially corrosive effects of credit card use on social values.[3] Analysis of the role of credit cards provides a window on the contemporary consumer credit system—its institutions, technologies and visions.[4] Institutions include credit bureaux and payments systems; technologies include credit scoring and the use of information technology in the assessment and control of credit risks; visions refers to ideas about the appropriate use of consumer credit. These visions may be found in the advertising of credit card companies, discussions of credit card use by the media, the literature of advice agencies, and the rhetoric of legal actors. Whatever the reality of credit card use, its development and regulation will be affected by these visions.

Credit cards are linked closely to bankruptcy in popular and academic discussion in several countries. Juliet Schor, a progressive critic of consumerism in

* Thanks to Johanna Niemi-Kiesiläinen, Bill Whitford, and Toni Williams for comments on a draft version of this chapter.

[1] See G Ritzer, *Expressing America: A Critique of the Global Credit Card Society* (Thousand Oaks, Ca., Pine Forge Press, 1995).

[2] This is the theme of one major text. See D Evans and R Schmalensee, *Paying with Plastic: The Digital Revolution in Buying and Borrowing* (Cambridge, MIT Press, 1999). See also G Cross, *An All-Consuming Century: Why Commercialism won in Modern America* (New York, Columbia University Press, 2000) at 175.

[3] A theme in R Manning, *Credit Card Nation: The Consequences of America's Addiction to Credit* (New York, Basic Books, 2000).

[4] These characteristics are borrowed from F Ewald, 'Insurance and Risk' in G Burchell, C Gordon, and P Miller (eds) *The Foucault Effect: Studies in Governmentality* (Chicago, University of Chicago Press, 1991).

the US, claims that credit cards result in irrational consumer behaviour and that 'the explosion' of personal bankruptcies in the US is evidence of this lack of control by some consumers.[5] In England, during Parliamentary debates on the insolvency reforms contained in the Enterprise Act, several Parliamentarians raised concerns about easy access to credit cards, and its relationship to bankruptcy and over-indebtedness. The following quotations provide a flavour of these concerns:

> These days, [credit cards], are enabling young people to accumulate massive debts in the hope that something will turn up to enable them to pay them off. I am aware of one young man who managed to run up debts of £250,000. Surely it is impossible for any credit company—or series of credit companies; I think that about 20 credit card companies were involved—to allow a debt of £250,000 to be run up in that way. There is great danger unless we seriously consider that matter. Borrowing has become a habit, and the use of easy access to credit is creating a penalty that many of the young will have to face in years to come.[6]
>
> To remove all the inconvenience and stigma of insolvency, particularly for individuals, would send a dangerous signal. That is particularly so now, at a time when we are seeing an explosion in consumer credit. We hear that people are borrowing more than ever, particularly on credit cards, but with less and less certainty that they will be able to repay the debt.[7]

The media in both North America and England are also sources of vivid accounts of the role of credit cards in an individual's downfall.

> It was the credit cards that finally pushed Liz, a 50 year old mother of three from Toronto, over the financial edge after a difficult divorce . . . Credit cards provided a quick fix and allowed her to maintain [her] standard of living . . . Within a year she had rung up a credit debt of $20,000 and reached the spending limit on 16 cards. She had no way even to make the minimum payments. Credit experts say Liz's story is one playing out across the country.[8]

These quotations illustrate visions of the relationship between credit cards and bankruptcy as well as assumptions concerning consumers and credit card issuers. For example, there is the imprudent or naïve individual unable to control her spending habits who racks up huge debts on numerous credit cards. The consumer protagonists in these stories are often female, reflecting a historical tendency to identify the overspending consumer as female.[9] There is also

[5] See J Schor, *The New Politics of Consumption* (Boston, Beacon, 2001) at 20–21.

[6] UK HL Parliamentary Debates, second reading, Enterprise Bill col 161 (2 July 2 2002) (Lord Boardman) <http://www.publications.parliament.uk/pa/ld199900/ldhansrd/pdvn/lds02/text/20702–04.htm#20702–04_head0>.

[7] UK HC Parliamentary Debates, Standing Committee, Enterprise Bill col 540 (9 May, 2002) (Mr Alexander) <http://www.publications.parliament.uk/pa/cm200102/cmstand/b/st020509/am/20509s01.htm>.

[8] J Thorpe, 'The Debt Trap' *Financial Post* (28 April 2001).

[9] See E Warren, 'What is a Women's Issue? Bankruptcy, Commercial Law, and Other Gender Neutral Topics' (2002) 25 *Harvard Womens Law Journal* 19 at 46.

the counterpoint of credit card companies aggressively marketing cards to consumers in an indiscriminate manner and not properly monitoring consumers' use of the card. Finally, there is, in the final quotation, the assumption that credit cards are a potentially uncontrollable and dangerous product, analogised to a drug. The assumption that credit cards are a potentially dangerous product persists even in a country, such as the US, which has a very high level of credit card use. A recent study identified an ambivalence among consumers concerning the use of credit cards with negative attitudes to credit cards more common now than they were in 1977.[10]

These visions deserve to be taken seriously since they undoubtedly influence the assumptions and decisions of officials, policymakers and judges, as well as the stories that individuals construct about the causes of over-indebtedness. In this chapter, I suggest that we should be sceptical of these visions of credit card use and more careful in drawing conclusions about the relationship between credit card use and bankruptcy. Part II summarises some of the large descriptive literature on patterns of credit card usage, drawing attention to the role of credit cards as a form of private insurance when individuals face an unforeseen change of circumstances. Part III explores potential failures in the credit card market, noting the role of adverse selection, moral hazard and consumer irrationality. I then sketch the important role of credit scoring and credit information in overcoming problems of adverse selection, expanding the breadth and depth of credit markets, and creating opportunities for the manipulation of consumer irrationality. I also relate the growth of credit bureaux and credit ratings to the development of norms of credit use and the importance of the reputation sanction in credit granting. The growth of these non-legal sanctions may be of greater significance than legal sanctions within a credit system. Part IV outlines the role of personal bankruptcy within this system of credit granting and places it in the context of other forms of regulation of the credit card market such as information disclosure and the creation of incentives for creditors to use prescreening information. I then turn to the heated debates on bankruptcy reform in the US and suggest that the issue of the relationship of credit cards to bankruptcy reflects symbolic conflicts about the role of credit in society, that this conflict has long historical roots, and that we should be careful to situate discussion of credit cards against the background of structural divisions within society.

I focus my analysis on examples drawn from the US, Canada and England . These are 'Anglo-Saxon' jurisdictions with which I have some familiarity. In comparative debates on the role of credit cards and bankruptcy, the United States is often held up as the model to be emulated or avoided, although the references to the US model are often based on myths and atrocity stories rather than close analysis of the underlying realities. Thoughtful analysts of the US system of consumer credit have underlined its importance to the vision of a

[10] See T Durkin, 'Credit Card Use and Attitudes 1970–2000' (2000) *Federal Reserve Bulletin* 623.

'consumers' republic,' a consumerist vision of citizenship and the state[11] where there is a residual welfare state and little role for public redistribution.[12] Within this vision, 'consumer confidence' means that consumers are fulfilling their duty of using credit to maintain a buoyant economy.

II. PATTERNS OF CREDIT CARD USE

The great majority of North Americans have access to a general purpose credit card and in Britain over 50 per cent of households own at least one credit card.[13] Credit cards provide both a payment mechanism and a credit facility. They offer several potential benefits to consumers, permitting the coordination of income and consumption, smoothing out volatility in income and expenses, and reducing the amounts that individuals need to maintain in a chequing account. Although the cost of borrowing on credit cards is high compared with other forms of borrowing, there are a number of non-price advantages associated with borrowing on a credit card. These include the reduction of transaction costs (applying for a loan, filling out forms, indicating what the loan is for) and the availability of a flexible form of financing without a fixed term or repayment schedule. Borrowing on credit cards has to some extent substituted for instalment purchase financing and small loan financing. David Evans and Richard Schmalensee note that in 1970 credit card debt represented 17 per cent of households' total consumer debt, whereas in 1995 this had almost doubled to 32 per cent of total consumer debt.[14] Credit cards are therefore a significant source of unsecured lending for consumers.

Credit card users may be divided between convenience users (sometimes referred to as 'transactors') who use the card as a payment mechanism and those who are carrying a balance on their card. In the US, about 60 per cent of consumers borrow on their bank credit cards,[15] and a Canadian study found that

[11] See L Cohen, 'Citizens and Consumers in the US in the Century of Mass Consumption' in M Daunton and M Hilton (eds) *The Politics of Consumption: Material Culture and Citizenship in Europe and America* (London, Berg, 2001) ch 10.

[12] Australia and New Zealand might also fit within this 'residual welfare' model. See P Alcock and G Craig (eds) *International Social Policy: Welfare Regimes in the Developed World* (London, Palgrave, 2001).

[13] US data show that in 1998 almost 75% of American families had one or more credit card, compared with 50% in 1970. Durkin, above n 10, at 624. In Canada, a recent survey found that 75% of individuals aged 18 or over owned at least one credit card. See Leger Marketing, 'Canadians and Credit Cards' (Montreal, 2001) at 5, <http://www.legermarketing.com/documents/spclm/011210eng.pdf>. For the United Kingdom see E Kempson, *Over-Indebtedness in Britain: A Report to the Department of Trade and Industry* (Bristol, Personal Finance Research Centre, Bristol, 2002).

[14] Evans and Schmalensee, above n 2, at 100.

[15] See D Gross and N Souleles, 'Do Liquidity Constraints and Interest Rates Matter for Consumer Behavior? Evidence from Credit Card Data' (2002) *Quarterly Journal of Economics* 149 at 151. D Laibson, A Repetto, J Tobachman, 'A Debt Puzzle' (Working Paper, National Bureau of Economic Research, September 2000) National Bureau of Economic Research <http://papers.nber.org/papers/w7879> at 2.

over 50 per cent of individuals surveyed admitted to carrying over a balance once in the past 12 months and 15 per cent carried a balance every month.[16] Consumers in Britain are increasingly using cards as a form of borrowing with about 40–50 per cent of consumers making a full payment on their card. Most credit card companies earn little income on convenience users apart from merchant fees (and annual fees) with one study indicating that Mastercard and Visa earn 78 per cent of their revenues from finance charges.[17] American Express, in contrast, generates a similar percentage of its revenue from merchant/ interchange fees[18] and card fees. Some writers have suggested that convenience users are referred to by some credit card executives as freeloaders or even 'deadbeats,'[19] although their prudent practises are applauded in public advice on the use of credit cards.

An important question is the distribution of convenience users and borrowers among different social and demographic groups. In Canada, research indicates significant differences between demographic groups in their likelihood of carrying a balance on their credit cards. Individuals in the 25–34 age group were much more likely to have outstanding balances than older consumers.[20] This is consistent with a life cycle approach to credit where individuals in the 25–34 age group are often in a period of asset formation. Evans and Schmalensee in the US indicate that 'transactors' have higher income and charge more than the average cardholder. Although they represent one third of cardholders they contribute to half the volume of charges.[21] Writers in the US have expressed concern about the inequalities in the cost and availability of credit by social class where more affluent convenience users are subsidised by less affluent consumers.[22]

Two further aspects of contemporary credit card use deserve mention. First, there is the use of credit cards to finance small businesses. Research conducted in Canada indicates that almost half of all small- and medium-sized businesses use credit cards to finance their operations and one third of this group report that they carry a balance from time to time.[23] Businesses owned exclusively by women are more likely to carry over a balance than male-owned businesses. Credit cards may be a necessary and expensive form of financing for some businesses and banks have marketed credit cards to small businesses as an

[16] See Press Release, Canadian Facts Group Credit Card Tracking Study (2001) based on telephone interviews with a nationally representative sample of Canadian adults 18 or older.

[17] See Evans and Schmalensee, above n 2, at 213.

[18] The American Express merchant fee is significantly higher than that charged by Visa or Mastercard. Coupled with a more affluent consumer base this results in higher revenues generated from transactions.

[19] See, eg Manning, above n 3, at 120.

[20] See *The Assets and Debts of Canadians: an Overview of the Results of the Survey of Financial Security* (Ottawa, Statistics Canada, 2001) at 26.

[21] Evans and Schmalensee, above n 2, at 211.

[22] See eg Manning, above n 3, at 18.

[23] See Thompson, Lightstone and Company, *Small and Medium Sized Businesses in Canada: An Ongoing Perspective of their Needs, Expectations and Satisfaction with Financial Institutions* (prepared for Canadian Bankers Association) vol 1 (Toronto, 1998) at 40–43.

alternative to a requirement that the business provide collateral for a loan. A second area of growth in both North America and Britain is the marketing of credit cards to students.[24] Consumer groups such as the Consumers Federation of America claim that students from affluent families who fall into debt are bailed out by their parents but that those from families with modest incomes are forced to cut back on course work or spend increased time on part-time jobs. In addition, it is claimed that students with high credit card debts are facing difficulties in obtaining jobs since some employers use credit reports to assess potential employees.

Credit cards differ significantly from traditional forms of loan credit. Repayment schedules are not fixed beyond a minimum payment (as low as 2–3 per cent), the total credit available is potentially variable, and the debt is incurred in small amounts (average transaction just under $100) over a period of time.[25] They provide a source of credit for instant gratification which is much simpler to access than traditional forms of lender or vendor credit. The hypothesis that there is a connection between credit cards and instant gratification is supported by research in behavioural economics (see further Schwartz in this volume), which suggests that individuals are willing to pay a high discount rate for immediate gratification when a small amount of money is at stake. Where the absolute amount of interest appears small (for example, the carrying costs of a credit card balance), the cost of waiting for a modest reward is viewed by individuals as foregoing an opportunity to consume rather than foregoing the opportunity to earn interest. Assuming that consumption is more tempting in this situation than foregone interest then a consumer may use the credit card to access immediate consumption.

The development of the instalment credit plan disciplined consumers to rational credit use through the requirements of regular payments and acted as a control on the potentially uncontrolled hedonism of consumer culture.[26] Credit cards loosen this discipline and the advertising vision of credit card use epitomised in the slogan 'just charge it' may encourage the irrationality identified by the behavioural economists. However, while these factors associated with credit card use may stimulate demand in the short run and reduce propensities to save, this irrational behaviour is not fatal to most consumers. It may result in temporary or long term over-indebtness for some consumers which is itself a cause for concern, but studies of bankruptcy outlined below suggest that hedonism accounts for a small percentage of consumer bankruptcies. In the most recent major US study by Teresa Sullivan, Elizabeth Warren and Jay Westbrook only 5.4 per cent of debtors identified credit card debt as a reason for filing for bankruptcy.[27]

[24] See generally Manning, above n 3, ch 6.

[25] See generally T Sullivan, E Warren and J Westbrook, *The Fragile Middle Class: Americans in Debt* (New Haven, Yale University Press, 2000) ch 4.

[26] See L Calder, *Financing the American Dream: a Cultural History of Consumer Credit* (Princeton, Princeton University Press, 1999).

[27] Sullivan, Warren and Westbrook, above n 25, at 132.

A. Credit Card Welfare: Credit Cards as a Substitute for Public Support Programmes

The idea of credit cards as insurance, substituting for public support systems where individuals become unemployed or face other changes of life circumstance such as family breakdown, is emphasised by a number of writers. It is highlighted in studies of bankruptcy in the US where there is an absence of a universal public health care system, limited unemployment benefits and the existence of a very modest residual welfare system. Melissa Jacoby in her chapter in this volume emphasises the extent to which credit cards are used to supplement private insurance and to pay for necessities when illness results in a reduction of income. In their recent study of US bankrupts, Sullivan, Warren, and Westbrook found that 60 per cent of bankrupt debtors who list bank card debt had experienced a job interruption during the two years before filing. They argue that:

> consumers now use credit cards to see them through a time of crisis for which public assistance is unavailable or inadequate. If they survive, as most do, they will pay high interest rates, but they will eventually get back on their feet. If they do not, they can nonetheless consume the goods and services they need and shuck the credit balances when the debt scheme eventually collapses.[28]

In their view, MasterCard and Visa may be the 'ultimate market-based social welfare program.'[29] In Britain, a study in the early 1990s found that a drop in income by consumers resulted in a number of responses by consumers in their use of a credit card. Some returned their cards, some kept them for emergencies and some relied significantly on their cards to pay bills and necessities.[30] It is unlikely that individuals in straitened circumstances would be able to obtain a loan from a mainstream lender so that credit cards play an important function in this situation. It is not surprising that a study of consumer bankrupts in Canada found that a significant number of debtors had been refused credit in the period before declaring bankruptcy but had survived by living on credit cards.[31] The ability to use credit cards in this manner will be related both to the availability of credit as well as the level of public safety net. The larger numbers of credit cards held by US consumers in comparison to British consumers mean that this may be a more important source of insurance in the US.

[28] *Ibid* at 137.

[29] *Ibid* at 138. See also Manning, above n 3, at 4; A Finlayson and S Martin, *Card Tricks* (Toronto, Viking, 1993) at 183; E Bird, P Hagstrom and R Wild, *Credit Cards and the Poor* Disccussion Paper no 1148–97 (Madison, University of Wisconsin, Institute for Research on Poverty).

[30] See K Rowlingson and E Kempson, *Paying with Plastic: A study of credit card debt* (London, Policy Studies Institute, 1995).

[31] See Compas Inc Multi-Audience Research, *Industry Canada Personal Bankruptcy Survey* (Ottawa, Industry Canada, 1997) at 20 describing the financial actions taken in two years previous to bankruptcy. Heading the list by a wide margin was the use of credit cards to pay other debts.

Bankruptcy provides the ultimate re-insurance for the use of credit cards as a substitute for social welfare. Given the possibility of discharging credit card debts in bankruptcy, there is the issue of moral hazard. This concept expresses the idea that because individuals are cushioned against the consequences of overuse through a bankruptcy discharge, they may be tempted to continue to use the card even when their position is hopeless. This tendency may be reinforced by two findings in behavioural economics. These are that individuals are loss averse and exhibit a *status quo* bias. In relation to loss aversion, repeated experiments show that individuals are willing to pay more to avoid a loss than they are to achieve an equivalent gain.[32] *Status quo* bias refers to the fact that individuals demand a large amount to change their existing circumstances. These factors may explain why individuals may use credit cards to maintain a lifestyle or a small business long after it would appear 'rational' to do so. Even those individuals who gamble with credit card advances or use the cards to purchase goods which are then sold to raise cash may be hoping, like Micawber, that something will turn up and that their financial circumstances will change for the better. The knowledge that debt default and bankruptcy may damage one's credit rating may reduce incentives to use the card in this way but it is probable that, given more immediate pressures facing individuals, this may not have a real impact until default seems inevitable. When this occurs, it is possible that individuals, overestimating the potential impact of bankruptcy,[33] may attempt to reduce their debt load. This is consistent with findings that credit card spending initially increases about 18 months before bankruptcy but eventually declines in the immediate period preceding bankruptcy, while the balance continues to increase during the entire period (presumably because of accrued interest).[34]

What are the costs and benefits of this 'credit card welfare'? The costs of those who fail after using credit cards as a substitute for public support will not be spread broadly and progressively among the public, but will be borne by credit card consumers in the same market segment. If an individual was originally in a higher risk category then the costs will be borne by other high-risk consumers. There may be some overlap here between higher risk, social class and gender. Unemployment, for example, which is highly correlated with default on credit payments, is experienced more by those who are less educated and have less earnings potential. A recent Canadian study concluded that falling behind with debt payments was most closely correlated with age (younger individuals), education and unemployment. In addition, lone parents, unattached men and previous bankrupts were also significantly more likely to fall behind in

[32] See D Kahneman, J Knetsch, and R Thaler, 'Experimental Tests of the Endowment Effect and the Coase Theorem' (1990) *Journal of Political Economy* 1325.

[33] See Note 'A Reformed Economic Model of Consumer Bankruptcy' (1996) 109 *Harvard Law Review* 1338 at 1343, citing to J Braucher, 'Lawyers and Consumer Bankruptcy: One Code, Many Cultures' 67 *American Bankruptcy Law Journal* 501 at 554.

[34] See Evans and Schmalensee, above n 2, at 97.

payments.[35] It is also possible that access to credit may reduce demand for public support and lessen pressures for progressive reform efforts in relation to public programmes of unemployment, health care or income support. It may also contribute to a view of the problems created by volatile employment patterns as a private trouble rather than a public issue[36]—to be addressed through the institution of consumer credit and bankruptcy.

This summary account of credit card use by consumers indicates that there are significant variations in patterns of use among different demographic groups and that simple stories of debtor abuse or creditor exploitation are unlikely to capture the complexity of credit card use and debt default. Use of credit cards as a borrowing mechanism is partly related to factors such as a particular household's life cycle, external shocks to a household budget, or running a small business. Certain groups are more at risk than others. It is useful to record these points as a corrective to the highly individualised and psychologised accounts of credit card 'misuse' which are popular in the media. They also suggest that any individualised attempt in bankruptcy law to sort credit card behaviour ex post into simple categories of fault/no fault is likely to be fraught with difficulty. Unfortunately, many bankruptcy systems attempt such an exercise. Behavioural analysis has developed the idea of hindsight bias where 'people constantly exaggerate what could have been anticipated in foresight . . . People believe that others should have been able to anticipate events much better than was actually the case.'[37] This bias might result in decision-makers either blaming debtors for imprudent borrowing or creditors for imprudent lending depending on the moral and political views of the particular decision-maker. The relative balance of decisions favouring one group or another may be relatively unpredictable.

III. MARKET FAILURES IN THE CREDIT CARD MARKET

Competition in the credit market in North America and the UK is focused on two issues: inducing consumers to charge more transactions on their cards and to carry greater balances but not default. To achieve these objectives credit card companies have tried many strategies, from automatically increasing credit limits, offering payment 'holidays,' reducing minimum payments,[38] shortening

[35] See W Pyper, '*Falling Behind*' *Perspectives on Labour and Income*, vol 3, no 7, (Ottawa, Statistics Canada, 2002) at 17.

[36] See Manning above n 3 at 96.

[37] See B Fischoff, 'For Those Condemned to Study the Past: Heuristics and Biases in Hindsight' quoted in J Rachlinski, 'A Positive Psychological Theory of Judging in Hindsight' in C Sunstein (ed) *Behavioural Law and Economics* (Cambridge, Cambridge University Press, 2000) at 95.

[38] A Consumer Watchdog group notes that the industry standard requiring cardholders to pay a minimum 4% of the balance has gone 'the way of the dinosaur' and that minimum payments are now 2–3%. See 'Consumer Action's 2002 Credit Card Survey', Consumer Action <http://credit.about.com/gi/dynamic/offsite.htm?site=http%3A%2F%2Fwww.consumer-action.org%2F> (last visited 21 January 2003).

grace periods, increasing late payments fees, and introducing rewards programmes and affinity cards which appear to induce greater use and higher borrowing among users.[39] There may be significant product differentiation with certain companies focusing on 'transactors,' attempting to maximise consumers' use of the card with the promise of rewards and in return charging significant fees. In contrast, other companies may focus on sub prime borrowers or attempt to develop a broadly based consumer portfolio.

The credit card market in the US presents the apparent paradox of a highly competitive market where issuers apparently earn supra-normal profits.[40] Whether the business of credit cards results in fact in supra-normal profits is a contested issue,[41] but during several years in the 1980s and 90s, the rate of return on credit cards exceeded those of other forms of lending. The potential failures in the credit card market are those of information and information processing failures, topics that have occupied a central place in economic analysis over recent decades.[42] Both consumers and creditors may face information problems in credit markets. It is possible that intense competition in the credit card market may focus around a number of highly visible terms with companies chiselling on subsidiary terms such as grace periods, late payment fees, and default fees, which consumers do not focus on at the time of entering the transaction. The literature on bounded rationality suggests also that consumers may deviate from rational models of economic behaviour in making credit decisions.[43] Lawrence Ausubel concluded that individuals' underestimation of the extent of their future credit card borrowing accounted for the supra-normal profits of credit card operations in the 1980s, notwithstanding the existence of a large number of credit card providers in the US market.[44] His central argument is that there are substantial numbers of consumers who do not intend at the outset to borrow on their cards, but who subsequently do so based on bounded rationality factors such as over-optimism. These consumers are unlikely to be interest rate sensitive since they do not intend to use the card as a borrowing mechanism. This seemed to be partly confirmed by the experience of credit card marketers who found that consumers are much more sensitive to increases in the annual fee than to increases in interest rates.[45] In later research, Ausubel argued also

[39] The world leader in affinity cards is MBNA, described as the 'King of the Affinity Cards.' A review of the company indicates that 'Vanity and loyalty to their groups lead card members to use their MBNA cards more frequently and carry average balances 60% higher than other cards.' KA Posner and AL Meehan, *The Internet Credit Card Report: A Primer on the Industry and its Role in E-Commerce* (New York, Morgan Stanley Dean Witter & Co, 20 July 1999).

[40] See L Ausubel, 'The Failure of Competition in the Credit Card Market' (1991) 81 *American Economic Review* 50; Sullivan, Warren, and Westbrook, above n 25 at 135.

[41] See Evans and Schmalensee, above n 2 at 251–62.

[42] See the review in J Stiglitz, 'The Contribution of the Economics of Information to Twentieth Century Economics' (2000) *Quarterly Journal of Economics* 1441.

[43] For overviews of the literature on behavioural economics see C Sunstein (ed), *Behavioural Law and Economics* (Cambridge, Cambridge University Press, 2000) and Schwartz in this volume.

[44] See Ausubel, above n 40.

[45] Ausubel's argument on this issue has been challenged by other writers. See T Cargill and J Wendell, 'Bank Credit Cards: Consumer Irrationality versus Market Forces' (1996) 30 *Journal of*

that evidence seems to support the argument that consumers do not act rationally in response to low interest introductory offers of credit, overrating the importance of the introductory rate as compared to its duration or the ensuing post-introductory rate.[46]

David Gross and Nicholas Souleles uncovered potential consumer irrationality in their study of consumers' response to an increase in credit card limits. Contrary to conventional economic analysis, the extra credit was not used solely by individuals close to their credit limit. Other consumers increased significantly their use of credit card debt. Individuals borrowed on credit cards even though they had access to alternative, cheaper sources of credit, such as low cost home equity debt and chequing and savings accounts.[47]

Credit card companies, as profit maximisers, will be seeking constantly to identify these systematic irrationalities in consumer behaviour and they regularly conduct 'experiments' on consumers to identify the most profitable selling techniques.[48] This is, of course, no different from the behaviour of many businesses selling goods to consumers. Businesses accumulate a large 'private sociology' of consumer behaviour as part of their attempt to influence consumer preferences.[49] In a recent article, Hanson and Kysar outline the many psychological techniques used by businesses to manipulate consumer preferences, coining the idea that there may be a market failure of 'market manipulation.'[50] The idea of credit card companies engaged in behaviour modification is captured neatly by the following explanation for the relatively slow expansion of MBNA into Europe:

> British consumers use credit cards much the same way Americans do, carrying outstanding balances, but many Continentals still pay off balances automatically each month . . . the challenge will be to change consumer behavior. MBNA has a marketing job ahead of it in Europe. But . . . the card giant has done it before. Half of British cardholders paid their balances in full each month when MBNA started there eight years ago. Now just 10 per cent of MBNAs customers do.[51]

Consumer Affairs 373; D Brito and P Hartley, 'Consumer Rationality and Credit Cards' 103 *Journal of Political Economy* 400; T Zywicki, '*The Economics of Credit Cards*' (2000) 3 Chapman Law Review 79.

[46] See L Ausubel, 'Adverse Selection in the Credit Card Market' (Working Paper, University of Maryland, 1999).

[47] See D Gross and N Souleles, 'Do Liquidity Constraints and Interest Rates Matter for Consumer Behaviour? Evidence From Credit Card Data' (2002) *Quarterly Journal of Economics* 149 at 180. 'Most puzzling of all, over 90 per cent of people with credit card debt have some very liquid assets in checking and savings accounts, which usually yield at most 1–2 per cent.'

[48] For example, the US credit card company Capital One continually experiments with fees or collection methods to understand how they affect different types of consumers. In 2000, it conducted 46,000 product, price, marketing and distribution channel and service tests. See 'Capital One: Fanaticism that Works' *US Banker* vol III Issue 8 (August 2001) at 24.

[49] I discuss this at greater length in I Ramsay, *Advertising Culture and the Law* (London, Sweet and Maxwell, 1996) ch 3.

[50] See J Hanson and D Kysar, 'Taking Behaviouralism Seriously: Some Evidence of Market Manipulation' (1999) 112 *Harvard Law Review* 1420.

[51] 'This Earnings Machine has Engine Trouble; Credit-Card giant MBNA's market isn't boundless after all' *Business Week* (17 June 2002) at 4.

Economic analysis of information markets indicates that credit card companies may also face significant risks. Credit cards are an unsecured form of lending of relatively small amounts where the costs of collecting an individual account might outweigh the recovery. There are the problems of adverse selection and moral hazard. Adverse selection refers to the problems that lenders may face in distinguishing between high and low risk debtors. It is argued that at a certain level of interest a lender will receive a lower rate of return by attracting more bad risks (who think they are getting a bargain) than good risks (who are driven away). This results in lenders refusing to lend above a certain interest rate rather than adjusting the interest rate. The credit market does not clear since some borrowers remain unsatisfied as to their credit needs. It is argued therefore that credit lenders 'ration' credit rather than adjust the price to meet consumer demand.[52]

Economic analysis of credit rationing was developed in relation to commercial loan markets and there has been very modest empirical testing of the concept of adverse selection in the context of consumer credit markets. Ausubel provides some support for the adverse selection argument. He found in an analysis of the offerings of a major credit card company that individuals who accepted inferior credit card offers (higher interest rates and fees) were more likely to default and declare bankruptcy.[53] Stavins found in a study of individual credit card issuers in the US between 1990 and 1999 that banks offering higher interest credit cards had more delinquencies than other issuers but there was little difference in charge off rates.[54] In addition, banks charging higher interest rates had higher net revenues. Thus although there was support for the adverse selection thesis, one could also conclude that the higher risk issuers had successfully segmented their market, with higher risk consumers being offered worse terms and issuers still capable of maintaining a healthy profit margin. However, Stavins' analysis concluded in 1999 that the increase in charge offs in 2002, particularly among sub prime lenders may foreshadow a retrenchment in lending.

A major antidote to problems of adverse selection and moral hazard has been the development of credit scoring and credit bureaux. The use of credit scoring allied to advances in computing has been crucial to the growth of the credit card market, permitting credit granters to reduce substantially their risks in this market.[55] Although credit scoring was originally used to minimise defaults, it is

[52] The application of the idea of adverse selection to credit markets is attributed to Stiglitz and Weiss. See J Stiglitz and A Weiss, 'Credit Rationing in Markets with Imperfect Information' (1981) 71 *American Economic Review* 393.

[53] Ausubel, above n 46.

[54] See J Stavins, 'Credit Card Borrowing, Delinquency and Personal Bankruptcy' *New England Economic Review* (July/ August 2000) at 15.

[55] See generally L Thomas, D Edelman, and J Crook, *Credit Scoring and Its Applications* (Philadelphia, Society of Industrial and Applied Mathematics, 2002); D Hand and W Henley, 'Statistical Classification Methods in Consumer Credit Scoring: A Review' (1997) *Journal of the Royal Statistical Society* 522.

also used now to maximise profits so that pricing of the card will take into account differential levels of default as one factor in calculating profit from a particular type of card. Credit card providers use information from credit bureaux records along with their own information on consumers to develop a variety of credit scoring regimes, which include predictors of delinquency and the likelihood that a consumer will file for bankruptcy. Companies also update their judgements on consumers using 'behavioural scorecards' based on consumers' use of credit and purchasing behaviour and several companies now use risk-based pricing with interest rates more finely tuned to an individual's profile. One traditional criticism of credit card companies has been that they are not interested in changes in a debtor's circumstances as long as the debtor maintains the minimum payment. But these developments in credit scoring suggest that companies monitor and react to changes in a debtor's circumstances. Credit scoring has facilitated the 'democratisation of credit' by permitting the prediction of risk and management of default and increased portfolio diversification. Those companies supplying credit cards to sub-prime consumers may charge higher fees to compensate for the perceived higher default rate. It has also enabled more targeted forms of collection of delinquent accounts.

Credit bureaux are most well established in North America and the UK with varying degrees of development in other European countries. There are significant differences between countries in the information held by these bureaux and the legislative framework of regulation. This information sharing reduces the level of default[56] and some economists argue that the breadth and depth of credit markets are related to the extent of information sharing in credit markets so that total bank lending to the private sector is larger in countries that have a greater degree of information sharing. The United States has, according to one study, the 'most complete credit files on the largest percentage of its adult population of any country'[57]; the authors claim that this has facilitated the 'explosion' (sic) of consumer credit since the mid 1980s in the US without any dramatic increase in defaults.

Credit scoring increases the significance of reputational sanctions in consumer credit markets.[58] Consumers may be increasingly internalising the norms associated with this system. It is not surprising that one of the first questions which a potential bankrupt asks a bankruptcy trustee in Canada is when her credit rating will be restored and whether she will have access to credit in the

[56] See T Japelli and M Pagano, 'Information Sharing, Lending and Defaults: Cross Country Evidence' (Working Paper No 22, Centre for Studies in Economics and Finance University of Salerno, 1999).

[57] See J Barron and M Staten, 'The Value of Comprehensive Credit Reports: Lessons from the US Experience' (Credit Research Centre, McDonough School of Business, Georgetown University, 2002) <http://www.privacyalliance.org/resources/staten.pdf> (last visited 21 January 2003).

[58] This was noted as early as 1970 by Arthur Leff. See A Leff, 'Injury, Ignorance and Spite: the Dynamics of Coercive Collection' (1970) 80 *Yale Law Journal* 1. For a recent discussion, see R Mann, 'Information Technology and Non-Legal Sanctions in Financing Transactions' (2001) 54 *Vanderbilt Law Review* 1627.

future. Exclusion from access to a credit card is for many, except the very poor, a significant sanction and potential source of embarrassment and shame. One of the most interesting developments in recent years is the increasing public access to credit scores and the assumptions on which these scores are based. The leading US credit scoring company, Fair Isaac, outlines on its web site the factors that are assessed in arriving at a credit score. Consumers are encouraged by private and public organisations to check their credit score regularly, in the same way perhaps that one has a medical checkup. And there is a whole industry devoted to 'credit repair' for those with problem files. There is also a significant industry of credit counsellors and media reports, which educate and inform individuals on the norms of credit use and the role of credit ratings. Within this system, there are the possibilities of both upwardly and downwardly mobile credit careers and it might not be odd to perceive the development of a morality of appropriate credit use within these systems, which those who wish to succeed in the use of credit should prudently follow.

IV. BANKRUPTCY AND THE REGULATION OF CREDIT CARD USE

In both Canada and the US the rise in the use of credit cards is associated with rises in bankruptcy rates. A recent Canadian study indicated a correlation between credit card balances per household and bankruptcies, and a strong positive correlation between credit card cash advances and consumer bankruptcies, suggesting that they are the lender of last resort.[59] These data do not mean, however, that credit cards are the cause of bankruptcy but rather that there is a link here which needs probing. My earlier discussion of credit cards as a form of public support suggest that it may be unemployment or changes of circumstances which are the ultimate cause of bankruptcy. There may also be other factors at work. This point is illustrated by an oft-cited study by Diane Ellis, who noted that after the entry of Visa in Canada in 1968 there was a dramatic increase in credit card loans and that from 1966 to 1976 there was also a dramatic rise of 340 per cent in personal bankruptcy rates in Canada.[60] However, this study did not take into account the introduction of state-subsidised processing of consumer bankruptcies in 1972. It is likely that this was a significant factor in the consumer bankruptcy rate doubling between 1972–74.

In the US, there has been a continuing debate over the relationship of consumer credit to the increased bankruptcy levels in the mid-1990s, a period when there was an apparently buoyant economy. Charge-off rates for credit cards increased during the 1990s, along with increases in the bankruptcy rate.

[59] See Informetrica, *Consumer Bankruptcies: Contributing Key Factors* (Ottawa, 1999) at 32.

[60] See D Ellis, 'Bank Trends—The Effect of Consumer Interest Rate Deregulation on Credit Card Volumes, Charge Offs, and the Personal Bankruptcy Rate' no 98–05 *FDIC Bank Trends* (March 1998), Federal Deposit Insurance Corporation <http://www.fdic.gov/bank/analytical/bank/bt_9805.html>.

Different explanations have been developed to explain this increase. One explanation is that the 'democratisation of credit' had led to increased lending to a more risky borrower pool with the consequence of greater numbers of defaults and bankruptcies.[61] The highly profitable nature of credit card lending meant that lenders were willing to accept higher write offs. In Canada, Saul Schwartz and Leigh Anderson have hypothesised a similar argument to Moss and Johnson, namely that increases in bankruptcy rates may be accounted for by lending to more vulnerable individuals.[62] Elizabeth Warren, however, argues on the basis of recent data that this thesis is not reflected in the current demographics of US bankrupts who continue to exhibit the characteristics of the middle class.[63] Over two-thirds of this group had substantial job problems before filing for bankruptcy and their continued use of credit after encountering these difficulties is consistent with my earlier discussion of the use of credit cards as a substitute for other forms of income support. Other writers have also argued that increased risk does not fully explain the rise in bankruptcies and that it is possible that something may have changed on the demand side of bankruptcy, such as the costs of declaring bankruptcy (reduced stigma, information costs, etc).[64] Given our current state of knowledge, the precise relationship of credit cards to the bankruptcy decision remains unclear.

From an economic perspective, the central questions in relation to bankruptcy and credit card use are those of risk allocation and its impact on debtor and creditor incentives. An additional aspect is the distribution of the benefits and costs among different groups. If bankruptcy is conceptualised as a form of mandatory insurance in all consumer credit contracts then the issue is to determine the optimal insurance contract.[65] Increased insurance may create problems of moral hazard so that it is necessary to model the effects of different levels of protection of income and assets on credit granting, interest rates and the substitution of secured for unsecured credit. In terms of distributional effects, protection of income rather than assets will have in general a distributionally progressive effect given the distribution of wealth in countries such as the US and Canada. In addition, it is necessary to also take into account externalities, such as the impact on productivity of limited protection for income in bankruptcy, and the possibility of a debtor requiring state support if she is unable to protect assets or income in bankruptcy.

[61] See D Moss and G Johnson, 'The Rise of Consumer Bankruptcy: Evolution, Revolution or Both' (1999) 73 *American Bankruptcy Law Journal* 311.

[62] See S Schwartz and L Anderson, *An Empirical Study of Canadian Seeking Bankruptcy Protection* (Ottawa, Carleton University School of Public Administration, 1998) at 38–45.

[63] See E Warren, 'Financial Collapse and Class Status: Who Goes Bankrupt?' (2003) 41 *Osgoode Hall Law Journal* 116.

[64] See D Gross and N Souleles, 'An Empirical Analysis of Personal Bankruptcy and Delinquency' (Working Paper No w8409, National Bureau of Economic Research, 2001), NBER Working Papers <http://papers.nber.org/papers/W8409>.

[65] See B Adler, B Pollak and A Schwartz, 'Regulating Consumer Bankruptcy: A Theoretical Inquiry' (2000) 29*Journal of Legal Studies* 585.

US bankruptcy law is unique in providing full wage insurance to a debtor who declares bankruptcy under Chapter 7. In contrast, Canada provides a limited protection for post-bankruptcy income and there is limited protection against a debtor reaffirming a credit contract. In Europe, debtors' income is also available for repayment since most European systems require a debtor to enter a repayment plan as a condition of discharge. The relative stringency until recently of European systems of debt-adjustment had a significant impact on debtors' willingness to continue working and also stimulated deviant behaviour among some debtors. The more generous state-provided insurance in these countries has the effect of spreading the costs of debtor protection among all members of society. This will also create moral hazard problems for creditors who will oversupply credit in the knowledge that they will be repaid by state-provided insurance. This problem may be addressed through greater control on credit granting, which does exist in a number of European countries.

The previous paragraphs outlines hypotheses. The hypotheses are based on rational actor models of debtor behaviour which assume that individuals know their preferences and the legal rules, maximise their self-interest, discount the future at marginal interest rates and are not subject to inconsistent preferences over time. The predictive power of economics is based on assuming that if the empirical evidence indicates that consumers behave *as if* they are rational calculators, for example, if the bankruptcy rate goes up when the price of bankruptcy falls, then it is not necessary to probe more deeply into consumers' motivations. However, it is difficult to isolate the effect of differences in bankruptcy rules on the credit market. The actual effects of bankruptcy on lending practices may depend on the institutional structure of credit card lending. Thus, although Canada has less generous protection for income in bankruptcy than the US, credit card lending in that country has not been extended to lower quality borrowers to the same extent as in the US. This is partly because of the traditionally more cautious approach to lending by the concentrated banking sector which dominates credit granting in Canada.[66]

Moreover, since the existing level of credit use in society is in part a function of a large number of laws, the institutional structure of credit granting, and social norms, it is a normative question whether any change in the existing level of credit granting in a society is desirable. For example, less generous protection of income in bankruptcy might induce unsecured lenders such as credit card companies to increase supply at the margin. Whether this is a desirable consequence may be answered differently in differing societies. As I have already indicated some European countries continue to control credit grantors in extending more risky forms of credit.

[66] See *Moody's Canadian Credit Card Index* Special Report, August 23, 2002 noting that charge offs and delinquency rates in the US are nearly double those in Canada. It attributes 'the large part of the difference in delinquency and loss performance between the two countries to the US's much earlier move to extend credit to lower quality borrowers.' *Ibid* at 5.

Bankruptcy law is part of the ground rules of credit markets and it might be useful to place it within a continuum of potential forms of regulation of the credit card market. Credit card companies are undoubtedly one of the losers in a bankruptcy. They are unsecured creditors for relatively small amounts and individuals are more likely to attempt to repay or renegotiate debts relating to major assets such as a home or car. Policy-making might proceed by attempting to affect the supply (creditor) or demand side (consumer) of the credit market and one might assume that if creditors are rational actors, it may be simpler to affect their behaviour than to alter consumer behaviour.

A direct response to information failures in the credit card market is through information disclosure, which is required in many jurisdictions at the time of entering into the credit contract. 'Truth in Lending' is a pervasive form of consumer protection and its attractiveness as a policy is partly because it supports the ideal of consumer autonomy through informed consumer choice, has limited costs for governments and may attract a consensus of support from business and consumer groups. There is, however, little evidence that the introduction of disclosure provisions has had significant impact on over-indebtedness (although it may have achieved other goals). Truth in Lending is based also on a 'rational consumer' model of decision-making and the literature on behavioural economics suggests that disclosures based on this model may be limited as a form of 'debiasing intervention.' If there are systematic irrationalities in consumer decision-making and these are deliberately targeted by credit card companies, for example, through automatic increases in credit limits, low introductory rates, etc, then policy-makers must either be much more careful in designing effective information policies or engage in direct regulation of the activity. For example, the psychological finding that individuals weigh losses more heavily than gains might suggest an information campaign directed at students which emphasises the long-term damage to a credit rating from imprudent use of credit cards.

A further limitation on disclosures is that they are often made before or at the time of entering the contract. Since empirical evidence suggests that it is often a change of circumstance which causes increased use of credit cards, and ultimately the necessity of declaring bankruptcy, disclosures at the time of entering into the contract are unlikely to affect the behaviour of those who had not anticipated this situation at the time of entering the contract. It is, however, possible that post-contractual disclosures could have an impact.[67] For example, individuals may not realise the consequences of making only monthly minimum payments on their credit cards. If a significant number of individuals are making these payments because of a change of circumstances, it is at this point that disclosures may be relevant. Recent California legislation would require warning of the period of time necessary to pay off an outstanding balance when

[67] See W Whitford, 'The Functions of Disclosure Regulation in Consumer Transactions' (1973) *Wisconsin Law Review* 400 at 466.

minimum payments are being made.[68] The disclosure would be triggered by an individual carrying a balance from a previous month. Although this state legislation has been struck down under Federal pre-emption jurisprudence, it provides a potential model for future regulation.

Controls on the supply side of the market might also be developed. In the early 1970s, Vern Countryman suggested the concept of 'improvident credit extension' as a method of regulating what he perceived to be the overextension of credit by high risk creditors.[69] His definition would have included a situation where credit was extended when a reasonable inquiry by the creditor would have revealed that there was no reasonable expectation that a debtor could repay the debt. Although this concept is recognised in consumer protection statutes, it has probably had little effect on creditor practices. Like the doctrine of unconscionability or the English concept of an 'extortionate credit transaction,' it is unlikely to have much impact on a broad range of transactions.

The more interesting question is what improvident credit extension or 'prudent lending practices' mean in the context of relatively sophisticated and computerised credit granting practices. In England, a recent task force on over-indebtedness proposed the improvement of credit scoring techniques and greater information sharing as one strategy to reduce over-indebtedness.[70] The European Directive on Consumer Credit proposes a concept of 'responsible lending,' which will place an obligation on a lender to determine whether a consumer may be reasonably expected to repay the obligations under an agreement. The creditor is required to consult any credit databases in making her judgement on this question.[71] This obligation represents a requirement that the lender take greater care in considering the interests of the other contracting party and could be said to reflect the idea that contracting parties should not treat each other as gamblers.[72]

As I noted earlier, the use of credit scoring to maximise profits may not necessarily result in a lower level of default. It may permit a higher risk company to predict the level of default and price the credit accordingly. However, even these companies will be interested in reducing levels of default since a reduction in defaults of only 0.25 per cent in bad debts results in savings of millions of dollars. It is possible to imagine 'default reduction' incentives in the area of consumer credit. Different levels of optimal default could be established and companies that exceeded this could buy the right to a higher level of default

[68] See Cal Statutes 2001, adding California Civil Code s1748.13, at ch 711.

[69] See V Countryman, 'Improvident Credit Extension: A New Legal Concept Aborning' (1975) 27 *Maine Law Review* 1.

[70] See *Report by the Task Force on Tackling Over-indebtedness* (London, Department of Trade and Industry, Consumer Affairs Directorate, July 2001).

[71] See *Proposal for a Directive of the European Parliament and of the Council on the harmonisation of the laws, regulations and administrative provisions of the Member States concerning credit for consumers* (Brussels, COM(2002) 443 final 2002/0222(COD)) at Art 9 (Responsible Lending), Art 8 (Central Database).

[72] See I Ramsay, 'Consumer Credit Law, Distributive Justice and the Welfare State' (1995) *Oxford Journal of Legal Studies* 177.

from companies that had a lower than average default level. This could create incentives to reduce default levels. A further role of the law might be to give greater incentives for creditors to develop and use information. For example, the ability of a consumer to transfer a debit balance from one credit card to a card which promises a low introductory rate means that a consumer may be able to double their borrowing capacity. If the consumer has a high bankruptcy predictor score then it might be regarded as improvident to make this further extension of credit. One could apply a presumption that receipt of a new credit card a short time before declaring bankruptcy when an individual had a high bankruptcy predictor score should result in the subordination of any debt incurred on the card.

A full investigation of the regulation of credit information is potentially quite complex in terms of its efficiency and distributional implications and cannot be explored in this paper. It might be dangerous to be too optimistic about the precision of creditor screening through credit scoring, the ability of creditors to scientifically predict default, and their willingness to act rationally on the basis of the information. Creditors may be subject to forms of 'irrational exuberance' in periods of apparent prosperity such as the 1990s. There is, however, a case for systematic analysis of this issue and the implications for privacy policies that cannot be viewed as distinct from issues of debt default and bankruptcy. One author points out how interpretations of the Fair Credit Reporting Act restricted the ability of credit card companies to pre-screen consumers.[73] Credit grantors in the US have opposed privacy legislation that could restrict their access to information on consumers arguing that credit reporting permits the widespread availability of credit and low default rates. Yet credit grantors also argue that there have been significant rises in defaults and reduction in stigma when discussing bankruptcy reform. In addition to exploring these connections between credit information and bankruptcy, there is a need for greater understanding of the role of credit information in facilitating exploitation of consumer irrationality, a part of the more general phenomenon of market manipulation.[74]

A. Bankruptcy Law as Expressive Law; the Construction of the Social Meaning of Debt Default

The previous section indicates that most disagreement in debates on bankruptcy in the US and Canada relates to the level of income and assets that a debtor may shield from her creditors. It is at this level not a debate about fundamental value conflicts in society. All agree that relief should be provided to individuals who

[73] See M Howard, 'Shifting Risk and Fixing Blame: the Vexing Problem of Credit Card Obligations in Bankruptcy' (2001) 75 *American Bankruptcy Law Journal* 63 at 127.

[74] See J Hanson and D Kysar, 'Taking Behaviouralism Seriously: Some Evidence of Market Manipulation' (1999) 112 *Harvard Law Review* 1420.

have suffered a change of circumstances, although there may be disagreement as to the exact scope of the concept of the 'honest but unfortunate' debtor. However, this account of the disagreement does not explain the heated debate over bankruptcy reform in the US and broader issues seem to be relevant. Much discussion relating to bankruptcy and credit card use focuses on the expressive or symbolic role of law in affirming morality or social norms. A rather extreme example of this perspective is found in a dissent to the report of the National Bankruptcy Review Commission, which feared that the existing US Bankruptcy law was encouraging promise breaking and leading to a breakdown in social cohesion and moral welfare.[75] The relationship of law to informal constraints and social norms is a topic much studied by sociologists and, more recently, economists. I have already concluded that the existence of credit scoring and other information make informal sanctions a powerful inducement to repay. There is also the existence of internalised social norms in relation to debt repayment. It would be surprising if a society heavily dependent on credit would leave the issue of repayment of debts to the contingency of rational cost calculation by its members accompanied only by legal sanctions.

Michelle White, an economist, argues that a majority of US households could benefit financially from bankruptcy if they acted 'strategically'.[76] She fears that given the liberal bankruptcy laws in the US, more consumers who learn of the benefits of bankruptcy will change their negative views about the process and file for bankruptcy. This analysis neglects, however, the significance of reputation, the continuing power of social norms, and the many social sites in contemporary society which communicate the proper norms of credit use. A typical example is a cover story for 'Newsweek' magazine entitled 'Are You Maxed Out?' which outlines the 'Seven Tips' for financial management with the first maxim being that 'you don't save money by borrowing more.'[77] Historical studies also suggest caution in making broad statements about the decline of stigma[78] and contemporary sociological research concludes that stigma remains a significant factor among US bankrupts.[79]

The expressive role of bankruptcy law remains very visible in judicial rhetoric on credit card abuse and the dischargeability of credit card debts. The conclusion that the courts in the US have 'made a muddle' of determining the issue of

[75] 'Additional Dissent to Recommendations For Reform of Consumer Bankruptcy Law submitted by Honorable Edith Jones and Commissioner James I Shepard' in National Bankruptcy Review Commission, *Bankruptcy: The Next Twenty Years* vol 1 (Washington, US Government Printing Office, 1997) at 13–14.

[76] See M White, 'Why it Pays to File for Bankruptcy: A Critical Look at Incentives under US Bankruptcy Laws and a Proposal for Change' (1998) 65 *University of Chicago Law Review* 685.

[77] See *Newsweek* (27 August 2001) at 34.

[78] See, eg Moss and Johnson, above n 61; Calder, above n 26; B Mann, *Republic of Debtors: Bankruptcy in the Age of American Independence* (Cambridge, Massachusetts, Harvard University Press, 2002).

[79] See D K Thorne, 'Personal Bankruptcy through the Eyes of the Stigmatized: Insight into Issues of Shame, Gender and Marital Discord' (Washington, Washington State University, PhD 2001).

fraud in relation to pre-bankruptcy credit card use[80] may reflect the tension between disapproval of a morality of 'easy credit' by aggressive credit card companies and irresponsible behaviour by debtors.[81] In the well-known case of *In re Dorsey*[82] the judge excoriates American Express for its irresponsible lending practices at the same time as disapproving of the debtor who had enjoyed a 'grand time' on her trip to Europe, financed through credit cards.

We should return at this point to the quotations at the beginning of this chapter concerning visions of credit card use and their relationship to bankruptcy. The lack of fit between these visions and the reality of credit card use suggests that debates about credit card use are often about whose vision of social reality will be made to stick in society. In his classic text on debt enforcement, Paul Rock suggested that historically laws on debtor-creditor relations were framed by 'people who believe that creditors are not always innocents, and debtors not always villains.'[83] The ability of many individuals with whom I discuss the topic of consumer bankruptcy to believe simultaneously that many individuals take advantage of the bankruptcy system and that credit card companies exploit consumers seems to fit this description. There is a continuing moral ambivalence about credit and the nature of debt default in society and it is in the interests of ideological entrepreneurs to convince legislators and the public of the validity of their vision of the reality of debt default.

In a different context Joseph Gusfield argued that the passage of Prohibition in the United States was primarily significant because of its affirmation of the norms of a particular group (the abstinent Protestant middle class) rather than in its actual impact on behaviour: 'even if the law was broken, it was clear whose law it was.'[84] Creditor financed attempts to roll back bankruptcy protections in the US may be viewed through this lens. If they are successful, bankruptcy law will become their law, debtors will be more subject to their mercy rather than being entitled to choose bankruptcy options, and the social meaning of bankruptcy might be affected. Of course, there might be material benefits to creditors and the bargaining power of debtors would be reduced, but it is important to see also the symbolic dimension of the conflict over bankruptcy protection.

[80] See M Howard, above n 73 at 86.

[81] See, eg Duncan Kennedy, *A Critique of Adjudication: fin de siècle* (Cambridge Ma, Harvard University Press, 1997) who describes what he perceives as the endless policy debate between liberalism and conservatism in US law. Jean Braucher also draws attention to the differing ideologies of US bankruptcy lawyers. See Braucher, above n 33.

[82] *In Re Dixie Lee Dorsey, Debtor, American Express Travel Related Services v Dixie Lee Dorsey* (1990) 120 BR 592.

[83] See P Rock, *Making People Pay* (London, Routledge, 1973) at 263.

[84] See J Gusfield, 'Moral Passage: The Symbolic Process in Public Designation of Deviance' (1967) 15 *Social Problems* 175 at 178. See also J Gusfield, *Symbolic Crusade: Status Politics and the American Temperance Movement* (Chicago, University of Illinois Press, 1963).

V. CONCLUSION

> Credit was blamed for promoting extravagance and encouraging fecklessness. It was alleged to cause individuals to lose a sense of who they were and what they could and could not afford, and to lead them to replace thrift and careful saving with the immediate gratification of trivial or even improper desires.[85]

This description of attitudes towards credit in eighteenth century England, the birthplace of the consumer society, has a remarkably contemporary tone. Debates on credit cards and bankruptcy seem to be a repetition of a historical pattern of concern about the 'explosive' growth of credit and its potentially corrosive effect on culture and morality.

Consumer credit may in fact be a conservative and potentially disciplining force in society. The French theorist Jean Baudrillard argued that:

> credit is a disciplinary process which extorts savings and regulates demand—just as wage labour was a rational process in the extortion of labour power and in the increase of productivity.[86]

This argument has been adopted recently by Lendol Calder in his history of consumer credit in the US where he concludes that the development of the instalment plan imposed a discipline on consumers not dissimilar to that of the factory discipline developed in Frederick Taylor's models of scientific management.[87] Pursuing the theme of credit as discipline, many writers have described contemporary society as a 'risk society'[88] where increasingly populations are classified and sorted on the basis of actuarial assessments of risk, which encode normative judgements about behaviour. Thus credit ratings, which are used to sort and classify credit risks, become embedded in norms of consumer behaviour to which consumers are expected to orient their conduct.

This broader perspective on the role of credit is valuable in drawing our attention to the relationship of consumer credit to social divisions within society. Credit scoring technology facilitates both the democratisation of credit and greater segmentation and discrimination among consumers, potentially reducing any sense of consumer solidarity. Whether access to credit cards provides greater freedom and autonomy to ordinary workers faced with insecurity than a well-functioning public safety net does is debatable. There is increasing inequality in North America and other industrialised countries. Manuel Castells has described the new class divisions associated with informational capitalism where there is a broad distinction between the new producers, such as managers, professionals and technicians, and generic labour that is replaceable by

85 See P Haagen, *Imprisonment for Debt in England and Wales* (PhD, Princeton, 1986) at 108–09.

86 See J Baudrillard, 'The Consumer Society' in J Baudrillard *Selected Writings* (Stanford, Stanford University Press, 1988) at 81.

87 See Calder, above n 26, at ch 4.

88 See, eg U Beck, *Risk Society: Towards a New Modernity* (London, Sage, 1992).

machines or other workers. The latter group often faces significant insecurity because of the loss of a stable relationship to work and is subject to a higher incidence of major crises such as loss of employability, assets and credit.[89] For this group, credit cards may provide within the 'consumers' republic' in the US 'a taste but not a share of the pie.'[90] Since this generic labour is easily replaceable, it may not be surprising that there is less public support for a generous safety net in bankruptcy for this group. The traditional concern that over-indebtedness leads to lost productivity is no longer as salient when labour is easily replaceable.[91]

It would be helpful if debates on credit cards and bankruptcy could proceed beyond distorted discussions of the decline of stigma and visions of hedonistic or foolish consumers lurching towards the bankruptcy courts. Current political debates on credit, debt and bankruptcy are often grounded in supposed histories of credit and debt, which like similar discussions of crime and punishment, are usually 'such gross misrepresentations of the historical record that they hardly deserve to be called debates at all.'[92] Moralisms are not a substitute for a political economy of the role of consumer credit and its institutions in contemporary consumer capitalism. History suggests that money and credit have often raised questions of power. We need greater exploration of the nature of this power whether it is reflected in the extent to which credit card companies manipulate consumer preferences or the creation of ideologies of credit card use.

[89] M Castells, *The Information Age: Economy, Society and Culture Vol III* (Oxford, Blackwell, 1998) at 344–45.

[90] Manning, above n 3 at 124 quoting from a consumer interview.

[91] A point made by Bill Whitford. See W Whitford, 'Changing Definitions of Fresh Start in US Bankruptcy Law' (1997) 20 *Journal of Consumer Policy* 179 at 194.

[92] D Hay, 'Foreword' in C Strange (ed), *Qualities of Mercy Justice Punishment and Discretion* (Vancouver, University of British Columbia Press, 1996).

2

Collective or Individual? Constructions of Debtors and Creditors in Consumer Bankruptcy

JOHANNA NIEMI-KIESILÄINEN*

Comparing the US and Finland:
When I first came to the US, the two most surprising things were peanut butter and having to pay for school lunch. This may sound strange but in Finland we have free dental care, free health care and totally free schools. This is because we have five times as many taxes on alcohol, tobacco and gasoline. Other taxes are normal.
Mikko Kiesiläinen, 10 years old, after one year in Madison, Wisconsin.

I. INTRODUCTION

THE DIFFERENCES BETWEEN an Anglo-Saxon or common law jurisdiction and a civil law jurisdiction can hardly be greater than in the matter of discharge in bankruptcy law. While Anglo-Saxon jurisdictions have historically granted a bankrupt a discharge of her debt, civil law jurisdictions have refused to acknowledge any discharge at all. Quite to the contrary, civil law countries have insisted on the full payment of all debts after a bankruptcy.[1]

Lately, these opposite views have moved towards more similar positions. Anglo-Saxon countries have attached conditions to the discharge, such as mandatory counselling before a discharge is granted in Canada.[2] In the United States, the

* Funding for the research was received from Finland's Academy. I am very grateful to Prof. William Whitford for his comments and encouragement. The discussions in the conferences in Toronto 1998 and Budapest 2001 have been essential for the development of the ideas presented in the article.

[1] Legally, the enforcement of debt has been limited to a period of 10 or more years. Even this period is renewable. Thus, the liability for debt, at least in theory, can be a lifelong burden. In practice, however, many banks and other creditors may choose to write off certain debts after futile attempts to enforce their collection. See J Niemi-Kiesiläinen, 'Consumer Bankruptcy in Comparison: Do We Cure a Market Failure or a Social Problem?' (1999) 37 *Osgoode Hall Law Journal* 473 at 480 ['Consumer Bankruptcy in Comparison'].

[2] J Ziegel, *Comparative Consumer Insolvency Regimes from a Canadian Perspective. A Report for Industry Canada* (2000); Mason and Duns in this volume; Telfer in this volume.

liberal discharge provisions have met with vehement criticism. The majority of the National Bankruptcy Review Commission (1997) did not propose mandatory payment plans or 'means testing' as conditions of a discharge, but the minority members of the Commission did. The subsequent discussion has almost exclusively concerned 'means testing' and partial repayment of debt as conditions of a discharge. Two bills concerning mandatory payment plans in consumer bankruptcy law were discussed in Congress, but they were not carried through during the Clinton administration. President George W Bush seems to be more willing to confirm the amendments of the Bankruptcy Code to curtail discharge.[3]

A development in the opposite direction has taken place in continental Europe. At the beginning of the 1990s, several Western and Northern European countries passed their first ever consumer bankruptcy laws, including provisions on the partial discharge of debts. The Danish bankruptcy law was already amended by 1984 to include a specific procedure for consumer debt adjustment and discharge.[4] This Danish amendment was an important example for other Scandinavian countries when they drafted their respective laws. The laws on judicial debt adjustment for consumers entered into force in 1993 in Finland[5] and Norway [6] and in 1994 in Sweden.[7] The French law on the prevention and regulation of individual and household over-indebtedness was already enacted by 1989[8], but its very restrictive discharge provision was substantially expanded in 1998.[9] In Austria, debt adjustment legislation was accepted in 1993.[10] The German insolvency reform proceeded to its final stages as a business bankruptcy law. The reform act, however, was amended by Parliament to include a chapter on consumer insolvency. Enacted in 1994, the German insolvency law came in force in 1999.[11] Finally, the Netherlands passed a law on consumer debt adjustment in 1997[12] and Belgium in 1998.[13]

[3] For discussion about the reform of US bankruptcy law, see M Jacoby in this volume.

[4] The amendment of the Danish Bankruptcy Code, *Konkurslov* (part IV, *Gældsanering* S 197–237) came into force 1.7.1984. See P Møgelvang-Hansen, 'Adjustment of Hopeless Debt' in *Consumer Debt in Europe: the Birmingham Declaration* (Proc Third Eur Conf on Over-indebtedness, Birmingham, 4 & 5 December 1992, 85, 1993). For an overview of European consumer bankruptcy laws, see 'Consumer Bankruptcy in Comparison', above n 1.

[5] *Lagen om skuldssanering av privatpersoner* (25.1.1993/57; entered into force 8.2.1993).

[6] *Lov av* 17. July 1992 *om frivillig og tvungen gjeldsordning for privatpersoner (Gjeldsordningloven)* came into force 1.1.1993. See, generally, H-P Graver, 'Consumer Bankruptcy: A Right or a Privilege? The Role of the Courts in Establishing Moral Standards of Economic Conduct' (1997) 20 *Journal of Consumer Policy* 161.

[7] About the Swedish law, see B Carlsson and D Hoff, 'Dealing with Insolvency and Indebted Individuals in Respect to Law and Morals' (2000) 9 *Social and Legal Studies* 293 at 295–319.

[8] *Loi 89–1010 relative à la prévention et au règlement des difficultès liées au surendettement des particuliers et des familles,* entered into force 1 March 1990. In 1993, the provisions were incorporated into the Consumer Protection Act as Articles L 331–1 to L 333–8.

[9] *Loi n 98–657, 29.7.1998.*

[10] *Konkursordnungsnovelle* 1993 (BGBl 974); *Abschöpfungsverfahren mit Restschuldbefreiung, Konkursordnung* § 199–216. Entered Into force 1.1.1995.

[11] *Insolvenzordnung* 5.10.1994, Bundesgesetzblatt Teil I, 2866. Entered into force 1.1.1999.

[12] See Huls, Jungmann, and Niemeijer in this volume.

[13] L Demeyere and J Everaert, 'Die Neue belgische Gesetzgebung über das Vergleichs- und Konkursverfahren' (1999) 2 *KTS, Zeitschrift für Insolvenzrecht* at 165–91.

The European consumer bankruptcy laws, however, differ from the Anglo-Saxon laws in at least three important respects.[14] Firstly, the European legislatures have not adhered to the principle of open access to consumer bankruptcy. Secondly, they insist on a mandatory payment plan as a condition for discharge. And thirdly, debt counselling and preliminary negotiations with creditors, albeit in different ways, have been incorporated into the judicial procedure in most European countries.[15] According to Nick Huls, these three features characterise the European consumer bankruptcy model.[16]

Despite the convergent tendencies of late, the Anglo-Saxon and the European continental jurisdictions are still so far apart that it is even appropriate to use different terminology. In the following text, I use the term *consumer bankruptcy* when referring to the Anglo-Saxon institution and *consumer debt adjustment* when referring to its European counterparts. Consumer bankruptcy is used also as an overall concept for all types of collective insolvency proceedings open to consumers and leading to the alleviation of the debt burden.

The international and comparative bankruptcy scholarship has frequently utilised the concept of *model* in comparisons. Depending on what features the author wants to emphasise, different models have been presented. Originally, Udo Reifner classified consumer bankruptcy models according to the political ideologies they represented.[17] Nick Huls, to the contrary, wanted to use politically neutral language when emphasising the differences between Anglo-Saxon and Continental jurisdictions.[18] Iain Ramsay has used a functional differentiation in his threefold classification of consumer bankruptcy: the consumer protection model, the control of deviant debtor behaviour and the social welfare model.[19] Finally, I myself have resorted to geographical differentiation in model building while, at the same time, emphasising the variety of legislative differences both within the models and among them.[20]

The use of ideal-type models always requires a certain degree of simplification. It is a methodological choice that necessarily leads to the reduction of the variety and complexity of phenomena under inspection to a few variables or criteria. The models we have built so far have illustrated the systematic differences among different legal regimes. However, they have not been able to reduce the

[14] J Niemi-Kiesiläinen, 'Changing Directions in Consumer Bankruptcy Law and Practice in Europe and USA' (1997) 20 *Journal of Consumer Law and Policy* 133 at 135; N Huls, 'Overindebtedness and Overlegalization: Consumer Bankruptcy as a Field for Alternative Dispute Resolution' (1997) 20 *Journal of Consumer Policy* 143 ['Overindebtedness and Overlegalization'].

[15] About different models of debt counselling, see J Niemi-Kiesiläinen, 'The Role of Consumer Counselling as Part of the Bankruptcy Process in Europe' (1999) 37 *Osgoode Hall Law Journal* 409; See also Gross in this volume; Braucher in this volume.

[16] See N Huls *et al*, *Overindebtness of Consumers in the EC Member States: Facts and Search for Solutions* (European Communities, Kluwer, 1994) [*Overindebtedness of Consumers in the EC*] and 'Overindebtedness and Overlegalization', above n 14.

[17] U Reifner in *Overindebtedness of Consumers in the EC*, above n 16, ch 6.

[18] See 'Overindebtedness and Overlegalization', above n 14.

[19] I Ramsay, 'Models of Consumer Bankruptcy: Implications for Research and Policy' (1997) 20 *Journal of Consumer Policy* 269.

[20] See 'Consumer Bankruptcy in Comparison', above n 1 at 499.

complexity, caused by different choices made by legislators,[21] nor have they been able to explain why the legislators have chosen such different approaches.

The approach I am proposing in this article focuses on the functions of consumer bankruptcy in the broader frame of the legal regulation. Instead of building models by classifying the similarities and differences among the legal institutions of bankruptcy law, I will start by analysing the different discursive approaches the legislators have taken, either explicitly or implicitly, vis-à-vis consumer bankruptcy and over-indebtedness. Since the difference between the Scandinavian welfare orientation and the American market approach seem to be the most obvious, I shall take it as my starting point. First, I will discuss how the liberal and welfare state paradigms are reflected in the *travaux preparatoires* of consumer bankruptcy laws. Then, I will argue that the different paradigms have a bearing on how the concrete institutions of bankruptcy law are formulated and interpreted. My central thesis is that different paradigms have contributed to the construction of quite different representations of subjectivity in bankruptcy law, both for debtors and creditors. These constructed subjectivities, for their part, have an effect on how central institutions of bankruptcy law are regulated and interpreted.

II. ABOUT MODELS AND PARADIGMS

This article may be understood as a revitalisation of functionalism in bankruptcy law. But it is exactly the functionalism of the consumer bankruptcy models that has called for a rethinking. Almost all models presented make statements about the functions of consumer bankruptcy and use the function as one of the criteria for classification. Reifner makes a differentiation among fresh start, educational and social protection models.[22] Ramsay distinguishes the models depending on whether they emphasise consumer protection, the control of a debtor's deviant behaviour or social welfare.[23] Niemi-Kiesiläinen has taken up, as the primary aims of different models, rehabilitation, repayment, prevention and efficiency.[24]

This kind of functional approach forces one to choose one overriding aim (or function) for the respective legislation of each jurisdiction. In reality, however, the legislators have had several, at times contradictory, aims in their minds when the consumer bankruptcy laws have been enacted. The actual consumer bankruptcy law, as finally accepted, is a compromise among different interests.

Moreover, the aims of the laws are not attributable to distinct models of consumer bankruptcy. The rehabilitation function is especially present in all

[21] No attempt of harmonisation has taken place even among the EU member states. See *ibid* at 479.

[22] U Reifner in *Overindebtedness of Consumers in the EC*, above n 16 at 17.

[23] Ramsay, above n 19.

[24] See 'Consumer Bankruptcy in Comparison', above n 1, at 499.

models of consumer bankruptcy and can hardly be used to distinguish one from another. In addition, the educational function, which seems to be discussed in all contemporary reform plans, seems to be compatible with any model.

The models presented by Huls and Reifner in 1994 deserve special attention because they connect the models with their ideological underpinnings. In Reifner and Huls' classification of consumer bankruptcy laws,[25] the fresh start model corresponds to the liberal, if not libertarian ideology, and the US bankruptcy law serves as an example of the model. As the economic value of the new start for both business and consumer debtors is emphasised, and the specific social and educational needs of the consumer debtor are not recognised, the model equates a consumer debtor with a business debtor.

The re-educational model is linked to the conservative attitude, according to which inability to pay debt is a personal and moral failure. Partial relief from debt is linked with accepting responsibility, especially through mandatory partial payment of debt. Moreover, according to the German law that exemplifies this model, 'good behaviour' is required by the debtor during the payment plan.

Reifner's social protection model is reflected in the European debt counselling schemes. The experience of these programmes is that the debtor has, besides over-indebtedness, other social problems that also have to be addressed. The connection between over-indebtedness and other social problems and the debtor's need for social support is the cornerstone of these models, and relates back to the social liberal ideology.

Even though the material Reifner used in 1994 is somewhat out of date, the analysis of how different ideological starting points are reflected in bankruptcy law still holds. My approach in this article is related to Reifner's, because I am also interested in the relationship between consumer bankruptcy law and the ideological orientation of the legislator. In the following, I take a constructivist look at how the legislators in the United States as opposed to those in Scandinavian countries have constructed the debtors and creditors in their discussion of consumer bankruptcy law. I look at these discourses in the context of Habermas' legal paradigms.

Jürgen Habermas uses the concept of legal paradigm to comprehend how we understand the role of law in the regulation of social and economic problems. According to Habermas, legal paradigms consist of implied knowledge about society, social actors and legal institutions.[26] While the implied knowledge of judges has a special status, the legal paradigm encompasses the implied knowledge of all citizens, including different actors in the judicial field, the clients, the legislature, the justice system and the administrative actors. Thus, a legal paradigm is a broader context than ideology, which is a product of a more explicit political deliberation. Legal paradigm can be utilised as a theoretical

[25] The models are presented by Reifner in *Overindebtedness of Consumers in the EC*, above n 17, at 117–20.

[26] J Habermas, *Faktizität und Geltung: Beiträge zur Diskurstheorie des Rechts und des demokratischen Rechtsstaats* (Frankfurt am Main, Suhrkamp, 1992) at 473–75.

and methodological tool that helps to explore unacknowledged assumptions about law and its functions.

Habermas distinguishes between two contemporary legal paradigms, the liberal paradigm and the welfare state paradigm. My central thesis in the following is that the differences in consumer bankruptcy laws can better be understood if we view contemporary laws as representatives of respective paradigms.

III. LIBERAL AND WELFARE PARADIGM IN CONSUMER BANKRUPTCY

A. Consumer Bankruptcy as a Tool for Market Regulation

It is somewhat unorthodox to claim that American bankruptcy law is not socially oriented. It is well known, both praised and cursed, for its pro-debtor nature.[27] The discharge of pre-bankruptcy debts is historically an inherent part of American bankruptcy law, especially since the federal Bankruptcy Act (1898).[28] The right to a *fresh start* has an ideological underpinning that reaches far beyond the fairly technical scope of bankruptcy law. As a part of the pioneer spirit of the nation, the fresh start has a strong moral content.

Notwithstanding its pro-debtor nature, American bankruptcy law reflects a liberal paradigm, as evidence of a more general approach to law in this culture. In Habermas' liberal paradigm, as in any other liberal thinking, the market is the central sphere of economic action. While the market, according to liberal thinking, is disconnected from the state, private law regulates the organisation of non-political economic actors there and provides for the legal institutions necessary to protect the interests of market actors, such as the enforcement of contract obligations and property rights.[29] While the tone of the Bankruptcy Laws Commission of 1973 was far from the voices of the most libertarian market ideologists,[30] it clearly took the market as its object of regulation. It defined

[27] In his comparative work, Philip Wood assessed the degree of the pro-debtor/pro-creditor nature of bankruptcy laws using several criteria. While the US Bankruptcy Code does not top the list as most pro-debtor regime, it gets high marks in the areas of discharge and reorganisation. See PR Wood, *Principles of International Insolvency* (London, Sweet & Maxwell, 1995).

[28] For a historical account, see C Tabb, 'The Historical Evolution of the Bankruptcy Discharge' (1991) 65 *American Bankruptcy Law Journal* 325; DA Skeel, *Debt's Dominion. A History of Bankruptcy Law in America* (Princeton, Princeton University Press, 2001).

[29] See Habermas, above n 26, at 477.

[30] Also, the reorganisation of businesses according to Chapter 11 and the other reorganisation chapters of the Bankruptcy Code is usually considered a debtor-friendly option. Characteristically, both the Bankruptcy Laws Commission in the 1970s and the Bankruptcy Review Commission in the 1990s have discussed bankruptcy in terms of balancing the different interests and social consequences of a business bankruptcy in a broad societal context. See Bankruptcy Laws Commission in Report of the Commission on the Bankruptcy Laws of the United States, HR Doc No 93–173 (1973) at 220 [Bankruptcy Laws Commission]; 'Bankruptcy: The Next Twenty Years,' National Bankruptcy Review Commission (1997) <http://govinfo.library.unt.edu/nbrc/report/01title.html> [Bankruptcy Review Commission 1997]. A new insight into this discussion has been made by Karen Gross who argues that the redistributive role of bankruptcy should be redesigned. See K Gross, *Failure and Forgiveness: Rebalancing the Bankruptcy System* (New Haven, Yale University Press, 1997) at 210.

consumer bankruptcy law as a market function, describing bankruptcy as an exit from the credit market and as a complement of the open access to the same market.[31]

The Bankruptcy Laws Commission was convinced of the beneficial effects of credit and risk taking. Its assessment of the use of credit was positive and, according to the Commission, the possibility of discharge in bankruptcy had an important role in reducing the risk and encouraging people to borrow and to be economically active.[32] Thus, bankruptcy served the efficiency of the market. As the right to fresh start also has a moral content, right to discharge was seen to serve both moral value and market efficiency.

Much of contemporary American scholarship is influenced by the liberal paradigm. Most pertinently, the law and economics school views consumer bankruptcy as a tool for risk allocation in the consumer credit market.[33] Since many of the risks in the credit market are beyond the reach of bankruptcy law, the law and economics approach has been concerned mainly with those provisions of bankruptcy law that may affect a debtor's behaviour. Law and economics scholars are concerned with moral hazards and incentives for debtors to avoid bankruptcy, such as how much property a debtor can keep in bankruptcy or the choice between a payment plan and a straight bankruptcy.[34]

The most important application of the law and economics approach is, however, the management and the calculation of credit risk by the major credit companies.[35] Actually, bankruptcy law plays only a minor role in this game, since it does not really matter to the credit company whether the non-paying debtor is formally bankrupt or not.[36] The criterion that matters is that the debtor is not able to pay her debts. Some authors have argued that the most important consequence of a discharge provision in bankruptcy law is that the credit issuers become more risk conscious.[37] In much of law and economics scholarship, however, the analysis of the incentives in bankruptcy law solely focuses on debtor behaviour, leaving aside possible incentives to the creditors. [38]

[31] Bankruptcy Laws Commission, above n 30, at 71–76.

[32] *Ibid* at 73–74.

[33] FJ Weston, 'Some Economic Fundamentals for an Analysis of Bankruptcy' (1977) 41 *Law and Contemporary Problems* 47 at 53; TH Jackson, *The Logic and Limits of Bankruptcy Law* (Cambridge, Massachusetts, Harvard University Press, 1986) at 229.

[34] See especially, B Adler, B Pollack and A Schwartz, 'Regulating Consumer Bankruptcy: A Theoretical Inquiry' (2000) 29 *Journal of Legal Studies* 585, and MM White, 'Economic Versus Sociological Approaches to Legal Research: The Case of Bankruptcy' (1991) 25 *Law and Society Review* 685, a book review of *As We Forgive Our Debtors*, by TA Sullivan, E Warren and JL Westbrook (see below at n 50).

[35] For a discussion about credit rating systems, see Ramsay in this volume.

[36] LM Ausubel, 'Credit Card Defaults, Credit Card Profits, and Bankruptcy' (1997) *American Bankruptcy Law Journal* 249 at 270.

[37] P Shuchman, 'Theory and Reality in Bankruptcy: The Spherical Chicken' (1977) 41 *Law and Contemporary Problems* 66 at 90; Jackson, above n 33, at 229.

[38] Most recent example of this focus is an article by Adler, Pollack, and Schwartz, above n 34.

B. Policy Goals in Welfare State Regulation

In contrast to the liberal state, the role of the welfare state is to pursue certain politically set goals. If the liberal state is characterised by formal justice, the welfare state seeks to realise material justice.[39] Among the most important acknowledged goals of the welfare state is the protection of citizens against risks caused by natural disasters, accidents, illness and economic misfortunes. It is for the state to actively promote the equality of citizens and legal regulation is one of the means by which the politically set goals are to be achieved.

Welfare regulation is mostly public law. Welfare policies are for the most part realised through redistribution, taxes, social security payments and social services. Reflections of welfare orientation are rare among commercial law or the law of procedure. In civil law, however, we can distinguish some well-established traces of welfare or social regulation. In labour law and in the regulation of apartment leases, for example, the protection of the weaker party is a generally accepted civil law principle. The development of consumer law is another example in which civil law recognises the different roles and power relations of contractual parties.[40] More generally, it has been argued that the possibility of adjusting an extortionate contract provision and the possibility of increasing the attention paid to the material equilibrium of the content of a contract are reflections of a welfare orientation in contemporary legal thinking.[41]

In civil law, the doctrine of social *force majeure,* developed by Thomas Wilhelmsson, has the closest connection to consumer bankruptcy law.[42] Social *force majeure* refers to situations where a debtor is unable to pay the debt because of illness, unemployment or another such unforeseen change in her life situation, which is beyond her control. For such reasons, the Scandinavian laws allow for the alleviation of interest, collection fees and other consequences for the delay in certain contract relations.[43]

The aims of the consumer debt adjustment laws in Scandinavia are quite similar to those aims presented in the doctrine of social *force majeure*. The explicit aim of the consumer debt adjustment laws is to alleviate the burden of a debtor who, for reasons beyond her own control, has ended up with insurmountable debt.[44]

[39] See Habermas, above n 26, at 480.

[40] T Wilhelmsson, *Critical Studies in Private Law. A Treatise on Need-Rational Principles in Modern Law.* (Dordrecht, Kluwer, 1992) at 80 [*Critical Studies*]; T Wilhelmsson, *Perspectives of Critical Contract Law* (Aldershot, Dartmouth, 1993) at 23 [*Perspectives*].

[41] J Pöyhönen, 'Contracts: Just Social Practice' in *Perspectives*, above n 40, at 311–24.

[42] See *Critical Studies*, above n 40, at 180.

[43] The doctrine has evolved along with the development of consumer law, but similar legal provisions may be found in other fields of law as well, for example, in tax law and other public law. See J Bärlund, *Sociala prestationshinder i konsumentavtal* (Göteborg, Nordiska Ämbtsmannakommittén för Konsumentfrågor. NÄK-rapport 1990:6, 1990).

[44] For example, Finnish law contains an explicit provision on the purpose of the law, which is 'to correct the situation of an insolvent private person (the debtor). . . .' S 1 of the Finnish Debt Adjustment Act.

This goal is highlighted in the *travaux preparatoires* of the European debt adjustment laws. Many of the laws were enacted during the first half of the 1990s when the European economy went through the worst depression since 1930s and, naturally, unemployment was mentioned as the most important cause of over-indebtedness. Also, the causal relationship between the overall economic situation and the economic plight of individual debtors was manifest in the preparatory works of the consumer bankruptcy laws.[45] Besides unemployment, other consequences of the economic situation that hit individuals and households, such as high interest rates, losses in income or overtime pay and abrupt changes in the housing market, were underlined.[46] Traditional welfare state risks, illness and disability were also mentioned.[47]

These social and economic risks endanger a citizen's welfare, social relations and her ability to act in society. A citizen who, because of overwhelming debt, is pushed outside society, endangers not only his or her own well being but the security of society as well. Therefore, debt adjustment legislation was needed.

The difference vis-à-vis the American market orientation is obvious. The object of regulation is not the market, but the protection against social risks. Some of the Scandinavian *travaux preparatoires* quite explicitly stated that the aim was not a matter of market regulation. They went as far as to say that the new law should not interfere with the functioning of the credit market at all or as little as possible.[48] It was emphasised that the payment plan generates repayment funds for creditors as much or more than a debtor would otherwise pay and that discharge, thus, concerns debts that the debtor would not be able to pay back, notwithstanding the discharge.[49]

In the following, I will discuss how these differences are reflected in the concrete institutions of bankruptcy law. My central thesis is that different paradigms have contributed to the construction of quite different representations of subjectivity, both for debtors and creditors, in bankruptcy law.

[45] HE 183/1992, Government Bill for the Debt Adjustment Act at 20–21 [Finnish Bill]; Regeringens proposition 1993/94:123 *Skuldsaneringslag* at 34 [Swedish Bill]; Norway, Report of Working Group, Family and Consumer Department, *Gjeldsordning for personer med betalningsvansker* at 13.

The Finnish Minister of Justice, Hannele Pokka expressed the general atmosphere at the time of accepting the law: '[o]ne has to say, in this situation, that indebtedness causes suffering for the whole country and for all citizens today when the amount of over-indebtedness is so high among businesses and households.' Protocoll of the Parliament 1992, 5528 (Translation JNK).

[46] Finnish Bill, above n 45, at 21.

[47] Swedish Bill, above n 45, at 34; Finnish Bill, above n 46, at 25.

[48] Swedish Bill, above n 45 at 36.

[49] Finnish Bill, above n 45, at 22; Betænkning om gældssanering (Denmark) 957/1982 at 76; Swedish Bill, above n 45, at 78.

IV. CONSTRUCTIONS OF THE DEBTOR IN BANKRUPTCY LAW

A. The Market Actor and Consumer Choice

When I started to study American bankruptcy law more than ten years ago, I was, like many of my European colleagues at that time, quite astonished by the institution of discharge. But the second surprise—like a bill for a school lunch after peanut butter—came when I realised that the debtor, whose biggest problem was that he did not have any money, had to pay for court fees and for legal help to get this remedy.

This started to make sense much later when I realised that when we talk about access to discharge in the market model, we talk about a consumer's choice. A consumer debtor makes a choice between filing and not filing for bankruptcy. She considers the price for filing and, if the benefits she gets from the bankruptcy exceed the price, she files. It is not a serious concern that the poorest debtors are excluded from bankruptcy because of the costs of the filing fees.[50] Bankruptcy would not improve their lot, because their income is so low already that their wages cannot be garnished.[51] They would not be able to pay their debts, in or out of bankruptcy, nor would (or should) they get new credit after a hypothetical bankruptcy. The poorest debtors do not benefit from bankruptcy, so they do not pay the price.

The consumer choice that has preoccupied scholars more than any other is the choice between Chapters 7 and 13 of the Bankruptcy Code.[52] In the studies concerning this choice, the central question is how the law should be written to give debtors appropriate incentives to choose the appropriate Chapter. Relevant incentives for the Chapter choice are legal provisions on how much assets the debtor has to relinquish, how much she has to pay to creditors through a payment plan and what debts are discharged in each alternative Chapter.[53]

According to the official policies and many of these aforementioned studies, the law should give the debtor incentive to file Chapter 13 because it generates a better outcome for creditors. This assumption has, however, been challenged by two arguments. The belief that Chapter 13 is a better alternative has led

[50] About the prohibitive effect of costs, see TA Sullivan, E Warren and JL Westbrook, *As We Forgive Our Debtors: Bankruptcy and Consumer Credit in America* (New York, Oxford University Press, 1989) at 23. For Canada, see Ziegel, above n 2, at 23.

[51] About the situation of these debtors, see S Kovac, 'Judgement-Proof Debtors in Bankruptcy' (1991) 65 *American Bankruptcy Law Journal* 675.

[52] The main difference between the two chapters is that in a Chapter 7 bankruptcy (straight bankruptcy), the debtor is required to use all of her non-exempt assets to pay off her debts, but does not have to encumber her future income. A debtor in a Chapter 13 bankruptcy is allowed to keep her assets, but has to allocate part of her future income to pay off her debts in accordance with payment plan. About the differences between the two chapters, see Jacoby in this volume.

[53] Examples of studies focusing on 'debtor choice' between the chapters are MM White, above n 34; RF Dole Jr, 'Selective Chapter 13 Plans: A Permissible Use or a Prohibited Abuse of Bankruptcy Code Following the 1984 Amendments?' (1986) *Bankruptcy Developments Journal* 511.

bankruptcy courts in many districts to develop policies that favour Chapter 13 payment plans. Empirical studies show that these policies, as local legal cultures, direct the debtor's choices more than rational calculation between alternative Chapters.[54] Furthermore, a large portion of debtors are not able to fulfil their Chapter 13 payment plans. Therefore, the preference for Chapter 13 plans has been questioned. This line of argument challenges the idea that debtor behaviour could be easily manipulated by a change of bankruptcy law and some of its proponents question the need for a Chapter 13 alternative.[55] The desirability of a Chapter 13 alternative has been questioned from another perspective recently. The possibility to choose Chapter has been perceived as too favourable to debtors because it allows for retaining assets and, therefore, it diminishes the incentive to avoid bankruptcy, decreasing efficiency.[56]

The actor in the market mode is the rational welfare maximiser of the microeconomic theory. According to liberal theory, the actors are interchangeable and equal. In bankruptcy law, this assumption is valid only as far as it concerns straight bankruptcy, which is regulated in Chapter 7 of the Bankruptcy Code for both business and consumer debtors. For rehabilitation processes, the Chapters and regulations differ.

In the market paradigm, the role of civil law is to protect the formal rights and positions of the actors. One of the most important media guaranteeing the functioning of the market is the equitable access to information about the market.[57] While most other interferences with a free market exchange have been considered inappropriate by the liberalists, access to information deserves special protection by the law. In bankruptcy law, the special status of information is highlighted in the regulation of access to discharge. While the access to bankruptcy historically has been and still is essentially free, important exceptions prevail when a debtor has withheld essential information from creditors. The most important exceptions to discharge are related to different kinds of fraud. A debt obtained by giving a false statement can be excluded from the discharge and, in more serious cases of fraud, discharge may be denied altogether.[58]

[54] J Braucher, 'Lawyers and Consumer Bankruptcy: One Code, Many Cultures' (1993) 67 *American Bankruptcy Law Journal* 501; W Whitford, 'The Ideal of Individualized Justice: Consumer Bankruptcy as Consumer Protection, and Consumer Protection in Consumer Bankruptcy'(1994) 68 *American Bankruptcy Law Journal* 397 at 406 ['The Ideal of Individualized Justice']; Sullivan, Warren, and Westbrook in this volume.

[55] See g, W Whitford, *Has the Time Come to Repeal Chapter 13?'* (1989) 65 *Indiana Law Review* 85; 'The Ideal of Individualized Justice', above n 54, at 415. About the discussion, see Sullivan, Warren and Westbrook, above n 50, at 232–34, and in this volume.

[56] Adler, Pollack, and Schwartz, above n 34 at 607.

[57] J Häyhä, 'Liability and Information in Private Law' in T Wilhelmsson and S Hurri (eds), *From Dissonance to Sense: Welfare State Expectations, Privatisation and Private Law* (Aldershot, Ashgate, 1999) at 301–48. See also Ramsay in this volume.

[58] US Bankruptcy Code § 707 and § 727. See also discussion on fraudulent borrowing connected to credit card below.

The abuse clause, which Congress added to the Bankruptcy Code in 1984[59] and which restricts access to discharge, has been used to channel debtors to Chapter 13 payment plans instead of straight discharge. 'Abuse' in this context covers both fraudulent behaviour and cases in which the debtor proposes a straight bankruptcy even though she would be able to pay a (substantial) portion of her debt after the deduction of living expenses.[60] The aim is not to curb access to discharge from the last mentioned group of debtors, but to guide them to Chapter 13.

The American legislator and American scholarship have not been particularly preoccupied with the reasons why debtors end up in bankruptcy.[61] The featureless, exchangeable market debtor only gets attributed with more personal features when she has misbehaved so fraudulently in the market that she should be excluded from the remedy.

Consequently, debtor education has not gained much attention. No mandatory counselling or education is tied with the consumer bankruptcy process as such. Only recently have new initiatives to start debt counselling programmes become common.[62] These programmes, however, are run by non-profit organisations and are funded by credit institutions or debtors themselves. The credit counselling has not been an educational policy connected by law to the consumer bankruptcy process. With the new consumer bankruptcy legislation, the debtor education seems to be getting more attention.

B. The Sociological Construction of the Debtor

The Nordic *travaux preparatoires* of debt adjustment laws were preoccupied with the reasons for over-indebtedness. Over-indebtedness was seen as a consequence of changes in circumstances, either in macroeconomic forces, which cause unemployment, small business bankruptcies, loss of income, abrupt changes in housing prices and increases in the cost of credit, or in individual circumstances, such as illness, disability and family relations.[63]

[59] US Bankruptcy Code § 707(b). The abuse clause may be invoked by the court *ex officio* or by the U.S. trustee supervising the bankruptcy trustee system, but not by the creditors.

[60] Whitford, above n 55, at 404. The American discussion was provoked by the so-called Purdue study in 1982, claiming that a considerable portion of bankrupt debtors could pay their debts. About the opposite view and research to back it up, see, for example, Sullivan, Warren, and Westbrook, above n 50; TA Sullivan, E Warren, and JL Westbrook, *The Fragile Middle Class: Americans in Debt* (New Haven, Yale University Press, 2000)[*The Fragile Middle Class*].

[61] When the reasons for filing bankruptcy have been studied, the studies usually reveal a picture that is not far from the experience of European debtors. See Sullivan, Warren, and Westbrook, above n 50; also *The Fragile Middle Class*, above n 60.

[62] See J Braucher in this volume; K Gross in this volume.

[63] Under Finnish law, the legitimate reasons are even mentioned in the text of the law. According to s 9 of the Consumer Debt Adjustment Act, to qualify for a discharge, the main reason for the indebtedness of the debtor should be illness, disability, unemployment or other change in the debtor's circumstances which is not her fault, or there should otherwise be serious reasons for the adjustment of the debt.

Therefore, the debtor is not reduced to a market actor, but has a fuller personality. Paramountly, she has, or rather, has had, a profession and a job. Her income is important because it has almost always decreased, but it is important not only for paying her debts but also for sustaining a family. Clearly, the debtor often has a family. In fact, the law is very preoccupied with the question of how much money a debtor needs every month to keep up with her monthly expenses. Her health is crucial and so is that of her family members. Sometimes, her family has broken up. Her housing seems to be of special interest since the lawmakers often discuss at length the possibility of keeping a home after a debt adjustment.

The preoccupation with the reasons for over-indebtedness does not stop with the *travaux preparatoires*. In all Nordic countries, the law now requires the court to take a stand on the reasons for indebtedness in each individual case. Thus, the regulation of access to consumer bankruptcy has become a moral statement.

The morality at issue is not so much that of helping individuals in need but the morality of paying one's debts. The Nordic *travaux preparatoires* contain strong statements about the importance of upholding the general morality to pay one's debts, notwithstanding the new legislation.[64] The emphasis on repayment of debt morality seems to be particularly strong in the Nordic countries.

The Danish debt adjustment law, already enacted by 1984, prescribes that when a court decides whether or not the debtor has access to debt adjustment, it should make an overall assessment of the debtor's situation. In this assessment, the court should take into consideration:

> whether the overall circumstances of the debtor speak in favour of the arrangement, such as the debtor's interest in the arrangement, the age of the debts, the origin of the debts, and the debtor's circumstances when the debts were incurred, the repayment history of the debts, and the debtor's circumstances while the application is pending.[65]

The courts have interpreted these requirements quite strictly and many applicants have not gained access to debt adjustment.[66]

Moreover, according to Swedish debt adjustment law, the court should make a broad assessment of a debtor's circumstances before any access to the procedure is granted. The Norwegian law uses indeterminate terminology also, but its assessment, whether or not debt adjustment would be *støtande*,[67] abusive, refers directly to the payment morality. In the Swedish and Norwegian systems, in addition to the legal regulation of access, the institutional organisation of the debt adjustment procedure is important. The debtor is required to file for a debt

[64] SOU 1990:74, Skuldsaneringslag (Sweden) at 14; Swedish Bill, above n 45 at 77; Finnish Bill, above n 45 at 25; Finnish Amendment Bill (HE 180/1996) at 3; Norwegian Bill Ot.prp.nr. 81(1991–92) at 3.

[65] *Konkurslov*, s 199 (Translation JNK). In essence, the provision was incorporated into the Swedish law.

[66] 'Consumer Bankruptcy in Comparison', above n 1; Møgelvang-Hansen, above n 4.

[67] *Gjeldordningsloven* § 5–4.

adjustment at a debt enforcement agent's office, not at the court. In Sweden, especially, this arrangement has led to a rigorous pre-screening of applicants.[68]

In Finland, the law enumerates specific grounds, the existence of which excludes the debtor from debt adjustment. The list includes fraud, economic crime, and other intentional activities to harm the creditors, as well as the breach of the rules of bankruptcy law. The most important ground for exclusion, however, concerns the debtor's reckless borrowing or that '. . . there are reasonable grounds to believe that the debtor has run into debt in an irresponsible way or with a debt adjustment in mind.'[69] More specifically, the debtor's borrowing is judged by her prudence in handling her finances, the source of the debts and the circumstances under which they were incurred. The cases concerning consumer households with heavy credit card debt or persons who have guaranteed another person's loan are numerous. In such cases, the case law has developed a 'bona fide test,' looking to see whether the debtor knew or should have known that she would not be able to pay the debt when it became due.

The mandatory payment plan can be seen as part of the project of upholding the repayment morality. The length of the payment plan, which is generally five years, has been discussed as a moral question, not as an economic issue. Even debtors who have no payment capacity at all are legally under a plan for five years.[70] In fact, the economic value that the plans provide to creditors is generally low.[71]

Interestingly, there seems to be a difference between the Nordic and continental European countries. In Scandinavian debt adjustment laws and discourses, paradoxically, indebtedness is seen in its social context more than elsewhere but, at the same time, the regulation of access to debt adjustment gives an expression to the sentiments of moral conservatism.

On the Continent, to the contrary, indebtedness is seen more in an individual context. The regulation of access, however, seems to be more open.[72] The moral tone of continental debt adjustment laws (*Restschuldbefreiung*) is expressed in the emphasis they put on repayment obligations according to the payment plan. In Germany, especially, the standard length of the plan, seven years, exceeds the

[68] *Riksskatterverkets statistik* 1998. *Utvärdering av skuldsaneringslagen, Konsumentverket* 1995/1996:34, 32 and 64. B. See also Carlsson and Hoff, above n 7.

[69] Judicial Consumer Debt Adjustment Act, § 10 para 7 (Translation JNK).

[70] See, for example, the Finnish Judicial Consumer Debt Adjustment Act § 30(4).

[71] For example, according to a Finnish study, debtors were able to pay approximately 14% of their debt, including contributions from the plan and the sale of the debtors' property. J Tala *et al*, *Velkajärjestelyt tuomioistuimissa* (Helsinki, National Research Institute of Research Policy, Research Communications 13, 1994). In Sweden, the plans confirmed by the enforcement officials generated 13% of the debt and 40% of debtors did not make any payments. In the court proceedings, the numbers were 4% of the debt, and 75% of the debtors who made no payments. Utvärdering av Skuldsaneringslagen, Konsumentverket 1995/96:34, at 36.

[72] Of course, this is again a matter of degree. According to German and Austrian laws, endangering the interests of a creditor is a ground for exclusion from debt adjustment (Schuldenregulierung). This exclusion clause is narrower than the general clauses in the Nordic debt adjustment laws.

period of time that is elsewhere considered reasonable. The plan is adjusted continuously to changes in the debtor's income. In addition, the completion of the plan is controlled by a debt enforcement agent and the creditors. The plan may be revoked in a case of debtor misbehaviour. Thus, the duration of the plan is called the 'well-behaving period' (*Wohlverhaltensphase*).

The welfare state orientation of the laws in Nordic countries is reflected in the way the procedures are organised. While all debt adjustment laws provide a full scale court proceeding with the possibility of oral hearings, the procedure is supplemented with administrative intervention. The debtor is not only a party, but is also a client of the welfare state.

How the administrative officials have been incorporated into the proceedings varies from one country to another. Counselling is offered to insolvent private persons in most, if not all, European countries that have introduced debt adjustment legislation. Participation in counselling is either mandatory (Sweden) or necessary in order to be able to fulfil the formal requirements for filing in court (Finland). Counselling is provided by the state and community officials in the Nordic countries and by different organisations funded by the state or other public bodies in continental Europe.[73] It is obvious, however, that the indigent debtor has no funds and does not pay for the counselling or for the filing.

V. THE OTHER PARTY: A COLLECTIVE OF CREDITORS OR A GROUP OF INDIVIDUALS?

All textbooks on bankruptcy law define bankruptcy as a collective proceeding in which the debtor's estate is used to pay all of her creditors. The equality of the creditors and the moratorium against any action by individual creditors are fundamental principles of bankruptcy.[74] The argument is that all creditors fare better if individual action is restricted to protect and preserve the estate to achieve a better overall dividend to creditors.[75] After a statement on the fundamental principles of bankruptcy, a bankruptcy scholar, however, admits that the debtor's whole estate is never available for a division among all the creditors and that in no legal order are all the creditors paid on the same footing.[76]

While these statements hold true generally, I will argue in the following text that the creditor as 'the other party' of the bankruptcy proceedings can be constructed in different ways by the legal system. The crux of the matter is to what degree the idea of the common and collective interest of the creditors is upheld and what infringements upon their rights the creditors are compelled to endure in the name of the collective proceedings. I claim that in American bankruptcy

[73] See Niemi-Kiesiläinen, 'The Role of Consumer Counselling', above n 15.

[74] See, for example, Wood, above n 27, at 2.

[75] TH Jackson, above n 33, at 5, 10–18, 25–27 and *Overindebtedness of Consumers in the EC*, above n 16, at 207–08.

[76] Wood, above n 27, at 2.

law, the collective nature of the bankruptcy proceedings is in the background and that, even in a bankruptcy situation, individual creditors and the debtor are seen as bargaining parties. European bankruptcy law, on the other hand, has never departed that far from the original idea of a common pool and collective enforcement. Recent reforms have even strengthened the old principles.

A. Individual Bargaining at the Cost of Bankruptcy Principles

American bankruptcy law offers several examples of how the interests of individual creditors override the collective creditor interest. Firstly, several debts do not belong to the collective of creditors at all. For example, taxes, fines, damages, debts incurred by drunken driving, debts taken for luxury consumption a short period of time before the bankruptcy filing, alimonies, educational loans and debts not disclosed by the debtor in the bankruptcy proceeding are all exempted from the discharge.[77] The debtor has to pay these debts in full, notwithstanding the discharge of other debts.

Secondly, some debts take priority. Taxes, salaries and certain prepayments by consumer debtors have to be paid before other debts in a bankruptcy.[78] There are good causes behind all these regulations, but from a bankruptcy point of view, they put the individual creditor before the collective of creditors.

Thirdly, debt obtained by a false representation may be excepted from discharge.[79] Unlike the abuse clause, which denies a debtor access to Chapter 7 bankruptcy, this provision concerns only the specific debt in relation to which the claim of false representation is made. It is thus possible that most of a debtor's other debts are discharged and the creditor who invokes exception for false representation collects payment post-bankruptcy. The false representation exception has been invoked frequently by the credit card companies and it has been concluded that this exception is used to get non-fraudulent credit card debt excepted from discharge.[80]

Fourthly, reaffirmation agreements are allowed. The debtor and an individual creditor are allowed to make an agreement in which the debtor binds herself to repay a pre-bankruptcy debt.[81] The agreement is subject to control by the bankruptcy court or the trustee, but the courts rarely reject these agreements. Also, the debtors often reaffirm without approval.[82] The goal of reaffirmation

[77] Bankruptcy Code § 523. The scope of exceptions is narrower in Chapter 13 bankruptcies, however (BC 1328 §). In other Anglo-Saxon countries, the exclusions vis-à-vis discharge are less numerous and most of them are related to the fraudulent behaviour of the debtor. See the table in Ziegel, above n 2, at 45–46.

[78] Bankruptcy Code § 507.

[79] Bankruptcy Code § 523(a)(2)(A).

[80] Bankruptcy Review Committee, above n 30, at 182.

[81] Bankruptcy Code § 524 (c) and (d) (1994).

[82] MB Culhane and MM White, 'Debt After Discharge: An Empirical Study of Reaffirmation' (1999) 73 *American Bankruptcy Law Journal* 709 at 733.

agreements may have been to facilitate the debtor to get post-bankruptcy credit or to continue some other contractual relationship.[83] Often reaffirmations concern secured debt and the purpose of reaffirmation is to keep the collateral.[84] In practice, however, many commercial unsecured creditors are using reaffirmations.[85]

Some of the above-mentioned exceptions and preferences can be defended by the argument that these creditors are not market actors and they have not been able to choose to become creditors. Therefore, those creditors merit priority. We see from the list of exceptions that such provisions have been enacted to advance various policy goals, ranging from discouraging drunken driving to encouraging the payment of alimony. As praiseworthy as these goals may be, one may wonder whether bankruptcy law is an effective or a just way of promoting them. The promotion of these goals is impaired by the fact that most bankruptcy debtors are so indigent that, notwithstanding any priority or exception, the creditor can hardly expect a substantial payment from the bankruptcy estate or post-bankruptcy income.

The fairness of bankruptcy exceptions and priorities is first called into question when different priorities are compared with each other or when exceptions are compared with dischargeable debt. Secondly, the fairness of these regulations is called into question when their effect on the fresh start is taken into account. As numerous as they are, the regulations seriously compromise the fresh start.[86]

These examples of priorities and non-dischargeable debt show that the promotion of policy goals through legislation is by no means alien to American law. In a bankruptcy context, however, the introduction of policy goals that are foreign to the rationale of bankruptcy seem to interfere with the more intrinsic goals of bankruptcy.

B. Revival of the Pro Rata Principle

In the European debt adjustment laws, very few debts are excluded from discharge.[87] If a debtor's behaviour does not warrant a discharge, the debtor is denied access to debt adjustment and all his debts remain intact. Excluding specific debts is hardly possible.

[83] Canada, for example, allows for reaffirmations but such agreements are enforceable only if supported by new consideration, such as the renewal of a credit agreement. Ziegel, above n 2, at 54.

[84] Secured debt has to be paid in full and reaffirmation has relevance when the debt is undersecured. See W Whitford, 'Secured Creditors and Consumer Bankruptcy in the United States' (1999) 37 *Osgoode Hall Law Journal* 339.

[85] Culhane and White, above n 82, at 737; Sullivan, Warren, and Westbrook, above n 50.

[86] W Whitford, 'Changing Definitions of Fresh Start US Bankruptcy Law' (1997) 20 *Journal of Consumer Policy* 178; Gross, above n 30.

[87] In some jurisdictions, criminal fines are excluded; alimony may also have a favourable treatment.

The idea of the reaffirmation agreement is alien in European bankruptcy law. To the extent of my knowledge, such an institution has not been seriously discussed in any European country. Quite the contrary, promises of payments that favour a certain bankruptcy creditor are forbidden under debt adjustment law and criminal law and can be voided according to bankruptcy law.

The need for the favourable treatment of private individuals as creditors has occasionally been discussed. In particular, the legal position of persons who have personally guaranteed the payment of another person's loan, typically family members, close relatives and friends, was heatedly discussed when the debt adjustment law was amended in 1997 in Finland. It was clear, however, that any remedy should be decided by law, not by agreement.[88] Criticism of the reaffirmation agreement has also been raised in the US. The National Bankruptcy Review Commission (1997) proposed that its scope be reduced drastically so that it would only be allowed for secured debt.

The most important difference is the treatment of the state creditor. In the market model, the state is excluded because it is not a market creditor.[89] In European countries, both the number of priorities in bankruptcy law and the amounts bankrupts owed to prioritised creditors had increased by the 1970s enormously. The growth of the public sector had generated new taxes, retirement fund contributions, mandatory insurance payments and other public and semi-public obligations that had been given a prioritised position in the bankruptcy. The reduction of priorities was demanded by all bankruptcy lawyers but, for a long time, it was far from being put into practice.

Under the debt adjustment laws, the state is more or less treated the same as all other creditors. The introduction of debt adjustment laws in the 1980s and 1990s has been accompanied by the removal of priorities for the state and many other creditors. In some countries, such priorities have been drastically reduced under general bankruptcy law and, thus, also in debt adjustment.[90] In other countries, priorities are not applied at all in debt adjustment.[91] And still in some places, the tax creditor's claims are processed separately, according to the same principles as other creditors in debt adjustment.[92] The curtailment of priorities seems to be connected to the development of rehabilitation processes in both business and consumer bankruptcy.

The state represents the welfare policy and, in the end, is liable for whatever benefits and social rights it guarantees its citizens. The state also has the broad-

[88] Finnish Amendment Bill, above n 64. The solution to this problem was that the payment plan may be extended for another two years for the benefit of creditors who are private individuals.

[89] About the different arguments in favour of the tax priority, see BK Morgan, 'Should the Sovereign Be Paid First? A Comparative International Analysis of the priority for Tax Claims in Bankruptcy' (2000) 74 *American Bankruptcy Law Journal* 461.

[90] The priorities in bankruptcy have been abolished or drastically reduced, for example, in Denmark, Austria, Finland (1993), and Germany (*Insolvenzordnung* 1994/99).

[91] Sweden, *Skuldssaneringslagen* 6 and 7 §. A radical reduction of the number of priorities in general bankruptcy law is also discussed in Sweden. See SOU 1999:1 (Nya förmånsrättsregler).

[92] Norway, *Gjeldsordningsloven* 4–8c §. H-P Graver, *Gjeldsordningsloven med kommentarer* (Tano, Oslo, 1996) at 88.

est possible capacity for risk sharing. Therefore, it is logical to include the state creditor in the discharge. It is equally logical that the state carries the burden of the costs of the proceedings. The state does not generally charge for its welfare services if the recipients are indigent.

VI. CONCLUSION

The purpose of this exercise has been to show that the fundamental beliefs about the role of law in society relate to how we construct debtors and creditors in consumer bankruptcy law and how the concrete provisions of bankruptcy law are formulated.

The exercise has shown that American and European consumer bankruptcy laws differ from each other, not only in detail, but also in their more fundamental paradigmatic orientations. While the American regulation represents an attempt to regulate the functioning of the market, the Scandinavian orientation has been towards social security, that is, towards the protection against economic risks and welfare.

In the liberal orientation, the debtor and creditors are primarily seen as market actors even in a bankruptcy situation. This view leaves room in bankruptcy law for bargaining between a debtor and individual creditors and for the privileged treatment of many creditors. A creditor has a chance to bargain for an exception from the discharge concerning his debt on numerous grounds, including false representations to the creditor. A debtor's choice is a self-evident starting point in the abundant scholarship on the choice of Chapter in consumer bankruptcy.

The welfare or social orientation has taken the debtor's social needs as a starting point. Debt counselling is emphasised. The debtor's rehabilitation is, however, only one of many common policies that are attempted to be realised by debt adjustment laws. Another is the upholding of a common policy of general payment morality. Therefore fraudulent or irresponsible behaviour is controlled through the access to debt adjustment by the courts and, if such behaviour is detected, access is denied. Exceptions for individual creditors are almost non-existent. The orientation towards common goals and policies has promoted legal solutions that require creditors' individual rights or privileges to yield before the common interest. To my own surprise, this welfare orientation seems to be more compatible with the traditional notion of bankruptcy as a collective enforcement of debts and a distribution of a debtor's assets among the creditors according to the *pro rata* principle.

In this article, I have juxtaposed legal regimes, labelling them as being either liberal or welfare; however, this categorisation does not seem to hold in the context of bankruptcy law. Consumer bankruptcy brings welfare policies to the market, be it in the form of the regulation of access to debt adjustment or in the form of creditor exemptions and privileges. Welfare law is often needs based. In Nordic debt adjustment law, we found an influence of social contract law in that the access to debt adjustment was reserved for debtors who had experienced a loss of income beyond their own control or whose circumstances otherwise warranted access to debt adjustment. Consequently, an individual assessment of need and reasons for the indebtedness require a considerable amount of time and resources. In American legislation, some of the creditors' priorities and exceptions are based on the creditor's needs or dependencies or on other social policies. Karen Gross has recently argued for increased needs-orientation in bankruptcy law. Taking the bankruptcy system as a means for social change and redistribution, she argues for a greater discretion for the courts to assess the needs of creditors and to make exceptions to the *pro rata* rule.[93] Obviously, both systems include considerations of welfare policies.

The introduction of welfare and other social policies into consumer bankruptcy law seems to have a price. The individual access evaluation and counselling of debtors in Nordic countries involves considerable administration costs. On the other hand, some of the policies designed to favour certain creditors in the US, such as the false representation exception and the reaffirmation policy, seem to cause noteworthy adjudication costs. In addition, the economic value of prioritised debts seems to be rather low because the payment capacity of the debtors is so diminished.[94] Even if a debtor's payments are allocated to one or two privileged creditors, a social policy based on bankruptcy law depends on a debtor's payment capacity and is, at best, quite arbitrary.

While adjudication costs and low economic yield of the plans are serious concerns for courts that are overburdened by case loads on both sides of the Atlantic, the real threat for consumer bankruptcy policy, however, is that these policies seriously limit the principle of a fresh start. When access to bankruptcy is restricted, many seriously over-indebted debtors fall outside this remedy. The creditor privileges and exceptions, to the contrary, restrict the fresh start for those debtors who go through bankruptcy. Notwithstanding bankruptcy, they will find that they have to pay certain pre-bankruptcy debts. The unfortunate consequence of bringing welfare policies into consumer bankruptcy appears to be the limitation of the principle of a fresh start.

[93] Gross, above n 30, at 247.

[94] 'Consumer Bankruptcy in Comparison', above n 1. In a similar vein, SF Norberg, 'Consumer Bankruptcy's New Clothes: An Empirical Study of Discharge and Debt Collection' (1999) 13 *American Bankruptcy Institute Law Review* 415 at 462, has asked whether the costs of Chapter 13 are justified in light of the low Chapter outcome.

3

Personal Bankruptcy Law: A Behavioural Perspective

SAUL SCHWARTZ*

I. INTRODUCTION

IN 1985, THOMAS Jackson published a paper that applied what has come to be called 'behavioural economics' to the analysis of bankruptcy law.[1] Jackson argued that individuals collectively recognise the need for a rule that provides for the discharge of most debts *and* a rule that prevents them from contracting with lenders to waive the right to discharge. This collective recognition is then translated into law by democratic lawmakers responding to the wishes of the voters.

This paper builds on the idea of applying behavioural economics to the analysis of bankruptcy in two ways. First, Jackson's analysis is explained and evaluated in light of recent ideas from behavioural economics, ideas well summarised in papers by Jolls, Sunstein and Thaler, and Hanson and Kysar.[2] Second, the behavioural perspective is applied to several aspects of bankruptcy law not fully discussed by Jackson—the reaffirmation of debts, the exempt status of various assets and the student loan exception to discharge.[3] Proposals concerning each of those aspects of bankruptcy law have been put forward by a taskforce on the reform of Canadian bankruptcy legislation and the discussion includes the specifics of those proposals.[4]

* This chapter has benefited from the comments of participants in the Collaborative Research Network on Personal Bankruptcy, sponsored by the Law and Society Association. In addition, detailed comments from my Carleton colleagues Philip Ryan and Warren Thorngate were very helpful.

[1] T Jackson, 'The Fresh-Start Policy in Bankruptcy Law' (1985) 98 *Harvard Law Review* 1393–448.

[2] C Jolls, CR Sunstein, and R Thaler, 'A Behavioral Approach to Law and Economics' (1998) 50 *Stanford Law Review* at 1471 and JD Hanson and D Kysar, 'Taking Behavioralism Seriously: The Problem of Market Manipulation' (1999) 74 *New York University Law Review* 630.

[3] Following Jackson, the paper focuses on the non-waivable right to discharge and on the nature of the fresh start provided, not on the discharge itself. As an editor suggested, however, this focus may be surprising outside of North America where discharge is itself controversial.

[4] Office of the Superintendent of Bankruptcy Canada, 'Personal Insolvency Task Force: Final Report' (Ottawa, 2002), Strategis.gc.ca <http://strategis.ic.gc.ca/SSG/br01221e.html> [PITF].

The paper is essentially an exploration of the usefulness of the behavioural perspective for understanding the content of bankruptcy law and for prescribing changes to it. This perspective cannot account for all or even most of the provisions of bankruptcy law. Other important influences on the evolution of bankruptcy law include societal norms, political expediency, special interest pressures and the desire to leave existing laws unchanged unless they are in great need of reform. The modest suggestion here is only that the behavioural perspective can contribute to the understanding of particular features of the law and to the prescription of particular reforms. The paper limits its analysis to the 'fresh start' provisions of bankruptcy law and does not address either the laws concerning the division of debtors' assets among their creditors or the laws governing the administration of the bankruptcy process.

The structure of the remainder of the paper is as follows. First, the major precepts of behavioural economics—bounded rationality, bounded willpower and bounded self-interest—are presented and examples given as to how the assumptions might bear on borrowing decisions. Second, Jackson's use of the behavioural perspective to explain the non-waivable right to discharge is summarised and evaluated, followed by an application of that same perspective to the reaffirmation of debts. Third, the behavioural rationale for exempting certain assets from seizure by creditors is described and then applied to the taskforce recommendations concerning exemptions. Finally, the rationale for excepting particular debts from discharge is presented and applied to the recommendation of the above-mentioned taskforce concerning the exception of student loans from discharge.

II. THE ASSUMPTIONS OF BEHAVIOURAL ECONOMICS

Behavioural economics differs from conventional economics in its assumptions about how individuals make decisions. In particular, where conventional economics assumes perfectly rational behaviour, unbounded self-interest and infinite willpower, behavioural economics assumes that human beings are not perfectly rational, not entirely self-interested and have limited willpower.

Jolls, Sunstein and Thaler present a framework for 'behavioural law and economics' and point to various situations in which its explanations are likely to be superior to those of conventional law and economics. In general, behavioural economics is most relevant in non-market situations, one of which is clearly personal bankruptcy.[5]

[5] In market settings, many economists assume that market participants who do *not* exhibit perfectly rational behaviour, unbounded self-interest, and infinite willpower will be driven out of the market and thus become irrelevant to the analysis of the market's functioning. For the contrasting view that market forces do *not* drive irrational actors out of the market, see S Mullainathan and R Thaler, 'Behavioral Economics' (October 2000) National Bureau of Economics Working Paper No. 7948.

The increasing influence of behavioural economics is founded on an extensive and growing body of research that clearly demonstrates that, in many situations, the conventional assumptions of neoclassical economics do not describe individual economic behaviour. Nonetheless, behavioural economics is not an attempt to reject economic analysis. As JST write:[6]

> Behavioural economics is a form of economics, and our goal is to strengthen the predictive and analytic power of law and economics, not to undermine it. Behavioural economics does not suggest that behaviour is random or impossible to predict; rather it suggests, with economics, that behaviour is systematic and can be modeled.

Behavioural economics shares with conventional economics the notion that the value of a theory is measured by its usefulness in predicting changes in behaviour resulting from changes in important characteristics of the economic environment (such as prices and income). The key difference between behavioural economics and conventional economics is that behavioural economics applies research from other disciplines—notably social psychology—to specify how economic agents will behave rather than using the theoretical assumptions normally used in economics.

This section briefly describes the three 'bounds' described by Jolls, Sunstein and Thaler—bounds on rationality, self-interest and willpower—in general terms.

A. Bounded Rationality

When individuals make decisions, they do so with 'limited computational skills and seriously flawed memories.'[7] Knowing this, decision-makers might make efforts to improve decisions; more information might be collected, calculations checked and double-checked, and outside experts consulted. Such 'deliberation costs,' however, might be quite high. To avoid deliberation costs, decision-makers systematically use of 'rules of thumb.' These rules of thumb, however, are themselves imperfect and lead to systematic errors. In particular, the research strongly suggests that decision-makers often underestimate future risks. In a borrowing situation, for example, decision-makers may systematically underestimate the probability of being unable to repay the debt.

This is not to suggest that markets do not 'work.' In many cases—Jolls, Sunstein and Thaler give the example of the market for foreign exchange—conditions exist which mitigate against widespread errors in decision-making. In such markets, transactions are repeated again and again so that decision-makers can learn, over time, to estimate probabilities as accurately as possible. Moreover, if prices stray from their 'correct' level, the professionals can make quick and certain profits (as in foreign exchange arbitrage). Significantly for a

[6] See Jolls, Sunstein, and Thaler, above n 2, at 1475.
[7] See *ibid* at 1477.

study of the application of behavioural economics to personal bankruptcy, Jolls, Sunstein and Thaler write that: 'these conditions render agents who do not conform to the standard economic assumptions irrelevant (because they will be bankrupt).'[8]

Rules of thumb or 'heuristics' are tools that human beings adopt in order to deal with the mass of information available to inform any particular decision. The three most prominent examples of rules of thumb are *availability, representativeness* and *anchoring*. While helpful in avoiding deliberation costs, these rules of thumb often lead decision-makers to overestimate the probability of success and underestimate the probability of failure.

Availability is a rule of thumb that leads decision-makers to estimate the likelihood of an event by the ease with which past occurrences of the event can be recalled. Availability is partly a function of how often something has happened in the recent past. Recent events are more 'available' to the decision-maker than past events so that too much weight is put on recent performance. Availability is also a function of salience—a recent deadly car crash along a particular stretch of highway increases the perceived probability of another accident among those who regularly travel that highway.

Another decision-making bias is created by false judgements about the *representativeness* of particular events. Robert Frank gives the following example.[9] Suppose you know that Steve is a shy person and are asked whether he is more likely to be a librarian or a salesperson. Most people think that shyness is a characteristic that is more representative of librarians than salespeople, and are thus likely to say that Steve is a librarian. Suppose that shyness is indeed more representative of librarians and that, say, 80 per cent of them are shy. Suppose that only a relatively small proportion—say, 20 per cent—of salespeople are shy. Even so, because there are so many more salespeople than librarians, Steve is more likely to be a salesperson than a librarian.

Another strategy for making decisions when complete information is either not available or is too voluminous to process is called '*anchoring and adjustment*.' Faced with a choice, we often make an initial guess (the 'anchor') and then adjust that estimate in light of whatever additional information comes to hand. Daniel Kahneman and Amos Tversky, two of the pioneers in this area, demonstrated, in the following experiment, the biases that anchoring-and-adjustment can sometimes create.[10] They told a group of students that each would be asked: 'What proportion of countries in the UN are located in Africa?' Before answering the question, each student was first asked to spin a wheel that generated a number between 1 and 100. Only then was the student asked to make a precise estimate. The median estimate of students whose number on the wheel was 10 or below was 25 per cent; the median estimate of students whose number on the wheel was above 65 on the wheel was 45 per cent. Clearly, the

[8] See *ibid* at 1486.

[9] See R Frank, *Microeconomic and Behavior,* 4th edn (Boston, McGraw-Hill, 2000) at 267–68.

[10] See *ibid* at 269.

students were using the number on the wheel as an anchor for their estimate and then adjusting the estimate up or down based on their knowledge of the proportion of UN countries from Africa. However, decision-makers systematically under-adjust from their anchor, even when they know, as in this case, that the anchor has been randomly determined.

Overall, as Jolls, Sunstein and Thaler write:[11]

> Many of the forms of bounded rationality . . . call into question the idea of consumer sovereignty. For example, overoptimism leads most people to believe that their own risk of a negative outcome is far lower than the average person's. Similarly, the effect of salience may lead to substantial underestimation of certain risks encountered in everyday life (for example, the risks from poor diet), since these harms may not be very salient. When overoptimism is combined with salience, people may underestimate risks substantially.

Such over-optimism is of obvious relevance to decisions about whether or not to borrow for personal investment purposes. Consider the case of student loans. Which recent high school graduates can predict the likely future earnings that might attach to any career choice? Success is extremely salient, made so by continual advertising by both governments and schools urging students to get as much education as possible. The downside—students who go to university but who never finish or who end up in jobs no better than they might have had without the education—is much less readily available.

B. Bounded Willpower

The conventional model of economics assumes that individuals make decisions in a way that is consistent over time. If A is preferred to B at time t, A will be preferred to B at all other times. Such preferences can be captured by a model in which rational decision-makers 'discount' (or translate) future costs and benefits into present dollars at a rate that is constant over time.

'Bounded willpower' is what Jackson called 'impulsiveness', what Hanson and Kysar called 'time varying preferences' and what economists sometimes call 'dynamic inconsistency.' In the contemporary literature on psychology and economics, it is now common to think of consumers as having multiple selves, each one 'in charge' at a different point in time. A decision-maker with (at least) two selves can exhibit 'dynamically inconsistent' or 'time inconsistent' choices, as illustrated by the following example. Suppose an individual is choosing between A, to be consumed at time t, and B, to be consumed at time t+1, and assume that t is far in the future; in that situation, the consumer prefers B to A. When time t arrives, however, the person actually chooses A over B. For example, in the evening, a person might set an alarm in order to wake up before dawn, preferring a walk with a friend in the peace of early morning to an extra hour of sleep;

[11] See Jolls, Sunstein, and Thaler, above n 2, at 1540.

when the alarm rings, however, it is quickly turned off, the extra hour of sleep now preferred to the morning walk. Experience may teach that preferences are dynamically inconsistent and, in the evening, the person may set several alarms or perhaps tell a friend to ring the doorbell at 6. Such actions are examples of 'commitment devices,' established in anticipation of time-inconsistent preferences.

In the context of borrowing, the 'planner self' sets aside money for the future and rationally thinks through alternative investment and consumption decisions. The 'impulsive self,' however, thinks only about the moment and therefore has a strong preference for current consumption; the future costs are heavily discounted. When the planner self is in charge, that self knows that the impulsive self will be in charge at some later point. Armed with that knowledge, the planner self takes actions to limit the consumption behaviour of the impulsive self.

The intuition for these ideas is both straightforward and consistent with common ideas about human behaviour. As Raymond Strotz wrote:[12]

> We are often willing even to pay a price to precommit future actions (and avoid temptations). Evidence of this in economics and other social behavior is not difficult to find. It varies from the gratuitous promise 'Give me a good kick if I don't do such and such' to savings plans such as insurance policies and Christmas Clubs which may be hard to justify in view of low rates of return.

C. Bounded Self-Interest

Conventional economics assumes that all individuals act rationally to maximise their individual self-interest. A substantial body of evidence (and intuition) suggests that individuals in fact behave as if they care about others, including strangers, in some circumstances. Moreover, individuals care about protecting their reputations and about behaving in ways that are consistent with their own self-concept.

A large number of experiments involving the 'ultimatum game' provide a convincing example of such concerns. In this experiment, a 'proposer' is given a sum of money (say, $10) and asked to propose a division of the money between him or herself and a second person called the 'responder.' If the responder accepts the proposed division of the money, both proposer and responder keep their allocation. If the responder rejects the proposed division, neither the proposer not the respondent gets any money at all. Conventional economics has a very clear prediction about the outcome of such a game. The proposer should offer a very small amount to the responder and the responder should accept that small amount, because something is better than nothing. In the event, proposers offer

[12] R Strotz, 'Myopia and Inconsistency in Dynamic Utility Maximization' (1956) 22 *Review of Economic Studies* 165.

considerably more than a small amount and, in those cases where only small amounts are proposed, the responder sometimes rejects the proposal, apparently to prevent the proposer from benefiting from behaviour perceived as unfair.

It seems that decision-makers care about being treated fairly and, in addition, are willing to be fair to others if others are fair to them. Decision-makers seem to be more generous than conventional models suppose (when they perceive the situation to be fair) and more spiteful when they perceive themselves or others to have been treated unfairly. 'Fairness' here is not 'a vague and ill-defined catch-all.'[13] For example, in transactions between consumers and firms, decision-makers seem to judge fairness with respect to a 'reference transaction', one that takes place on a regular basis. Transactions that vary from these market norms are judged unfair. The use of behavioural norms extends beyond fairness to a whole set of activities involving the reputation and self-concept of decision-makers.

D. The Scope of Behavioural Law and Economics

Behavioural law and economics focuses on bounded rationality, bounded willpower and bounded self-interest. Nonetheless, not all bankrupts are bankrupt because of these bounds. Empirical analyses of personal bankruptcy in the last 20 years have established that the majority of bankruptcies occur because of unanticipated events—job loss, illness, marital dissolution and others. By and large, bankrupts are ordinary citizens with ordinary levels of debt who have experienced unanticipated and serious economic setbacks. The focus of behavioural economics is on those cases—perhaps a minority—that are affected by bounded rationality, willpower and self-interest.

Jolls, Sunstein and Thaler point out that their framework can be used for several distinct purposes. Foremost among them is the positive analysis of how the law affects the economic behaviour of individuals. This is a typical goal of the economics of public policy—to predict how a change in policy will change the decisions made by economic agents. In the words of Jolls, Sunstein and Thaler: 'what will individuals' likely response to changes in the rules be?'[14] A second, prescriptive, purpose is to design the law so that the aims of public policy can be attained. That is, how might the law 'be used to achieve specific ends, such as deterring socially undesirable behaviour'?[15]

[13] Jolls, Sunstein, and Thaler, above n 2, at 1496.

[14] *Ibid* at 1474.

[15] Jolls, Sunstein, and Thaler also note that behavioural law and economics can address normative issues. Their example is the possible conflict between the principle of consumer sovereignty that is part of the normative structure of conventional economics and the 'anti-antipaternalism' that is arguably implied by behavioural law and economics. This normative issue is not a major part of this analysis and is thus not discussed further.

The next section of the chapter revisits Jackson's 1985 justification for the 'fresh start' in bankruptcy, in light of current research on decision-making biases. In the remaining sections of the chapter, several of the proposals of a Canadian bankruptcy taskforce will be presented and discussed from a behavioural perspective. In constructing those proposals, the taskforce members had both positive and prescriptive goals. It was their positive understanding of how the current law worked that led them to prescribe particular changes. The taskforce (called the Personal Insolvency Task Force, or PITF) was formed in 2000 in order to advise the Superintendent of Bankruptcy in advance of a round of legislative reforms scheduled to occur in 2002–03. Members included bankruptcy trustees, lender representatives, bankruptcy judges and several academics.[16]

III. JACKSON'S APPLICATION TO THE RIGHT OF DISCHARGE IN PERSONAL BANKRUPTCY

The bounds on rationality, willpower and self-interest summarised by JST have been the subject of widespread testing in the 1990s and have come to play a prominent role in several areas of economic and legal research. The outline of the new assumptions has been known for many years, however, and in 1985, Thomas Jackson applied some of the findings to the laws around personal bankruptcy.[17]

Under bankruptcy law in both the US and Canada, the right to discharge of most debts, in most circumstances, is a central element of bankruptcy law. In addition, borrowers cannot agree, at the time of borrowing, to waive their right to discharge the debt. Jackson's first contribution was to develop a normative rationale for the existence of a *nonwaivable* right of discharge.

Jackson's argument is that most citizens, knowing that bounded willpower and bounded rationality might lead them to underestimate the probability of failure and to then waive their right to discharge unwisely, favour the limitation on their right to contract implied by the nonwaivable right to discharge.

Why would citizens agree to limit their own rights in advance? Jackson's answer is that individuals realise, if faced with a situation in which their borrowing could only be accomplished if they waived their right to discharge, that their bounded willpower (which he calls 'impulsive behaviour') and bounded rationality ('incomplete heuristics') might lead them to waive their

[16] The current author was a member of the PITF. The proposals discussed in this paper are those in the final report of the Taskforce issued in August 2002.

[17] Several recent papers have referred to behavioural economics in their empirical studies of the economics of credit card usage. These papers are cited in I Ramsay in this volume, at 25–30.

right to discharge when they should not.[18] The nonwaivable right to discharge is the best way to eliminate the negative effects of bounded willpower and rationality.

The bounded rationality explanation proposed by Jackson is almost exactly paralleled by the discussion in Jolls, Sunstein and Thaler. The central point is that decision-makers systematically overestimate the probability of success (here, that the borrowing will 'pay off') and underestimate the probability of failure (in this case, that they will be unable to pay the loan).

Borrowers could try to adjust for their systematic over-estimation of the probability of successful repayment by simply avoiding borrowing—always paying credit card bills on time, self-financing home improvements, never buying a new car until the necessary cash is on hand. Counselling and education could lead potential borrowers to seek more information than they might first be inclined to collect. These potential solutions clearly have not worked for everyone and the problem of systematic errors in decision-making remains. As Jackson writes, the problem is one of 'incomplete information – an incompleteness unknown to the individual.'[19]

Viewed from the perspective of contemporary scholarship, Jackson's analysis of borrower's underestimation of the risks of borrowing holds up quite well, even though the psychological research has now documented a much wider range of decision-making biases.

The wider range of decision-making biases has been extensively discussed in the context of product liability law, where the research on decision-making biases has been especially influential.[20] In some ways, bankruptcy can be seen as the negative outcome—the 'accident'—associated with the use of a particular product—in this case, consumer credit. The key question is whether consumers systematically under-estimate product risks. If so, there is agreement that the liability for defects in products should be placed on manufacturers who, it is assumed, will respond by designing safe products. In product liability law, researchers accept the importance of decision-making biases but differ about the implications of the research. Some believe that decision-making biases lead consumers to under-estimate product risks while others believe that consumers over-estimate product risks.

In discussing this disagreement, Jon Hanson and Doug Kysar enumerate a number of reasons why it is not easy to apply the lessons learned from the behavioural research to product liability law:[21]

> First . . . it seems likely that different cognitive anomalies may simultaneously bias consumer risk perceptions in different directions. For instance, consumers might fail

[18] They 'should not' in the sense that, were they not subject to bounded rationality and willpower, they would not have made the same decision.

[19] See Jackson, above n 1, at 1414.

[20] See, for example, HA Latin, '"Good" Warnings, Bad Product, and Cognitive Limitations' (1994) 41 *UCLA Law Review* 1193.

[21] Hanson and Kysar, above n 2, at 722.

> to realise the significance of product safety warnings when presented in statistical fashion but also overreact to similar information when presented in a vivid television news account. Second, it appears impossible to tell, ex ante, which cognitive effect will be most pronounced in any given context. That is, when analysing a consumer product setting, it is impossible to know whether representativeness, anchoring, dissonance, overconfidence, or any other cognitive bias will exact the greatest influence on consumer perceptions. Even if the existence of their effect can be predicted, the relative impact cannot.

Jackson's argument is that individuals systematically under-estimate the product risk—here, the risk of borrowing. What about the biases that might work in the opposite direction? In the analysis of product liability law, those who argue against strict product liability (because they believe consumers over-estimate product risks) believe that a particular pattern of risk perception errors exists.

First, some events are extremely unlikely, so much so that they are effectively hidden from the view of consumers and are therefore ignored. Second, there are events that occur with a 'low' probability but are highly publicised when they do occur. The probability that such events will occur is thought to be overestimated because of availability bias. As discussed above, availability bias can cause the over-estimation of the risk of low probability but highly 'available' events—highly available because they are widely publicised or especially memorable.

Third, there is a category of relatively high probability events that are under-estimated because they are not particularly salient. For example, even though the probability of dying from an automobile accident may be far greater than the probability of dying in an airplane crash, people routinely underestimate the probability of traffic fatalities.

Those who argue that consumers overestimate product risks place product-related accidents in the second category of 'low probability but highly available' events. If so, there is no need to make manufacturers strictly liable.

Might the same argument be made in the credit market? If personal bankruptcy falls into the second category, then Jackson's justification of the right to discharge would be unconvincing. The cases in which borrowing had especially negative consequences would be highly available to potential borrowers and the resulting bias would lead to the over-estimation of the risk of the negative consequences. Borrowers would therefore be overly careful in their borrowing and there would be no need to encourage creditor monitoring by means of a nonwaivable right to discharge.

The consequences of over-borrowing are certainly not invisible. Negative consequences associated with two kinds of borrowing are especially well-publicised—credit card borrowing and student loan borrowing. In both cases, it is easy to find mass media stories of borrowers who have fallen on hard times.

My view is that the argument for over-estimation is not particularly strong and that the cognitive biases leading to under-estimation are more powerful than those leading to over-estimation. In addition, following Hanson and

Kysar, there is another important reason to assume that borrowers underestimate the risks of borrowing, even if the a priori impact of the decision-making biases is indeterminate. The reason is that, in a competitive market, it is in the interest of lenders to manipulate the decision-making biases of borrowers in order to induce them to underestimate the risks of borrowing, as long as that underestimation leads to greater profits. This argument is developed at length by Hanson and Kysar in the context of product liability law, but a full application to the credit market is beyond the scope of this paper.[22] Regardless, the existence of the biases that might lead to over-estimation means that, as in the case of product liability law, there is room to argue about the direction of the a priori biases.

I believe that Jackson's 1985 partial justification for the nonwaivable right to discharge is supported by later psychological research. From a policy point of view, however, it is clear that any policies that make the negative consequences of bankruptcy more salient could reduce the need for a nonwaivable right to discharge because the increased salience would reduce the extent to which borrowers under-estimate the probability of being unable to pay the debts.

IV. DOES JACKSON'S ARGUMENT EXTEND TO THE REAFFIRMATION OF DISCHARGEABLE DEBTS?

Reaffirmation, in the context of personal bankruptcy, occurs when a former bankrupt agrees to pay a debt that has already been discharged or when a bankrupt agrees to pay a debt that is likely to be discharged at the end of the bankruptcy process. In Canada, there is nothing in the bankruptcy law that stops debtors from reaffirming particular debts. By contrast, in the US context, reaffirmation is governed by rules that allow reaffirmations only before discharge, and only with the approval of a court or the recommendation of the debtor's lawyer.

There is as yet little empirical evidence as to the frequency with which reaffirmation occurs in Canada. In the PITF deliberations, several trustees gave examples of particular cases in which reaffirmation was requested by creditors, but no evidence was presented that suggested that reaffirmation was a widespread problem. In the US, by contrast, a high profile (and therefore highly 'available') example of reaffirmation occurred when the large retailer, Sears Roebuck and Company, was the focus of a class action suit concerning systematic and unauthorised reaffirmation. In the end, Sears paid over $165 million to 190,000 debtors.[23]

[22] See P Ryan and S Schwartz, 'The Fresh Start in Bankruptcy: Expanding the Role of Lenders', 2002, mimeo available from the authors.

[23] See M Hoffman and J Cymrot, 'Disaffirming Reaffirmation' 52 *Commercial Law Journal* 53 at 65.

Jackson's rationale for the existence of a nonwaivable right to discharge also justifies a ban on reaffirmation. Jackson noted that one alternative to the nonwaivable right to discharge was identify those borrowers who were *not* prey to impulsive decisions and bounded rationality and then to allow those individuals to waive their right to discharge if they so chose. He rejected that alternative as impractical, and illustrated that impracticality by referring the US reaffirmation rules and how those rules do not successfully identify those who could benefit from reaffirmation:[24]

> . . . the cases applying these [reaffirmation] rules contain little evidence that judges do anything other than impose their own view of the individuals' best interest in deciding which reaffirmations to permit. Similarly, we might expect that a case-by-case attempt to single out individuals who need the protection of a right of discharge might well result not in the identification of individuals whose choices do not accurately reflect their personal desires, but rather in the identification of individuals whose choices strike judges as somehow odd or aberrant.

These same considerations led Hoffman and Cymrot to recommend that 'Congress . . . make reaffirmation agreements unenforceable.'[25]

Bans on the waiver of the right to discharge and on reaffirmations constitute what JST call 'blocked trades.' They argue that bounded self-interest is 'part of the causal mechanism' that establishes the laws that ban economic practices such as usurious lending, price gouging, ticket scalping and, presumably, reaffirmation in bankruptcy.[26] The general idea is that, in these cases, there is a 'reference transaction'—a widely available interest rate, a long-standing price. Large variations from that reference transaction are perceived as 'unfair' by most people and are thus disallowed.

The argument for banning reaffirmation is that the 'reference transaction' is the discharge of most debts. The reaffirmation of debts that would otherwise be discharged seems 'unfair' even when the reaffirmation is voluntary. In the same way, usury is thought to be unfair even though the borrower feels that paying a very high interest rate is better than not being able to borrow at all. In creating such laws, 'legislators may be responding to community sentiments about what kinds of things are properly subject to market arrangements.'[27]

The PITF did not find this argument convincing and did not recommend a blanket ban on reaffirmation agreements. Instead, the PITF proposal concerning reaffirmations recommends limits on the availability of reaffirmation that vary according to whether the debt is secured or unsecured.[28] Reaffirmation of unsecured debt would be prohibited. Under the proposal, secured debt can be reaffirmed without a court order only if the amount reaffirmed is less than or equal to a certain percentage—specified by a sliding scale—of the value of the

24 See Jackson, above n 1, at 1416.
25 Hoffman and Cymrot, above n 23, at 75.
26 See Jolls, Sunstein, and Thaler, above n 2, at 1510.
27 See *ibid* at 1516.
28 See PITF, above n 4, at 29–33.

secured asset. For example, reaffirmation of up to 150 per cent of the value is allowed if the asset is worth between $5,000 and $20,000 but only up to 110 per cent of the value of assets worth more than $50,000. Any other reaffirmation of secured debts would be subject to the approval of a bankruptcy official. Failure to abide by these reaffirmation rules would generally be an offense under the relevant legislation.

Even though the PITF did not recommend a ban on reaffirmation, the assumptions of behavioural economics played a part in the formulation of its proposal. In particular, the bounded rationality and bounded willpower of bankrupts (as opposed to potential debtors) was thought by some PITF members to create the possibility that bankrupts might unwisely reaffirm debts that, were the situation fully explained to them, they would never choose to repay. The requirement that a bankruptcy official approve many reaffirmations as being in the best interests of debtors is clearly intended to discourage unwise reaffirmation both by imposing a cost and by allowing the judgement of the bankruptcy official to override the debtor's.

The argument against a ban on reaffirmation is that situations where reaffirmation is in the best interest of all parties can be identified and should therefore be allowed. In the discussion of the Canadian proposal, one participant described such a situation. Suppose a couple borrows $15,000 to buy a new car; in the new car market, asymmetric information leads to an immediate drop in the resale value of the car to, say, $12,000 (or to some level such that the amount owed is considerably more than the fair market value of the car). Now suppose that the loan is jointly guaranteed by the husband and the wife and that the husband files for bankruptcy but the wife does not. If the husband cannot reaffirm the $15,000 debt, the creditor can seize the vehicle and sue the wife for the difference between the market value and the amount borrowed. In this case, it would seem than a reaffirmation would involve no objectionable creditor behaviour and would be in the best interests of the couple, assuming they do not want to lose their car. It was this kind of example that led to the adoption of the 'sliding scale' that defines the kinds of reaffirmation of secured debt that can occur.

Note, however, that the same argument could be made against the nonwaivable right to discharge; there are surely cases where waiving the right to discharge would be in the best interest of all parties, even assuming that all parties are acting in a rational, self-interested way.

V. BEYOND THE NONWAIVABLE RIGHT TO DISCHARGE

Jackson notes that simply establishing the rationale for a nonwaivable right to discharge 'does little to define the proper contours of bankruptcy's fresh start.'[29]

[29] See Jackson, above n 1, at 1424.

The second half of his article is thus concerned with some of the particulars surrounding the fresh start offered by the right of discharge. Similarly, this paper takes up two particular issues under discussion in the current round of bankruptcy law reform underway in Canada. These reforms involve several issues that bear on the contours of the fresh start offered by the law and that can be informed by the insights of behavioural economics.

A. Which Assets Should be Exempt from Seizure?

Under bankruptcy laws in both the US and Canada, some assets are exempt from seizure by the bankrupt's creditors. Most importantly, the nonwaivable right to discharge exempts human capital by not allowing creditors access to post-bankruptcy earnings or by imposing strict limits on that access.

In Canada, the extent to which creditors were entitled to the debtor's post-bankruptcy income remained unclear until the reforms of 1997.[30] As a result of the 1997 reforms, Canadian bankrupts are now required to pay their creditors part of the 'surplus income' they earn during the period between the filing of their bankruptcy and the discharge of their debts. An administrative edict defines 'surplus income' as a function of Canadian poverty lines. After discharge, however, no payments are required from the former bankrupt's income.

By contrast, American bankrupts have never been required to make payments to their creditors from post-bankruptcy income. If proposed bankruptcy reforms are enacted, however, 'means-testing' may force some US debtors who would have filed for bankruptcy under Chapter 7 to file proposals under Chapter 13 that would require payments over the ensuing several years.

Jackson argues that human capital should be protected because it is the least diversifiable form of wealth, because it is crucial in determining the future well-being of the bankrupt and his or her family, and because the garnishment of future wages would create an externality in the form of reduced productivity of the individual.

Nonetheless, the exemption of assets clearly conflicts with the goal of bankruptcy law to liquidate debtors' assets and divide them equitably among creditors. Given the need to balance the rights of debtors and creditors, which other assets should be protected, if any?

One rationale for exemption lies in making sure that, after discharge, the debtor can still be a productive member of society. The behavioural perspective, however, suggests that exemptions might also be the result of the efforts of the 'planner self' to protect its future well-being from risks created by the rash behaviour of the 'impulsive self.' The thrust of these efforts is to create assets

[30] For a fuller comparison of the US and Canada provisions on this issue, see J Ziegel, 'Comparative Consumer Insolvency Regimes from a Canadian Perspective: A Report for Industry Canada', Mimeo, September 2000 at 31–40, 76–83, and 168–70.

that are beyond the reach of the impulsive self. In particular, the 'planner self' purchases illiquid assets (including locked-in savings plans and durable consumption goods) which then operate as commitment devices to ensure its future well-being.

Jackson seems to be adopting a similar view when he writes:[31]

> The rationale for protecting durable goods may be that they constitute a form of savings, in the sense that their value is consumed over time. Because the main problem caused by impulsive behaviour, incomplete heuristics and externalities is the tendency to overconsume today and undersave for tomorrow, the decision of exemption law to protect savings for future consumption follows reasonably closely from the core notion of the fresh-start policy itself. Individuals may underestimate the extent to which they jeopardize their future consumption of existing durable goods when they borrow money in order to consume today.

From this perspective, *wage substitutes* should be protected and the cost of that protection absorbed by all members of society in the form of higher credit costs. The most important wage substitute is illiquid retirement savings, usually held in formal pension plans or in tax-deferred retirement savings vehicles.[32] After retirement, individuals must either have savings to substitute for the earnings that had been generated by their exempt human capital or they must rely on government-sponsored pension plans. By exempting retirement savings, the 'planner self' completes the protection of future income by providing for income after retirement. Moreover, protecting individual savings limits the extent to which tax-financed government pensions will be utilised.

The other form of assets that are commonly exempt are those deemed essential to ensuring a meaningful 'fresh start.' As Jacob Ziegel writes:

> Modern bankruptcy systems agree that the debtor must not be stripped of all his assets. The debtor and his family must be allowed to keep the basic necessities of life and . . . to pursue his livelihood.[33]

For example, 'tools of the trade' are exempt because lacking the tools necessary to exploit one's human capital—being a carpenter without carpentry tools—would impair the fresh start.

Using the behavioural rationale, one might argue that *all* assets should be exempt since almost all represent forward-looking behaviour and most might be deemed essential (at least by the bankrupt debtor).

However, another crucial factor here is the balance between costs of bankruptcy and the availability of credit. As has been argued above, bounded rationality and bounded willpower imply that a nonwaivable discharge be available

[31] See Jackson, above n 1, at 1434.

[32] Laibson writes that 'all illiquid assets provide a form of commitment . . . a pension or retirement plan is the clearest example of such an asset. Many of these plans benefit from favorable tax treatment, and most of them effectively bar consumers from using their savings before retirement.' D Laibson, 'Golden Eggs and Hyperbolic Discounting' (1998) *Quarterly Journal of Economics* 444.

[33] Ziegel, above n 30, at 25.

to provide bankrupts with a fresh start. But it is also true that society values, and is willing to pay for, the availability of credit. If it becomes too easy to default on loans, creditors will undoubtedly limit the availability of credit. The 'ease' with which default can occur is a function of the cost of defaults, measured by the value of what must be given up to obtain a discharge. The primary costs of bankruptcy are the value of non-exempt assets, limitations on post-bankruptcy credit, the stigma of becoming bankrupt and the out-of-pocket costs of the bankruptcy process.

Conventional economists have argued strenuously that lengthening the list of exempt assets lowers the cost of bankruptcy, therefore increasing the number of bankruptcies, and raising the cost of credit. Empirically, however, most studies have found no impact of differential exemption rules across American states.[34]

Regardless, it seems evident that some assets must be available to creditors because they are neither essential to the immediate post-discharge well-being of debtors nor essential to their long-term well-being, as defined by the 'planner self.' Debtors, however, are unlikely to correctly identify assets that are non-essential. The typical compromise has been to formulate a relatively short list of assets that are exempt.

In Canada, each province has its own list of exempt assets. The PITF formulated a proposal concerning exempt assets. I first discuss the proposal concerning retirement savings before turning to the proposal concerning tangible assets.

1. *Retirement Savings*

The two most common financial instruments used for retirement savings in Canada are registered pension plans (RPPs) and registered retirement savings plans (RRSPs).

RPPs are usually related to an individual's employment; they are often mandatory and often involve pre-defined contributions by both employee and employer. Pension fund investments are often not controlled by the beneficiary and, crucially, are 'locked in' so they cannot easily be cashed in prior to retirement. RPP contributions are exempt from seizure by a bankrupt's creditors.

For those without employment-related pension plans—including self-employed individuals and non-working spouses—Canadian law allows contributions to registered retirement savings plans (RRSPs). Conventional RRSPs offer immediate tax benefits (in the form of deductions from taxable income) and can be invested at the discretion of the individual. Even though intended as retirement savings, conventional RRSPs can be 'cashed in' if the holder is

[34] See R Hynes and EA Posner, 'The Law and Economics of Consumer Finance' (2001) John M Olin Program in Law & Economics, Working Paper No 117, 2D Series at 22–24, <http://www.law.uchicago.edu/Lawecon/index.html>.

willing to incur a tax penalty. Currently, funds held in conventional RRSPs can be seized by creditors in the event of bankruptcy.[35]

RPPs and RRSPs are both assets intended to finance retirement by acting as wage substitutes. In the current situation, however, RPPs are exempt and RRSPs are generally not. In the discussions about exemptions, the inconsistency in the treatment of these assets was taken up. The alternative of making both non-exempt was considered but quickly rejected.

If pension plans were to retain their exempt status, then it seemed logical that similar retirement savings vehicles—conventional RRSPs—should also be exempt and such a recommendation is part of the PITF final report.[36] In terms of behavioural law and economics, it makes a great deal of sense to protect savings for retirement. Retirement savings are clearly the work of the 'planner self' and represent a substitute for future wage income, already protected by bankruptcy law.

While the exemption of retirement savings is interesting from the behavioural perspective, it should be noted that few bankrupts hold RRSPs at the time of filing for bankruptcy and the value of their holdings is relatively small. In a summary of the assets of approximately 900 bankrupts filing in 1999, the Office of the Superintendent of Bankruptcy reported that at most 58 had non-exempt RRSPs, with a mean value of $2,130.[37]

2. *Tangible Assets*

By tradition, certain physical assets have been deemed exempt. The exempt status of these assets is an attempt to give meaning to the idea of a fresh start—to leave bankrupts without their tools of trade, without clothes and household effects, and without a vehicle would give lie to 'a fresh start.' Other assets are deemed non-exempt and therefore can be sold and the proceeds turned over to creditors.

[35] For the purposes of this discussion, two other types of RRSPs are important. First, 'insurance-type RRSPs' take the form of annuities held with insurance companies and are exempt from seizure if the beneficiary of the RRSP is the individual's spouse, parent or child. Second, 'locked-in' RRSPs come into existence when individuals leave jobs in which they had vested pension rights. The result is an RRSP that cannot be cashed in until the individuals retire. Locked-in RRSPs are exempt from seizure.

[36] See PITF, above n 4, at 17–24. The PITF reform proposals dealt with several practical objections to the extension of exempt status to conventional RRSPs. First, it would require bankrupts to lock-in their RRSPs until retirement, much as converted RPP benefits are locked-in. This provision ensures that the now-exempt RRSP will indeed be used as a wage substitute during retirement. Second, it proposes a condition that is intended to avoid abuse. Any RRSP contributions made in the three years prior to bankruptcy would *not* be exempt; the reasoning here is that such contributions should have gone to repay debts and should therefore not be available to the bankrupt.

[37] 'At most' because the asset category is labelled 'life insurance/RRSPs' and may therefore contain assets that were not RRSPs. It should be noted that it is likely that debtors cash in their RRSPs prior to declaring bankruptcy. If RRSPs become exempt, the RRSP holdings of future bankrupts may increase.

Each province in Canada (and each state in the US) has its own list of exemptions. There is considerable variation across these jurisdictions, particularly in the way in which home equity is treated. Here, the relevant issues are: (a) whether debtors should be able to waive their right to claim some assets as exempt; and (b) whether the exemption list should be national in scope or remain provincial.

Debtors might waive their right to claim an asset as exempt by granting a creditor a security interest in the asset. For example, an individual might use the tools of his or her trade as collateral in order to borrow the money needed to purchase the tools or for some other purpose. In such cases—where a creditor holds a security interest in exempt assets—Jackson argues that a distinction should be drawn between non-purchase money security interests and purchase money security interests.

In the former case, he argues that bounded rationality will cause borrowers to systematically underestimate the probability of default and, therefore, non-purchase money security interests should not be enforceable in bankruptcy. In practice, the case for the non-enforceability of non-purchase money security interests in bankruptcy seems to be based on the desire to avoid undue pressure by creditors on debtors. Since 1978, in the US context, non-possessory, non-purchase money security interests have been invalid insofar as they affect the exempt status of an asset. According to William Whitford, this provision:[38]

> had an impact on a lending pattern that was commercially significant . . . in some instances, a lender took a security interest in a large number of the debtor's previously acquired personal possessions, sometimes called a 'blanket security interest'. Such security interests allowed the lender to threaten the debtor with repossession of large amounts of the debtor's possessions. Even if these possessions had little resale value, such threats could be effective in inducing the debtor to make payments—even after a bankruptcy filing—to avoid repossession.

In Canada, some trustees believe that particular lenders—usually consumer loan companies rather than banks or individuals—use the threat of repossession to unfairly pressure debtors into reaffirmation or repayment. In the US, the 1985 Credit Practices Rule of the Federal Trade Commission prohibits non-purchase money security interests in a range of exempt assets as 'unfair.'

Jackson argues that purchase money security interests should be treated differently:[39]

> Unlike general security interests, purchase money interests are secured by the same asset that the extension of credit helped the debtor to obtain. Because the debtor's ability to acquire—and hence to consume—the asset in the first place derives from his 'waiver' of the property's exempt status vis-à-vis the purchase money loan, purchase

[38] W Whitford, 'Changing Definitions of Fresh Start in U.S. Bankruptcy Law' (1997) 20 *Journal of Consumer Policy* 179 at 342.

[39] See Jackson, above n 1, at 1436.

> money security interests should be excepted from any general rule barring secured creditors from reaching exempt assets in bankruptcy.

This rationale seems obscure. There is no reason to think that the bounded rationality that leads borrowers to over-estimate the probability of success differs according to whether or not the creditor has a purchase-money interest in the asset. Moreover, if the assets are necessities of life, they are necessary whether or not a creditor holds a security interest of any kind. For example, as the PITF wrote:

> Such a security interest enables lenders to threaten to repossess household goods or motor vehicles in hopes of obtaining better treatment. That is, debtors may be intimidated into giving preference to the lien holder. Even if the items have no commercial value, they may be essential to the debtor's welfare.[40]

Instead, from a behavioural perspective, the rationale for making non-purchase money security interests in exempt assets invalid is bounded willpower, not bounded rationality. The fear is that the 'impulsive self,' anxious to borrow money for immediate consumption, will grant security interests to creditors who will later take advantage of the security to threaten the debtor unfairly.

On the issue of federal versus sub-national exemption lists, Jackson notes that when a problem is national in nature (as is, in this case, the problem of borrowers under the influence of bounded rationality and bounded willpower), it is appropriate to have national policies (in this case, a national list of exemption). The non-waivable right to discharge protects human capital and its exemption should therefore not be left to provinces or states. On the other hand, provinces and states might be best placed to know which types of assets are most important to their citizens, thus justifying different lists.

The PITF proposed two changes to the treatment of physical assets.[41] First, it proposes a federal exemption list and would allow debtors to choose whether to use the federal or the relevant provincial list (but not to pick and choose among specific items on each list). The proposed federal exemptions are modest—they include a $3,000 vehicle, $5,000 in home equity, 'tools of the trade' worth up to $10,000.[42]

Second, it proposes making non-purchase money security interests in exempt assets unenforceable. In particular, 'the BIA should be amended to avoid non-purchase money security interests in personal property that would otherwise be exempt from seizure.'[43] Such a provision would bring the Canadian system into line with the similar US provisions.

[40] See PITF, above n 4, at 27.

[41] See PITF, above n 4, at 24–28.

[42] In a dissent from the PITF proposals, Iain Ramsay noted that home equity is often the most important form of retirement savings held by Canadians. For such individuals, the $5,000 exemption for home equity is paltry compared to the large exemptions offered for other forms of retirement savings.

[43] See PITF, above n 4, at 28.

B. Which Debts Should be Excepted from Discharge?

Not all debts are dischargeable. The list of those that are not varies from country to country.[44] Non-dischargeable debts are often those that arise from intentional wrongdoing or because of the nature of the obligation. For example, no country exempts debts arising from pre-bankruptcy criminal behaviour (including damages awarded to victims) or those that arise from alimony orders.

The dischargeability of student loans has been a contentious issue in both the US and in Canada. In the US, government-subsidised student loans are non-dischargeable in bankruptcies filed within seven years of the time when the first payment was due. In Canada, student loans are non-dischargeable in bankruptcies filed within 10 years of the last period of full- or part-time study. In both countries, however, a court determination of hardship can lead to discharge. A major difference between the US and Canada is that the Canadian hardship hearing cannot occur until 10 years after the former student left school whereas the US hearing can occur much more quickly.

From the behavioural perspective, the same arguments that justify the non-waivable right to discharge—bounded rationality and bounded willpower—are relevant in the case of student borrowing. Potential students are inexperienced with credit and, influenced by exhortations to stay in school, may borrow to finance unwise educational investments. Ziegel writes that

> regard should also be paid to the findings of observers that students are often not adequately advised before a loan is granted on the appropriateness of their study programme and their job prospects on completing the programme . . .[45]

The opposition to allowing the discharge of student loans seems rooted in one of two views. The first is that society must balance its attempt to account for bounds on rationality and willpower with its desire to have well-functioning credit markets. Jackson uses the non-dischargeability of student loans as an example of negative consequences of making discharge 'freely available,' arguing that the too-easy discharge of student loans may limit their availability. The second argument is that the discharge of student loans is 'unfair' since students are thought to be likely to have high future incomes.

It seems clear that the provision for discharge in cases where repayment would cause hardship is an attempt to distinguish between those student loan borrowers who are thought be acting unfairly (by seeking discharge of their loans when their future incomes would allow repayment without undue hardship) and those who are honest but unfortunate. If the student loan exception

[44] Ziegel summarises the non-dischargeable debts in Canada, Australia, England and Wales, and the US. Ziegel, above n 30, at 44–49.

[45] See *ibid* at 185. Apart from this behavioural argument, the arguments against the student loan exception are: (a) that it discriminates against individuals who, by going to school, have done exactly what they have long been encouraged to do; and (b) that it gives preference to those who have made or guaranteed the loans.

were simply an attempt by lenders to put themselves in a preferential position vis-à-vis other creditors, there would be no need for the hardship provisions in the US and in Canada.

In both the US and in Canada, judges have not been quick to allow discharge as the result of hardship hearings. In the US, for example, the courts have imposed a variety of tests for 'hardship' that have resulted in cases where discharge was denied to individuals living below the poverty line, with heavy student loan debt and little prospect of high future earnings.[46] But if the behavioural perspective is correct, the criteria used to test whether a debtor seeking discharge on hardship grounds should not be very stringent. The goal should be to identify egregious cases of unfairness—the young professional with large student loans and the prospect of high future income—but to allow discharge for most others. In effect, the hardship hearing should result in the discharge of student loans for all except those who demonstrate a likely *lack* of hardship in the post-bankruptcy period.

Prior to 1997, student loans were an empirically significant part of the liabilities of those filing for bankruptcy.[47] Saul Schwartz reports that roughly 25 per cent of bankrupts had at least one student loan among their debts with the median value (among those with the debt) of $10,000. Just under 20 per cent of the bankrupts either reported that their student loans had 'triggered' their bankruptcy or that the loans comprised more than 50 per cent of their debts. The empirical evidence further suggested that many would have had their student loans discharged if the definition of hardship in the last paragraph were adopted. Many of those with student loans among their debts had attended post-secondary institutions without graduating and did not reap large returns from their education. Moreover, many had low current earnings (even some years after leaving school) and had relied on other social programmes.

In the discussion of the treatment of student loans, the PITF felt strongly that[48]: (a) the 10-year period, after leaving school, in which discharge is not currently allowed should be reduced to five years and that (b) an American-style hardship clause should be adopted. Part of the reason for choosing the five-year period, rather than removing the exception completely, was the feeling that student loans should not be easily discharged because the loan was, in effect, a purchase money security interest in the debtor's future earnings.

VI. CONCLUSION

This chapter has explored the usefulness of the behavioural perspective, as summarised by Jolls, Sunstein and Thaler, for the study of personal bankruptcy law.

[46] R Salvin, 'Student Loans, Bankruptcy, and the Fresh Start Policy: Must Debtors Be Impoverished to Discharge Educational Loans?' (1996) 71 *Tulane Law Review* 139.

[47] S Schwartz, 'The Empirical Dimensions of Consumer Bankruptcy: Results from a Survey of Canadian Bankrupts' (1999) 37 *Osgoode Hall Law Journal* 83.

[48] See PITF, above n 4, at 13–17.

Following the lead of Jackson, who used the perspective some years ago, the chapter extends the analysis to the reaffirmation of debts, the exemption from seizure of retirement savings, the enforceability of non-purchase money security interests in exempt property and the student loan exception to discharge.

The basic argument about the effect of bounded willpower is that the 'planner self' desires laws that constrain the behaviour of the 'impulsive self,' knowing that the 'impulsive self' will be in charge at key decision-making points. Moreover, bounded rationality may lead even the non-impulsive individual to over-estimate the probabilities of successful investments. This individual desire is assumed to be translated into law by a democratic political structure that responds to widespread citizen demands for various laws.

The behavioural perspective seems quite useful in describing the desire of policy-makers—here exemplified by the Canadian Personal Insolvency Task Force—to limit reaffirmations, to exempt retirement savings (while locking them in until retirement age) and to make unenforceable non-purchase money claims in exempt assets. On the other hand, the perspective suggests that student loans should be dischargeable and they are not; indeed, Canada has moved to tighten the rules that limit the dischargeability of student loans.

This fact highlights a problem with the behavioural perspective. Each individual is not only a borrower, but also a taxpayer and a potential creditor. At the same time that a non-waivable right of discharge is desired, so are limits on the right to discharge. The empirical result—the law that comes to exist—reflects the balance between the desires of society as potential bankrupts versus the desires of society as borrowers who bear at least some of the cost of bankruptcy. Since the outcome of this balancing is unknown, the result is theoretically ambiguous.

Part II

Consumer Over-indebtedness in Countries Without Bankruptcy

4

Consumer Bankruptcy and Over-indebtedness in Brazil

JOSÉ REINALDO DE LIMA LOPES

I. INTRODUCTION

THIS PAPER SEEKS to assess the problem of consumers' over-indebtedness from a social-legal and critical point of view. It starts by pointing out the political aspect of indebtedness: debts are a component of wealth and power distribution in society. Consumer law, on the other hand, is part of a legal-political arrangement through which welfare policies, that is, distributive policies, are implemented. I am primarily concerned with consumer credit. I am basically interested in passive over-indebtedness, even if active over-indebtedness may be a problem. Active over-indebtedness in itself bears the assumption that consumers may be partially responsible for their difficult position. Passive over-indebtedness is more clearly a matter of involuntary situations of default. This is the foundation of Section One.

In Section Two, I move on to describe the institutional framework in which insolvency of consumers may be understood. I try to show that some traditional instruments of legal reasoning have a distributive effect and help maintain a certain balance between creditors and debtors without regard to considerations of the fairness or justice of such balance. I also claim that most of these institutional devices were created to be applied between professional business people and may be criticised from the consumer protection perspective. I also argue that the uselessness of personal insolvency in Brazil is the rational result of a system that naturally imposes negotiation on an individual basis, both for economic and cultural reasons. In the third section, I make use of some data collected by other studies to give a general view of consumers' indebtedness. It is clear from these data that consumers who look for help tend to be passively over-indebted. Section Four shows that passive over-indebtedness may be partly caused by an irresponsible lending policy. This will lead to Section Five, where I propose the use of collective non-contractual remedies to stop or limit some aggressive market strategies used by banks, credit card companies and financial institutions.

This paper is a critique of the current situation. No statute has been passed or is being discussed in Brazil to rearrange personal insolvency; personal or civil insolvency is not a viable solution for over-indebted consumers.

The development of consumer credit in Brazil has taken place in the last 50 years, along with the development of industrialisation policies. Retail dealers had advanced consumer credit in general on a traditional, personal basis, until the 1960s and 1970s brought along a new wave of industrialisation (of which the automobile plants established in the country in the late 1950s were the most visible) and the need for a more general system of credit for consumers. During some 20 years, consumer credit blossomed under the name of '*financeiras*,' which were authorised to issue '*letras* de *câmbio*' in the name of consumers at the exact amount of credit they would advance. Besides these firms, car manufacturers soon entered this market to facilitate credit to their potential consumers. Due to the *Banking Act* of 1964, car manufacturers had to organise separate corporations to advance credit, but soon enough they all had their own 'banks.' American legal creations, such as leasing, fiduciary sales and the credit card, were imported a few years later.

The attraction of a potential market of 170 million people, as is roughly the population of Brazil estimated by the census of the year 2000, and the prospective growth of this market, have attracted not only industrial and public services (utilities) corporations but also foreign banks. However, almost two decades of high inflation—even of hyperinflation in the early 90s—had some effect on the credit market, such as allowing the banks to gain from the difference in rates of inflation instead of on their productivity in terms of business policy (credit extension, interest rates, etc). When hyperinflation was finally brought under control in the mid-1990s, consumers felt that they could make plans for the future and started to buy on credit. A boom in credit expenditure followed and the immediate consequence was a boom in default.[1] In spite of the negative consequences, it is clear that the Brazilian economy has definitely shifted to a massive economy of credit and consumers will need credit to function in the contemporary consumer market place.

II. INDEBTEDNESS AND POLITICS

Forgiveness of debts has been a frequent factor in revolutionary discourses. Perhaps the best example of the association of political revolution and the struggle between creditors and debtors is the Athenian legal revolution directed by Solon, in the VI Century BC, who fought the unlimited accumulation of land. Debts in the ancient world would often be paid either by the seizure of one's land or by slavery of the debtor, or both. Seen from a historical perspective it is

[1] AC Pinheiro and C Cabral, 'Credit Markets in Brazil: the Role of Judicial Enforcememnt and Other Institutions' (1998) *Ensaios BNDES* at 17, n 9. According to Pinheiro, using data of the Banco Central, overdue loans peaked in 1995. The average of overdue loans was 18.8% in 1998. *Ibid* at 16.

clear that the relation of creditors and debtors has a distributive aspect. Essentially, this means that the credit system can not be separated from a social process in which it helps to determine who will and who will not accumulate wealth. In many historical examples, debtors enraged by a continuous concentration of wealth and inequitable repayment conditions joined forces with other social groups to put an end to that situation.

It is very well known that in many places in Brazil a modern form of slavery has developed in situations where farm workers can not repay their debts to the boss (*patrão*) who brought consumers goods from town and resold them at his farm to his workers. Unable to repay their debts, due to the negative balance between their salary and their consumption needs, workers find themselves trapped in a dead end. For all intents and purposes they become modern slaves. Would it be an exaggeration to say that over-indebted consumers—if not given a form of release—can become similarly enslaved to bankers? Any approach to present day consumer credit should therefore emphasise that distributive matters are a first order element of the discussion.

Another factor in the social aspect of consumers' indebtedness has to do with the general social arrangements of a society. Some of the aspects that interest us are structural and some are cultural, but both are intertwined. Structurally speaking, industrial societies—even if semi-peripheric[2] societies—tend to destroy traditional forms of support, personal and family ties. Irrespective of cultural aspects, this is so in any industrialised and urbanised society. Consumers′ indebtedness and over-indebtedness reflect the need for money to support one′s basic needs in contexts of depersonalisation and of a lack of strong, solidaristic ties by individuals.

Culturally speaking, industrialisation and individualism have been considered more at home in the Protestant, Calvinist countries. Following Max Weber's much cited (and frequently contested) thesis, the United States of America is the ideal type of individualistic, Protestant and Calvinistic culture. 'The United States is *par excellence* the nation of ascetic Protestantism.'[3] When put together, structural and cultural elements result in certain arrangements, including legal arrangements. The bankruptcy system will then seem natural and rational in these countries.

In semi-peripheric countries, where social ties are developed differently, this legal solution does not necessarily apply. Even if less frequently than a few decades earlier, personal ties still count as a social protection network. Family members may not be affectionate to one another, but it is still fairly unthinkable that they will not, in time of great financial distress, give a helping hand to family. This is also true for personal friendship ties: friends will still lend money

[2] B de Sousa Santos uses the term semi-periphery to distinguish societies or countries (nation-states) with intermediate levels of 'modernisation.' B de Sousa Santos, 'Estado e Sociedade na Semiperiferia do Sistema Mundial: O Caso Portugues' *Analise Social* 87/88/89 869.

[3] J de Souza, 'A Etica portestante e a ideologia do atraso brasileiro' (1998) 13 *Revista Brasileira de Ciencias Sociais* at 104.

to friends in extreme cases. Cultural aspects may well help to explain the relative de-emphasis of consumer bankruptcy as a public, rather than private, problem. Personal ties, or communitarian ties of this kind, tend to provide, especially to consumers of lower income levels, a network of material support that includes financial support in cases of extreme need. Of course, one may legitimately ask if such personal ties and support networks are adequate for survival in complex societies.

A. Consumer Credit

The second half of the 20th century has seen a sharp rise of consumer credit in Brazil. Until the late 19th century, credit was a special sort of business between bankers and their clients who were for the most part, if not totally, businessmen and corporations, either in the industrial or the commercial fields. Credit was also widely used in agriculture, where land served as security.

It is only with the industrialisation in the second half of the 20th century that consumer credit actually developed. Industrialisation, as is widely known, increased significantly in the war years, when manufacture of heavy industrial goods to substitute for imports became essential. In the 1950s, the country was ready for its second phase of industrialisation: the manufacture of consumer goods to substitute for imports. Nevertheless, how could the middle classes and the working class[4] afford to consume this new production? The answer was the general reorganisation of the banking system in 1964 and the continuous creation of legal instruments allowing creditors both to advance credit and to have special procedural rights to recover it. In very simple terms, consumers gained broad access to legal instruments that were previously the exclusive interest of businessmen. Not only was there an increased use of chequing accounts, but also a growing use of promissory notes and letters of exchange, and an ever-growing variety of contracts. This may seem an ordinary event, but from a historical perspective, it represented an extraordinary revolution in the everyday life of millions. Legal theory—the doctrines concerning commercial papers or *credit titles* (*títulos de crédito*)—so far regarded as a matter of commercial law, that is, the law of professional business people, treated ordinary individual borrowers (*pessoas físicas não comerciantes*) the same way it had treated professional businessmen for the last 500 years of legal history. As is widely known, commercial law, in continental Europe and this 'other Europe' as Fernand Braudel calls South America, had developed as the law of professional business men, and was different from civil law, the law of ordinary people.

Another important, well-known, phenomenon relates to the development of credit in society in general. Credit advanced by financial institutions was basi-

[4] This is a loose use of the concept of class. The Marxist conceptual framework does not accept the middle class as a class per se, but in this case we can use class in the sense of groups with similar income.

cally industrial and commercial credit (at least until some decades ago). Ordinary consumers would not be the subjects of much interest to bankers, except for the acquisition of real estate. But since the 1950s, housing has basically been a social right that government-run banks (or pension funds) invest in, so that low interest and long-term loans were provided by public financial agencies in most cases. For other ordinary needs, consumers would benefit from a well-established and familiar relationship with small businessmen. They would sell on credit all sorts of items a household would need. Small businessmen would sell *fiado*—short for *confiado*, trusting one's ability to pay and keep his word. All this has changed with the fast industrialisation of the country since the 1950s. Financial institutions then took the lead in advancing credit to the growing needs of consumers.

B. Consumer Law as Distributive Justice

Consumer law is clearly a by-product of the welfare state or, in other words, of *social law*.[5] It is also clear that any field of consumer law, and consumer credit in particular, deals with distributive issues. I have made this point in an earlier work[6] and others make it as well,[7] insisting in various ways on the distributive or 'social' aspects of consumer law. Consumer law, as Gustavo Ghidini puts it,[8] may be well described as labour law for those outside the factories: consumer law acknowledges the uneven power and position of producers and consumers and addresses this difference.

C. Is Credit a Collective Good?

The distributive character of consumer credit law is even more relevant when we take into account the fact that consumer credit deals with money. Money, as many legal scholars have mentioned, is not one commodity among others. It has a special nature because of the problems it poses in terms of monetary units, currency and the global amount of exchange in an economic system. John M Keynes made it clear that money and its value are especially important because

[5] F Ewald, *L'Etat Providence* (Paris, Grasset, 1986).

[6] JR de Lima Lopes, *A Responsabilidade civil do fabricante e a defesa do consumidor. Sao Paulo: Revista dos Tribunais* (1992) at 21–22.

[7] See T Wilhelmsson, 'Consumer Law and Social Justice' in T Wilhelmssohn *Twelve Essays on Consumer Law and Policy* (Helsinki, University of Helsinki, 1996); I Ramsay, 'Consumer Credit Law as Distributive Justice' in SS Rachagan (ed), *Developing Consumer Law in Asia* (Kuala Lumpur, IOCU, 1994); and GG Howells, 'Whose Responsibility to plan for future changes in circumstances—debtor, creditor or the state?' in T Wilhelmsson and S Hurri (eds), *From Dissonance to sense: welfare state expectations, privatization and private law* (Aldershot, Ashgate, 1999).

[8] G Ghidini, *Per I Consumatori* (Bologna, Zanichelli, 1977).

a change in money value is always an instrument of wealth distribution or concentration.[9]

The distributional effects of the price of money are at the centre of a series of essays published by J P Dawson in 1934–5.[10] Tullio Ascarelli was intrigued by the same phenomena that attracted Dawson's attention: the devaluation of money, the political consequences of inflation, and the contribution that legal scholars could make to the solution of distributive conflicts that appeared in society at large but which had a devastating effect on private relations, contractual relations in particular. Ascarelli insists that anything that functions as money is money (that is any commodity that plays the role of standard of values and instrument of exchange). Law does not define money (that is the job of economics), but in the end he concedes that the legal system determines what is to be the money *(valuta* in Italian) in a given time and place.[11]

Arthur Nussbaum was also interested in the legal theory of money. Nussbaum's definition of money has two important aspects to be emphasised: (1) money is an ideal unit, and as a unit it refers to a part of a whole: to hold money is to hold a part of all assets that may be 'translated' into money; (2) money is money due to a 'common usage.'[12] I would like to stress that money is money due to a general convention and this 'convention' is sustained, in modern industrial societies, not by private parties alone but also by the state. In this logic, money becomes a 'public or collective good' (goods whose provision can not be made in individual terms), as described by economists and provided by state authority. Even if use by private individuals and business corporations affects the value of money, it is only the state authority that creates money. The point of this argument is to stress that money is a public good, and as such, it is and must be regulated.

Even if this seems obvious, Brazilian legal scholarship has not dealt with the point so directly. In the hyperinflation years, courts tended to treat money as an ordinary commodity and ignored arguments of social or collective relevance. Based on the German theory of indexation—used with devastating effects by German courts in the 1920s—courts invested themselves with the power to arbitrate the value of money by choosing the devaluation rate to be used in contracts. Different courts used different rates, and the same person would have different rates applied to her credits and her debts, resulting in a mismatch in one's personal or corporate balance sheet. Individual arbitration of monetary issues would be very problematic.

[9] JM Keynes, 'Conseqüências das alterações no valor da moeda para a sociedade' in T Szmrecsányi (ed) *John Maynard Keynes* (São Paulo, Ática, 1978) [original title in English: 'The consequences to society of changes in the value of money'].

[10] JP Dawson, 'Effects of inflation on private contracts: Germany, 1914–1924' (1934) 33 *Michigan Law Review* 171; JP Dawson and F Cooper, 'The effect of inflation on private contracts: United States, 1861–1879' (1935) 33 *Michigan Law Review* 706; JP Dawson, 'The gold clause decisions' (1935) 33 *Michigan Law Review* at 647.

[11] T Ascarelli, *Saggi Giuridici sulla Moneta* (Milano, Giuffre Ed, 1952) at 38–40.

[12] A Nussbaum, *Money in the Law* (Chicago, Foundation Press, 1939).

The same idea applies to the regulation of consumer credit. The fact is that so far, Brazilian legal scholars, for the most part, and the Brazilian legislature have not paid particular attention to this fact. Credit, a special complex of obligations in which the provision of money is the central aspect, should be seen, from this point of view, as a collective or public concern and should fall naturally under the scrutiny of public authorities.

This conceptual framework is the background against which legal institutions—concerning credit and consumer protection—should be criticised.

III. INSTITUTIONAL FRAMEWORK

A. Bankruptcy and the Limits to Debt Collection

Bankruptcy is a traditional commercial law remedy. According to Brazilian law—as in most Roman law derived systems—it applies exclusively to *comerciantes*, either as individuals or incorporated legal entities. This has a systemic as well as a historical explanation. From the historical point of view, bankruptcy has developed from commercial law since the late Middle Ages. From a systemic point of view, it is part of a series of legal institutions of limited liability offered to venture capital since the rise of bourgeois 19th century statutes (an example is the 1863 French Act of limited liability partnerships). One of these legal institutions is, of course, liability of capital holders who invest their money in corporate entities. In case of failure (bankruptcy), they will not lose anything beyond the investment made; creditors cannot seize their individual personal assets. Historians have pointed out that this legal system provides a strong incentive for investment and technical development, and facilitates wealth concentration.

Bankruptcy can also be seen from this perspective: once all corporate assets are sold, creditors of the incorporated firm will support their own losses and the law will put an end to the debt. Some jurists still refer to bankruptcy as a sort of 'civil death.' Bankruptcy does not imply, in the civil law tradition, the idea of a fresh start. Quite the contrary, it implies the idea of a loss of rights, a *capitis diminutio*.

Bankruptcy (*falência*) is applied to a very restricted group of corporations: only 'commercial' corporations can become bankrupt. Non-commercial corporations—schools, associations, co-operative corporations, and personal professional (liberal) activities, such as a medical or legal office—do not qualify for bankruptcy remedies. *Falência* (the word derives from the Latin word for failure) as a legal procedure can be filed either by creditors or by the debtor (*falido*) himself. Once accepted, the liquidation of all the assets of the debtor will necessarily follow. It brings, as its necessary legal consequence, the end of the business of a corporation. In the case of individual business people (*pessoas naturais comerciantes*), it results immediately in the suspension of one's capacity to enter another business activity; essentially, this means the *falido* is not allowed to establish another individual firm and be a registered *comerciante*. He can work only in professional activities that do not require registration with the Trade Board (*Junta Comercial*). He can be a partner or a shareholder in commercial partnerships or corporations, but will not be allowed to be the manager or representative of the partnership or corporation.

In short, a person's legal capacity will be diminished; the comparison with the status of a minor would be an appropriate analogy. It is therefore not a surprise that being a *falido* will impose enormous difficulties and bankrupts will have to make use of other people's help (in associating with them or making use of their businesses) to develop their activities. These negative aspects will be part of the collective imagination: if similar effects are found in personal insolvency, as will be described below, it is almost certain that personal insolvency (civil insolvency) will not be attractive to most, if not all, consumers.

Concordata gives the debtor a relief for a period of two years, after which it is supposed to be suspended. It is a relief plan filed by the debtor that, once accepted by the court, binds all her unsecured creditors. A very large number of *concordatas*—possibly the vast majority—are never successful, in the sense that they eventually become bankruptcy procedures. In a *Concordata*, the debtor must make the first payment (half of the amount due) within the first year, and by the end of the second year she should be able to complete the payment of all her unsecured debts. If she does not do so, the court may immediately find her bankrupt.

One important aspect of both *falência* and *concordata* is that despite statutory provisions allowing creditors to organise the procedure in the court of law, they usually do not do so. The usual practice is that the court will appoint a lawyer to act as a *síndico* or *comissário* (trustee). The chances of debt recovery tend to be very low. Only in extraordinarily important cases (involving large banks in large credit transactions) do the creditors take any interest and move on to try to reorganise the business or transfer the assets as an entirety, lest they deteriorate with time.

B. Civil Insolvency

Falência and *Concordata* do not apply to consumers. Traditional remedies provided to consumers are limited to the restriction on attachment (*penhora*) of specified property or assets. The Civil Procedure Code (CPC) provides a list of 'unattachable property' (*bens impenhoráveis*), among which one finds the following: food and fuel that a person can usually consume in one month, wedding rings, salaries and wages in general, tools and instruments used in professional earnings, life insurance policies and a few others. The residential building where the person or family is currently living is also unattachable property.[13] The legal

[13] Law no 8009/90.

system applied to individual consumers will protect the minimum assets, but this does not affect the validity of the creditors' claims: the credit itself will be valid for the time provided in each case by the statute of limitations.

Nonetheless, the Civil Procedure Code (enacted in 1973) does provide for a 'civil insolvency' procedure. This procedure, as its structural place within the Code shows, is no more than a form of collective, judicial debt collection (*execução coletiva*) on an individual debtor's assets. In spite of its legal existence, this procedure is seldom used.

Both the creditors and the debtor may file the insolvency claim before a civil court (like all bankruptcy suits, civil insolvency is handled by regular State courts). The debtor *confesses* her insolvency, whereas the creditor has to show evidence that there are no available assets to secure her credit.[14] Even though she confesses her insolvency, the debtor immediately risks most, if not all, of her possibilities of dealing with creditors on a one-by-one basis. She is immediately dispossessed of her right to administer all of her assets in favour of a court-appointed trustee, and all her debts automatically become due.[15] The debtor only keeps her unattachable property and the right to have a certain amount of money for living expenses (if she has any source of income). The debtor will not be allowed to sell any of her assets and all the goods that she may acquire pending the civil insolvency procedure may be sold by the trustee for the benefit of the creditors.

If there is an insolvency procedure, no statute of limitations applies to any debt. The insolvency procedure is closed once after the trustee has sold all the debtor's assets and the creditors have received their share. However, if there is any balance left, the debtor does not get immediate relief. Only five years after the end of the insolvency procedure will the debtor obtain general relief and then be able to restart her ordinary civil business life. This general relief means that the *insolvente* will once again have full capacity in civil and business life.

In the course of the insolvency process, the debtor may enter into an agreement with her creditors.[16] The court may approve the agreement and render it enforceable, but before that the agreement has to be unanimously accepted by the creditors.

It is clear that the debtor will lose more than she will gain by filing her own insolvency suit. The five-year period provided by the Civil Procedure Code, which involves the final liquidation of all the debtor's assets, will only start to run from the end of the insolvency procedure. If the liquidation process lasts more than five years, a debtor would then be excluded from ordinary economic life for at least 10 years. This is a considerable length of time. For 10 years or more the consumer will be practically excluded from some everyday transactions: he would be unable to have a credit card and he would be unable to make all the uses ordinarily made by others of their chequing accounts. Time is

[14] Civil Procedure Code (CPC), Art 754 and 759.
[15] CPC, *ibid* Art 761–63, Art 751,1.
[16] CPC, *ibid* Art 783.

therefore one important cost in the civil insolvency procedure. Civil insolvency can mean that for a long time all of one's living expenses will be under the scrutiny, if not under the direct administration, of a trustee. This seems too long a period for one to be considered, and to consider himself, a 'minor.'

Another relevant aspect is that in order to file a civil insolvency claim, the debtor has to make use of the services of a lawyer. Small claims courts are presently open to cases that amount to approximately US$ 2,500.00. Lawyers normally charge a fee of 10 to 20 per cent of the value of the object of litigation. This can be less in many cases, and the usual agreement is that part of the payment be made at the end of the procedure, *ad exitum* (in case of success). It is very unlikely that debtors will have the money to start a law suit if they are truly insolvent, and it is even more unlikely that lawyers will be willing to wait such a long time to receive any payment, assuming the consumer recovers financially. This is another important factor in making civil insolvency a practically non-existent institution.[17]

There is no incentive for creditors to file bankruptcy claims against debtors either: they risk losing all possibility of receiving any of the debtor's assets outside of bankruptcy. The system as designed is a typical case of a prisoner's dilemma, where co-operation seems to be a more costly solution for everyone.

All these factors indicate that the institutional design of civil insolvency is in need of reform if it is to become attractive to consumers. Time-consuming procedures, long periods of diminished civil capacities, the need for professional legal services, and the cultural symbolic notion that a case of bankruptcy is a case of failure, add to the historic uselessness of civil insolvency.

C. What Consumers Really Do

Contrary to a long established tradition in certain societies, most typically in the United States, certain other societies make use of non-judicial and more informal means of dispute resolution. Alexis de Tocqueville had already noticed that United States citizens tend to take all their disputes to the courts.[18] In addition, Max Weber commented that the United States constituted the ideal type of sectarian and Calvinist society,[19] in which a general system of horizontal relations was the counterpart of a process to segregate social interaction. In this respect, judicial solutions tend to be naturalised, as social organisation will naturally help people to consider an affirmation of rights as very acceptable. In non-typical Calvinist (in the Weberian sense) societies, continuous negotiation will probably be more acceptable, as the ideal of church-like societies

[17] Courts will not charge any fees in such cases, as the general statute on free judicial services (*justiça gratuita*) gives the courts discretion to consider cases on an individual basis and extend to individuals the benefits of free litigation. Brazilian courts tend to be fairly generous in this respect.

[18] A de Tocqueville, *Democracy in America* (New York, Harper Perennial, 1988) at 99, 270.

[19] M Weber, *A Etica protestante e o espirito do capitalismo* (S Paulo, UnB-Pioneira, 1981) at 198.

(Weber opposes sects and churches as two ideal types of social interaction) is the permanent attempt to avoid separation.

The Consumers Protection Agency of São Paulo *(Fundação PROCON-SP)* has collected some data from consumers who sought out the Agency. The data were collected in May 1998 and surveyed the situation of all consumers (120 in total) who voluntarily sought the advice of PROCON in one given week of that month. The result may not be generalised to all consumers,[20] but the findings may be useful as a first source of information, especially as this is the only survey of its kind currently conducted by a consumer protection organisation. The data show that before looking for a more formal and legal solution, 65 per cent of all debtors try to negotiate individually with their creditors in search of longer payment schedules, and reduced penalties and interest rates. On the other hand, most creditors who deal with consumer credits do not seem to be interested in sharing with other creditors their possibilities of collecting their credits individually. If they are lucky enough to conduct their own negotiation and get a few instalments ahead of the others, they will not file insolvency suits either. Thus, insolvency seems a fairly irrational choice for everyone involved and it is seldom used.

It is no wonder that individual negotiation has been the most frequent way of dealing with situations of over-indebtedness. Such negotiation presumes the generally slow motion of court proceedings, and in this respect it is a rational alternative to judicialisation. Time-consuming judicial processes may be a powerful argument to convince creditors to wait and negotiate. In this respect, not confessing, that is, not taking the initiative to file an 'auto insolvency suit', is at first sight a better strategy for the individual consumer. Data collected by *Fundação PROCON* confirm this trend: in 53.33 per cent of cases, consumers were in doubt about the value of their debt. They were looking for information to start negotiations. Approximately 25 per cent (25.83 per cent) admitted that what they wanted from the consumer agency was advice on how to conduct negotiations. Of all of those who contacted the consumer agency, only one third (35 per cent) had not tried any negotiation with their creditors.

Most, if not all, credit providers may access databases relating to consumers' ability to pay, such as the *Serviço de Proteção ao Crédito* (SPC) or *Serasa*. In addition, consumers know that if their name ever appears in one of these databases they will probably be excluded from the institutional credit market. In case of need, they will be pushed into a marginal market (*agiotas*) that will submit them to both an extremely high rate of interest and forceful, unlimited coercion to ensure repayment. Creditors can threaten to report a debtor to one of

[20] The research covered only consumers who had spontaneously looked for help from Procon at its premises in the city of São Paulo. It does not offer a comprehensive view of consumers of Brazil. However, São Paulo may be considered a paradigmatic case, as it is a place where traditional family and neighbourhood bonds have to give way to impersonal forms of interaction. On the other hand, it is a city with a considerable and visible working class who need access to credit to be able to buy consumer durables.

these databases, in the hope of securing an agreement to repay and it is likely this approach will be much more successful than initiating a civil insolvency proceeding. All these factors put together help to explain how and why insolvency has never been seen as a response to deal with consumers' over-indebtedness.

D. Legal Incentives and Privileges of Professional Creditors

Other historical factors have undeniable importance in the ideology present in the imagination of legal scholars and others involved in consumer credit in Brazil. Contrary to common-sense assumptions made by liberal ideologues, Brazilian law has historically been very favourable to creditors. As early as 1837, Brazil had totally liberalised interest rates and private parties were totally free to agree on any rate they wanted. It was only in the 1930s, during the Vargas regime (1930–1945) and along with a wave of social, welfare and labour protection statutes, that a maximum interest rate was established. In 1965, however, the Banking Act did not repeat these provisions and courts have since understood that banks were free to charge any interest rate, as long as the Central Bank did not establish any administrative regulation.

Brazil has also lived through decades of high inflation. In the 1980s, especially after 1982 (the beginning of the foreign debt crisis—*crise da dívida externa*), inflation soared from 100 per cent a year to over 1,000 per cent a year in the mid-90s. A general indexation system developed, and it became increasingly difficult to distinguish in the 'price of money' what the real interest rate was and what the indexation device (*correção monetária*) was. During these last decades, the financial market could not rationally discuss limitations on interest rates. Inflation, as is widely known, is a system of reverse distribution that ends up concentrating wealth in an irrational way.

In the meantime, creditors were given judicial procedural privileges in many instances by specific statutory provisions. Banks, credit card companies and other 'professional' credit providers enjoyed special and more expedient collection procedures, some of which were directly 'imported' from the Anglo-American legal system. The case of *leasing* is a typical example: it was introduced in Brazil in the 1970s and it gives the creditor some rights of seizure of debtors' property that were unknown under the traditional civil law and in fact contradicted constitutional provisions (a private party should not be able to seize another party's property without a previous judicial order). As a practical matter, these special procedures can be used only by financial institutions. The rationale behind these special statutory provisions seems to be that court procedures make judicial credit recovery slower and costlier than some people would wish. To compensate for the courts' slow pace and time-consuming formalities, professional creditors get increased procedural privileges as a sort of incentive.

IV. OVER-INDEBTEDNESS—WHO AND WHY

Data on consumer over-indebtedness [21] are scarce. Some of the best available data were collected by Fundação PROCON of Sao Paulo, as described above. It is fairly clear that the majority of cases of consumer indebtedness originated in cases of *social force majeure*. When asked why they defaulted on their payments, the majority of consumers listed unemployment in the first place (37.5 per cent), and 'lack of control' of one's expenses in second (35 per cent). The third and fourth largest causes of default were unemployment of a member of the family (10.83 per cent) and health problems in the family (5 per cent). In short, unemployment and health problems add to 53.3 per cent of all the cases. Two other *social force majeure* cases may be added: drop in income (for 'autonomous workers') adds another 4.16 per cent, and reduction in wage (0.83 per cent). That is almost another five per cent so we have a figure of 58 per cent of typical *force majeure* cases. These are cases of *passive over-indebtedness* (*superendividamento passivo*).

Moreover, among those who complained of their own 'lack of control,' we can find explanations that are nothing to do with their own fault. Some of them (20 per cent) reported a sudden increase in the price of public utilities (which is true, as prices were fixed at higher levels to attract foreign investors to the privatisation programme, the so-called *tarifaço*). One must also remember that advertisement of credit is very common. This is done through the media and on the streets by handing out attractive leaflets and pamphlets to passers-by. Some banks have had their employees distributing these pamphlets on the pavements in front of their branches, or in their vicinity of branches. As a consequence, 'lack of control' of one's expenses has to be measured against aggressive and irresponsible lending.

The question of the origins of their debts shows the following picture of the goods that consumers usually buy on credit. The most significant were:

—19.16%—cars
—15.83%—electric or electronic household appliances
—12.50%—personal/revolving credit
—10.83%—house
—9.16%—furniture
—9.16%—clothes

[21] I am not drawing a sharp distinction between indebtedness and over-indebtedness in this paper. Data on over-indebtedness of consumers are not available as such. Data on indebtedness have been collected from the perspective of the creditors (banks and financial institutions in general). Therefore, it is fairly reasonable to know the level of debt. No social service and no consumer agency—except for the survey conducted in São Paulo—have made precise studies of the profile of indebtedness of consumers. There is no court dealing specifically with consumer insolvency and there is no social service giving financial help to families in financial difficulties caused by over-indebtedness.

—8.33%—credit card
—5.0 %—rent
—3.33%—telephone bills
—1.66%—education/schooling
—1.66%—water bills

More than one third (approx 35 per cent) of the credit was used to buy typical consumer goods (durable goods), the acquisiton of which has been generally stimulated by public policies. The consumer credit market has been organised to provide credit exactly for this purpose and many of the new legal rights attributed to creditors have to do with seizure of these 'durable' goods.[22] The third most important origin of indebtedness is 'personal/revolving credit.' A closer look would probably confirm the hypothesis that consumers have been given easy access to personal credit and tend to use it in some *social force majeure* cases. As seen above, the reason for default was mostly *social force majeure* (unemployment, health problems) and the significant use of personal credit (12.5 per cent) and credit cards (8.33 per cent) may show that in case of financial distress consumers will obtain unsecured credit from the financial system. Individual consumer credit is then used to replace a very inefficient social insurance system. A significant percentage of financial problems is caused by a series of household expenses: rent payments, telephone and water bills together represent 10 per cent of the complaints.[23] Living expenses in a large city tend to go up, and at the same time the restructuring of business has created structural unemployment.

The total amount of debts were distributed within the groups listed in Table 1.[24]

Among those who were defaulting, in 56.65 per cent of the cases the monthly instalment was somewhere between approximately 43 and 170 US dollars; in 31 per cent of the cases, it was between approximately 43 and 85 US dollars. Of course, consumer credit is only a small part of the whole debt within the financial system. Forty-two per cent of all credit transactions are under 10,000 US dollars. This is the equivalent of only 0.1 per cent of all credit.[25]

[22] A historical survey of the credit market in Brazil shows that consumer credit was largely facilitated by a series of statutes contemporary with the industrial boom of the 60s. The Banking Act of 1965 (Law nr 4.595 of 1965) was followed by the Financial Institutions and Capital Market Act of 1967 (Law nr 4728). The latter gave banks special privileges to collect their credit. The idea behind the law was that banks with greater privileges in collection would be more inclined to advance credit to consumers who would then be more inclined to buy the manufactured goods of the new industries. The collection system has remained basically the same for the last 30 years.

[23] Numbers are still insufficient to establish a connection between the financial stress of consumers and the privatisation programme (privatisation of public utilities), but it is clear that privatised utilities occupy a large part of consumer organisation efforts due to their aggressive practices, including price increases.

[24] The exchange rate between the American Dollar and the Brazilian Real varied around U$ 0.85 per R$ 1.00 in 1998. R$ 5,000 equals approximately U$ 4,250, R$ 1,000 equals U$ 850.

[25] Cf Monthly reports of Banco Central do Brasil, Banco Central do Brasil online <www.bcb.gov.br>.

Table 1 Percentage of consumers per class of debts

Amount due	% consumers in the group
R$ 5,000–R$ 1,001 (U$ 4,250–U$ 850.85)	36.66
R$ 501–R$ 1,000 (U$ 425.85–U$ 850)	25.83
R$ 201–R$ 500 (U$ 170.85–U$ 425)	18.33
R$ 101–R$ 200 (U$ 85.85–U$ 170)	7.5
R$ 10,001–R$ 20,000 (U$ 8,500.85–U$ 17,000)	5.0
Up to R$ 100 (U$ 85)	4.16
Over R$ 20,000 (U$ 17,000)	0.83

Source: Fundação PROCON-SP.

V. AGGRESSIVE CREDIT POLICIES AND THE LEGAL RESPONSIBILITY OF CREDITORS

Credit card companies have developed aggressive marketing strategies. They are proud to announce a considerable increase in numbers of clients and annual transactions.

The number of credit cards has tripled in less than one decade. In 1991 there were 7.9 million credit cards, whereas in 1999 the number increased to 23.6 million cards. Between November 1999 and November 2000 there has been an increase of 37.36 per cent in the total amount of transactions with credit cards. The number of transactions in the same period increased by 43.02 per cent.[26] In 1991, the total transactions of credit cards were 1.29 per cent of the Brazilian GDP; by 1997, it had increased to 3.47 per cent.

This growth has been the result of aggressive and sometimes illegal marketing practices. The entry of credit cards into the consumer market has been in association with banks. Payment of workers' salaries is usually made by deposit in chequing-accounts (*contas-salário*), so that the association of credit card companies with banks provides them with inside information on the financial lives of consumers. They send offers of credit cards and frequently send credit cards. The Consumer Defense Code (CDC) prohibits certain forms of unrequested offers of products and services to consumers, but credit card companies and banks have continually violated this provision.[27]

Banks have also increased and fostered the use of plastic money. A growth in transaction fees has forced clients to choose between having a cheque book or a plastic card. And plastic cards include credit cards. Even if the credit card

[26] Associação Brasileira de Empresas de Cartão de Crédito e Serviços, ABECS web site <www.abecs.org.br>.

[27] CDC, Law no 8078, 1990, Art 39, III. The banks have also been found guilty of continually violating the CDC provisions on the limits of fines to be collected by the creditor in case of default or arrears. By November of 2000, Diners Club, Mastercard and Visa, in different association with several banks, were subject to administrative penalties enforced by the Federal Bureau of Consumer Protection (*Departamento de Proteção e Defesa do Consumidor*).

contract is not valid without the clients' acceptance, the electronic access to a password works as a first step towards credit card acceptance.

Another aggressive practice used by banks in general is the continued advertisement of credit in all media and on the streets. In spite of its uniqueness and despite the fact that credit is part of a regulated market and is an essential part of the creation of money (and currency), credit is freely advertised everywhere. As a rule, provisions of the CDC would apply to the credit market, but so far there has been no action on the part of either government or civil society to curb general advertising of credit. In fact, it is not seen as a potentially hazardous good even if used by naive consumers.

More than half of all credit given by professional lenders (financial institutions) is based on an unsecured transaction. This of course has a tremendous negative impact on the price of money for consumers; for example, it has a negative impact on interest rates. In April 2000, the interest rates for secured loans for consumer goods varied from 1.032 per cent to 11.623 per cent per month.[28] Personal unsecured loans varied from a monthly rate of 0.83 per cent to 14.54 per cent.[29] Revolving credit transactions (also unsecured) had an interest rate between 1.569 per cent and 16.714 per cent per month.[30] In addition to these sky-high rates, an indebted consumer would also be charged a series of other costs, including attorney's fees, usually at a rate of 10 per cent of the total debt to be collected.

Aggressive credit offers can also be measured against the level of income of consumers. Even though banks do rank and screen their clients in terms of income, they do offer credit to consumers with extremely low incomes. This is done most especially by *bancos múltiplos* or *companhias financeiras*, who have developed the habit of placing their employees on the sidewalk distributing small advertisement papers with messages such as: 'easy credit,' or 'easy money—no bureaucracy, no red tape, no collateral' and similar attractive phrases. This 'street market' of credit is clearly directed towards the lower classes who need to avoid red tape, as they may be unemployed, or only recently employed. They may use this money for personal and everyday expenses. This 'street credit market' is obviously a by-product of some of the social effects of the so-called 'structural adjustment' policies. In this respect, many of the agreements and contracts entered into by consumers would very likely be rendered invalid under provisions of consumer law. If not under any particular provision, then certainly under the general principles, among which are the following:

—Article 6 of the CDC—the basic right of all consumers to: education about reasonable consumption and detailed information on the goods and services, a general protection against abusive or deceitful advertisement, the change of abusive contractual clauses;

[28] Banco Central do Brasil <www.bcb.gov.br/htms/taxas/14prefist.htm>.
[29] *Ibid.*
[30] *Ibid.*

—Article 39 of the CDC– the right to be protected against abusive practices such as: sending or delivering to the consumer an unsolicited service, the abuse (*prevalecimento*) of a consumer's weakness or ignorance (in view of the consumer's age, health, knowledge or *social conditions*).

Another aggressive marketing strategy can be seen in the monthly reports all banks send to their clients. They usually include a reference to a pre-approved personal credit, informing the consumer that he does not have to go through any selection process to obtain the amount of credit mentioned in the report. Some of these companies need only a phone call to get the money ready for the consumer. In recent years, consumer credit has been made easier still by the operation of 'factoring': these semi-financial institutions have granted retail commerce a higher degree of liquidity and consumers have, so to speak, benefited from a general disposition of smaller business to sell to them in instalments. It is credit made easy.

Interest rates have a large variety of factors behind them. One of these, constantly brought up in discussion, is the high level of default in payments. But numbers show at least two important factors that should not be overlooked: first, banks insist on advancing unsecured credit, and second, consumer default rates are lower than the general default rates that affect industrial and commercial credit.[31]

VI. REMEDIES

Consumer credit is not currently regarded as a social phenomenon or as a social problem. Although it is rather obvious that credit is a general and public good, to legal scholars, courts and consumer protection organisations (public or private), the problem still appears as a matter of contractual relations. To put it in traditional, but still illuminating terms, it is not seen as matter of distributive justice, but of commutative justice. This will give consumers a few remedies to be found in the Consumer Defense Code (*CDC—Código de Defesa do Consumidor: Law n 8078/90*). If seen as a matter of distributive justice, there would be other possibilities, such as the filing of class actions to alter some market practices of banks[32] and credit card companies.

[31] Some of these numbers can be found in Pinheiro and Cabral, above n 1. The average figure of default for private national banks between 1988–1997 was 16.8% and 9.6% for foreign banks: *ibid* at 18. In 1997, a period of high default following the economic boom of 1994–5 (Plano Real—the stabilisation plan), there was a general default rate of 53%, but for household credit (typical individual consumer credit) it was 34.2%: *ibid* at 17. Industries and commerce in general defaulted at higher levels than consumers, whereas rural and housing credits had the best performance rate. The general figures for default can be found at IPEA web page <www.ipea.gov.br>.

[32] For further discussion of the CDC, see above n 27 and accompanying text. The general term in Brazil is 'financial institution' (instituição financeira); it is the phrase used by the Banking Reform Act of 1964. Financial business has expanded and created other forms of money-dealing corporations, which have been subjected to the supervision of the Central Bank and, in this respect, have been acknowledged as part of the financial market. There are very few

Class actions were introduced into the Brazilian legal system by a statute of 1985. The statute was partly altered by the Consumer Defense Code of 1990 (CDC) to accommodate a collective action. In the original class action system, the object of litigation should have a single aim: environmental issues and the protection of consumers against discriminatory or abusive advertisements were typical cases of interests with a single aim to be protected by the class action. The 1990 changes created the collective action, in which consumers who had individual rights could be represented by only one claimant and benefit from the outcome of the suit. The difference between the two sorts of class action is often blurred, but from the conceptual point of view a 'social issue' is a single aim issue: the decision on it will affect all members of a class. The collective action will affect those who are involved in similar contractual relations. Thus, a collective action (one of the possible forms of a class action) can be used in very traditional ways to determine the contractual rights of several debtors of one given bank, or to recover damages for a specific group of consumers. A class action could also be used in a broader way—for example, to force banks to review their lending practices. The latter use is clearly a distributive use of the class action; the former is basically a collective use of the suit but still framing the legal issue in terms of contractual or commutative justice.

The general provisions concerning invalid clauses in all consumer agreements are listed in Article 51 of the CDC. They can be divided in three broad classes: (a) provisions concerning the equivalency or commutative balance between the parties; (b) provisions prohibiting different forms of unilateral changes in the agreements or on their perfomance; (c) provisions prohibiting the consumer from disposing of his fundamental rights as granted in the CDC or other statutes. Some of these clauses are frequently present in credit agreements. The case of interest rates seems to be most obvious: in many cases interest rates may vary, either because the loan has been made with foreign currency funds (and exchange rates will vary) or because of different provisions that index interest rates. Lenders will argue that these contractual provisions are not illegal because interest rates are not altered unilaterally by the lender himself: the conditions under which variation is accepted are universal and independent of any individual bank. Courts are still dealing with this issue: in some cases they have granted preliminary remedies to consumers, but final judgements have not yet been passed.

Another important controversial case concerns the so-called *cláusula mandato* by which the creditor is given the right to issue a commercial paper in the name of the debtor. These clauses have been considered abusive by the majority of Brazilian courts. To avoid this cláusula mandato, banks started to force consumers to execute blank promissory notes. Blank promissory notes are legally valid for some ordinary commercial transactions, but they would be void

exceptions: credit card companies and factoring are not considered financial institutions, or at least have been struggling to stay out of the Central Bank regulations. However, as they operate in association with banks, they naturally depend on credit regulation in general.

as far as consumers' rights are concerned. In both cases, consumers can get protection from the CDC and invalidate some of the claims made by their creditors (the credit agreement will be acceptable, but the 'abusive' clause or the blank promissory note will not).

Both contractual remedies and non-contractual remedies can be used on a commutative basis. Contractual remedies have been used both in individual and collective law suits. Of course, the problem with judicial protection of consumers in a contractual—and therefore commutative—basis is the inequality in the treatment of consumers that may be caused by such suits. Certain classes of consumers may get some relief, while others may not get any.[33] This criticism does not invalidate the judicial protection of groups of consumers; it only shows that consumers are not being protected as a class and emphasises that the welfare dimension of consumer law may be lost.

Non-contractual remedies can be divided in two different groups. Let us call them the semi-contractual group and the non-contractual *senso stricto*. They both have a collective dimension. Semi-contractual remedies—already available in the legal system—would try to curb pre- or post-contractual relations with consumers: for instance, class actions could be used to prohibit advertisements in certain forms or to obtain general damages in cases of abusive market practices contrary to the consumer protection code. One can think of class actions against credit providers who try to 'seduce' consumers with the ideas of 'cheap and easy' money. Non-contractual remedies, or regulations, are a more difficult matter. They would interfere more directly with the credit market as a whole.

Indebtedness and over-indebtedness have not been publicly discussed by lawyers as a social phenomena. That was the opening statement of this section. Objections might be raised to this statement: the Central Bank has been trying to impose greater responsibility in lending on banks and financial institutions, as a sign of its preoccupation with the excessive cost that indebtedness adds to the functioning of a healthy credit system. This is at least partly true, but it's emphasis is the perspective of the lender. Borrowers who are heard are basically industrial and commercial business corporations. Consumer credit is only a small part of the credit system and has been neglected.

I have tried to show that there is an alternative perspective to be taken into account. It is the perspective of consumers as a class and as subjects of social law. Globalisation and liberalisation of markets take place in societies that are still structurally divided and this division should be the starting point for any consumer protection analysis.

[33] Class, economic resources and other differences in bargaining power may lead to different treatments of consumers. In this respect, Marc Galanter's argument, that the 'haves come out ahead', is valid for groups of consumers too. *Cf* Marc Galanter, 'Why the "Haves" Come Out Ahead: Speculations on the Limits of Legal Change' (1974) 9 *Law & Society Review* 95 (1974).

5

Development of Consumer Credit in China and Concerns about the Underlying Legal Infrastructure

XIAN-CHU ZHANG*

THE DYNAMIC ECONOMIC reform and development of markets in China since the end of the 1970s have dramatically changed people's life and their attitudes towards consuming. In the period 1978–95, the average sum that people spent on consumption increased by over 12.5 times. The major consumption goods like watches, sewing machines and bikes in the 1970s were replaced by air conditioners, colour televisions and washing machines in the 1980s, and further upgraded to private cars, residential apartments and modern communication means in the 1990s. Overseas holidays and higher education have also been included in the budgets of many families today. Thus, China is becoming a new consumer society in the world.[1] The awakening of the consumer market has not only played a crucial role in modernising the Chinese economy, but has also attracted huge amounts of foreign investment into China.[2]

However, the development of a consumer society has been seriously hindered by a defective legal infrastructure. At the time of writing, the Chinese Government is facing a dilemma: on the one hand, the recovery of the national economy from a long deflation strongly demands more consumer spending; on the other hand, a lack of legal rules, including legal mechanisms for effective

* This article is a revised version with updated materials of the conference paper the author presented at the Law & Society Conference in Budapest, Hungry in June 2001. The author would like to express his gratitude to Professor Bill Whitford of Wisconsin University School of Law and Professor Iain Ramsay of Osgoode Hall Law School, York University, for the very valuable comments and materials they kindly provided in the course of revision.

[1] Xu Zhongwei (ed), *Dangdai Zhongguo Ruogan Jingji Wenti* [Certain Issues of Contemporary Chinese Economy] (Beijing, Huawen Publishing House, 1998) at 248–60.

[2] Before 1998, China had the second largest annual foreign direct investment in the world. However, since the Asian financial crisis, China's rank has slipped to fourth place behind the United States, the United Kingdom and Sweden. See C Gelb, 'Foreign Investors Wise Up' (Nov/Dec 2000) *The China Business Review* at 8. China presently anticipates a new wave of foreign investment resulting from its accession to the World Trade Organization. Direct foreign investment is expected to exceed US$ 50 billion in 2002, a new record high. See Pan Qing, ' 2002 Nian 1–6 Yuefen zhongguo Xingpi Sheli Waishang Touzi Qiye 15155 Jia' [Between January and June 2002 15155 New Foreign Investment Enterprises were Established] *Shichang Bao* [Market Daily] (19 July 2002) 1.

collection of debts as well as personal bankruptcy laws, has troubled both consumers and banks in dealing with consumer loans. This article examines the current situation in China. Part I highlights the change of consumer policy in China in the past two decades and the present consumer market conditions; Part II examines the current legal environment of consumer credit in China; Part III considers some difficulties in developing reforms of consumer credit and bankruptcy law in China; and Part IV draws some conclusions.

I. THE CHANGE IN CONSUMER POLICY AND CURRENT MARKET CONDITIONS

When the People's Republic of China was established in 1949, a planned economy was introduced and developed over three decades. In this period, the top priority of the totalitarian government was to strengthen the national economy through more production and accumulation of the profits of production; as a result, consumer rights and private property rights were totally ignored and consuming activities were harshly restricted through rationing and salary control. For instance, the average salary of workers in 1976 was even lower than in 1957.[3]

The implementation of economic reform and the open-door policy of the late 1970s has dramatically changed the government's consumer policy. By drawing a hard lesson from the failure of the planned economy, the government realised that the merit of a social system should ultimately be judged by the living standards of the people. The paramount leader, Deng Xiaoping, pointed out that based on the hard lessons of the past, peoples' living standards had to be raised, together with the development of productivity; otherwise, the merits of socialism over capitalism would not be apparent.[4] Consequently, the basis of the national development has slowly shifted from production to consumerism.

This ideological change has led to a consumer revolution in China. As compared with 1978, by 1997 the per capita disposable income of urban and rural residents across China had jumped 200 per cent and 285 per cent to reach Rmb 5,160 (about US$ 620) and Rmb 2,090 (about US$ 250) respectively. In the same period, per capita consumer spending of urban and rural residents increased by 10.7 and 13.9 times respectively.[5] However, these increases were not distributed evenly across the population. By 1997, the middle and 'comfortable' classes accounted for more than 65 per cent of the consumer market in China's main

[3] For a discussion of the policy in this period, see Xu, above n 1, at 239–43.

[4] See Dai Zhou (ed), *Deng Xiaoping Lilun yu Dangdai Zhongguo* [Deng Xiaoping's Theory and Contemporary China], vol 1 (Beijing, Red Flag Publishing House, 1998) at 266–67.

[5] Research Department of Hong Kong Trade Development Council, *China's Consumer Market* (Hong Kong, Hong Kong Trade Development Council, 1998) at 1 [Hong Kong Trade Development Council].

cities, up from 35 per cent just since 1992.[6] There were more than 7.6 million households with an annual income exceeding Rmb 30,000 that represented, and continue to represent, the dominant force of the Chinese consumer market.[7]

According to conventional per capita GDP measures, China remains one of the poorest countries in the world, with an enormous disparity between its urban and rural consumers.[8] However, the huge size and potential of a market with a population of 1.3 billion, and the presence of income not reflected in conventional GDP figures,[9] have lured both domestic and foreign investors. By 1997, the number of shopping centres with an annual turnover exceeding Rmb 1 billion had soared to 17 from only two in 1992. There were over 1000 chain store enterprises with over 15,000 chain stores in 1997, up 54 per cent and 67 per cent from the previous year.[10] According to a recent survey, private car, housing purchases and holiday spending have become the key areas for boosting consumption. Among them, rising private car ownership alone will on average add 0.52 percentage points to China's annual GDP growth in the next 10 years.[11] As such, a consumer revolution is apparently taking place in China.[12]

However, since 1997 when the Asian financial crisis broke out, China has suffered serious deflation, together with other neighbouring countries. By April 2001, deflation had caused national retail sales and the consumer price index to fall for 24 and 19 successive months respectively. Despite the government's efforts to curb this negative trend, the latest national statistics have recorded a further fall.[13] Worse yet, the new round of economic recession across the world is further slowing down the development of the Chinese economy.

[6] The State Statistical Bureau divides consumers across the country into five classes: wealthy class, middle-income class, comfortable class, subsistence class and poverty class. *Ibid* at 2–3.

[7] *Ibid* at ii of the Summary Pt.

[8] L Sklair, 'The Cultural-Ideology of Consumerism in Urban China' in NR Goodwin, F Ackerman and D Kiron (eds), *The Consumer Society* (Washington DC, Island Press, 1997) 320 at 323. Also see Y Wu, *China's Consumer Revolution, The Emerging Patterns of Wealth and Expenditure* (Cheltenham, Edward Elgar Co, 1999) at 132. It was estimated that consumption of rural households lagged about 10 years behind their urban counterparts.

[9] One study found that most incomes in China arise from three sources: formal salaries; 'grey income' referring to wages derived from informal or concurrent work; and 'black income' resulting from illegal, corrupt or immoral activities. See Yuan Wang, Xin Sheng Zhang and R Goodfellow, *Business Culture in China* (Singapore, Butterworth-Heinemann Asia, 1998) at 125–26. As a result, China has rates of ownership of consumer durables that compare favourably with countries that have three times China's official per capita income. Sklair, above n 8.

[10] Hong Kong Trade Development Council, above n 5, at i–ii of the Summary Pt.

[11] Bei Hu, 'Capitalist Road to Prosperity' *South China Morning Post* (20 June 2001) B4.

[12] For some detailed discussion, see Wu, above n 8 and D Davis (ed), *The Consumer Revolution in Urban China* (Berkeley, University of California Press, 2000).

[13] The statistical figures are quoted from Yuan Mingang, 'Kuoda Neixu Haishi Dangwu Zhiji' [Expansion of Domestic Consumption Is Still a Pressing Matter of the Moment] *Zhongguo Jinji Shibao* [China Economic Times] (19 June 2001) 1; Fan Jianping, 'Zai Fazha Zhong Ezhi Tonghuo Jinsuo' [Curbing Deflation in the Course of Development] in Writing Group *Jinji Baipishu 2000nian Zhongguo Jingji yu Zhanwang* [Economic White Paper: Forecasting and Prospects of China's Economy 2000] (Beijing, Economic Publishing House of China, 2000) at 87; and see Deng Yiwen, '2002 Nian 7 Yue Zhongguo Jumin Xiaofei Jiage Zongshuiping bi 2001 Nian Tongyue Xiajiang 0.9%' [Consumer General Price Index (GPI) of July 2002 in China dropped 0.9% as compared with that in January 2001] *Economic Times of China* (19 August 2002) 1.

The government has adopted a series of policies to combat deflation and increase consumer spending. For example, the People's Bank—the central bank of China—has thus far lowered the interest rate of domestic bank deposits eight times since 1996 in order to discourage saving and encourage spending. Further, in 1999 the government implemented a new tax on bank deposit interest, and three one-week long holidays were created as a means of encouraging consumption. According to Mr Qiu Xiaohua, a deputy director of the State Statistical Bureau, in order to maintain the growth rate of the national economy over seven per cent in 2001, there must be more domestic consumption to offset a decline in the export of Chinese goods. He called domestic consumers the new engines of the national economy.[14] Other officials have considered whether encouraging consumption should represent a development strategy in the new century to fuel the long-term growth of the country.[15]

What the government expects, however, is by no means an easy job to be done. By May 2002, resident deposits in Chinese banks reached a historical high of over Rmb 8 trillion, rising from Rmb 2.1 billion in 1978, and these deposits continue to increase at a rapid pace.[16] But domestic consumption has not increased as much as the government had hoped. The gap between resident deposits and loans granted by financial institutions has become even larger than it had been.[17] In addition, industrial production showed a slowdown in May 2001.[18] Apparently, deflation and insufficient domestic demand will continue to challenge the Chinese economy in the near future.

Quite a few social reasons have been identified to explain the phenomenon. The three most important appear to be the under-developed rural consumer market, the polarisation of social wealth and the uncertainties of the reform. A recent investigation found that by the end of 1999, the average rural household had an income of approximately Rmb 2,000. Individual purchasing power averaged less than Rmb 200 per rural resident.[19] Since China is a country with over one billion in rural population, the consumer revolution may not be sustainable without greater purchasing power on the part of farmers.

The polarisation of social wealth is another key to understanding the decline of consumer spending. A report of the State Statistical Bureau in 1999 showed

[14] See report: *Qiu Xiaohua Said Consumers Were the New Engine of China's Economy*, <http://www.peopledaily.com.cn/GB/jinji/20010520/469220.html> (visited on 21 May 2001).

[15] See Fan Jianping and Yang Dakan (ed), *Jumin Xiaofei yu Zhongguo Jingji Fazhan* [Private Consumption and Economic Development of China] (Beijing, Planning Publishing House, 2000) at 113–38.

[16] See Zhang Weimin, '2002 Nian 5 Yue Mo Zhongguo Chengxiang Jumin Chuxu Zunkuan Yuer Wei 80.4 Wanyi Yuan' [By the End of May, 2002 the Deposit of Urban and Rural Residents Reached 8.04 Trillion] in *Zhengquan Ribao* [Securities Daily] (25 June 2002) 1.

[17] The difference between deposits and loans for all financial institutions in China increased from Rmb 741.84 billion in 1996 to Rmb 1654.36 in the first quarter of the 2000. Lu Wei, 'Jinru Hou Duanque Shiqi de Zhongguo Jingji' [China Economy in the Post-Shortage Period] (March 2001) *Caijing Wenti Yanjiu* [Study on Financial and Economic Issues] 11.

[18] Yuan, above n 13.

[19] *Ibid* at 4.

that approximately 66 per cent of bank deposits were owned by 10 per cent of the population.[20] Because of this high concentration of social wealth, the repeated lowering of interest rates cannot affect the behaviour of most consumers. At the other extreme, at least 60 million people, including farmers in poor areas and laid-off urban workers, are still living below the poverty line.[21]

The uncertain future of economic reform, placing greater reliance on markets to determine investments, has also affected consumer confidence. In recent years, the reform of state-owned enterprises has resulted in more than 15 million urban employees becoming redundant. The government has also been trying to withdraw its subsidies of public housing, medical service, education and retirement services. The implementation of these reform measures has inevitably driven people from spending to saving.[22] In 1999, retail sales rose by just 6.8 per cent while personal savings climbed 11.6 per cent. Workers on average are estimated to already save 40 per cent of their salaries, and growing worries about unemployment and heavier social-welfare burdens may continue to act as a deterrent to spending.[23]

Despite impressive growth in recent years, the consumer credit market is still in its infant stages. Some recent investigations in major cities in China found that merely 19.6 per cent of urban residents have ever used consumer credit.[24] Over half of the urban population has no intention of purchasing on a credit basis.[25] The People's Bank of China has a strong policy of encouraging the extension of personal consumer credit, which exceeded Rmb 250 billion in 2000.[26] Yet such lending constituted approximately only one per cent of all the bank loans, no comparison with the average 30 per cent level of consumer credit in all bank lending in developed countries.[27] Nonetheless, the policy remains to expand consumer credit. According to the forecast of the People's Bank,

[20] See Wang Shuiping, 'Zhongguo Tongji Jiu Yifen Baogao Biaomin Jiangxi Nanneng Youxiao Qidong Jiqi Xiaofei' [One Document of the State Statistical Bureau Shows That Lower Interest Unlikely Starts Instant Consumption] *Zhongguo Gaige Bao* [China Journal of Reform] (22 November 1999) 1.

[21] Lu, above n 17, at 5.

[22] For a discussion, see Sun Liping, 'Neixu Buzu de Shehuixue Fengxi' [A Sociological Analysis of Insufficient Domestic Demand] (2000) 6 *Zhongguo Qingnian Zhengzhi Xueyuan Xuebao* [Journal of Political College of Chinese Youth] 72 at 72–76; also see Fan, above n 13, at 89.

[23] T Saywell, 'Mrs Wang Gets a Taste for Credit' (27 April 2000) *Far Eastern Economic Review* 56.

[24] See Dong Min and Wang Xing, 'Zhonguo Xindai Xiaofei de Fanzhan Zhuangkuang ji Qushi Diaocha Fenxi' [A Survey and Analysis of the Condition and Development Trend of Consumer Credit in China] *Zhongguo Baoxianbao* [Insurance Journal of China] (27 June 2002), <http://www.chinainfobank.com/IrisBin/Text> (visited on 6 July 2002).

[25] Mei Deping, '*Zhonguo Xiaofei Xindai Shengji Cunzai de Wenti*' [Problems of Consumer Credit in China] (27 September 2000) *Zhongguo Chengxiang Jingrongbao* [Urban Finance Journal of China] 1.

[26] The figure represents a 25-fold increase between 1997–2000. See the report, 'The New Spendthrifts' (18 April 2002) *The Economist Print Edition*, <http://www.economist.com/displayStory.cfm?Story_ID=1089716> (visited on 1 July 2002).

[27] Su Qin, *Xiaofei Xindai* [Consumer Credit] (Beijing, Auditing Publishing House of China, 2001) at 253.

personal credit consumption will reach Rmb 2 trillion by 2005, representing 12 per cent of all domestic credit consumption.[28]

The discussion in this section clearly demonstrates that the economic reform of encouraging markets over the past two decades has significantly changed government policy on consumption. With an emerging middle class, a consumer revolution is taking place in China. However, further development of the consumer market is facing some fundamental problems. Long running deflation, triggered by the Asian financial crisis, has made the situation even worse. Having highlighted the development of the consumer market in China, we now turn to the legal conditions of the market.

II. THE LEGAL CONDITIONS OF THE CURRENT CONSUMER MARKET

With the modernisation of the national economy in China, there has been an unbalanced development of consumer legislation. On the one hand, numerous rules have been adopted to provide consumers with legal protection. The Law of Protection of Consumer Interest[29] and the Law of Anti-Unfair Competition[30] were enacted in 1993 and the Law of Advertising[31] in 1994. Recently, the amendment of the Law of Contract[32] in 1999 and the Law of Product Quality[33] in 2000 reflected the continued efforts to enhance the legal protection of consumers.[34]

On the other hand, legal rules governing consumer credit, consumer bankruptcy and protection of the creditor of a consumer/debtor are virtually undeveloped. Currently, the application of bankruptcy rules in China is limited to enterprise debtors. The Bankruptcy Law of State Owned Enterprises of 1986 (on Trial Implementation)[35] is only applicable to state-owned enterprises and a

[28] The report: *2005 Nian Zhongguo Xiaofei Xindai Guimo Yuji Jiangda 2 Wanyi* [The Scale of Consumer Credit Is Estimated to Reach 2 Trillion by 2005], <http://www.chinainfobank.com/Irisbin/Text.> (visited on 16 May 2001).

[29] For an English translation of the Law, see The Laws of the People's Republic of China (vol 5: 1993) (compiled by the Legislative Affairs Commission under the Standing Committee of the National People's Congress of China) (Beijing, Science Press, 1995), at 203–16.

[30] *Ibid*, at 193–202.

[31] For an English Translation of the Law, see The Laws of the People's Republic of China (vol 6: 1994), (Compiled by the Legislative Affairs Commission under the Standing Committee of the National People's Congress of China) (Beijing, Science Press, 1996), at 129–40.

[32] For an English translation of the Law, see The Laws of the People's Republic of China (vol 11: 1999), (Compiled by the Legislative Affairs Commission under the Standing Committee of the National People's Congress of China) (Beijing, Science Press, 2000), at 10–76.

[33] For an English translation of the Law, see The Laws of the People's Republic of China (vol 12: 2000), (Compiled by the Legislative Affairs Commission under the Standing Committee of the National People's Congress of China) (Beijing, Science Press, 2001), at 64–81.

[34] For example, the new Contract Law includes rules relating to standard form contracts for the first time and the Law of Product Quality extends its coverage and introduces more severe penalties.

[35] For an English translation of the Law, see Laws of People's Republic of China (vol 1:Civil–commercial laws) (Compiled and translated by the General Office of the Legal Affairs

considerable part of the law has become outdated.[36] Company bankruptcy is governed by Chapter 8 of the Company Law of 1993[37] and the bankruptcy rules of other enterprises with legal personality are set out in Chapter 19 of the Civil Procedure Law of 1991.[38]

Personal bankruptcy laws have yet to be enacted. Current law provides for unlimited liability of individuals. Article 107 of the General Principles of Civil Law of 1986[39] stipulates that debts shall be repaid. If the debtor is unable to repay the debt immediately, the repayment may be made in instalments with the creditor's consent or following a court judgment. Further, Article 233 of the Civil Procedure Law provides that the debtor shall continue to repay debts remaining unpaid after execution of the judgment in favour of the creditor. The creditor may apply to the court at any time for further execution if additional assets are acquired by the debtor or become available.

Yet there may be a need for personal bankruptcy. The Partnership Enterprise Law of 1997[40] and the Law of Sole Proprietorship Enterprises of 1999[41] have imposed unlimited liability on partners within business partnerships and on sole proprietors. A legal regime may be needed to deal with these individuals' inability to repay debts. In fact, certain cases in the past have sent a warning message concerning personal debt payment to the legal system. A young college girl from a poor village was ordered by the People's Court to pay a sum that she might never be able to pay to a victim who was injured in a fire that the student had accidentally caused. The lack of a personal bankruptcy system not only subjected this young girl to a 'life sentence' in terms of the debt, but it also hindered her ability to get married, since, given the current economic condition in China, few men would be willing to marry a girl with a debt she might never be able to pay in her lifetime.

Commission under the Standing Committee of the National People's Congress of China) (Beijing, Legal Publishing House, 1998), at 684–95.

[36] See also, R Winston Harmer, 'Insolvency Law and Reform in the People's Republic of China' (1996) 64 *Fordham Law Review* 2563; and R Tomasic, 'Insolvency Law Principles and the Draft Bankruptcy Law of the People's Republic of China' (1998) 3 *Australia Journal of Corporate Law* 211.

[37] Ch 8 of the Company Law is entitled Bankruptcy, Merger and Liquidation of Company. However, the 10 Articles in the Chapter merely provide some general principles, whilst overlooking many issues. For an English translation of the Law, see The Laws of the People's Republic China, vol 5 above n 29, at 267–318.

[38] Ch 19 is entitled Procedures of Bankruptcy and Debt Repayment of Enterprise Legal Persons. The rules are mainly applicable to non-state enterprises and foreign investment enterprises. For an English translation of the Law, see The Laws of the People's Republic of China, (vol 4: 1990–1992) (Compiled by the Legal Affairs Commission under the Standing Committee of the National People's Congress) (Beijing, Science Press, 1993), at 183–239.

[39] For an English translation of the Law, see Laws of the People's Republic of China (vol. 1: Civil-commercial Laws) above n 35.

[40] For an English translation of the Law, see The Laws of the People's Republic of China (vol 9: 1997) (Compiled by the Legal Affairs Commission under the Standing Committee of the National People's Congress) (Beijing, Science Press, 1998), at 3–19.

[41] For an English translation of the Law, see The Laws of the People's Republic of China, vol 11 above n 32, at 131–41.

The harsh results of this judgment and the current defective system have been strongly criticised by scholars.[42] Some argue that personal bankruptcy should be introduced to protect debtors' legitimate interests.[43] Further, as discussed in the first part of this paper, the recovery from deflation and the high speed development of the country demands further encouragement of consumer spending. Introducing a personal/consumer bankruptcy system would play an important role in increasing consumer confidence and reducing the risk of debt.

On the other hand, limitation of consumer liability in a country like China, which is still poor, may jeopardise the future of many creditors, including manufacturers of consumer goods and service providers. The condition of the car loan market may serve as a warning and a good example of this. Between 1998–2000, the banks found that more than 50 per cent of car loan debtors failed to make repayments in accordance with their loan agreements.[44] A car sale promotion in Beijing in 1997 saw not only the purchase of about 2000 cars on credit, but also later more than 400 defendants in debt collection proceedings and losses of several million Rmb on the part of the sellers.[45] In the Guizhou Province, the speedy growth of default has recently forced all except one of the banks to suspend the bank loan business.[46] In the Zhejiang Province, a bank investigation found that more than 10 per cent of borrowers had never deposited any money in their self-pay accounts which acted as the repayment facility, once they had taken out their loans.[47] Further, the newly opened telecommunication industry has reported Rmb 20 billion of arrears of customers' payments in 2001 alone.[48] Currently in Beijing, all the banks except one have cancelled their credit card overdraft service due to rampant fraud and reckless overdrafts.[49]

The dilemma between encouraging repayment and encouraging consumers to borrow has been clearly reflected in recent government action. From the banks' perspective, there are strong incentives to increase consumer lending. In the

[42] Cao Siyuan, *Pochan Fengyun* [Storm of Bankruptcy], (Beijing, The Central Publishing House of Compilation and Translation, 1996) at 365–68.

[43] Tang Weijian, *Pochan Chengxu yu Pochan Lifa Yanjiu* [A Study of Bankruptcy Procedure and Legislation] (Beijing, People's Court Publishing House, 2001) at 84–92.

[44] See the report: 'Qiche Xiaofei Xindai Jiujing Nengzuo Duoyuan' [How Far Can Car Loan Go?] on Shenzhen Tequbao, *Shenzhen SEZ Daily* (30 October 2000) 5.

[45] Mei, above n 25.

[46] The report: 'Yuqi Buhuan Pinfa, Guizhou Yinhang Beipo Yasuo Qiche Xiaofeo Daikuan' [Frequent Default Has Forced Guizhou Banks to Cut Down Auto Loans], <http://www.chinainfobank.com/Irisbin/text.> (visited on 21 February 2001).

[47] Cao Zhongxuen, 'Geren Xiaofei Xindai Lutu Yaoyao' [Still a Long Way to Go to Personal Consumption on Credit] (2001)3 *Jingji Zhanwang* [Economic Prospect] 37.

[48] See the report on *Beijing Qingnian Bao* [Beijing Youth Daily] (22 July 2002), <http://www.peopledaily.com.cn/GB/news/8410/20020722/781341.html> (visited on 23 July 2002).

[49] See the report: 'Zhongguo Youguan Renshi Huyu Zhendui Geren Xinyong Jianli Geren Pochan Zhidu' [Some Public Figures Called for the Establishment of a Personal Bankruptcy System] by the central news network of China (25 January 2002), <http://www.chinainfobank.com/IrisBin/Text> (visited on 6 July 2002).

past, lending by financial institutions has been tightly controlled by the mandatory government policy of supporting state-owned enterprises, regardless of their market potential and performance. This politically biased policy has dragged all major state-owned banks into deep financial trouble. Their bad debts have accumulated somewhere between 20 to 50 per cent of their total lending, depending on different analyses.[50] Against this backdrop, the banks are very eager to take advantage of the state policy of developing the consumer credit market to improve their loan portfolio. Various provisions have been adopted at both central and local levels. For instance, the Operational Procedures of Administration of State Assisted Education Loans (the 'Education Loan Measures')[51] were promulgated by the People's Bank of China, the Ministry of Education and the Ministry of Finance jointly in 1999 and the Trial Measures of Administration of Residential Housing Mortgages (the 'Mortgage Measures')[52] were issued by the People's Bank of China and the Ministry of Urban Construction in 2000. In these regulations, the issues of consumer inability or failure to pay and of bankruptcy are not considered at all, however. The Education Loan Measures only require a borrower to execute a guarantee of repayment with the lending bank at the time of graduation; otherwise, the borrower is unable to obtain his or her graduation certificate from the university.[53] However, the measures fail to provide any remedy for the borrower's default. Article 41 simply states that the loans that cannot be recovered shall be dealt with according to the relevant state provisions,[54] which have not yet been enacted.

The Mortgage Measures, on the one hand, recognise the rights of the lender and the guarantor by allowing them to dispose of the property in case of serious default. On the other hand, Article 29 (2) states that in case of foreclosure, if the mortgagor has real difficulty in finding a residential place to live, the guarantor shall provide assistance.[55] This vague provision thus places the guarantor in a very difficult position between the default risk and the responsibility for taking further care of the defaulter.

A similar problem is reflected in local enactments. For example, the Beijing Municipal Government adopted a decree concerning the administration of mortgages for personal housing loans in 1997. In 1999, by an emergent notice,

[50] J-F Huchet, 'Non-Performing Loans in the Banking Sector: A Chinese Shadow Theater' (1998) 20 *China Perspective* 69; and P Loong, 'What WTO Means for Chinese Banking' *Asiamoney* (July/August 2000) 21.

[51] The Operational Measures on State Education Loan Administration (on Trial Implementation) of 2000 is available at 4 Zhonghua Renmin Gongheguo Guowuyuan Gongbao [Bulletin of the State Council of PRC] 2000, at 24–26 [Operational Measures].

[52] The Trial Measures of Administration of Residential Housing Mortgages of 2000 is available at 34 Zhonghua Renmin Gongheguo Guowuyuan Gongbao [Bulletin of the State Council of PRC] 2000, at 30–33 [Trial Measures].

[53] Art 37 of the Operational Measures, above n 51, at 26.

[54] *Ibid.*

[55] Article 29 (1) of the Trial Measures, above n 52, at 32.

the decree was amended to incorporate a new provision stating that the monthly repayments by borrowers should not exceed 70 per cent of the mortgagor's family income and, for a family of three, minimum living expenses of Rmb 800 should be retained.[56] Clearly, the local government has to adopt some rules to limit the creditors' right against the defaulted debtors in circumstances where personal bankruptcy law is not available.

Against this backdrop, the absence of consumer bankruptcy law in China has been considered as at least one cause of the problems of the consumer credit market. In a well-developed country like the United States, consumer bankruptcy law is now seen less as a creditor remedy than as a debtor protection.[57] But in China, as an emerging economy, the development of a consumer credit market apparently also needs institutional support to encourage or force debtors to make repayments. In practice, as compared with legal provisions that will spell out the rights and obligations of creditors and debtors, the moral culture may play an even more influential role in controlling consumer behavior. With the long tradition of Confucianism in Chinese society, people may try to avoid personal bankruptcy partially because they do not want to be subject to the legal consequences and partially because they do not want to be stigmatised.[58] At the same time, consumers may not suffer very much from default. This is partly because of their limited wealth, but it is also because they do not have to worry about carrying any social 'stigma of being a deadbeat,'[59] as will happen in many other market economies. In China, there has been little development of credit reporting systems and, consequently, there is little notoriety attached to non-payment of debt.

The failure to find solutions to these legal dilemmas is apparently causing difficulties for the government's aim of stimulating the consumer credit market. A recent investigation showed that, despite the government's promise to help, many poor students were still unable to obtain education loans from the banks. In Chongqing, among 2,401 applicants who lived in poverty in two major universities, only 102 had received loans by November 2000. In Xian, 312 of 10,250 applicants from 12 colleges received loans. A similar situation is found in the Gansu Province, which has 18 universities and colleges where merely 611 poor students were granted loans.[60]

[56] The emergent notice with the amendment is available at <http://www.chinainfobank.com/Irisbin/text.> (visited on 16 May 2001).

[57] For a recent discussion, see DA Skeel, Jr, *Debt's Dominion: A History of Bankruptcy Law in America* (Princeton, Princeton University Press, 2003); see especially, ch 7 'Credit Cards and the Return of Ideology in Consumer Bankruptcy,' at 187–211.

[58] Audrey Eu SC, 'Pochanfa' [Insolvency Law] in Association with Hong Kong People (compiled), *Xianggang Falu 18 Jiang* [18 Lectures of Hong Kong Law] (Hong Kong, Commercial Publishing House, 1997) 71 at 84.

[59] DG Baird, *The Elements of Bankruptcy* (Westbury, The Foundation Press, 1993) Reserved edn at 28.

[60] See the report: 'Quanguo 12 ge Shengshi Guojia Zhuxue Daikuan Fafang Qingkuang Gaishu' [A Survey of State Education Loans in 12 Provinces and Cities] *Nanfang Zhoumo* [Southern Weekend] (7 December 2000) 7.

In the residential housing loan market, the People's Bank has banned zero down payment loans for the purchase of residential property. The scheme was developed to boost the market. However, the central bank justified its strict prohibition because of the financial risks associated with the defective personal credit system. At the same time, the Bank has also prohibited banks from issuing loans to consumers without specifying the purpose of the borrowing.[61] As a result, a new banking product of 'free loans' terminated after a short life of just one year.[62]

The development of the consumer credit market in China urgently needs a sound legal framework, including both better enforcement mechanisms and a consumer bankruptcy law. Otherwise, the paradox of government policy favouring consumer credit and the reality of the defensive market will continue.

III. DIFFICULTIES IN IMPLEMENTING CONSUMER CREDIT AND BANKRUPTCY REFORM IN CHINA

The introduction of personal bankruptcy into China was advocated years ago. For example, Mr Cao Siyuan, a leading bankruptcy expert in China, believed that implementation of personal bankruptcy would protect the lawful interests of not only the debtor, but also the creditor, because the institution would put pressure on the debtor to repay the debt. He further argued that a bankruptcy regime without personal bankruptcy violates the fundamental principle of market equality.[63]

The passage of time, however, has not helped this argument to be accepted by the drafters of the new Bankruptcy Law, which is supposed to unify the current individual pieces of bankruptcy legislation applicable to different kinds of enterprises.[64] The drafters are divided on whether individual debtors should be included into the new law. At least three opinions were articulated. Some argued that the new law should be equally applied to enterprises as well as individuals, and personal bankruptcy should be adopted. Others opposed the inclusion of personal bankruptcy on the ground that the conditions were not ready. The third group suggested a compromise of limiting individual bankruptcy to those

[61] The report is available at <http://www.peopledaily.com.cn/GB/jinji/34/165/20010518/467975.html> (visited on 18 May 2001).

[62] Free purpose loans were first marketed in Shanghai in May 2000 and received a very warm reception from consumers. Liu Shen, 'Zhongguo Geren Xinyong Zhidu Yudai Guifan' [Individual Credit System In China Needs To Be Streamlined] *Zhongguo Qiyebao* [Enterprise Journal of China] (5 December 2000) at 1.

[63] Cao, above n 42, at 365–68; see also Tang, above n 43, at 84–86.

[64] The drafting of the new Bankruptcy Law started in 1994 and a comprehensive first draft was completed in 1995. However, government concerns with unemployment of large numbers of workers and potential social instability caused the draft to be shelved by the national legislature. The drafting process resumed in 1998. Wang Weiguo, 'Adopting Corporate Rescue Regimes in China: A Comparative Survey' (1998) 3 *Australia Journal of Corporate Law* 234 at 234.

who engage in business, such as partners of partnerships and commercial households.[65]

The latest draft of the Bankruptcy Law of 2002 seems to adopt a bisectional approach. According to the Drafting Group, all enterprises, regardless of their nature and form and due to the business risk they undertake, should be subject to the bankruptcy law. Even individual business person would be open to bankruptcy. However, the draft does not provide for other types of individual bankruptcy. The Drafting Group held that the infrastructure problems, such as the absence of a system of personal property registration, would render it appropriate not to set out legal rules governing non-business personal bankruptcy.[66]

Unlike developed countries where banks share information about their customers through various credit bureaux, personal credit reference and rating systems, as well as property registration systems, have not yet been established in China. As such, effective enforcement of creditor rights in bankruptcy proceedings may be difficult, as a debtor may easily transfer and hide his assets. At the time of writing, a personal credit reference system only exists in Shanghai and Guangzhou, and in both cities it is on a trial basis with a very short history.

In Shanghai, the system was launched in July 2000 and has been managed by the Shanghai Credit Reference Company with a network connecting 15 commercial banks in Shanghai and their 300 branches. The data centre for the system provides basic personal information, personal credit records and special recorded information like offences and violations.[67] Since June 2001, the system has established personal credit records of 2.4 million people and handled 140,000 inquiries.[68] In October 2000, Guangzhou established its local system with the government initiative by involving banks, insurance companies, the taxation authority and the public security bureau to supply information to the system. As a result, the Guangzhou system seems to include more reliable information.[69]

In Shenzhen, the first provision for personal credit reference agencies became effective on 1 January 2002. The Administrative Measures on Personal Credit Reference and Rating[70] authorised the establishment of personal credit reference firms responsible for providing financial institutions and other potential creditors with information and evaluation services. The coverage of the relevant information includes personal background data, credit conditions, taxation and

[65] For a discussion of these opinions, see Wang Weiguo, *Pochan Fa* [Bankruptcy Law] (Beijing, People's Court Publishing House, 1999) at 192–94.

[66] Drafting Group of the Bankruptcy Law of the People's Republic of China, *Guanyu Zhonghua Renmin Gongheguo Pochanfa (Caoan) de Shuoming* [Legislative Notes on the Draft Bankruptcy Law of the People's Republic of China] April 2002, at 3–4, on file with the author.

[67] For an introduction to the personal credit system in Shanghai, see Liu, above n 62.

[68] Zhao Peixin, 'Zhongguo Jiangjianli Geren Xinyong Tixi' [China will establish a personal credit system] *Zhongguo Qingnian Bao* [Beijing Youth Daily] (13 March 2002) 6.

[69] Liu, above n 62.

[70] The Administrative Measures of Personal Credit Reference and Rating is printed at *Shenzhen Tequ Bao* [Shenzhen SEZ Daily] (26 December 2001) 3.

insurance records as well as a history of involvement in legal proceedings and administrative penalties. Records can be kept for up to seven years.[71]

Apparently, these systems, with limited local coverage, are far from being sophisticated and afford no comparison with the tried and tested systems of other jurisdictions where credit reference agencies, some of them being profit-making bodies and trade protection associations, play an important role in preventing reckless or dishonest people from obtaining credit, while at the same time stimulating trade by facilitating the ready granting of credit in appropriate cases.[72] The current experiments with reference systems in China will no doubt provide the government with important experience. In fact, based on the Shanghai experience, the State Council and the People's Bank have formed a task force to develop a national personal credit reference system in early 2002.[73] However, the national system will take many years to become fully functioning and the current systems can hardly be very effective since they are very local with only limited coverage. An investigation in Shanghai has already found that the Shanghai credit system could not effectively prevent a credit crisis and that more needed to be done.[74]

Moreover, the legal basis to support the development of personal credit reference systems still needs improvement. Presently, credit information collection in Shanghai is carried out in accordance with some circular issued by the Shanghai Branch of the People's Bank, which has no legislative power at all.[75] In addition, necessary rules concerning consumer privacy and other protection, such as a right to copies, the service standards of reference and relevant legal liabilities, all need to evolve. For example, in Shanghai, some banks have refused to provide information to the credit reference firms by relying on certain provisions of the Law of Commercial Banks.[76] Lack of legislation concerning credit reference agencies has become a factor restricting the development of consumer credit in China.[77]

[71] See Yi Yunwen, ' Shenzhen Shi Zhengshi Shishi Geren Zhenxin Zhidu' [Shenzhen Officially Implement Personal Credit Reference System] *Guangming Ribao* [Guangming Daily] (14 January 2002).

[72] The Report of Younger Committee on Privacy (Cmnd 502 (1971)) at 78; also see C Scott and J Black, *Cranston's Consumers and the Law* (London, Butterworths, 2000) at 244–45.

[73] Zhao, above n 68.

[74] Liu, above n 62.

[75] Zhao, above n 68.

[76] For instance, Art 29 of the Law requires commercial banks to keep their customers' information confidential in the operation of their business and Art 30 entitles commercial banks to refuse to answer any inquiry concerning deposits, except where the law or regulations provide otherwise. For an English translation of the Law, see The Laws of the People's Republic of China (vol 7: 1995) (Compiled by the Legal Affairs Commission under the Standing Committee of the National People's Congress) (Beijing, Science Press, 1996), at 169–89. For the report, see Liu Fang, 'Shanghai Shehui Zhengxin Tixi Jianshe Zaoyu Falu Pingjing' [The Construction of Credit Reference System in Shanghai Encounters Legal Restrictions] *Jiefang Ribao* [Liberation Daily] (4 July 2002) 3.

[77] Wang Zhengyu and Yu Jiang, 'Zhongguo Xiaofei Xindai Qidai Tupo Pingjin' [Some Breakthrough Needed for Consumer Credit in China] *Jinji Ribao* [Economic Daily] (31 October 2001) 1.

The introduction of consumer credit and personal bankruptcy into China may be made difficult by two cultural traditions. On the one hand, Chinese traditional culture may not accept the ideology of debtor protection. Historically, failure to repay a debt was treated as a crime. Even the debtor's death could not bring the obligation to an end; rather, it would pass to the next generation.[78] In addition to the historical view, a modern theory holds that in a socialist country like China, subject to tight government control, individual consumers should have little access to and little need for excess debt. Such limited exposure to financial vulnerability suggests less need for financial relief as part of the personal bankruptcy regime.[79] The notion of 'fresh start' under bankruptcy law may need a long time to take root in China.

Modernisation of these cultural attitudes is complicated by the poor credit environment in China, as a result of an emerging market economy without well-established consumer morality. Currently, the total defaulted sum owed by state-owned enterprises has reached Rmb 1600 billion[80] and state-owned enterprises defrauded the state bank in 2000 alone of as much as Rmb 185.1 billion.[81] With regard to personal credit, as mentioned earlier, the situation is equally poor. Most consumers have very limited understanding of the importance of a credit system to a market economy and fraudulent activities are extensive. Moreover, some local criminal tribes also exploit opportunities presented by consumer credit. For example, 17,126 phoney credit cards were seized in April 2002 when police in Guangdong Province busted a piracy gang.[82] Worse yet, very few enactments and supervisory schemes have been developed to counteract these trends.[83] As a result, many worry that the introduction of personal bankruptcy into China may further fuel debt evasion.

Another Chinese tradition that may not favour the development of a consumer bankruptcy regime is the psychology of Chinese consumers. It has been observed as one of the outstanding dimensions of the Chinese market that consumers insist on basing consumption upon past savings, not borrowing. Many in China still believe that borrowing money to buy goods is a form of public embarrassment. One explanation of this mentality is that for most Chinese consumers, the act of purchasing is not just a simple transaction, but also a

[78] Zhang Jinfan (ed), *Zhongguo Fazhishi* [Legal History of China] vol IV (Beijing, Legal Publishing House, 1999) at 476–78.

[79] R Efrat, 'Global Trends in Personal Bankruptcy' (2002) 76 *American Bankruptcy Law Journal* 81 at 94–98.

[80] Shou Beibei, 'Womei li Xinyong Jinji yu Duoyuan' [How Far Are We From A Credit Economy—Interview with Credit Management Expert Lin Junyao] *Southern Weekend* (31 May 2001) 2.

[81] Liang Yanjun and Yan Ning, 'Xinyong Tafang Huisun Jinji' [Credit Collapsed, Economy Damaged] *Beijing Evening* (13 April 2001) at 46.

[82] 'The New Spendthrifts', above n 26.

[83] For a recent discussion of these concerns, see Wang Aijian and Meng Hao, 'Jianli Woguo Geren Xinyong Zhidu Duice Yanjiu' [A Study of Strategy To Establish A Personal Credit System in Our Country] 2 *Jinjixue Dongtai* [Trend of Economic Study] (2001) 15 at 15–19.

demonstration of the individual's financial capacity and social status.[84] Today, the fact that cash remains 'king' in China, with a credit card penetration rate of less than one per cent of personal expenditure on consumption, at least partially illustrates consumer behaviour and psychology there.[85] The success of consumer credit market development in China, perhaps a necessary precursor to the successful introduction of consumer bankruptcy, may be conditional on breaking-down this negative psychology about borrowing.

Last but not least, insufficient judicial resources adds to the difficulty of the development of consumer bankruptcy in China and is one of the major barriers to its introduction.[86] The rapid economic and social development in China have subjected the People's Courts to a very heavy caseload pressure. The number of civil and economic cases has increased from just over one million in 1986[87] to approximately five million in recent years.[88] In the past decade, the People's Courts at all levels in China handled nearly 10,000 bankruptcy cases.[89] As compared with over a million existing enterprises of different types of ownership in China, this number does not look very great. However, the defective legal regime and the lack of supporting social infrastructure have made the handling of these cases very difficult and slow. According to a senior judge in Shenzhen, a Special Economic Zone of China, the average completion time of a bankruptcy case is normally two years.[90] As such, a general formula has been developed to calculate the approximate number of man-hours needed for a bankruptcy case: the handling of one bankruptcy case is treated as the equivalent of eight other cases. In small bankruptcy cases, the ratio is reduced to the equivalent of four.[91] Against this backdrop, it seems difficult to open the door for a flood of personal bankruptcy cases at the present time when the workload of the People's Courts may not allow them to handle the new type of cases competently.

IV. CONCLUSION

The consumer market and consumer credit in China have developed rapidly and have great potential. However, the slow development of the necessary legal infrastructure, including consumer bankruptcy, may hinder the smooth and

[84] For a discussion of these points, see Wang, Zhang, and Goodfellow, above n 9, at 115–17.

[85] Visa International Asia-Pacific, *Changing the Way We Pay: A Report on the Development of Payment Industry in Asia-Pacific Region* (Singapore, Sema Group Pte Ltd., 2000) at 41.

[86] Wang, above n 65, at 194.

[87] See 'The Working Report of the Supreme People's Court of 1987' Issue 2 (1987) *Zuigao Renmin Fayuan Gongbao* [Bulletin of the Supreme People's Court] at 7.

[88] See 'The Working Report of the Supreme People's Court of 2002' Issue 2 (2002) *Zuigao Remin Fayuan Gongbao* [Bulletin of the Supreme People's Court] at 40.

[89] Wang, above n 65, at 238.

[90] Xu Liandong, *Pochan Anjian Shenli Chengxu* [Trial Procedures of Bankruptcy Cases] (Beijing, People's Court Publishing House, 1997) at 35.

[91] *Ibid* at 427.

healthy growth of the market. In particular, the latest legislative development has showed that the introduction of consumer bankruptcy into China is not likely to take place in the near future, due to the lack of supporting institutions, the current economic conditions and the influence of certain old traditions. However, further delay in introducing the necessary legislation consumer credit and bankruptcy may prove costly to national economic development; what is needed is the legislation to protect creditors from non-payment, as well as to relieve debtors from overwhelming debt. Such legislation would increase the confidence of both parties in the consumer marketplace. As such, the preparation for future enactment and implementation of the reform legislation are urgently needed.

6

Searching For an Over-indebtedness Regulatory System for Portugal and the European Union

MARIA MANUEL LEITÃO MARQUES AND CATARINA FRADE

I. INTRODUCTION

ACCESS TO CREDIT has become 'democratised' in virtually all the most developed market economies, becoming available to debtors and families from almost all social strata. In Europe and the USA alike, rates of indebtedness among families have not stopped growing, giving greater visibility to the problem of over-indebtedness. In these economies, indebtedness and over-indebtedness are now expressions in everyday use.

By *indebtedness*, we mean the amount owed by a family unit. This may result from one credit commitment, or from more than one source. In cases where there is more than one debt, the concept of *multi-indebtedness* is frequently used.

Indebtedness may lead to payment default, that is, situations where the debtor fails to pay an instalment of his/her debt on the due date. Such failure does not necessarily imply inability on the part of the debtor to fulfil the payment. It may be a purely opportunist decision by the debtor, based on a cost-benefit calculation of non-payment. Nevertheless, non-payment frequently results from over-indebtedness. Consumer over-indebtedness includes cases where families are in a situation such that they are totally unable to pay one or more debts. Some authors also regard as situations of over-indebtedness those in which the debtor manages to meet his/her commitments, but with serious difficulties.

In Portugal, consumer credit is a relatively new phenomenon. Its expansion began in the 1990s, but its growth has been very fast. The rate of family indebtedness rose from 20 per cent in 1990 to 95 per cent in 2001. It has had a deep effect on the way Portuguese society has come to deal with credit and consumption. A sense of taking advantage of an opportunity—using credit that has become accessible and cheaper—exists alongside one of cultural rejection—consuming before saving is contrary to the cultural habits of many Portuguese.

This contradiction is reflected in the discussion on public initiatives for regulating over-indebtedness, either supporting them or categorically rejecting them.

In this paper we shall examine this change and show how it is related to other economic indicators that have been favourable to it, such as interest rates and levels of employment. We shall start by showing how consumer credit rapidly expanded during the 1990s. We shall give up-to-date data on credit extended to consumers, both for housing and for consumption, and also the rates of payment default for Portugal. In addition, we shall paint a picture of household over-indebtedness, based on the data we obtained from the biggest Portuguese consumers' association. Afterwards, we shall present the main options being discussed in Portugal on regulating over-indebtedness: the judicial *versus* non-judicial approaches (a mediation/arbitration system).

Finally, a commentary will be made on the current situation in the EU with respect to preventive measures and solutions for the problem of consumer over-indebtedness. The way discussion has evolved in Europe could either have a pro-regulatory impact in Portugal if, for example, it were to go ahead with a directive to harmonise the law for remedying over-indebtedness, or it might be neutral in terms of domestic regulation, if the idea still prevails that this is not an issue which the European Commission should regulate.

II. THE OPEN CREDIT SOCIETY

The expansion of consumer credit has not occurred at the same time, nor in the same circumstances, in every European country. A variety of different factors have influenced its development: the laws governing credit; the level of social and economic development; household income and the availability of consumer goods; government monetary and financial policies. Consumer habits, their social and extended family relationships and the cultural context (particularly the dominant religion) have strongly influenced credit expansion.

These factors usually form the basis for explaining the difference between Northern Europe, mostly Protestant and more open to credit, and Southern Europe, where Roman Catholicism largely prevails, with its negative image of credit and historic condemnation of money-lending. But in both the north and south of Europe, the 'democratisation' of credit has been influenced by changing habits of consumption and the availability of forms of credit already widespread in the USA.

With this expansion, being in debt ceased to be seen as synonymous with poverty. Credit became a common way of acquiring a house or a car. This familiarisation of credit is a late 20th century phenomenon. Prior to this, the social connotation of debt was very different. The Biblical condemnations of usury only very gradually lost their force from the middle ages, and their influence continued up to the second Vatican Council. Along the way came periods of racism which was directed towards the groups most involved in money-lending, especially the Jews, and the condemnation of loans with interest by different social and religious codes, notably in Catholic countries.[1]

Also to blame for the negative image of credit are informal forms of lending that developed at the end of the 19th century, especially in towns, among lower income earners. Dickens and Balzac painted a dramatic picture of creditors and debtors. The US loan sharks and the UK pawnbrokers are often identified with the practice of levying extortionate interest rates and exploiting the hardships of people of slender means.[2]

This historical overview is important to better understand the different credit regulation models, setting them in the respective economic and cultural context. In Portugal, the development of consumer credit started relatively late. Recently there has occurred converging changes on the side of supply—deregulation of the credit market—and the side of demand—changing attitudes and the favourable social and economic climate of the 1990s. The result has been dramatic expansion of credit for consumption and housing, to be detailed in the next section. Even though consumer credit has been replacing other forms of anticipating income in order to acquire consumer goods, such as post-dated cheques and payment in instalments, there is no doubt that the expansion of consumer credit is a significant phenomenon, with economic, social and cultural consequences associated with it.

The discussion that all this change has stimulated has sometimes been overdramatised, reflecting traditional cultural values that are still strongly embedded. The demonisation of borrowing ('borrowing is usury and usury is a sin'), particularly of consumer borrowing—implicitly regarded as something that is only used to buy unnecessary goods, as opposed to credit for housing, which is a necessity—pervaded the discourse about incurring debt.

The very novelty of the phenomenon is, however, relative. In the first place, a great deal of what the Portuguese are now concerned about has already been studied and resolved in other countries. Second, the scale of the problem of over-indebtedness does not yet seem to be reaching worrying proportions, as has happened in other countries, since it has taken place in a favourable economic climate, which has combined an increase in real incomes with a steady fall in interest rates.

The fact that the rate of payment default is limited enables us to take the time to look at the foreign models for regulating over-indebtedness more calmly, considering their virtues and flaws, to avoid making the same mistakes. Above all, we should not confine ourselves to copying systems that are unsuited to the legal system in which they are incorporated and inappropriate to the reality that they are meant to regulate, as so often happens.

[1] For the history of consumer credit, see R Gelpi, *Histoire du crédit et de la consommation: doctrines et pratiques* (Paris, Éditions de la Découverte, 2000).

[2] Mutualist associations, eg the French *mont-de-pieté*, also sought to respond to the most deprived classes' demand for loans.

Moreover, it is especially important to know, as far as the information available permits, what the exact size of the problem is in Portugal for both indebtedness and over-indebtedness in comparison with other countries. This knowledge is, at the very least, extremely important for choosing the model to prevent and treat over-indebtedness. We have relatively precise statistical information on the level of indebtedness, but neither multi-indebtedness nor payment default can be measured with the same degree of accuracy. The problems are far greater when we move on to over-indebtedness, which can only be measured in Portugal by means of very imperfect and indirect indicators.

III. CONSUMER CREDIT AND OVER-INDEBTEDNESS IN PORTUGAL

A. Consumer Credit Evolution

Consumer credit, both for consumption and housing acquisition, started to increase in the beginning of the 1990s. Graph 1 shows the increase of credit for consumption. This type of credit has been used especially to buy cars and furniture. Graph 2 shows the evolution of housing credit, which absorbs 75 per cent of all household credit.

In December 2000, credit for consumption represented 14.9 per cent of GDP, compared to 2.3 per cent in December 1990 (Table 1). Housing credit represented nearly 40 per cent of GDP in December 1999, whereas in 1990 it represented only 13 per cent (Graph 3).

Graph 1 Evolution of banking credit for consumption[(a)]
Balance at year end (10^6 Euros)
1977 prices[(b)]

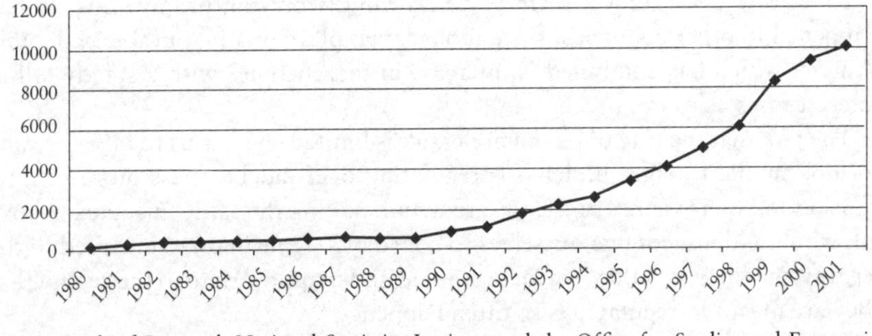

Source: Bank of Portugal, National Statistics Institute and the Office for Studies and Economic Prospects (Ministry of the Economy)
Calculations: Observatory of Consumer Indebtedness
Notes:
(a) purposes other than housing
(b) series deflated by private consumption (1977 = 100)

Graph 2 Evolution of bank lending for housing
Mortgage contracts for housing acquisition, 1978–1999

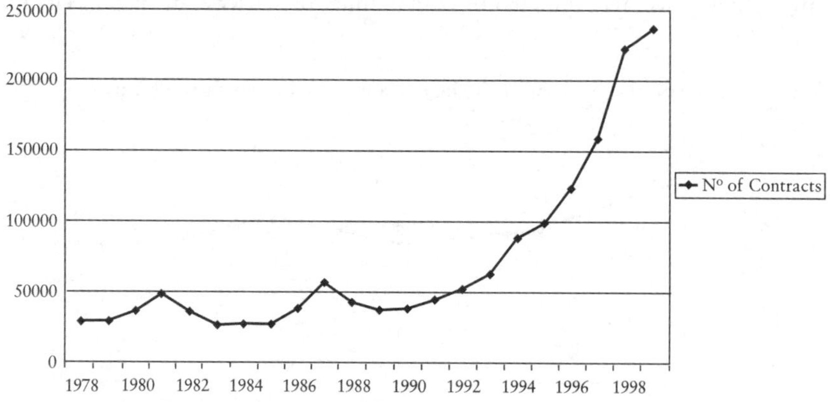

Source: Bank of Portugal and Treasury Office

Table 1 Consumer credit as percentage of GDP and Household Disposable Income Balances at year end

YEAR	1990	1991	1992	1993	1994	1995	1996	1997	1998	1999	2000
% GDP	2.3	2.6	3.2	4.7	5.1	6.4	7.5	9	10.7	13.9	14.9
% HDI	3	3.3	4.2	6.2	6.8	8.8	10.4	12.5	15	20.2	21.2

Source: Bank of Portugal, Observatory of Consumer Indebtedness and Ministry of Planning

Graph 3 Consumer credit as percentage of GDP and Household Disposable Income Balances at year end

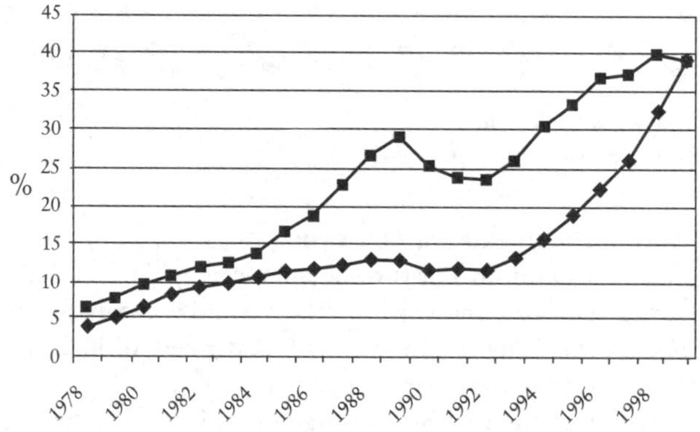

Source: Bank of Portugal and Treasury Office

There was a significant fall in interest rates during this period, during which average real wages rose at an average rate of three per cent (Graph 4). The rate of saving also fell, though the drop in inflation partly explains this change

Graph 4 Interest rates (per cent) for bank consumer credit (weighted average)

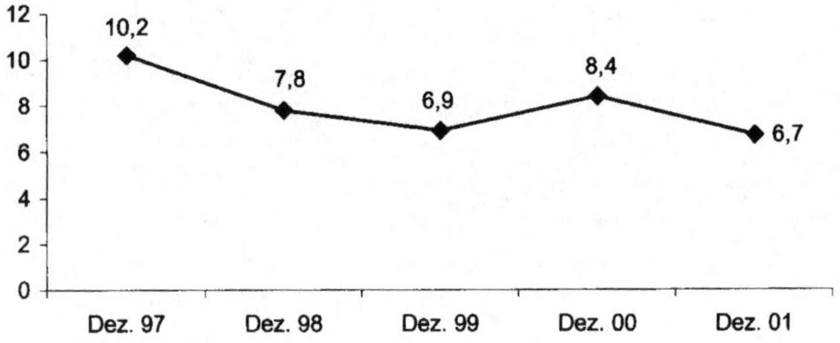

Source: Bank of Portugal

Graph 5 Household saving rates (percentage of disposable household income)

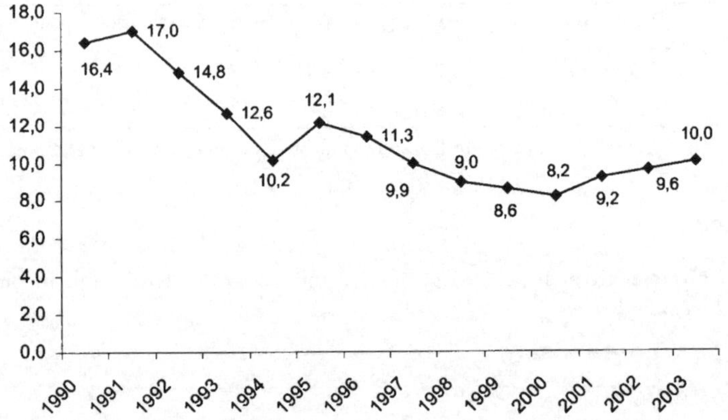

Source: OECD, Economic Outlook no 71
Note: The values for 2002 and 2003 are forecasts

during the 1990s, making consumption easier and more tempting (Graph 5). The attraction of consumption was further enhanced by the fact that consumption levels among the Portuguese were relatively low compared with other European countries (for instance, in 1990 only 7 per cent of households had a dishwashing machine and 5.2 per cent had a computer).

Consumer credit is dominated by housing loans (Table 2). Home loans represent 75 per cent of total consumer credit. Cars are the second most common

Table 2 Consumer credit and mortgage credit and as percentage of total household credit balances at year end

Year	1990	1991	1992	1993	1994	1995	1996	1997	1998	1999
C Cred	16	17	20	25	24	26	25	25	24	26
M Cred	84	83	80	75	76	74	75	75	76	74

Source: Bank of Portugal and Ministry of Planning (*Departamento de Prospectiva e Planeamento*), 2000

item purchased with consumer credit, followed by household appliances and fittings. Credit extended via credit cards is not yet a very substantial percentage of total consumer credit, but it is increasing.

The growth in household mortgage credit seems to reflect the following basic features of the Portuguese situation in recent decades[3]:

—*A clear policy option encouraging home ownership*. Home ownership has been made possible mostly through public support of the mortgage credit system.[4]

—*A close relationship between home ownership policies and macroeconomic conditions and policies*. In the 1970s and 1980s, these were in conflict in several aspects, notably the application of strict credit limits because of very high inflation and nominal interest rates. In the 1990s, inflation showed a steep decline.

—*Financial deregulation in the last decade*. The highly regulated and poorly developed financial system (including the mortgage markets) has been subjected to extensive changes, aimed at innovation and liberalisation. This has also influenced other types of consumer credit.

These changes in financial markets have resulted from Portugal's membership of the European Union, linked first to the need to integrate itself in the single market and then to its participation in the euro project. Financial deregulation has had a tremendous impact on the Portuguese housing finance system. The spread between the interest rate for consumer saving accounts and home

[3] The question of housing policy in Portugal is related to its semi-peripheral situation; that is, it has tended to reconcile and combine features of housing policies and conditions from the more developed countries with those existing in under-developed countries. See N Serra, *Estado, Território e Estratégias de Habitação* (Coimbra, Quarteto, 2001) at 134. The weaknesses and limitations of the housing market can be explained in terms of late industrialisation and urbanisation, and the delay in the capitalist development of productive forces. Thus, it is not surprising that in a semi-peripheral country like Portugal, 'community strategies for the provision of housing are still relevant. In this case, they derive particularly from the fact that they are developed by families, which articulate and reconcile their direct earned income and that from the limited State benefits (indirect income), with the synergies deriving from family, friends and neighbourhood relationships.' *Ibid* at 136.

[4] At this moment, in Portugal, government subsidies for home loan systems will finish by the end of September (Law No 16-A/2002, 31 May 2002). Individuals, who apply for subsidised credit in writing from a credit institution and submit the house purchase agreement by 30 September, may still benefit from subsidies.

mortgages, which was very high, has been considerably reduced. The long waiting times, which used to be endured before obtaining a loan, are a thing of the past.

These factors have helped to ensure that families' *rate of indebtedness* has risen from 18.1 per cent in 1990, to 88 per cent of disposable income in 2000 (Table 3). In European terms, the rate of indebtedness in Portugal is now one of the highest, as the table below shows (Table 4).

The *rate of indebtedness* is an important indicator of indebtedness in the economy. It is the ratio between the total amount of credit awaiting settlement (also known as 'balance outstanding') and household disposable income per year. This is different from the *debt servicing rate*, which is the ratio between the debt payments due in one period—interest plus amortisation of the loan(s)—and disposable income for the same period (usually a year). It is the debt servicing rate and not the indebtedness rate that makes it possible to analyse the sustainability of the growth in credit and the solvency of the households. A high indebtedness rate does not necessarily mean over-indebtedness. The latter is overwhelmingly dependent on the debt servicing rate, which in Portugal has never exceeded 25 per cent.

Table 3 Household indebtedness as percentage of GDP and of household disposable income

YEAR	1990	1991	1992	1993	1994	1995	1996	1997	1998	1999	2000
% GDP	13.7	14.2	15.3	18.8	21.1	25.1	29.7	35.5	44	52.5	59.6
% HDI	18.1	18.4	20	24.4	28.6	34.5	41.3	49.5	61.8	79	88

Source: Bank of Portugal, Observatory of Consumer Indebtedness and Ministry of Planning

Table 4 Rate of indebtedness as percentage of household disposable income

	1990	1995	1999
Germany	84%	88%	97%
France	na	37%	41%
Holland	76%	90%	140%
United Kingdom	92%	91%	101%
Belgium	na	29%	42%
United States	90%	94%	99%
Portugal	na	38%	79%

Source: Observatory of Credit and Indebtedness (Belgium)—General Report 2000

B. Over-indebtedness in Portugal

The increase in interest rates for consumer credit at the end of 1999 created the expectation of a significant change in payment defaults and bankruptcy cases as a new area of social conflict. But this has not yet occurred. Economic data from the Bank of Portugal show that only about 4 per cent of total consumer credit contracts were in default in 1999 (with only 1 per cent of the total contested) and this figure has remained the same despite increased indebtedness. This conclusion is also confirmed by information from the judicial system. While figures for judicial debt collection cases more than quadrupled between 1991 and 2000, this generally involved small amounts (less than 1250 euros). Moreover, most of these cases do not arise from credit agreements, but from other contracts for the provision of services, such as a mobile phone service or insurance. Debts for houses and cars, the two items most often bought on credit in Portugal, are the very last to be defaulted on, even if other commitments are delayed for this purpose. Housing credit is always secured, and car credit is often secured. The lower rates of default for these types of credit may be explained partly by the fear of loss of this collateral upon default to the secured creditor. Housing and cars are considered essential assets of daily life.

The number of consumers currently making demands on public or private institutions for support because of over-indebtedness is still very limited. The available data are indirect and very incomplete. They come from DECO, the most important Portuguese consumers' association.[5] We received a synopsis of all the 203 files of over-indebted consumers, who had asked DECO for support between January 2000 and January 2002. Although the results cannot be fully extrapolated to consumers in general, the findings may nonetheless be useful as a first source of information.

This is the profile of the over-indebted Portuguese consumer that we obtained from the analysis of those files (Graph 6). Most insolvent individuals are men between 36 and 55 years of age, married, and who have only completed their secondary school education. Their household income is fairly low. In fact, 58.6 per cent of the families have a monthly income of less than 1250 euros. Nearly 85 per cent have several debts. Loss of income, unstable employment and health problems are the three main reasons for payment default.[6]

Other information provided by various case studies carried out in collaboration with some of Portugal's more important financial institutions seems to bear

[5] DECO is not only the biggest, but also almost the only Portuguese consumers' association, which makes its data more significant.

[6] This rough profile of over-indebted individuals in Portugal is not substantially different from that for other countries, especially regarding its causes. Karen Gross indicates the chief reasons for bankruptcy among North American consumers as the 'increased extension of consumer credit and inadequate monitoring of that credit; job downsizing and the need for job retooling; changes in family structure, such as a spouse, grandparent, or child moving in or out; increased uninsured medical expenses; and a lack of financial management skills.' K Gross, *Failure and Forgiveness* (New Haven, CT, Yale University Press, 1999) at ix. Both the figures given by the Bank of France or by Belgium's *Observatoire du Crédit et de l' Endettement* report that passive over-indebtedness predominates, caused by unemployment, divorce and separation, and health problems. Banque de France, *Surendettement:enquête typologique* (Paris, Rapport général, 2001) at 16; Observatoire du Crédit et de L'Endettement, *La Consommation et le Crédit aux Particuliers* (Charleroi, Rapport général, 1999) at 169.

Graph 6 Profile of over-indebted individuals in Portugal

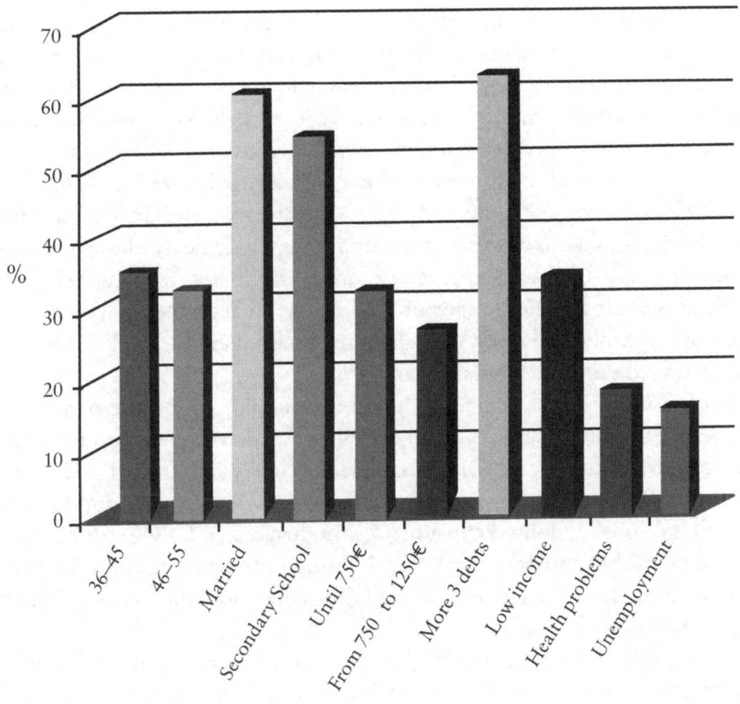

Source: Observatory of Consumer Indebtedness and DECO

out the conclusion that over-indebtedness is a not yet a serious problem.[7] The following reasons help to explain why the over-indebtedness situation is still under control. First, during this period, the labour market was very healthy, almost reaching full employment. Legally guaranteed job stability helped families to cope with the increase in their credit repayments, albeit with some sacrifices being made. Second, Portuguese consumers had taken advantage of the drop in interest rates, increasing their credit purchases. When the rate increased, they reacted immediately, and there was a significant cut in the growth of demand for consumer credit.

[7] We have analysed the data on payment default to two banks. One bank is the largest issuer of housing credit and is also a very important lender for other types of credit. We have the distribution of all the credit extended and payment default by the amount of credit, its duration, purpose and some features of the debtor (age, marital status, etc). We have also accessed the number of debtors registered in Credinformações, a private credit bureau connected to Equifax. The bureau registered only the debtors in default to some financial institutions that are members of Credinformações. The reported payment default rate is usually a little higher than the rate reported by the Bank of Portugal for the entire household credit system. The financial institutions grouped in Credinformações do not work with housing credit, perhaps explaining this disparity.

The few figures available on over-indebtedness should, however, be interpreted with a certain amount of caution, since the number of over-indebted families may be underestimated, for two reasons. On one hand, there is no legal system in Portugal for dealing directly with the issue of consumer over-indebtedness. That is why there are no official data on the significance of over-indebtedness in Portuguese society. On the other hand, the 'propensity for resignation', that is typical of Portuguese consumers in several areas of conflict, together with the problems of gaining access to institutional assistance, itself limited, equally apply to this domain. Furthermore, if Portugal is entering a recession (as data from the central Bank for the first half of 2002 show), and if the employment laws and cuts in the number of Civil Servants are achieved as announced by the current government, then it is likely that the number of individuals sliding into over-indebtedness will increase.

This potential situation makes a discussion on the implementation of a range of preventive measures and remedial systems for over-indebtedness more urgent. Indeed, as we shall show, although the first project on consumer insolvency law was present in 1998, none has yet been approved.

IV. THE REGULATION OF CONSUMER INSOLVENCY

A. Introduction: Risk and Regulation

Regulation of over-indebtedness may, broadly speaking, be divided into three complementary parts: that of *observation* and description of indebtedness and over-indebtedness; that of *prevention* of over-indebtedness; and that of *treatment* of household over-indebtedness or insolvency, via mediation and/or a judicial procedure. The three aspects have the common aim of correcting the way in which the market imputes risk to the various agents and, in particular, how it spreads it among the credit institutions and consumers.

Frequent resort to credit by all sectors of society may be regarded as presenting a problem of consumer risk regulation. State regulation of indebtedness and over-indebtedness is one way of managing the risk, seeking a balance between individual responsibility and socialisation. The appropriate balance is hard to achieve but is increasingly a central issue in the regulation of consumer risks ranging from food consumption to radical sports.

Risk regulation is defined as governmental interference with market or social processes to control potential adverse consequences to health or other aspects of individual security.[8] The institutional geography of risk regulation varies as a function of factors such as the scale, international or local, the number of public services with risk control functions, or the specialisation. The regulatory

[8] C Hood, H Rothstein, and R Baldwin, *The Government of Risk: Understanding Risk Regulation Regimes* (Oxford University Press, 2001) at 3.

regime depends on whether risks may or may not be predicted. If we are looking at unpredictable risks, such as natural disasters or other inevitable incidents, they cannot be managed beforehand. In other domains, however, such as pollution, food, or over-indebtedness, attention should be focused on precaution and anticipatory solutions. The importance given to the precautionary principle varies considerably in accordance with the type of risk and the cultural context in which it is regulated. Some regulatory cultures are more in favour of action based on prevention, with all the associated costs, while others incline more towards remedial intervention of a compensatory nature.[9] The cultural context also influences the shared risk model. This may be more individualised, with risks being transferred to the citizen, or it may be socialised, with society shouldering the main burdens, even when risk is assumed on an individual basis (over-indebtedness, radical sports).

These general aspects of risk regulation may be observed when we look at the regulation of the risk of over-indebtedness, in particular. First, it may be regulated at the international level (for example, in the framework of the EU) and/or at the domestic level. Second, a specialised body may be allocated to this function (eg, a credit and indebtedness observatory), or it may be shared among several non-specialist public departments (eg, social security, consumer protection, courts). Risk regulation could also be shared among public and private organisations (consumer protection groups or financial institutions).

The regulatory regime for over-indebtedness could focus on prevention. Although there are risks for which prevention is shown to be more effective, there are others for which it is not. Over-indebtedness can be *active*, if the debtor has actively contributed to being in a situation where he/she finds it impossible to pay; for instance, by failing to plan the commitments undertaken. Or it can be *passive*, when, due to unforeseeable but unavoidable circumstances (divorce, unemployment, illness, etc), he/she has been put in a situation where payment is impossible. Active over-indebtedness may be prevented by regulatory insistence on financial education, but such actions would not prevent passive over-indebtedness linked to unavoidable events.

But insistence on prevention does not depend solely on the type of risk. It also depends on the cultural context and political options that influence the shared risk model adopted by the regulator. The tendency to individualise over-indebtedness risk, such as we find in models where there is no chance of debt forgiveness, or socialising it, when forgiveness is accepted (eg as happens with the American 'fresh start' model and the European models based on payment plans, though these are less widespread and more demanding with respect to conditions for such socialisation).

In Portugal, the discussion of a regulatory model for over-indebtedness could be analysed in terms of these different options, looking at the three aspects of observation, prevention and remedy.

[9] *Ibid*, at 3–5.

B. Observation and Prevention of Over-indebtedness

Observation is designed to characterise indebtedness by means of an ongoing diagnosis of the situation, formulating intervention proposals and overall assessment. Observation requires various public and private bodies to cooperate with one another. Such bodies would include central banks, consumer protection groups and the financial institutions that operate in the consumer credit market. As an example, we may point to the observatories that some countries have established in the sphere of consumer indebtedness, such as the *Observatório do Endividamento dos Consumidores* (Observatory of Consumer Indebtedness) in Portugal, the *Observatoire de l'Endettement des Ménages* (France), and the *Observatoire du Crédit et de l' Endettement* (Belgium).

Prevention of over-indebtedness also requires public and private bodies in the area of consumer credit and protection to cooperate with one another. Forestalling the harmful effects of excessive and poorly considered indebtedness implies action on several fronts, of which the following are the most important:

a) *Education* about consumption and individual borrowing, including educating consumers who are already over-indebted.

b) Promoting *consumer credit counselling*, both just before a credit agreement is signed and in situations where fulfilling financial commitments has become difficult.

c) Adopting *deontological norms* which, through self-regulation, could discipline the relations between financial institutions and their customers, and which could prevent improper behaviour at the contract phase and non-fulfilment phase alike.[10]

d) Encouraging the use of *credit insurance* to mitigate the negative effects that unforeseen events in the life of the debtor could have on timely payment of instalments.[11]

e) Creating *credit files* as databases containing information on the asset and liability situation of individuals, and then encouraging financial institutions to consult them in assessing the ability of prospective consumer borrowers to repay. Credit files may be negative or positive. Negative files only contain data relative to debtors who incurred payment default. Positive files contain the entire credit history of the debtor, even if no default has occurred. There is a need to safeguard the privacy of personal data, but credit files, especially those

[10] For examples of codes of conduct relevant to the domain of over-indebtedness, see the code of conduct of the Netherlands Association of Money-lending Institutions (NVVK), described in N Huls, N Jungmann and B Niemeijer in this volume, and the UK's Code of Mortgage Lending Practice described in MML Marques et al, *O endividamento dos consumidores* (Coimbra, Almedina, 2000) at 207.

[11] Credit insurance should be used with some caution, to ensure that it does not represent an excessive cost and that it effectively covers the main risks.

of a positive nature, are an important instrument for preventing payment default.[12]

f) Finally, another effective preventive action that should not be ignored is the need to exercise a certain amount of control over the *advertising* put out by banks and finance companies, which has sometimes been excessive. There should be greater transparency and disclosure of information to consumers, enabling them to assume risks in full awareness of what is entailed in signing a credit agreement.

C. Treatment of Over-indebtedness

The situation in various countries has shown that over-indebtedness does not simply depend on macroeconomic changes, although these may be very important for determining the extent of the problem. Even in favourable circumstances, over-indebtedness is the other face of the opening up of credit to all social levels. Confirmation that situations of over-indebtedness have been multiplying has led some governments to adopt recovery measures for over-indebted individuals. These measures have been based on certain principles. First, over-indebtedness ought to be managed as a mixed problem, with both social and economic dimensions. Second, extra-judicial solutions, with independent mediation, are always preferable to strictly judicial solutions. Finally, effective regulation of over-indebtedness needs to balance the interests of the debtor, creditors and society.

In Portugal, there is no legal system to deal with the problem of consumer over-indebtedness. Nevertheless, two proposals have been put forward, which represent two distinct regulatory models. The unfolding debate revolves around a legal approach versus an extra-judicial mediation solution.

Everything started about seven years ago (1996), when the Ministry in charge of consumer protection set up a Commission to draw up a consumers' code. The Ministry submitted the part of the Commission's proposal corresponding to the remedy for over-indebtedness for public discussion. During this consulting process, another Ministry, the Ministry of Justice, asked the Permanent Observatory of Justice (*Observatório Permanente da Justiça*) for another proposal. As members of the Permanent Observatory of Justice, we were the authors of that proposal.

The Commission's proposal creates a judicial-based system with a supporting office that has a mission to establish a voluntary payment plan or, in the absence of agreement, to help the judge to prepare a judicial payment plan. This proposal presents a classical civil procedure, extremely formal and slow, such that

[12] In Portugal, there are two institutions authorised to keep personal information files on the solvency of private individuals. They are the Bank of Portugal and Credinformações. The first is a public, positive file and the second is a private, negative file. They both comply with the law on the protection of personal data (Law No 67/98, of 26 October).

the court will take at least a year to come to a decision. The Commission argues that this procedure, although relatively slow, has the advantage of being legally secure, as well as having the authority and independence that only courts can provide. Debts may be discharged when the creditor's conduct is censurable.

Our proposal, submitted by the *Permanent Observatory of Justice* (OPJ), is based on a non-judicial mediation system. Mediation would be provided by public or private institutions (most of which already exist), recognised by the Ministry of Justice, to deal with consumer indebtedness conflicts. The proposal would require the establishment of mediation network centres, able to give information and debt counselling to consumers, and to help in negotiations with creditors when they become bankrupt. The proposal would permit court intervention, as an appeal mechanism, only when the debtor and his/her creditors are unable to reach an amicable payment agreement.

This proposal would necessitate the expansion of some existing institutions such as social security offices and consumer protection agencies. These institutions have accumulated experience in social problems and would be rather more efficient than courts and considerably less expensive. Both debtors and creditors would have the opportunity of resolving the payment default problem non-judicially. As with other types of Alternative Dispute Resolution (ADR), this procedure gives a kind of 'sweet justice,' more readily acceptable to the parties, whereas the courts, with all their remoteness and inaccessibility, offer a more stigmatising and cruder answer to disputes. Further, OPJ research has shown that ADR mechanisms work as a filter for the judicial system, unloading the pressure on it, thereby helping that system to work better.[13]

The main features, the advantages, and the inadequacies of each proposal are summarised in Table 5. The recent political change in Portugal (from a social democrat government to one of the centre-right) led to suspension of the analysis of these proposals at the end of 2001.

V. EUROPEAN UNION: RECENT ACHIEVEMENTS CONCERNING CONSUMER CREDIT AND OVER-INDEBTEDNESS

Over-indebtedness poses many questions for Community institutions. Should the problem be dealt with by the Member-States, considering the subsidiarity principle (Art. 3.° b) of the EC Treaty, or by the Commission, as a necessary measure for the smooth running of the internal market? Is hard or soft regulation preferable? Should it be regarded as an economic problem or as a social one? We must remember that the powers of the Commission and the way it may intervene will differ according to the answer given to the last question. It has wider powers for dealing with an economic problem than it does for one that is regarded as just a social problem.

[13] B De Sousa Santos, MML Marques, J Pedroso, and PL Ferreira, *Os Tribunais nas Sociedades Contemporâneas: o Caso Português* (Coimbra, Edições Afrontamento, 1996) at 694.

Table 5 Two legal proposals for a consumer bankruptcy law

Proposal	Main characteristics	Advantages	Disadvantages

Proposal A *Proposed by the Consumer Code Commission to the Ministry for Consumer Affairs(1st version—1998; 2nd version—2000)*	• Judicial procedure
	• Court decision supported by an administrative office
	• Debt Discharge after fulfilling repayment scheme
		• High degree of protection of litigants' rights
		• High degree of enforcement
			• Extremely complex both technically and procedurally
			• Extremely formal
			  • Immediate judicialisation
			  • Decision delay
			  • High litigation costs
			  • Remote from the litigants
			  • Difficult to negotiate this proposal with all social actors

Proposal B *Proposed by the Permanent Observatory of Justice to the Ministry of Justice (2001)*	• Extrajudicial procedure, to be implemented via counselling already-existing services • Voluntary extrajudicial mediation • Admissibility of a judicial phase as a recourse of voluntary mediation	• Close to litigants • Quick decision • Simpler and more informal procedures • Encourages compromise • Less stigma • More readily accepted by the social actors, including financial institutions • Easier to test • Less costly to implement	• Less protection of litigants' rights • Less enforcement • More demanding in terms of negotiations • High demand for mediator training • In some cases, a judicial procedure may be required later (duplication of initiatives and institutions)

Source: Observatory of Consumer's Indebtedness

None of these questions has so far received a firm answer, though various initiatives have emerged, having differing methods and goals. The first came in 1994. The Commission asked for a report on the problem of over-indebtedness in general, and this was prepared by the Leiden Institute of Law and Public Policy.[14] Even today, this work is a European reference on the topic, and it has opened the way for reflections and subsequent studies.

Three significant initiatives have recently emerged from Community institutions: the Recommendation by the Economic and Social Committee (ESC) on the regulation of over-indebtedness in Member-States; the approval of the voluntary Code of Conduct relative to pre-contract information on credit for housing; and the yet unfinished review of the Directive on consumer credit.

[14] N Huls, *Overindebtedness of Consumers in the EC Member States: Facts and Search for Solutions* (Leyden, Leyden Institute for Law and Public Policy, 1994).

A. Regulation on Over-indebtedness

In 1999, the Economic and Social Committee (ESC) decided to instruct the Section for the Single Market, Production and Consumption to draw up an information report on household over-indebtedness. The three reasons underlying this initiative are summarised in the *Revised Preliminary Draft Information Report* of 10 April 2000. They are the convergence of competition conditions between those granting credit to private individuals, the way the single market itself works (while it is 'single' from the point of view of opportunities for cross-border transactions, it is split between various national legal systems when dealing with issues generated by this market like, for instance, e-commerce) and finally the reinforcement of consumer protection through measures which support, supplement and monitor the policy pursued by the Member States.

After a number of meetings attended by all the social partners represented (employers, unions, consumers and experts), the working group of the ESC published its final report in April 2002, which contained some recommendations for the Member-States and the European Commission alike.

With respect to the Member States, the working group recommended that they should consider the possibility that some legal aspects of over-indebtedness be dealt with in regulations similar to those covering business insolvency arrangements. Some tasks are appointed by the Commission to the Member States, like, for instance, education campaigns, harmonisation of information about consumers, the use of data on their solvency, the role of credit intermediaries and financial companies, procedural arrangements for dealing with payment default, special procedures for payment recovery, etc. Finally, the setting up of voluntary codes of conduct is also recommended.

The aim of the working group was not that all the EU countries should have exactly the same law and the same procedures. They should have a common objective, which would be to provide consumers with measures to solve problems of over-indebtedness. It would be very difficult for them to have the same law with the same results, considering the varied cultural contexts, and the differing levels of judicial performance and legal systems.

The working group also made some recommendations to the Commission. In particular, it urged it to propose measures for harmonising the legal framework for preventing and dealing with over-indebtedness, relating to matters of both substance and procedure, in accordance with the principles of subsidiarity and proportionality. It is also important to set up a network for exchanging information between Member States and the Commission, aimed at establishing a European Over-indebtedness Observatory.[15]

[15] The report, whose author was Manuel Ataíde Ferreira, is available at The European Commission: Consumer Affairs <http://www.toad.esc.eu.int/scriptsces/viewdoc.asp?doc=ces\int\int083\ces511–2002_ac.doc&lang=EN&terms>.

B. Pre-Contract Credit Information

In 1996, the European Commission published a Green Paper on Financial Services that tried to identify the main consumer concerns regarding financial services provided within the European Community, especially when those services were provided on a remote basis. In the debate stimulated by the Green Paper, the Commission received countless suggestions from consumer associations, which allowed the Commission to identify the actions that needed to be taken to ensure a high level of protection for consumers.

In 1997, via a joint initiative by Commissioners Mário Monti (Financial Matters) and Emma Bonino (Health and Consumers), the Commission issued a Bulletin/Communication on the pre-contractual information that should be provided on contracts for home loans. In the Bulletin/Communication on financial services, Monti and Bonino informed the credit institutions' associations that they would have two alternatives relative to pre-contractual information that should be included in home loan contracts: either the adoption of a voluntary code of conduct or submission to a directive issued by the Commission. The Commission indicated that it favoured the self-regulatory approach, as it was a more flexible regulatory method than the traditional one. The Commission therefore organised a meeting between financial sector associations and consumer associations. The proposal to adopt a Conduct Code was unanimously accepted in June 1997.

An agreement was finally signed between the European Consumers' Associations and the European Credit Sector Associations on 5 March 2001. This agreement was preceded by the Commission's Recommendation regarding the information to be provided by the creditors to the clients prior to the signing of home loan contracts. The role of facilitator played by the European Commission was reinforced when the Commission agreed to participate in implementating the Code by compiling a file of all the financial institutions, indicating those that had subscribed to the Code and those that had not. Compliance with the Code is voluntary and is open to all financial institutions, regardless of whether they belong to the associations subscribing to the agreement or not.

The Code harmonises the information on credit for home acquisition all over Europe, with the aim of helping consumers to choose a product that is best suited to their personal requirements and permitting a better comparison between the loan proposals made by the various financial institutions that operate within the internal market. The voluntary Code of Conduct is, as a *first step*, extremely important to the harmonisation of domestic law and to the globalisation of the market for home acquisition credit.[16]

[16] Concerning the negotiation and approval process for the Code of Conduct, see C Frade (2001) *O Código de Conduta Voluntário relativo à informação pré-contratual rnos empréstimos para a compra de habitação*, Observatory of Consumers' Indebtedness.

C. Directive on Consumer Credit

The Commission is also working on a number of concrete consumer policy initiatives that will try to reduce the risk that individuals will find themselves in a situation of over-indebtedness. Ensuring that consumers receive the information needed to assess the real cost of credit is one of the aims of the Directive on the Distance Marketing of Financial Services.

However, the most significant initiative is the proposed modification of the 1987 *Directive on Consumer Credit*, which has already been amended twice. This legislation covers more or less all aspects of a consumer credit agreement, including advertising and pre-contractual information, the transparency and conditions of the agreement, and various post-contractual aspects, such as early repayment. The Commission is now considering further amendments to the Directive to introduce minimum common rules on consumer protection, to include regulation of new forms of credit that have become widespread in recent years, and to improve the balance of rights and obligations between borrowers and credit institutions. The creation of databases to store consumer credit history, the possibility of insurance to prevent payment default situations, and the redefinition of the role of credit intermediaries are also being considered.

The negotiation phase for approving the text of a new Directive has proved to be quite difficult, and it will be some while before there is agreement on the final version.

VI. CONCLUSIONS

In Portugal, consumer indebtedness has increased, moving towards general European levels over the last few years. At the moment, default on consumer borrowing and home loans, and consumer over-indebtedness, are at levels that do not create big social problems. Nevertheless, the rapid increase in indebtedness means that preventive measures should be taken, particularly bearing in mind the experiences of other countries, and the favourable economic and social conditions in which indebtedness has expanded, especially the fact that interest rates are at an all-time low. Against a background of rising interest rates and economic recession, as is forecast for the Portuguese economy, it is likely that many households will be struggling with problems of liquidity and solvency.

Accordingly, it would be sensible for Portugal not only to strengthen mechanisms for prevention, but also to engage in a balanced and broad discussion about regulation of over-indebtedness. The idea of 'democratising' access to credit and allowing those who probably most need it to obtain it, means dealing with over-indebtedness without prejudicing access by the less affluent. In other words, a risk management model for over-indebtedness should be designed, which can spread the risk fairly among consumers, credit institutions and even society in general.

In the Portuguese context, considering the excessively slow and bureaucratic functioning of the courts, we believe that it would be better to adopt an approach to remedying over-indebtedness that is less judicial and based more on mediation and arbitration, at least in a first phase. In this way, a solution can be found that will satisfy creditors and debtors more quickly and at less social and financial cost.

In the European Union, the problem of consumer bankruptcy has finally succeeded in engaging the attention of the public and politicians alike. But the European institutions (particularly the Commission) are far from showing any commitment to preparing a common legal framework, either in the form of a Regulation or a Directive, to tackle the problem of consumer over-indebtedness. For the moment, the discussion will remain focused on two points: taking preventive measures, and gathering information on over-indebtedness (statistical data and the domestic law of the Member-States).

To sum up, over-indebtedness regulation in Portugal and in other EU Member-States will continue, for the next years, to obey a variable geometry. It will be much more extensive in northern European countries than in the countries of the south. In all locales, that regulation will continue to lag behind the growth in credit activity and overall consumer indebtedness. However, the harmonisation of financial market regulation is occurring faster than that concerning consumer protection rules.

Part III

New Consumer Bankruptcy Systems

7

'Thou shalt pay thy debts' Personal Bankruptcy Law and Inclusive Contract Law

UDO REIFNER

I. INTRODUCTION

CONSUMER CONTRACTS ARE contracts between unequal partners: businesses that seek to maximise profit and individuals who try to mobilise their unstable income in order to reproduce and enjoy their lives. Lack of profit will induce businesses to give up or seek other areas of investment, but lack of income does not terminate consumer needs.

The welfare state and the credit society have created different ways of addressing individuals' needs by either subsidising unproductive labour or facilitating the mobilisation of future income. The shift from the welfare state to the credit society in continental Europe resulted in the development of social consumer protection regulation with new forms of inclusive contracts. They are a form of recognising unemployment, divorce, illness and other risks in contractual relations in a profit-maximising society.

A subsequent stage in this development has been the rise of consumer bankruptcy schemes in the 1980s and 1990s. While it was initially a limited instrument of last resort to give relief to those few for whom contract law had no remedies, since the late 1990s its mass application has gradually replaced consumer protection law. It has not abolished substantive social rights but rather frustrated their application within a bankruptcy procedure that is focussed only on discharge from debts instead of the terms of the contracts in question. The judge can give discharge from debts which otherwise would have provided an opportunity for the development of more socially adaptive contract law. The reflexive learning model of contract law, which, using good faith and good morals, created labour, tenants and consumer protection law and many other corrective measures guaranteeing its survival in the industrialised society, is gradually given up within legal procedures where judges no longer care about the terms of contracts that have failed. Over-indebtedness as a mass phenomenon is thus no longer a sign of the failure of contract law but only for the failure of people who cannot cope with its inadequate terms. This chapter argues that we need to reintegrate consumer bankruptcy into socially inclusive contract law, which incorporates social needs throughout the life of a credit contract and provides for adaptation to changes in an individual's circumstances caused by events such as unemployment. The basis for inclusive contracts can be found in those general principles that seem to be generally accepted but remain abstract and inapplicable to individual contracts.

II. BANKRUPTCY AND CONTRACT LAW

A. Death of Debt Doctrine

'I know how to liquidate over-committed businesses but I cannot imagine how I should liquidate an individual.' This is how Jobst Wellensiek, the most renowned insolvency administrator in Germany, expressed his surprise to the German parliament in 1993 about including consumers within bankruptcy law. The traditional purpose of bankruptcy procedures, the 'liquidation' of capital for distribution to its creditors, can be compared with life and death. A legal person is 'dead' when it is bankrupt and can no longer participate in economic life. The core principle of competition, namely that the stronger party should prevail, requires the death of those who fail. Bankruptcy is therefore an economically productive selection process of the market and reflects the natural evolutionary model.

From this perspective, consumer bankruptcy is internally contradictory. A consumer survives bankruptcy in every respect: as a legal person, as a natural person, and as functional capital in the market. Only her existence as capital is an issue since all bankruptcy schemes liquidate a consumer's assets. However, significant assets and income that serve to sustain individual reproduction are exempt from liquidation.[1] Assets that serve the earning capacity, such as farmers' lands in the southern states of the US[2] or all tools in Europe, are exempt. In fact, only interest-bearing capital is liquidated.

Empirically, the distribution of assets plays a minor role in consumer bankruptcy. Most over-indebted households have never had investment capital or they have already lost it to creditors. Consumer bankruptcy is aimed at the only capital most consumers have: their earning capacity.

This form of capital can be used (or 'exploited') by creditors, but it cannot be distributed to them. The concept of bankruptcy as linked to liquidation does not

[1] See US Bankruptcy Code §522; German Code of Civil Procedure § 811. The German Code excludes items according to their function, the American code excludes them according to their function up to a certain money value, emphasising their dual application as labour and as investment capital.

[2] For a specific regulation on an Adjustment for a Family Farmer see Chapter 12 of the US Bankruptcy Code.

fit earning capacity. Workhouses and peonage in the 19th century can be conceptualised as 'labour as capital.' The US Supreme Court declared lifelong debts with a lifelong threat of garnishments equivalent to peonage and slavery.[3]

The free-market society of the USA and the welfare state society of continental Europe have developed significantly different solutions to over-indebtedness. In the USA, decisions abolishing peonage through the doctrine of bankruptcy have led to a reversal in the case of individual insolvency: it is not the individual who dies, but his or her debts. It is not the debtor who comes to an end but the claims by his or her creditors.

This 'straight bankruptcy' approach promises a 'fresh start.'[4] The debt is extinguished over a relatively short period. This is a logical transference of the concept of the legal person to the natural person. The individual is seen as an economic entity that invests capital. In the case of failure, there are two choices: abolish the person or abolish the debt. If the person is freed from his or her debt, he or she can legitimately live on—this is the 'fresh start' doctrine. It is simple and falls in line with the general view of economic activity in the marketplace.

Inherent in that view are, however, certain assumptions, listed below, which have been called into question by the extensive sociological research[5] conducted since the pioneering work of David Caplovitz.[6]

[3] *Local Loan Company v Hunt* (1934) 292 US 234 at 244. In Germany, the expression 'Modern Workhouse' ['*Moderner Schuldturm*'] dominated the campaign for debtors' relief.

[4] Chapter 7 of the US Bankruptcy Code §727.

[5] For a European overview, see U Reifner and J Ford (eds), *Banking for People, Vol 2: Consumer Debts and Unemployment in Europe—National Reports* (Berlin, New York, de Gruyter, 1992) at 315–648; see also from the same source the follow-up conference in Birmingham: G Hormann (ed), *Consumer Debt in Europe—The Birmingham Declaration: Proceedings of the Third European Conference on Over-indebtedness* (Birmingham Settlement, 1993); for the UK, see J Ford, *The Indebted Society:Credit and Default in the 1980s* (London, Routledge, 1988); R Berthoud and E Kempson, *Credit and Debt:The PSI Report* (London, Policy Studies Institute, 1992); Lord Crowther, *Consumer Credit: Report of the Committee* (London, HMSO, 1971); for Austria see Institut für Gesellschaftspolitik der Arbeiterkammer, *Privatverschuldung in Österreich—Konsumentenkredite zwischen Wunderwelt und Offenbarungseid* (Vienna, 1990) with a response from the Bundeskammer für gewerbliche Wirtschaft; P Mosslechner and P Brandner, *Ökonomische Aspekte der Verschuldung privater Haushalte* (Vienna, Österreiches Institut für Wirtschaftsforschung, 1992); for Germany see D Korczak and G Pfefferkorn, *Forschungsvorhaben zur Überschuldungssituation und Schuldnerberatung in der Bundesrepublik Deutschland—Final Report* (Stuttgart, Kohlhammer, August 1990); Institut Für Finanzdienstleistungen, *Schuldenreport 1993—Die Verschuldung der privaten Haushalte in Deutschland* (Kriftel, Luchterhand, 1994); Institut Für Finanzdienstleistungen, *Der neue Schuldenreport—Kredite der privaten Haushalte in Deutschland* (Kriftel, Luchterhand, 1995); K Holzscheck, G Hormann and J Daviter, *Die Praxis des Konsumentenkredits in der Bundesrepublik Deutschland—Eine empirische Untersuchung zur Rechtssoziologie und Ökonomie des Konsumentenkredits* (Köln, Bundesanzeiger, 1982); for Belgium see F Domont-Naert, *Le Surendettement des Consommateurs en Belgique, Rapport Final 1993* (Louvaine-La-Neuve, Centre de Droit de la Consommation) with support from Febecoop and the National Bank of Belgium; see also *L'Observatoire du Crédit et de l'Endettement, Prévention et Traitement du Surendettement en Region Wallone* (Charleroi, L'Oberservatoire de Crédit et de l'Endettement, 1996); J Niemi-Kiesiläinen, J Tala and Th Wilhelmsson, *Kuluttajien Velkasaneeraus—Tarve ja mahdollisuudet* [English Summary: Consumer Debt Advising, Restructuring of Debts and Discharge in Finland—an Analysis of Consumer Debt Situation and a Proposal for a Model of Legislation] (Helsinki, Oikeuspoliittinen Tutkimuslaitos No 106, 1991)

[6] D Caplovitz, *The Poor Pay More—Consumer Practices of Low Income Families—The Cost of*

1. Over-indebtedness is not the cause of the financial failure of a household. The causes are loss of income, unemployment, divorce or illness. Discharge does not remedy these problems, it merely affects the symptoms they produce.
2. Over-indebtedness is not even a common feature of situations such as unemployment, which may result in insolvency. Debt-free individuals who are unemployed or ill are significantly worse off than those with debts. Economic and social exclusion are more pressing concerns for this group than over-indebtedness as such.
3. Discharge from current debts does not address future debts. It may even stigmatise poor consumers when the new draft of the EU consumer credit directive comes into force, which makes creditors responsible for the extension of credit to such persons in cases where they are not convinced that the debt will be paid back. Presently, consumer bankruptcy is already seen as a negative qualification on the labour market.

Market ideology, as reflected in the US fresh start doctrine and its assumptions, is therefore only helpful as far as the individual's economic circumstances are primarily defined by over-indebtedness and not by other problems.

B. European Developments

In continental Europe, up until 20 years ago market theory related to capital had not been applied to the consumer, at least not in terms of law and jurisprudence. Neither the debt nor the consumer 'died' in the old bankruptcy law. The law tacitly assumed that discharge was unnecessary and only beneficial to those living irresponsibly at the expense of the wider community.

The welfare state had not needed consumer bankruptcy as a social safety net. Over-indebtedness had not deprived people of basic services or livelihood. Under prevailing social welfare doctrine, each individual was and is still guaranteed minimum income to cover the basic costs of living. This income should be primarily derived from work, but it is guaranteed through state support in the event of illness, unemployment and old age. Public services, such as health care, schooling, university education and kindergarten had also been free. Social welfare agencies could also pay rent in financial crises so that people could keep their homes. Statutory exemptions, adjusted with welfare law, prevented state benefits from going directly to creditors.

Indeed, loan accounts of heavily over-indebted consumers remained permanently dormant because creditors were unable to attach their assets. Although these debtors had not been discharged, creditors were unable to extract any money from them. For this reason, many banks would have quietly closed down

Paying Later, The Instalment Plan (New York, Free Press of Glencoe, 1963); D Caplovitz, *Consumers in Trouble—A Study of Debtors in Default* (New York, The Free Press, 1974).

their accounts after relatively short periods, writing off the debts in order to reduce wasted administration costs.

Thus market forces themselves created de facto discharge, especially at a time when data storage and its continuous monitoring was still costly. New information technology and debt collection services as a branch of personal investigation services put an end to the writing-off of consumer debts and these are now referred to special agencies which fish for Euros from the debtors through loopholes in the legislation protecting debtors.

The continental European economy developed into a credit economy significantly later than the USA. Consumers must now increasingly become investors in order to maintain general living standards. Credit is now used to buy consumer durables, to finance holidays and household equipment, to pay for further education, and to bridge liquidity crises. The need for investment capital has grown. Regular income is no longer sufficient guarantee of access and participation. Since the 1960s, the banks have reacted by increasing consumer lending to its current level of per capita debt of about €2.500, or about €10.000 per indebted household, in Germany.

C. 'Responsabilisation de l'Èconomie'

In the 1980s, over-indebtedness and the sharp rise of consumer credit became a public issue, especially in Germany. While research uncovered exorbitant interest rates[7] and fraudulent marketing practices, the traditional explanation of over-indebtedness as individual misbehaviour and irresponsibility was replaced by one which held banks and creditors as responsible for the circumstances of poor families. The rise in welfare spending funded through general taxation became a source of concern among the better-off. One consequence of these developments was a dominant view that the economy should solve the problems caused by the credit society.

This integration of welfare state functions into the economy, which the then President of France, Mitterand, called the 'responsabilisation de l'économie,' was achieved principally through a new approach to contract law. The court had the power to interfere with contracts or duties created by contract terms that may contribute to over-indebtedness. While states such as France, Norway, and Finland granted this discretion directly to the judge, others, such as the Netherlands and Sweden, introduced special courts or imposed self-regulation on banking business. In Finland and Sweden, the Consumer Ombudsman played a pivotal role in supervision of standard contract terms. In Germany, the courts applied the general clauses of good morals and good faith creating strict usury rules, reducing incentives for refinancing, voiding the co-liability of

[7] Interest rates of specialist instalment banks were between 15% and 30% pa, while the average of all banks in the late 1970s had been at 8%. Default interest rates were as high as either 18% or 28.9% for the two banking groups uniformly.

spouses and children, restricting default interest, abolishing collection fees, and awarding damages to those who had been wrongfully coerced or counselled into loan agreements beyond their means. This development was unified by the EU consumer credit directive of 1987, the first and perhaps the most significant European regulation of contract law.

The German Constitutional Court,[8] deciding on the co-liability of ex-spouses in credit contracts, gave this approach a constitutional foundation. The court asserted that, if the weakness of one party is clear and the solutions offered to this problem by the contract are inadequate, 'the civil courts must investigate whether the wording of the contract results from a structural imbalance in bargaining power and, if this is the case, rectify the position under civil law through the application of general clauses.'

The emerging continental European consumer insolvency schemes are based on the obligations arising from the original contracts, which are adapted to the debtor's ability to pay, on the provision of debt counselling and support, on assistance for the debtor's family, on protection of the debtor's home, and on attempts to offer information and education to the debtor.

French law contains the clearest expression of the idea that insolvency law remains a form of contract law. Until 2003 it did not provide for a compulsory discharge, nor did it prescribe any maximum repayment period. It leaves debt adjustment to special commissions, administered by the central bank, in which creditors' and debtors' organisations participate. They adjust the original contracts to the debtor's new social circumstances. The success of such voluntary procedures with creditors is assured through the authority of the central bank and the threat of a referral to the court system, where the judge does not apply bankruptcy procedures, but exercises the power to adjust contracts, stop payments, reduce a mortgage to the true value of a house, write off default interest and do many things which purist contract lawyers in other countries would not imagine in their worst nightmares. The effects resemble the adaptation of contracts to the over-indebtedness caused by unemployment, divorce, income reduction and illness according to the tradition of consumer protection law in Germany, the Benelux, and Scandinavia.

D. From Consumer Protection to Social Discourse

In the 1990s, public debate shifted in Europe. While in the 1980s, over-indebtedness had concerned consumer lending legislation (as well as landlord and tenant law and the sale of goods and services), in which consumer organi-

[8] Bundesverfassungsgericht 1 BVR 696/96 (2 May 1996) *Neue Juristische Wochenschrift* 1996 at 2021; for a general theory, see E von Hippel, *Der Schutz des Schwächeren im Recht* [The protection of the weaker party under the law] (Tübingen, Mohr, 1986); for a similar doctrine in Scandinavian law, see T Wilhelmsson, ' "Social Force Majeure"—A New Concept in Nordic Consumer Law' (1993) 16 *Journal of Consumer Policy* 435.

sations, the civil courts and the Ministry of Justice were involved,[9] the new focus was on the social implications of over-indebtedness. Welfare organisations usurped consumer organisations in counselling over-indebted families. In the German *Länder*, subsidised by the ministries of social affairs, social workers replaced lawyers and attorneys. Instead of civil law, the (administrative) bankruptcy law and welfare law became the focus of all debate and solutions. Even at EU level, the DG SANCO (Consumer Protection) lost its competence in the area of over-indebtedness to the DG Social Policy. The same had previously occurred in Germany, where political competence shifted from the Ministries of Justice to the Ministries of Social Affairs in all *Länder*.

Over-indebtedness had changed from an economic problem into a social problem. Consequently, legal debate has focused on bankruptcy law, and resulted in the conclusion that society should channel the over-indebted from ordinary economic life into a bankruptcy shelter, where they would be subject to guidance and supervision.

European countries also began to introduce laws on judicial debt adjustment. These laws did not, however adopt the US ideology of bankruptcy in their goals, procedures and terminology. The German legislation was entitled 'Insolvency Law' ('Insolvenzordnung').[10] The 1990 French enactment no 89–1010 was entitled: 'Law concerning the prevention and regulation of problems linked to the over-indebtedness of individuals and families.'[11] The Belgian regulations of 1998 were entitled 'Law on the collective regulation of debts and sales opportunities for real estate under seizure.'[12] Part IV of the Danish bankruptcy code, which deals with consumer over-indebtedness, was entitled 'financial rehabilitation'[13] and the Norwegian 'Law on voluntary or obligatory financial rescheduling for individuals'[14] adopted the same ideas as in Sweden in terms of its

[9] A good description can be found in Chapter VI entitled 'The Instalment Debt of Sylvia Farrenkopf' in R Dubischar, *Prozesse, die Geschichte machten—Zehn aufsehenerregende Zivilprozesse aus 25 Jahren Bundesrepublik* [Lawsuits that Wrote History—The Famous Civil Cases from 25 years of Federal Republic of Germany] (München, Beck, 1997) at 119–58. In 1983, the author led an EU-sponsored action research project on mobilising consumer law for bank clients, which laid the basis for financial services advice centres in the German consumer unions. See U Reifner and Volkmer, *Neue Formen der Verbraucherrechtsberatung* [New Forms of Consumer Legal Advice] (Franfurt/Main, Campus, 1989). For a response by the German Instalment Banker's Association to this project, see BKG (eds) *Irreführende Verbraucherberatung* [Misleading Consumer Advice] (Bonn, Fachverband Konsumenten- und gewerbliche Spezialkredite, 1984).

[10] *Insolvenzordnung* (*InsO*) 5.10.1994, Bundesgesetzblatt Teil I, 2866. In force 1 January 1999.

[11] *Loi relative à la prévention et au règlement des difficultés liées au surendettement des particuliers et des familles*. In force 1 March 1990. In 1993, incorporated in articles L331–1 to L333–8 Consumer Protection Code.

[12] *Loi du 5 juillet 1998 sur le règlement collectif des dettes et la possibilité de vente de gré à gré des biens immeubles saisis* (Moniteur belge, 31 July 1998) at 24.613 and *Loi du 5 juillet 1998 modifiant les articles 628 et 1395 du Code judiciare* (Moniteur belge, 31 July 1998) at 24.623.

[13] *Gældsanering*, Danish Bankruptcy Code, *Konkurslov* (part IV, *Gældsanering* p 197–237) from July 1984.

[14] *Lov av 17 July 1992 om frivillig og tvungen gjeldsordning for privatpersoner (Gjeldsordningloven)*

'regeneration' and 'debt consolidation' proposals.[15] Austria alone, where the first, very conservative draft of German consumer bankruptcy legislation was adopted before it was fundamentally revised in Germany, retained the traditional wording. The introduction of a clause, requiring a minimum offer of repayment of 10 per cent and a repayment period of seven years, the longest in Europe,[16] was consistent with the traditional view that over-indebtedness was an error committed by irresponsible consumers who must earn their discharge.[17] The German system gives consumers and small entrepreneurs with no employees and no more than 29 creditors a right to file for bankruptcy. The debtor has to present a certificate to the relevant court, issued either by one of the approximately 2000 licensed free public debt advice agencies or an attorney, stating that he or she had tried in vain to reach an agreement with the creditors. A failure is assumed if one of the creditors continues collection efforts. Furthermore, the debtor has to submit a repayment plan proposal and a list of all assets, debts and creditors.

After the file has been admitted by the court, no further enforcement of claims is possible. The judge will submit the plan containing a discharge provision to all creditors who may object to it within one month. If all creditors agree the plan will come into force. If more than 50 per cent of the creditors representing also more than 50 per cent of the total liabilities agree, the judge may overrule the minority and enforce the plan. Creditors may then still object by claiming that they will receive less through the plan than through the legal procedure. The reforms introduced in 2002 reduced the repayment period from seven to six years, shortened the time for preferential treatment of secured debts, and introduced a system of deferred payments for court fees. It also gave the judge discretion to proceed directly with the legal insolvency procedure if he or she assumes that the plan will not be accepted by a majority of creditors.

If a majority objects or the judge accepts the objections to the plan, the debtor's plan has definitely failed. The judge will then initiate the bankruptcy procedure prescribed in the bankruptcy code where first all assets will be distributed and then a repayment over six years from the time of the filing will be ordered. During this time all seizable income will be distributed equally to all creditors under the supervision of a fiduciary. Creditors such as banks, which commonly hold an assignment of wages from the debtor, remain preferred creditors for the first two years. In the fifth year, an additional 10 per cent and in the final year 15 per cent of the debtor's seizable income will be exempted in addition to the initial exemption from seizure to provide an incentive to the debtor to earn more.

[15] Regeringens proposition 1993/1994,123 *Skuldsaneringslag*, 22; The Finnish Law of 1993 is entitled *Laki yksityishenkilön velkajärjestelystä (25.1.1993/57)*. My language skills find their limits here.

[16] Periods vary from 7 years in Austria, 6 years in Germany, and 5 to three years in all other countries that have enacted such procedures.

[17] *Konkursordnungsnovelle 1993* (BGBl 974); s181–216 KO came into force 1 January1995.

Finally, the judge will grant a discharge if no creditor has proved that the debtor intentionally did not earn money or rejected work. Claims arising from injuries or child support are excluded from the scheme. The fee for the legal procedure can be paid in instalments out of the assigned wages or after the end of six years, while debt advice itself is free of charge.

In practice, most debt advice agencies present a first repayment plan that is already modelled after the legal repayment principles in order to minimise objections. In principle, within this procedure, the validity of claims can be challenged but in practice it never happens. The prospects of a total discharge replace all activity to void individual claims.

Although these European laws with their long rehabilitation periods differed significantly from the fresh start doctrine, they at least adapted the American way of thinking of consumer over-indebtedness as an individual problem of consumers and not of contracts.

E. Exit and Earned Start: the New International Wave

The new basic message was 'exit.' The over-indebted have failed in the market and are compelled to leave it, at least temporarily. Under the 'rehabilitation' doctrine, they may recover in a shelter (the European answer) and try again after three to seven years or, under the 'fresh start doctrine,' they may gain immediate free re-admission through straightforward bankruptcy.

The shift in focus was followed by a shift in legal thinking. After consumer bankruptcy procedures had been introduced into German law, the Supreme Court started to reformulate its jurisdiction in relation to contract law, partly reinventing free consumer choice as the leading paradigm. As over-indebted consumers now had procedural remedies with which to protect themselves from their creditors, they needed less protection within the contracts themselves. The jurisprudence on usury almost disappeared,[18] doorstep sales were permitted, linked transactions became irrevocable, co-liability of spouses, once nearly forbidden, became legally possible again, anatocism (interest on interest) was permitted, and prescription periods for money claims were prolonged.

The courts as well as the ministries referred directly to bankruptcy law to keep remedies for over-indebtedness out of contract law. Purified contracts and less social consumer protection went hand in hand with the introduction of consumer bankruptcy schemes, at least in Germany.

[18] At first glance it seemed as if all banks now comply, while loan sharks have vanished. At a second glance, it became obvious that usury had to a large extent been transferred to less controllable areas such as combined products, repeated refinancing and by-products such as insurance products. See U Reifner, *Harmonisation of Cost Elements of the Annual Percentage Rate of Charge, (APR) EU Project No.: AO–2600/97/000169 Final Report* (Hamburg, March 1998), Institut Für Finanzdienstleistungen <www.iff-hamburg.de>.

It would appear that the creditors' approach to contract law has prevailed in both systems. The missing eleventh commandment in the Bible, 'Thou shalt pay thy debts,' has been added to 19th century civil codes and is protected against the rising threat of over-indebtedness by the consumer bankruptcy schemes of the late 20th century. When this principle was questioned,[19] legal doctrine came unequivocally to its defence. Civil law would not be possible if lack of income could be raised as an excuse.[20]

However, this principle has only survived in theory, not in practice. Under contract law, debts must still be paid. However, under bankruptcy law, the same consumer is discharged from his or her debts. Civil law doctrine provides assistance through the concept of unenforceable claims, known as 'natural obligations,' which uphold the theory of a lifelong debt in contract law while bankruptcy law pays tribute to the economic reality that human beings survive even if there are only debts left. The anachronism of the eleventh commandment is hidden behind two ideological walls: The wall between substantive (contract) and procedural (bankruptcy) law and the additional wall between public and private law in civil law countries. Thus private law has been kept 'clean' from social poison. Private law is market law where freedom and individual choice prevail. Public (administrative law) is non-market law with its concepts of subordination, obedience, and care. When the state orders a discharge, the relationship between citizen and state comes to the foreground, instead of the relationship between private individuals in the market. Not your creditor, but 'God' has to forgive your debts.

There is, however, an important difference between the ideologies of 'fresh start' and 'rehabilitation.' Continental European bankruptcy law is modelled mostly on contract law rather than the American doctrine. While the 'death of debt' doctrine frees contract law from the cancer of insolvency and the parties continue to exist, the 'sheltered non-market economy' approach creates a kind of 'eternal life.' The debtor is granted a court-imposed quasi-contract in which debts are reduced, adjusted to income and limited in time. This new contract can be 'paradise' or 'hell' depending on how paternalistic (Austria), liberal (Netherlands), or socially minded (Scandinavia) the design of the system in question is. The debtor's 'life after death' is not as clearly distinct in theory or in practice from the life before as it is the religious concept of a debt-free heaven in the 'fresh start' doctrine.

[19] U Reifner, *Alternatives Wirtschaftsrecht* [Alternative Commercial Law] (Neuwied, Luchterhand, 1978) at 308 ff.

[20] D Medicus, *'Geld muß man haben'—Unvermögen und Schuldnerverzug bei Geldmangel* ['Money you Must Have'—Impossibility and Default for Lack of Money] AcP 188(1988) at 489 ff, 492, with a reply from U Reifner, 'Geld hat man haben—soweit nichts anderes vereinbart' ['You must have money—if not otherwise agreed'] in L Krämer, H Micklitz and K Tonner, *Recht und diffuse Interessen* Festschrift N Reich, (Baden-Baden, Nomos, 1998).

F. Bankruptcy of Consumer Bankruptcy

All involved—state, banks, debt collection agencies and debt counselling institutions—demand more preventive measures to cope with the enormous costs of bankruptcy procedures. Once designed for a few payment mishaps, they now form a huge battlefield of millions of cases.

Consumer over-indebtedness, affecting between four per cent and 10 per cent of all households, is no longer an incidental phenomenom but is an integral part of a market economy. There are annually approximately 1.2 million bankruptcy procedures in the US, several hundred thousand procedures in France, and 400,000 people seeking advice from debt counselling agencies in Germany. While there were less than 1000 bankruptcies in the first years of its existence, the first official number for individual bankruptcies after the 2001 reform indicated that 25,697 filed for bankruptcy in the first half of 2002.[21]

In 2001, the EU council made over-indebtedness a policy priority and asked explicitly for preventive as opposed to merely corrective measures.[22] The recent EU draft consumer credit directive[23] requires that all creditors use a central database to assess the solvency of their clients. They will even become liable for improvident lending, although it is unclear to whom, since the directive assumes that over-indebtedness is basically a function of improvident credit extension and not a function of unstable income and increasing liquidity strains of large parts of the population.

In the US, restrictive interpretation of the bankruptcy code denying access for many of those who formerly had no difficulty to get relief has been actively supported by major banks. Citibank in particular has led an enormous and partially successful campaign to restrict the access of debtors to the American fresh start system. German and Dutch bankers, on the other hand, are somewhat reluctant to participate in the non-litigious procedures provided by the relevant bankruptcy schemes.

[21] Media Release (22 November 2002), Federal Ministry of Justice, Press Release No 62/2002.

[22] See M Alexopoulos and I Domowitz, 'Personal Liabilities and Bankruptcy Reform: An International Perspective,' (1998) 1 *International Finance Journal* 127–59; J Niemi-Kiesilainen, 'Changing Directions in Consumer Bankruptcy Law and Practice in Europe and USA,' (1997) 20 *Journal of Consumer Policy* 133.

[23] EC, Proposal on Council Directive on the harmonisation of the laws, regulations and administrative provisions of the Member States concerning credit for consumers, COM (2002) 443 final of 9 September 2002 at 8: 'The directive will improve stability by putting in place a raft of provisions on responsible lending, on providing information and protection both when the credit agreement is concluded and during its performance (or in the event of its possible non-performance) that will reduce the probability of a creditor or credit intermediary being able to mislead consumers in another Member State or jeopardise their financial situation or even of acting irresponsibly. The directive being proposed, and in particular its provisions relating to the prevention of over-indebtedness, together with the rules on consulting central databases, will further improve the quality of loans and lessen the risk of consumers falling victim to disproportionate commitments that they are unable to meet, resulting in their economic exclusion and costly action on the part of Member States' social services.'

But abolishing both effective credit contracts which are able to cope with social problems through mechanisms of adaptation and denying access to a fresh start bankruptcy system has directed responsibility back to the creditors.

In a case between the American Federal Trade Commission and Associates First Capital Corporation, AFCC's new owner Citicorp was fined $215 million for predatory mortgage lending practices,[24] such as unnecessary refinancing and misrepresentation. Both practices have been identified as major factors contributing to over-indebtedness in surveys on consumer debts in Germany.

> 'The Associates engaged in widespread deceptive practices,' said Jodie Bernstein, Director of the FTC's Bureau of Consumer Protection. 'They hid essential information from consumers, misrepresented loan terms, flipped loans, and packed optional fees to raise the costs of the loans. What had made the alleged practices more egregious is that they primarily victimised consumers who were the most vulnerable—hard working homeowners who had to borrow to meet emergency needs and often had no other access to capital . . . In addition to The Associates, the complaint also names as defendants Citigroup Inc. and CitiFinancial Credit Company, Citigroup's consumer finance arm, as successors to The Associates.'[25]

G. A New Saviour: Financial Literacy

While consumer advocates challenge the 'eleventh commandment,' arguing for rehabilitation and adaptation instead of exit, politicians and creditors have looked to a third area, defined as 'education.'

The educational approach is easy to understand and sell. If all consumers were cautious, there would be no problem. Literacy, however, refers to 'letters,' which are the basis of written information. Reading and writing are necessary skills for participation in social life. Credit, to the contrary, is a product on the market that can be purchased without special skills. It is designed by the credit industry and not by culture or general institutions. While language is a public good, credit is a private product.

Banks design credit according to their client's needs only if the client has adequate market power. For those permanently at risk, creditors have a power to design their products to maximise their own return, even when their clients fall into difficulty. Teaching the impoverished consumer the complex language of such products will not produce the desired outcome. Furthermore, such knowledge will not help a poor person if it is the only product available.

It is cynical to make 'avoid credit by saving first' the main message of financial literacy. Credit is an integral part of economic life and those who do not use it are prevented from increasing their productivity. Financial education would be immensely beneficial if it were to teach people how to use credit contracts,

[24] News Cc) *dpa-AFX Wirtschaftsnachrichten GmbH* 19 September 2002.

[25] 'FTC Charges One of Nation's Largest Subprime Lenders with Abusive Lending Practices' (6 March 2001), Federal Trade Commission <http://www.ftc.gov/opa/2001/03/associates.htm>.

how to make good choices (if they are available), how to use consumer protection law, how to claim adjustments in social need and how to resist the self-serving offers of help in the form of additional credit and refinancing.

Financial education should be directed at the education of both parties. Creditors need education for the development of adequate products that are easy to understand and safe to apply. They also need to learn about the position of debtors and how debtors could make more productive use of credit. Finally, creditors need to acquire skills for preventive action and adaptation of contracts to the social situations of clients. The consumer's financial education would mean learning how to communicate confidently with creditors, knowing their rights and exercising their collective power.[26]

The creditors, however, will learn only if education reduces costs, increases profits or if they are forced into it by the state. For this reason, social consumer protection legislation is necessary to regulate the terms of standard loan agreements.

H. Towards a Productive Use of Credit

Over-indebtedness is a problem arising from contract law, and a solution to it should be found within the structures of contract law. Insolvency law is a necessary tool when it is too late for contractual remedies. Consumer bankruptcy, 'fresh start,' and 'liquidation' do not fit with consumer finance. Instead 'rehabilitation' and 'adaptation' underline the fact that the debtor will remain part of the game, continue his or her relations with the economy and thus 'prolong' contracts in the shadow of the welfare state. The concept of rehabilitation reconciles consumer bankruptcy with social consumer protection in contract law. Just as in French law, there should not be a fundamental difference between insolvency and default law, between contractual adaptation and consumer bankruptcy.

Bankruptcy law is therefore only the last arena of contract law. The more it buys into the commercial doctrine of liquidation, the more it reflects the failure of contractual remedies and contract law to cope with consumer needs. Socially blind contract law leads to straight bankruptcy approaches. This is why the problems of unstable income should be solved primarily in contract law. Consumer contracts must be adapted to real life and to the income cycles of consumers, just as the entire economy ultimately has to serve the consumer. This can only be done by adapting financial service agreements (loans, savings and insurance) to consumer needs through specific legislation and a needs-based interpretation of contracts.

[26] These thoughts have been developed in the book by U Reifner, *Finanzielle Allgemeinbildung* [General Financial Education] (Baden-Baden, Nomos, 2003).

III. INCLUSIVE CONTRACTS

A. Over-indebtedness and Social Justice

'Money thou shalt have' rules keep poverty outside contractual considerations. This applies both to common law and the civil law system. However, social protection legislation and jurisprudence do exist, and they introduce the values of social protection through general clauses contained in the civil codes.

Protection of employees, consumers, and tenants, environmental and health protection, education and other non-profit activities are well integrated into civil law. This stems from the historical compromise in continental Europe between the police and welfare state on the one hand and civil society on the other, and the split between Common Law and Equity in England. Such welfare aspects play a much greater role in the civil law tradition, while the American law has become, over recent decades, far more a pure expression of commercial law.

Over-indebtedness is significantly different from consumption, housing and labour. While the latter address specific interests, over-indebtedness addresses the borrowers' lack of money, characterising this group as poor and unable to participate in the market.

The concept of 'social justice' in continental European law implies a contractual approach. The German application of this notion distinguishes between '*sozial*' and '*gesellschaftlich*', which may be translated into social and societal. '*Sozial*', in the context of justice, state, and responsibility,[27] refers to the positive approach towards those who are disadvantaged, excluded and poor. The quest for the 'Sozialstaat' (Social State), a term too narrowly translated as 'welfare state,' is part of the unalienable principles contained in Article 20 of the German Constitution and also is defined in Article 1 of the Italian constitution. Similarly, the French concept of '*solidarité*' describes legal elements that compensate for shortcomings in the market. The German language makes a distinction within the social contract between the *Gesellschaftsvertrag*[28] and the *Sozialer Vertrag* (ie *soziales Arbeits-, Miet-, und Verbraucherrecht* [social labour, tenants and consumer law]).

In the Anglo-Saxon context, theoretical legal discussions on social justice refer to the social contract as the general *Gesellschaftsvertrag*. Revitalised by Rawls and the economics and law movement, the contract-based philosophical school links social justice[29] to equality[30] and anti-discrimination. John

[27] *Soziale Gerechtigkeit*, *Sozialstaat*, *soziale Verantwortung* [Social justice, Welfare State, social responsibility].

[28] *Gesellschaftsvertrag* is also often cited in Rousseau's language as '*contrat social*' or written in one word '*Sozialvertrag*.'

[29] See J Mill, 'Social Justice and Utility,' Chapter V from *Utilitarianism* (1861), reprinted in RC Solomon and MC Murphy (eds), *What is Social Justice? Classic and Contemporary Readings*, 2nd edn (New York, Oxford University Press, 2000) at 167 ff.

[30] C Sunstein, *Free Markets and Social Justice* (New York, Oxford University Press, 1997) at 4,

Rawls'[31] allusions to substantive justice are logically linked to *Gesellschaft*. This approach may require the poor be taken into account, but it does not address the mechanisms producing social injustice. Solidarity and the 'Social State' are even denounced as socialist.[32] Instead of this approach, poverty has to be seen as a structural threat within an equal market society. Equality alone will not help to overcome this deficit. Solidarity is a separate principle with its own collective history and merits that have to be applied.

Poverty law, as it is called in the USA, that is, welfare law and equal access to justice, accepts poverty as the result of individual choices. It addresses only the fundamental contradiction that equal opportunities are guaranteed by the law, but access to the law is left to the market. The result is 'legal poverty.'[33]

While American contract law has mostly ignored 'poverty,' legal poverty has been seen as critical to the foundations of democracy and the rule of law. Consequently, 'lawyering for the poor'[34] in the US concerns essentially legal poverty. It focuses on state oppression of the poor (immigration, criminal prosecution, eviction) or entitlement by the poor to state subsidies (welfare, rent subsidies, food stamps). Rights and access to rights must be guaranteed by the internal logic of common law. The old dispute about whether access to justice helps or deters the poor from meeting and enforcing their true needs[35] has still

refers to 'social norms' (*ibid* at 4 and 32 ff) which means '*Gesellschaft*' but then links it to 'discrimination' (*ibid* at 152) which refers to 'so*zial*'; for social as '*gesellschaftlich*' see P Atiyah, *The Rise and Fall of Freedom to Contract* (Oxford University Press, 1979) at 36–37; D Gauthier, 'The Social Contract as Ideology' (1977) 6 *Philosophy and Public Affairs* 130 at 155; D Richard, 'Allen's Social Contract Theory in American Case Law' (January 1999) 51 no 1 *Florida Law* Review 1–40; M Rosenfeld, 'Contract and Justice: The Relation between Classical Contract Law and Social Contract Theory' (May 1985) 70 *Iowa Law Review* at 769 ff.

[31] J Rawls, *A Theory of Justice* (Cambridge, Harvard University Press, 1971) at 60 ff.

[32] See F Hayek, *Law, Legislation and Liberty:The Mirage of Social Justice* (Chicago, University of Chicago Press, 1978) at 185 [*Law, Legislation and Liberty*]; TW Simon, *The Democracy and Social Injustice:Law,Politics, and Philosophy* (Maryland, Ryman & Littlefield, 1994) at 30: 'Social injustice consists of an infliction of social harm upon relatively powerless individuals because of their negative group identity.'

[33] See C Mirsky, 'The Political Economy and Indigent Defense: New York City, 1917–1998' presented at Chester L Seminar at NYU (see the accompanying essay in (1997) 4 *Annual Survey of American Law* at 891 ff) ['Political Economy and Indigent Defense']; See also M McConville and C Mirsky, 'Criminal Defense of the Poor in New York City' (1986–7) 15 *New York University Review of Law and Social Change* 581.

[34] For an overview, see the essays and discussions in *Lawyering for Poor Communities in the Twenty-First Century: Seventh Annual Stein Center Symposium on Contemporary Urban Challenges*, (summer 1998) 25:4 *Fordham Urban Law Journal* at 673–995: L Trubek and J Nice, *Cases and Materials on Poverty Law Theory and Practice* (St Paul, West, 1997). For specific areas like criminal law, see 'Political Economy and Indigent Defense', above n ; for environmental law, see L Cole, 'Empowerment As the Key to Environmental Protection: The Need for Environmental Poverty Law' (1992) 19 *Ecology Law Quarterly* 619; for civil rights, see S Cahn and J Camper Cahn, 'The War on Poverty: A Civilian Perspective' (1964) 73 *Yale Law Journal* 1317; on health care, see *Symposium, Urban Bio-ethics: A Symposium on health Care, Poverty, and Autonomy,* (1997) 24 *Fordham Urban Law Journal* 663.

[35] See John Griffith on the poor's claim to bread and butter and not to legal rights and Gary Bellow's cautious statements in 'Turning solutions into problems: the legal aid experience' (August 1977) 34:4 *National Legal Aid & Defender Association Briefcase* at 106ff; Richard Abel, *The Politics of Informal Justice* (New York, Academic Press, 1982); Charles Revon on the French *Boutique*

not been resolved by institutional solutions, such as legal aid schemes, clinics and societies, or pro bono work.

Poverty law is therefore not only the wrong answer to poverty but even acts as a diversion. Lawyers open a door to a room for hungry people in which there is nothing to eat. Similarly, over-indebted consumers are diverted into a process in which they learn to blame themselves for their own fate, such as occurs in financial education ideology.

A contract approach to over-indebtedness based on the principle of solidarity accepts the fact that free contracts systematically create poverty under certain market conditions. The split between anti-discrimination and solidarity has its philosophical tradition. Continental European philosophers taking the contract-based approach to a modern (market) society, such as Georg Hegel, Immanuel Kant and Jean-Jacques Rousseau, all predicted that individualism and competition would necessarily produce an accumulation of wealth on the part of some members of society while a significant number of others would face poverty. They attributed this process to the market mechanism itself. *Morality* (Kant), a *strong state* defending general interest against individual egoism (Hegel), or *pity* leading people back to nature (Rousseau) were seen as forces that would overcome the inherent vices of market society. Thomas Hobbes, David Hume and John Locke, on the other hand, came to the conclusion that the market alone could cope with these problems.[36]

In civil law, anti-discrimination law plays a minor role in poverty prevention. Article 3 (discrimination) is juxtaposed by Article 20 (social responsibility) of the German Constitution. Article 3 merely redistributes poverty more evenly within society as between races, sexes, ages and abilities without reducing poverty as such while Article 20 creates collective responsibilities for the poor.

Only if discrimination law is enriched by the principles of social responsibility and *solidarité* (Article 20) to form a principle of 'social discrimination' directly addressing the mechanisms by which 'the poor pay more,' will contract law be able to address the problem of over-indebtedness.

du Droit; and the discussion on the *Rechtswinkel Amsterdam* by Nik Huls and Gerrit Schep at their annual meeting in the beginning of the seventies. Much of the discussion, as well as its historical development, is reported in E Blankenburg and U Reifner, *Rechtsberatung* [Legal Aid] (Darmstadt, Luchterhand, 1981). For further reading, see G Bellow and J Kettleson, 'From Ethics to Politics: Confronting Scarcity and Fairness in Public Interest Practice' (1978) 58 *Boston University Law Review* 337; A Sparer, 'Gordian Knots: The Situation of Health Care Advocacy for the Poor Today' (1981) 15 *Clearinghouse Review* 1; S Wexler, 'Practicing Law for Poor People' (1970) 79 *Yale Law Journal* 1049 at 1054.

[36] For a juxtaposition, see M Rosenfeld, 'Contract and Justice: The Relation between Classical Contract Law and Social Contract Theory' (May 1985) 70 *Iowa Law Review* 769 at 847 ff. The texts considered are: J Locke, *Two Treatises on Government* (Cambridge, Cambridge University Press, 1088); D Hume, *Enquiries Concerning the Principles of Morals* (Oxford, Oxford University Press, 1978); T Hobbes, *Leviathan* (Indianapolis, Hackett, 1994); I Kant, *Methaphysical Elements of Justice* (Indianapolis, Bobbs-Merrill, 1965); GF Hegel, *The Philosophy of Right* (Oxford, Oxford University Press, 1977); J-J Rousseau, *On the Social Contract. Discourse on the Origin of Inequality and Discourse on Political Economy* (Indianapolis, Hackett, 1983). Related excerpts can be found in Solomon and Murphy, above n 29.

B. Unproductive Consumption and Equal Opportunities

'To them that hath, shall be given.' Discrepancies in the productivity of labour are reflected in different outputs per working hour. This productivity depends on the amount of capital that can be applied to the labour of the individual. Such capital includes all forms of prior investment made by others, such as education, inherited fortune and state support. It may be derived from the environment, in the form, for example, of a developed community or state, and it may come from the organisation of the production.

The increasing social discrimination between those who can save and those who can not is shifted more and more into the area of consumption, where purchasing power is distributed even more unevenly between income groups. A dollar earned by the investment household has higher purchasing power than a dollar from a cash-based household or an indebted household. Caplovitz' 'The Poor Pay More' and data disclosed through the US Home Mortgage Disclosure Act demonstrate that increased wealth follows increased income and this rule works against the low income investor through reduced choice, higher prices and additional costs. In the US, lower classes presently spend more than they earn compensating for the rising gap between rich and poor by an increased use of consumer credit. So-called 'credit socialism' postpones the discussion of income distribution to the future where even minor rises in interest rates or unemployment may have devastating social and economic effects.

The various aspects of this mechanism are discussed in both systems. Regular publication of statistics through the Reports of the Census Bureau[37] in the USA and the poverty reports of governments, trade unions or labour administrations in Europe provide the basis for what Friedrich Hayek asked the Americans to admit as inevitable in order for individual freedom to be upheld: 'some unworthy will succeed and some worthy fail'.[38] American presidents, Theodore Roosevelt and Lyndon Johnson, had stressed this issue and conservative states Texas and Florida have looked to it in their redefinition of the goals of affirmative action in the educational system.[39]

A fair concept of contract law would take these social inequalities into account at every stage of the contractual relationship. This would require not only the provision of information to the consumer but also adapted contracts that take consumer needs and hardship into account. There would also have to be a more even distribution of the cost of inequality to all contracting parties within society.

[37] Other institutions are the Economic Policy Institute, Center of Budget and Policy Priorities

[38] F Hayek, 'The Mirage of Social Justice' (1978) in *Law, Legislation, and Liberty*, above n 32, reprinted in Solomon and Murphy, above n 29, at 180, 185.

[39] It replaces race criteria by criteria of income and wealth. Whether this will lead to less justice for the poor black or improve his or her fate is a subject of controversy between minority leaders.

This contract law is neither compensatory nor a communal or social welfare response to consumer weakness because it attacks a contractual concept which creates consumer weakness.

In an unpublished paper, Caplovitz transformed the quest for solidarity into a call for general compulsory insurance against over-indebtedness. The law is able to fulfil this function as an insurance system in itself. If certain problems must be resolved by all lenders alike, lenders are left with only two choices: to exclude customers or to distribute costs equally among all customers. The law thus has the same effect as a compulsory insurance scheme. Contract law therefore will become social if it learns to be inclusive.

C. Inclusive Contracts as Incomplete Contracts

An inclusive contract must combine two apparently contradictory elements: equal access and social risk distribution for all members of society.

If the private economy reacts to the inclusion of over-indebtedness, it will react by excluding those who are at risk. This is why inclusive contracts cannot be the only elements of one individual contract. No single contract is able to regulate access to itself. Moreover, there is no reason why the individual should regulate the access of other members of the same group. An inclusive contract is therefore a collective element within each individual contract and is expressed by its reference to standards, morals, duties and rights extrinsic to the particular contract and independent of the parties who implicitly or expressly refer to it.

Management theorists and institutional economists already view individual contracts ('one-shot contracts') as manifestations of a long-term relational management[40] and banking, in which new credit contracts are continuously made.[41] When the relationship commences, the individual contract is an 'incomplete contract,'[42] a contract underlying the 'one-shot game' contract. As only the individual contract is legally defined and binding, economists denounce the danger that the unenforceability of the incomplete contract will succumb to the opportunism of the stronger party. From a macroeconomic perspective, the (external) values contained in the incomplete contract, such as reputation, trust

[40] H Hakannsson, *Industrial Technological Development: A Network Approach* (London, Routledge, 1987) at 10.

[41] J Süchting and P Stephan, *Bankmanagement*, 4th edn (Stuttgart, Schaeffer Poeschel Publishing, 1998) at 634.

[42] RG Rajan, 'Insiders and Outsiders: The Choice between Informed and Arm's-Length Debt' (1992) 47:4 *Journal of Finance* at 1367–1400. For an application of this theory to credit contracts, see U Reifner, I Grössl and U Krüger, *Kleinunternehmen und Banken in der Krise—Produktive Konfliktbeilegung durch Recht* [Banks and Small Business in Crisis—Productive Conflict Resolution through Law], Final Report of a Research Project financed by the Volkswagen Foundation, B II 4 a, (Baden-Baden, Nomos, 2003).

and confidence, should become more important in the interests of the economy as a whole.[43]

While 'incomplete contracts' extend individual contracts in terms of time and values, 'social contracts' extend them to collective relationships between creditors and consumer-debtors in general. Such relationships have been evident in collective labour agreements since the beginning of the 20th century. Their actual power over individual labour contracts is not in question, although they were accepted as legally binding contracts, enforceable through the courts in Germany only in 1914, and in the UK not until the second half of the 20th century.

Civil and common law theory has never truly incorporated the phenomenon of collective agreements into contract law. Blinded by the organisational background, theorists have assumed that these agreements were contracts between associations and enterprises, despite their normative effects that were directly visible in the terms and interpretation of individual and incomplete labour contracts.

Stripped of the organisational framework, the idea of collective agreements as incomplete contracts amounts to a general concept of social contracts to be implied into individual contracts. There are many instances in which these 'social contracts' become apparent; when, for example, banks in Alsace agreed with consumer organisations that they would give unemployed debtors an extension of 12 months, or when German banks, in the wake of the severe flooding in East Germany in August 2002, publicly declared that they would not cancel any credit agreement until 2003 if the delayed payment was caused by the floods.

In the USA, a loan agreement can be embedded into a number of community development agreements made under the US Community Reinvestment Act between banks and community groups for the promotion of investment in low-income areas. Such agreements are presently restricted to general figures and promises of investment. They could, however, also bind a contracting party to carry the risk of unemployment of other parties within the same community up to a certain limit. The contract could also have clauses deferring payments in circumstances of ill health for the period of recovery or, in the case of educational loans, until the student is earning an income. It could waive default interest where there is no 'fault' (in circumstances such as the recent floods in Germany) and create rights and duties of solidarity. In cases of insolvency, the contract could regulate rehabilitation. Non-financial duties of advice and mutual information, co-operation, and even pro bono work could be incorporated. These contracts would also contain a 'most favoured' clause applicable to certain groups and institute monitoring procedures in relation to the operation of the elements ensuring access.

[43] C Shapiro, 'Premiums for High Quality Products as Returns to Reputations' (1983) *Quarterly Journal of Economics* 97 at 659–79.

Whenever collective problems become public issues, such as the Exxon Valdes accident or the Los Angeles riots, providers are pressed by public opinion into declarations about social responsibility. These declarations have no legal status whatsoever. They could, however, be seen as part of social contracts, whose principles could be incorporated into individual contracts through interpretation and general legal clauses.

The Woodstock Institute in Chicago holds 300 'contracts' between community organisations and banks, whose impact on individual contracts is apparent in the products and prices offered in relation to mortgage loans in low-income areas of Chicago and Philadelphia. Effectively, these social contracts are sanctioned outside the legal system, but they have no repercussions in terms of contract law theory. Islamic banks in Malaysia, motivated by their desire to uphold the usury interdiction contained in the Koran,[44] offer 'credit contracts' in the form of stakeholder participation. Its legal effect consists in a debtor's right to make a lender participate in his or her social risks. Legally, he or she pays a 'share' out of the more broadly defined profit derived from the productive use of this loan. The lender accordingly also shares the risk of failure of the investment in the debtor's earning capacity as a result of unemployment or illness. Close communities such as those in Alsace, or Mondragon in the Basque country, have concluded collective agreements in which loan agreements are embedded. In case of unemployment and illness, they provide interest-free periods and payment holidays.

The court system uses these social contracts quite irrationally by referring to good morals, the *Anstandsgefühl aller billig und gerecht Denkenden,* unconscionability and good faith.[45] In a manner reminiscent of lender liability jurisprudence in the USA, a German judge will find that a lender is bound by the principle of good faith to offer refinance without seeking to make a profit from it. He or she will go on to refer to the general principle that one should not seek to profit from the misfortune of others.

Strangely enough, such decisions, while referring to a broad consensus within society as to what a party should or should not do, are captured in legal theory by the so-called *Einzelfallgerichtigkeit* [justice based on the circumstances of the individual case] following the Latin principle of *summum ius summa iniuria*. In

[44] 'What is usury?' A variety of injunctions can be seen to influence the course that commercial activity may follow in an Islamic economy, of which those relating to usury [*riba*], gambling [*maisir*] and deception [*gharar*] are extremely important. These injunctions are embodied in both the Qur'an and the ahadith. The literal translation of the Arabic word *riba* is increase, addition or growth, though it is usually translated as 'usury'. Usury is not to be regarded solely as the practice of taking interest on a loan. Two major forms of *riba* are defined in Islam. They are *riba al-qarud*, which relates to usury involving loans, and *riba al-buyu*, which relates to usury involving trade. *Riba* is mentioned in a number of Qur'anic verses (2:275 279, 3:130, 4:161, and 30:39) and is sometimes referred to as the 'devouring' of others' wealth' (taken from Islamic-Finance.com <http://www.islamic-finance.com/item5.htm>).

[45] See U Reifner, '"Good Faith": Interpretation or Limitation of Contracts? The Power of German Judges in Financial Services Law' in R Brownsword, NJ Hird and G Howells, *Good Faith in Contract* (Dartmouth, Ashgate, 1999) 269–310 ['Good Faith'].

reality, these decisions are much less individual than the formal contract; it is their very rules and references that make them partly incompatible with legal individualism.

D. Inclusive Contracts and Social Contracts

Freedom to contract is defined in civil law in terms of a threefold basic right: to contract with whom one wants to contract (*Abschlussfreiheit*), to determine the contents of the contract (*Inhaltsfreiheit*) and to choose its form (*Formfreiheit*). Inclusive contracts would significantly interfere with the first two and most important elements of it.

If the suppliers of goods, services or labour are not interested in making the contracts more inclusive, there appear to be only three options:

—the legislature uses its authority to set social rights;
—the judge applies general standards of good faith and unconscionability; or
—organised interests force the supplier side to sign collective agreements which also define the contents of each individual contract.

Historically, all three approaches have severe limitations. The legislative approach leads to inflexible constellations, in which a particular protective right may hinder the adaptation of contracts to new developments and generate high transaction costs.

Interference through the courts in terms of general principles raises the question of legitimacy and autocratic behaviour, 'the emperor's new clause,' as Arthur Leff described the unconscionability doctrine.[46] The misuse of judicial power under authoritarian regimes has already stigmatised as 'intra-pretation' the uncontrolled erosion through general clauses of the freedom to contract.[47]

Collective agreements must rely on the organisation of social interests. They generate additional bureaucratic power which may be exercised for other goals if the members are unable to control it democratically. However, the main objection stems from the fact that such organisations must, as Olson has shown,[48] exclude non-members for their own survival. Closed-shop agreements and clauses discriminating[49] against non-members are designed to impede free riding. In any case, the existence and history of collective agreements is a milestone in the development of inclusive as well as incomplete contracts in labour law. Any further research will have to focus on the conditions under which truly

[46] A Leff, 'Unconscionability and the Code: The Emperor's New Clause' (1967) 115 *University of Pennsylvania Law Review* 485.

[47] See 'Good Faith', above n 45.

[48] M Olson, *The logic of collective action: public goods and the theory of groups* (Cambridge, Mass, Harvard University Press, 2000).

[49] The so-called '*Spannenklausel*' (non-members must receive at least a certain percentage less than the salary increase agreed) has been voided by the German Supreme Court on the basis that it offends against the negative right to coalition (ie not to join a union). See Bundesarbeitsgericht Urteil vom 21.3.1978 *Arbeitsrechtliche Praxis* No 62 regarding art. 9, German Constitution, '*Spannenklausel*'.

inclusive elements have been generated since collective agreements, in a less organised form, have become more and more apparent in community, consumer and housing movements.

Key questions will be how the relationship of an individual contract to all other social contracts in society can be formulated, and how it can be introduced into the product of negotiations between the parties.[50] None of these three options can be applied alone. Undeniably, however, all three approaches do exist and operate to create aspects of contract law with inclusive effects.

There is an abundance of employment, consumer and tenant legislation in both legal systems, which have many similarities and interfere effectively with the freedom to contract by setting minimum standards. Increasingly, European legislators have also included questions of access to services for poor people into statutory contract law in 'services of basic necessity' officially designed by the EU. American anti-discrimination and lifeline legislation also shows that the question of access is to some extent removed from the sole prerogative of the individual under the freedom to contract.

The increasing reference to general standards of good faith and morality [*Treu und Glauben*, *bonnes moeurs*] for the protection of socially disadvantaged contracting parties already characterises every fourth legal decision relating to financial services in Germany and this undeniably reflects a trend towards the use of this tool to make contracts more inclusive.

It is up to legal scholarship to begin to collect social contracts and to formulate them in various declarations, public agreements and public promises, in the same way as in the development of international human rights law. A committee of experts from all countries should come together to develop the principles of how over-indebtedness should be treated in contract law, drawing examples from different laws and practices. Elements of the community reinvestment declarations in the US could be combined with voluntary codes within the German banking industry or the agreements on treating unemployment in parts of France. In addition, the case law on consumer credit should be researched to identify the general principles.

E. A Social Contract on Over-indebtedness

Over-indebtedness in the credit society is closely connected with consumer credit and the law relating to it. All industrialised societies have extensive consumer credit regulation. It is the first and only private product that has been regulated by the EU and in the USA. The US Consumer Credit Protection Act has long been federal legislation complementing existing state legislation. But these regulations do not address the principles of the creditor-debtor relation-

[50] For a broader approach to the Freedom to Contract Theorem, see also M Trebilcock, *The Limits of Freedom to contract*, 2nd edn (Cambridge, Mass, Harvard University Press, 1997).

ship, but instead the techniques and incidents that have given rise to public concern.

A model of a social credit contract to guide the interpretation of individual credit agreements could be based on the following principles[51]:

—Article 1: Consumers should have a fair opportunity of access to all available services and products, to lifeline accounts and protection against all discrimination based on the source or the amount of income.
—Article 2: Consumers should obtain an accurate picture of the costs and consequences of a loan. The disclosure of the cost of borrowing should be complete, exhaustive and correct. It should meet fully the evidentiary and warning functions of formalities and provide details of future payments.
—Article 3 Consumers should have time to reflect on a credit commitment through the provision of cooling-off periods and independent advice covering the product and its consequences.
—Article 4: Consumers' privacy should be sheltered from intrusion. His or her bank account and private life must be protected from debt collection practices. Debtors' relationships with family and friends should be protected against exploitation (restrictions on guarantees and co-liability).
—Article 5: Debtors' social lifeline must be protected. Creditors must respect minimum income and double the average interest rate should be the limit of rates (usury).[52]
—Article 6: Creditors should not profit from default but encourage credit adjustments through limitations on default interest. Repayment of debts must always be possible, free of charge and should reduce the interest-bearing capital first. There should be no extra profit from refinancing.
—Article 7: Consumers should be supported in the productive investment of the loan. No interest should be taken if no effective use of credit is possible and interest pyramiding should be prohibited.

IV. SUMMARY

Unlike capital, consumers do not die when they are insolvent. This is why consumer bankruptcy ideology is not adequate to describe their fate. In legal terms, their continuous life means that the contractual relation between creditors and debtors goes on under different terms. Accordingly, continental European legal

[51] The principles are elaborated in my paper given at the 1st Inter-American Conference on Consumer Law Gramado, Rio Grande do Sul State, Brazil, 8–11 March 1998 on *Principles of Consumer Protection in Financial Services*. The paper is available at iff@iff-hamburg.de.

[52] In *Toker v Westerman* 274 A.2d 78 (NJ 1970) the court held: 'Suffice it to say that in the instant case the court finds as shocking, and therefore unconscionable, the sale of goods for approximately 2 1/2 times their reasonable retail value.' The German Supreme Court (Bundesgerichtshof 4 May 1993 IX ZR 9/93) held that 'extortionate credit has to be assumed if the contracted interest rate is about double of the average market rate.'

thinking is based on the idea of a continuous relationship between creditor and debtor after bankruptcy. Both are still responsible for the outcome of the credit relationship. This responsibility can lead to a rethinking of the original contract and its inability to cope with those circumstances which, although socially predictable, have been ignored in the making of the contract. Instead of creating only remedies for those who are already in default or insolvent, contract law should no longer ignore unemployment, illness, divorce and other statistically significant and socially undeniable events and include these risks in the contents of the contract.

Such 'inclusive contracts' do not seem to be in the short-term interest of creditors who govern the making of the individual contract. This is why the legal system has to provide for it by defining consumer credit contracts as incomplete contracts that need additional input and adaptation through a form of interpretation. Using general clauses, the judge can refer to publicly acknowledged social contracts that contain rules and procedures for mechanisms against social discrimination and poverty. Thus the moral power of consumers as a collective could be mobilised for the construction of individual contracts.

8

The Political Economy of Personal Bankruptcy in Israel

RAFAEL EFRAT

I. INTRODUCTION

IN THE EARLY 1990s, Israel experienced a massive increase in imprisonment orders being issued and executed against non-paying debtors. Partly in response to the plights of those individual debtors, in 1996, the Israeli legislators passed a bankruptcy reform law aimed at revolutionising the fresh-start policy for financially troubled individuals. One of the purported goals of the reform law was to provide a meaningful opportunity for responsible and honest, yet financially troubled individuals to successfully resume their place in society free from their overwhelming debts. This bankruptcy reform marked the first ideological shift in Israeli history from a relatively conservative view to a more liberal view of the fresh-start policy.

This chapter begins with a brief summary of the evolution of the fresh-start policy in Israel. First, it traces the attitude toward debt repayment and financial fresh start in the Jewish tradition. The chapter then picks up the chronicle from the pre-statehood years in Palestine during the British Mandate period and traces the evolution of the fresh-start policy in Israel over its first 50 years.

Following the narrative of the historical evolution of the fresh-start policy in Israel, this chapter summarises the finding of a recent empirical study examining the extent of uniformity across the four judicial districts in Israel in implementing the recently reformed bankruptcy laws. Lastly, the chapter explores the role that internal legal culture in Israel has had on the implementation of the bankruptcy reform.

II. HISTORICAL EVOLUTION[1]

Long before the establishment of the State of Israel in 1948, Jewish communities around the world struggled with how to treat financially troubled individuals.

[1] The following section is based in part on R Efrat, 'The Evolution of the Fresh-Start Policy in Israeli Bankruptcy Law' (1999) 32 *Vanderbilt Journal of Transnational Law* 49.

Initially, the Jewish communities were strong advocates of the freedom and dignity of financially troubled debtors. When many non-Jewish legal institutions regularly imprisoned defaulting debtors, Jewish communities originally prohibited such practices. However, beginning in the seventh century, social and economic changes brought about more tolerance towards punitive debt-collection practices in many Jewish communities. The continuing growth of commerce and the persisting custom of debtor's prison outside the Jewish communities culminated, by the 16th century, in widespread acceptance in most of the Jewish communities of imprisoning financially able debtors for failing to pay their debts.[2]

The emerging practice in Jewish communities of imprisoning defaulting debtors, deemed to have financial ability to satisfy debts, was formally adopted in the newly established Jewish state in 1948.[3] Under the new law, a debtor who had the ability to pay her debts but failed to do so was subject to imprisonment for up to 91 days.

Similar to this creditor-oriented debt-collection mechanism, the leaders of the young Jewish State adopted a largely pro-creditor bankruptcy regime modelled after the British Bankruptcy Act of 1914.[4] While this early bankruptcy law recognised the right of the bankrupts to obtain debt forgiveness, it reserved this valuable benefit to financially troubled individuals who were able to repay substantial sums of their outstanding debts.[5]

During the first 30 years of the State of Israel, the legislature and the courts were largely unsympathetic and at times even hostile, to the plights of financially troubled individuals who pursued bankruptcy relief. The legislature's hostility towards bankrupts was initially manifested in the adoption of laws aimed at penalising the bankrupts and indirectly impairing their ability to resume a new chapter in their lives. Beginning in the 1950s, the government banned all individuals who were declared bankrupt from serving as a member of any city council or municipality.[6] In the early 1960s, financially troubled attorneys who

[2] See M Elon, *Herut Hapr at Bedarche Gveyat Hov Bamishpat Ha'Ivri* [Freedom of the Debtor's Person in Jewish Law] 16 & 255–6 (Hotsa 'at sefarim ' a1 shem YL Magnes, ha-Universitah ha—' Ivrit,964 [Jerusalem, Magnes Publication] 1964). See also M Elon, 'The Sources and Nature of Jewish Law and its Application in the State of Israel–Part II' (1968) 3 *Israel Law Review* 88 at 108.

[3] See R Harris, 'Nefilato Ve'aliyato Shel Ma'asar Ha'chayavim' [The Fall and Rise of Debtors' Prison] (1996) 20 *Tel-Aviv University Law Review* 439 at 460–2.

[4] See S Levin, *Pshitat-Regel* [Bankruptcy] 13 (Hotsa ' at Hevrah Yisre ' elit le-hahsharah miktso ' it, [Jerusalem, Israeli Society for Professional Training Publications] 1984); see also CW Fassberg, 'Cross-Border Insolvency in Israeli Law' in *Israeli Reports to the XIII International Congress of Comparative Law* 113–5 (Celia W Fassberg ed, 1990).

[5] Pursuant to the bankruptcy law, a court was precluded from granting the debtor an unconditional discharge if the bankrupt's assets were 'not of a value equal to five hundred mils in the pound on the amount of his unsecured liabilities.' Bankruptcy Ordinance, 1936, Official Gazette, Supp 1, § 26(3).

[6] See The Municipal Ordinance Code (new edition), 1964 § 120(7) (a member of any city council or municipality would be able to resume his position two years after obtaining order of discharge); see also The Local Municipal Ordinance, 1950 § 101(8); Local Municipal Ordinance, 1958 § 11(a)(10).

were declared bankrupt were prohibited from ever practising again.[7] A few years later, the government declared that any contractual agency relationship automatically terminates upon the bankruptcy declaration of either principal or the agent.[8] In the early 1970s, the government announced that a bankrupt individual could no longer enter into any binding contractual relationship.[9]

This belligerent attitude towards bankrupts culminated in 1976, when the Israeli legislature severely restricted financially troubled individuals' access to bankruptcy protection by precluding debtors from bankruptcy relief unless the debtors could demonstrate that their petition was likely to benefit creditors.[10] The legislature curtailed debtors' access to the bankruptcy process because it believed that the recent increase in debtor-initiated bankruptcy petitions, as opposed to creditor-initiated petitions, was inconsistent with the original bankruptcy mandate, which was intended to serve creditors' interests.[11] The legislature was also persuaded that it was critical to curtail debtors' access to bankruptcy protection because the recent increase in the number of voluntary petitions was violating fundamental moral norms of society, was too expensive for the government to administer and was harmful to the debtors themselves.[12]

Following the 1976 legislative bankruptcy reform, bankruptcy relief was no longer available to debtors who had few assets or limited potential for post-petition earnings. Courts began interpreting the 1976 legislative reform in a way that foreclosed the door of bankruptcy to numerous overly encumbered and financially distressed individuals unable to repay a meaningful portion of their debts within a reasonable period of time.[13] In routinely turning down the

[7] See Chamber of Advocates Law, 1961, 15 L.S.I. 48(3) (1961).

[8] See The Agency Law, 1965, 19 L.S.I. 14(a) (1964–65).

[9] See The Contracts (General Part) Law, 1973, 27 L.S.I. 4 (1972–73).

[10] First, the Israeli legislature added three procedural requirements for commencing bankruptcy protection with the aim of reducing the frequency of voluntary bankruptcy petitions. Second, courts were granted the authority to deny an application for bankruptcy protection unless the court is satisfied that, 'taking into consideration the judgment execution proceedings, which have been taken or can yet be taken against the debtor, bankruptcy proceedings are the appropriate course of action.' Lastly, a court was granted the power to annul the bankruptcy adjudication of an individual if it found that the continuation of bankruptcy would not benefit the creditors. See the 1936 Bankruptcy Ordinance, § 7 & 29 as amended by 797 SH 106 (1976).

[11] See DK (1975) 311 ('Today the bankruptcy process is used by many for illegitimate purposes. During the past few years, more than ninety percent of the bankruptcy petitions were initiated by the debtors and not by the creditors.')

[12] See, eg, Proposed Amendment of the Judgment Execution Law, 1974: Hearings Before the Judiciary Comm., 8th Knesset 4 (1974) (statement of the chairman, Mr Verheptig: 'Bankruptcy ruins a person economically. It also ruins the morals in the economy.'); Draft bill amending the Bankruptcy Ordinance (no 8), 1975 H.H., 279 ('[Allowing individuals to resort to bankruptcy amounts to] a burden on the courts and the taxpayers.'); D K (1976) 1612 (statement of Mr Verheptig: '[I]t is unjustified to ruin someone's source of income . . . and to cause him to be left out of the normal course of life once he becomes bankrupt and he cannot do anything.').

[13] See, eg, C A 3488/93, *Official Receiver v Almochtasev*, 95(2) T E 1330 at 1330. The court of appeals reversed a lower court's decision granting the debtor's application for commencement of bankruptcy protection. The court of appeals reasoned that since the debtor lacks any significant assets for distribution to creditors, there was no place for the debtor in bankruptcy. See also, C A 5877/92, *Shafir v. Official Receiver*, 47(4) P D 710, 712: 'When are [bankruptcy proceedings] appropriate. . . ? The intent is [that the bankruptcy process is appropriate] where it assures the creditors

bankruptcy relief applications of financially troubled debtors, the courts redirected the debtors back to the judgment execution process.[14]

Unfortunately for those financially troubled individuals who were disqualified from the bankruptcy process, the judgment execution process was not much more hospitable to their needs because it imposed the constant threat of imprisonment for failure to pay. During Israel's early years, several attempts were made to liberalise debtor prison law inherited from the Ottoman Empire; every attempt failed as there was strong resistance coming from the powerful community of judges and the bar association. These well-established groups believed that liberalisation of debtor prison law would impair the only effective tool for dealing with the perceived chronic problem of debt-repayment avoidance by certain segments of the newly formed society in Israel.[15] During parliamentary debate on the reform of debtor prison law, several legislators echoed this sentiment, arguing that existing social conditions in Israel simply made the country ill-prepared to deal with unethical and opportunistic tendencies in some segments of Israeli society. Some legislators were even more explicit and specifically referred to the Sephardic Jews as the problematic segment of Israeli society.[16]

Faced with the strong opposition to any liberalisation attempts towards debtor prison law, the advocates for liberalisation reform eventually settled for a reformed version of the law that in many ways was even more punitive than before. Specifically, in 1968, one newly adopted regulation shifted the burden of proof to a defaulting debtor, desiring to avoid the issuance of an imprisonment order, to establish that there was another way for the creditor to collect his debt. Further in 1968, the legislature made it procedurally much easier for a creditor to obtain an imprisonment order against a defaulting debtor. From then on, creditors no longer needed to obtain a judgment from a court to proceed with a request for the debtor's imprisonment on account of a defaulting promissory note, a returned check, or a bill of exchange.[17] Instead, the creditor would simply need to present the judgment execution officer with any of those documents, and such documents became executable as if they represented a final judgment of a court.[18]

To avoid imprisonment and other collection procedures, the debtors were also required to strictly fulfill the terms of a repayment order issued by an

of at least a reasonable repayment of their claims in a process that will eventually be beneficial to the entire group of creditors.'

[14] See 4892/91, *Ashkenazi v Official Receiver*, 48(1) P D 45 at 61.

[15] A typical argument against a reform proposal of the debtor's prison law was stated in a letter dated April 24, 1955, from the District Court Judge Kistner to the Attorney General. In the letter the judge asserted that: '[o]ne should not forget that our nation is in a period of massive immigration and that there are many people who do not have permanent jobs and are making a living out of daily temporary jobs and there are not effective avenues available to the creditor to collect the debt'. See Harris, above n 3, at 474.

[16] See, eg, DK (1957) 96; see also (1960) 1864; D K (1960) 1786.

[17] See Harris, above n 3, at 485.

[18] See HE Baker, 'Legal System' in *The Israeli Year Book 1970*, 119 (L Berger *et al* eds, 1971).

over-burdened judgment execution officer. However, as the rigid and at times unrealistic repayment demands made by those orders became increasingly more difficult to satisfy, more debtors found themselves subject to the impending threat of an imprisonment order.[19]

Hence, as a result of these various changes in the law, by the late 1980s insolvent individuals with few assets and limited future income potential were in practice excluded from both the bankruptcy process and the repayment options traditionally available under the judgment execution process.[20] Consequently, an increasing number of insolvent individuals faced an impending fate of imprisonment. Indeed, by the early 1990s, the number of imprisoned debtors had grown from 30 individuals per year in 1963 to over 24,000 individuals.[21]

The massive and almost indiscriminate use of debtor's prison in Israel as a tool for collection of unpaid debts ceased almost entirely in 1993. Acting in response to an appeal brought by a recently established grassroots debtor's organisation, the Supreme Court held that imprisonment orders could be issued only when the *creditors* can clearly demonstrate that the debtor has the means to repay the outstanding debt. This very activist decision overturned a tradition dating from the 1968 legislation that required the debtor, in order to avoid imprisonment, to prove that the creditor could collect in some other manner.[22] The Court further found that the judgment execution officer could no longer issue an imprisonment order without first conducting an adequate investigation of the debtor's financial affairs to determine whether the debtor indeed had the financial ability to repay the outstanding debts.[23]

The massive increase in the utilisation of debtor's prison in the early 1990s triggered an ad hoc protest by many who perceived the system to be inherently unfair. The protest took the form of a letter writing campaign, the development of an interest group dedicated to helping financially troubled debtors, a litigation strategy, and, apparently, some suicides. The public pressure resulting from this ad hoc protest movement was the catalyst of the above-mentioned landmark Supreme Court decision on the debtors' prison law in 1993. And the Court's decision was quite effective. Creditors were unable or chose not to meet the burden of proof assigned to them by the decision to obtain an imprisonment order. The practice of imprisoning debtors decreased sharply, though not entirely.[24]

[19] See eg, CA 5503/92, *Kirtzman v Official Receiver*, 49(1) PD 749 at 755–6.

[20] See Ashkenazi, 48(1) PD at 57; CC (TA) 2404/90, *Official Receiver v Ron*, 1992(2) PM 182, 184: 'This case is an example of many cases . . . of financially troubled debtors where one judicial system turns them to another judicial system and the other judicial system returns them back to the first, in a continuing cycle. This situation resulted from the recent reform in the judgment execution law . . . .'

[21] See DK (1965) 2528; HC 5304/92, *Perach Foundation v Justice Minister*, 47(4) PD 715 at 723–32.

[22] See the text preceding n 17.

[23] See Perach Foundation, 47(4) PD 715 at 763–4.

[24] See Harris, above n 3.

Evidently, the same public pressure was also the catalyst for the reform of the bankruptcy law in 1996.[25] The public pressure for a legislative reform to address the plight of the financially troubled individuals prompted the establishment of a high profile bankruptcy reform commission. While the commission failed to come up with any concrete reform proposal, the commission's deliberations seem to have cultivated some of the basic principles of the landmark 1996 bankruptcy reform. Indeed, the fundamental changes to the fresh-start policy, which were adopted in the 1996 reform, were outlined in a memorandum to the Justice Minister, written by his charismatic and highly influential deputy who herself was a member of the reform commission.[26]

The bankruptcy reform of 1996 was intended to promote two seemingly contradictory goals; while the reform was designed to expand the fresh-start opportunities for certain insolvent individuals, it also had the objective of penalising certain insolvents who pursued the bankruptcy option.[27] The reform broadened the opportunities for a financial fresh start by lifting the restrictive access limitations to bankruptcy relief placed on the financially troubled 20 years earlier. Furthermore, the reform dismissed the requirement that certain debtors formally apply for a discharge of debts and significantly liberalised the standard by which a court evaluates whether to grant a bankrupt an unconditional discharge of debts.[28]

However, to deter the individual from an abusive pursuit of the bankruptcy option, the reform adopted several provisions aimed at restricting the bankrupt's ability to engage in business transactions or to undertake further consumer debt upon the filing of his bankruptcy petition. Among other penalties, the bankrupt was prohibited from holding a credit card, retaining an interest in any corporate entity, or maintaining chequing account.[29] These seemingly inconsistent objectives of the bankruptcy reform demonstrated the legislature's persisting preoccupation with neutralising any attempt made by individuals to take unfair advantage of the more liberalised bankruptcy system.[30]

[25] See Efrat, above n 1, at 102–03.

[26] See Memorandum from Davida Lachman-Messer, Deputy Justice Minister, to Dan Meridor, Justice Minister (5 Aug 1992) (on file with author).

[27] See DK (1996) 72, the statement of Yitzhak Levi, chair of the bankruptcy reform, urging the Knesset members to approve the proposed bankruptcy reform as it not only considers the creditors' interests but also serves the legitimate interests of financially troubled individuals.

[28] See the 1980 Bankruptcy Ordinance, §§ 17(b), 18, 63 as amended in 1560 SH 60, (1996).

[29] See the 1980 Bankruptcy Ordinance, §§ 42a as amended in 1560 SH 60, (1996).

[30] In her introductory comments to the bankruptcy reform subcommittee, the Deputy Justice Minister generally described the objectives of the proposed bankruptcy reform to include broad expansion of the debt-forgiveness mechanism for the financially troubled individual who has acted in good faith in incurring his debts and who has no assets to distribute to his creditors. While broadening the fresh-start policy, 'we are not covering our eyes with respect to the fraudulent debtors, and in this [reform proposal] we want to worsen the condition of the debtors in general, and to worsen the condition of fraudulent debtors in particular . . . On the one hand we give the debtor access to bankruptcy but on the other hand, we demand from him many and serious things.'

Proposed Amendment of the Bankruptcy Ordinance: Hearings Before the Subcomm. on Bankruptcy Reform of the Judiciary Comm., 13th Knesset 4 (23 May 1995) (statement of Davida Lachman-Messer, Deputy Justice Minister).

Nonetheless, the 1996 bankruptcy reform evidenced a significant departure from the rather restrictive and conservative approach to fresh-start policy in Israel. By lifting the access limitations and by liberalising the standards for obtaining debt forgiveness, the legislators demonstrated their commitment to a bankruptcy regime with some opportunity for a financial fresh start. While the reform retained and even intensified the penalties associated with filing for personal bankruptcy, the overall departure signalled a new vision for financially troubled individuals in Israel.[31]

III. THE ISRAELI BANKRUPT

The liberalisation of bankruptcy law in 1996 did not result in a dramatic increase in the number of bankruptcy petitions filed. Israel has a relatively low per capita rate of bankruptcy filing. Every year in Israel there is considerably less than one bankruptcy filing for every 1,000 people.[32] The bankruptcy filing rate in Israel is three times lower than the personal bankruptcy filing rate in England and Wales, four times lower than New Zealand,[33] at least seven times lower than the consumer bankruptcy filing rate in Australia,[34] 19 times lower than the personal bankruptcy filing rate in Canada and 32 times lower than the personal bankruptcy rate in the United States.[35] While the limited relief and the high costs of bankruptcy may have contributed to the lower rate of bankruptcy filing in Israel, Israel's low bankruptcy rate might also be attributed to stringent consumer credit standards employed by the financial sector, high personal saving

[31] See eg, *Proposed Amendment of the Bankruptcy Ordinance: Hearings Before the Subcomm. on Bankruptcy Reform of the Judiciary Comm.*, 13th Knesset 2 (30 May 1995) (statement of Davida Lachman-Messer, Deputy Justice Minister). In arguing in favour of imposing limitations on bankruptcy petitioners, Ms Lachman-Messer stated '[i]t seems to me that this is the way we can accomplish the balance that is needed between the dignity and respect of the individual on the one hand, and the need to deter people from abusing the bankruptcy system . . .'.

[32] The personal bankruptcy rate in 1997 was 0.16 per 1,000 Israeli citizens. This figure was calculated by dividing the number of personal bankruptcy filings in Israel in 1997 by the total number of individuals residing in Israel in 1997 that were 20 years old or older. The number of personal bankruptcy filings in 1997 was 587. See Computerized Printouts from the Official Receiver of the Central, Jerusalem and Southern districts (July–September 1998) (on file with author). The number of individuals that were 20 years old or older in 1997 was 3,617,000. See State of Israel Central Bureau of Statistics, Statistical Abstract of Israel 2000, Figure 2.19 (2000).

[33] See TA Sullivan, E Warren and J Lawrence Westbrook, *The Fragile Middle Class: Americans in Debt* (2000) 259, reporting that in 1997 the personal bankruptcy filing rate per 1,000 citizens was .47 in England and Wales; P Heath, 'Consumer Bankruptcies: A New Zealand Perspective', (1999) 37 *Osgoode Hall Law Journal* 30: 'By 1997, [the personal bankruptcy] figure had reached 70 per 100,000 of population.'

[34] See R Mason and J Duns, 'Developments in Consumer Bankruptcy in Australia' 2 (July 6, 2001) (unpublished manuscript, on file with author reporting a national personal bankruptcy rate of 1.1 per 1,000 head of households).

[35] See Sullivan, Warren and Westbrook, above n 33, at 259, reporting that in 1997 the personal bankruptcy filing rate per 1,000 citizens was 3.0 in Canada and 5.1 in the US.

rates, limited public awareness about the availability of bankruptcy relief and expansive social welfare programmes.[36]

As mentioned earlier, financially troubled individuals in Israel generally begin the journey of dealing with their financial crisis in the judgment execution system. Under that system, financially insolvent individuals are ordered by a clerk of the judgment execution court to make monthly payments to the creditors and, in exchange, the creditors are prohibited from pursuing any collection activities against the debtors. However, once a debtor becomes unable to go along with the ordered monthly payments, he becomes vulnerable to various collection remedies, including imprisonment.To escape the draconian nature of imprisonment, some debtors find it necessary to obtain relief under bankruptcy. Indeed, the typical petitioner in Israeli bankruptcy is, by and large, in a terrible financial condition. Most bankrupts are former small business owners. One study showed that, on average, debtors in bankruptcy had assets and income worth half of that owned or earned by the general population, but that bankrupt debtors owe crushingly more, nearly 15 times more than their average annualised income. Moreover, with their lower income, the Israeli bankrupts tend to support larger families, while having only a tenth as much net income as the general population.[37]

Bankruptcy, however, does not necessarily provide many of these financially troubled individuals with a fresh start. A recent study found that the rate of debt forgiveness in the bankruptcy sample was just under four per cent.

IV. LEGAL CULTURE

A. Introduction

The dramatic reform of the bankruptcy regime in Israel in 1996 signalled the beginning of an emerging favourable view toward the plight of financially troubled individuals in Israel. However, the legislature's intent aside, a recent empirical study of over 200 personal bankruptcy cases that were commenced after the 1996 reform suggests that, to a large extent, key reform provisions of the recent bankruptcy legislation have not been implemented, but, in fact, ignored. The study indicates that legal culture has had a powerful impact on the actual implementation of legislative reform. More specifically, the findings suggest that the values, attitudes and beliefs shared by key government officials from the Official Receiver's office seem to be playing a critical role in shaping practices in the Israeli bankruptcy system.

36 See R Efrat, 'Global Trends in Personal Bankruptcy' (2002) 76 *Bankruptcy Law Journal* 81 at 101–08.

37 See generally R Efrat, 'The Rise & Fall of Entrepreneurs: An Empirical Study of Personal Bankruptcy in Israel' (2002) 7 *Stanford Journal of Law, Business & Finance* 163.

B. Legal Culture in the American Bankruptcy System

Studies have also documented the pervasive and systematic influence legal culture has had on the operation of American personal bankruptcy system. A number of studies have found serious disparities in the implementation of bankruptcy law in different locales in the United States.[38] The authors concluded that these differences could not be explained by differences in formal law or by variations in the economic circumstances of debtors in the different localities. Instead, the authors asserted that the pervasive and systematic disparities are the product of differing local internal legal cultures in bankruptcy.[39]

The authors found that the local legal culture in personal bankruptcy in the United States is cultivated by attitudes, perceptions and beliefs held by a number of key repeat players. Since attorneys represent the vast majority of petitioners in the United States,[40] attorneys play a key role in influencing the decisions of their mostly uninformed clients. The authors persuasively argued that the attorney's own financial interests as well as moral convictions clearly affect the way in which they influence their clients.[41] However, the attorney's own financial interests and moral convictions are shaped, to a large extent, by other dominant forces that make up the local legal culture. These other dominant forces include judges,[42] the United States Trustee and the Chapter 13 Trustees[43] and the local bar.[44]

[38] For example, one study has found personal bankruptcy filing rates vary significantly among the various judicial districts across the United States. After accounting for economic differences, the study observed statistically significant variation in the filing rates of more than 100% among districts within Texas, Florida and Oklahoma. The study also found substantial geographic variation in the rates by which individual petitioners pursue bankruptcy pursuant to Chapter 7 liquidation option versus its Chapter 13 repayment plan option. Finally, the study was further able to detect dramatic variations in Chapter 13 practices among various districts. See TA Sullivan, E Warren and J Lawrence Westbrook, 'The Persistence of Local Legal Cultures: Twenty Years of Evidence from the Federal Bankruptcy Courts' (1994) 17 *Harvard Journal of Law and Public Policy* 801, 828–9. See also J Braucher, 'Lawyers, and Consumer Bankruptcy: One Code, Many Cultures' 67 *American Bankruptcy Law Journal* (1993) 501 at 532.

[39] See Sullivan, Warren and Westbrook, above n 38, at 806. See also WC Whitford, 'The Ideal of Individualized Justice: Consumer Bankruptcy as Consumer Protection, and Consumer Protection in Consumer Bankruptcy' (1994) 68 *American Bankruptcy Law Journal* 397 at 406, 408.

[40] See S Block-Lieb, 'A Comparison of Pro Bono Representation Programs for Consumer (1994) Debtors' (1994) 2 *American Bankruptcy Institute Law Review* 37 at 41 (finding that less than 15% of bankruptcy petitioners were not represented by an attorney).

[41] See Braucher, above n 38, at 546–7, 550–1; Sullivan, Warren and Westbrook, above n 38, at 852; WC Whitford, 'Has the Time Come to Repeal Chapter 13?' (1989) 65 *Indiana Law Journal* 85 at 91.

[42] Judges' attitudes and perceptions about personal bankruptcy have significant influence on how the attorneys exercise their power over their clients. For example, judges have reportedly set attorneys fees that provide financial incentive for attorneys to influence their clients to file under one chapter as opposed to another. See Sullivan, Warren and Westbrook, above n 38, at 843–5.

[43] The United States Trustee and the Chapter 13 Trustees also influence how attorneys advise their clients in bankruptcy and have helped formulate the local legal culture. An attorney's nonconformity with the United States Trustee or Chapter 13 Trustees' preferred practices may result in holding up the client's plan confirmation and/or examining with a high degree of scrutiny the

C. Legal Culture and Uniformity in Bankruptcy Practice in Israel

The findings of an empirical study of personal bankruptcy undertaken recently in Israel[45] are consistent in some fundamental respects with the empirical findings relating to the operations of the American bankruptcy system. The studies in both countries have demonstrated the impact of legal culture on the lack of uniformity in the practices among various localities in the implementation of the formal bankruptcy law. Similar to bankruptcy practices in the United States, there is substantial variance in bankruptcy practices among the four judicial districts in Israel. While none of the four districts in Israel employ exactly the same practices, there seems to be a major divide between two camps. The dominant creditor-oriented camp is characterised by practices that are primarily aimed at furthering the interests of the creditors in bankruptcy. The central, southern and northern judicial districts all belong to the creditor-oriented camp. In contrast, the emerging debtor-oriented camp is distinguished by the various practices that are predominantly aimed at enhancing the debtor's fresh-start opportunities. The only judicial district that belongs to this camp is the Jerusalem District.

A sharp difference between the creditor-camp versus the debtor-camp in Israel is the method by which courts arrive at debtors' repayment orders. In Israeli bankruptcy, most benefits awarded to debtors, such as a commencement order,[46]

attorney's fee application. As a result, most lawyers only propose Chapter 13 plans that satisfy the United States Trustee and/or Chapter 13 Trustees' preferred practices relating to the minimum debt repayment percentage. See Braucher, above n 38, at 532.

[44] The bar's collective norms have influential power over the attorneys' action because of the small size of the local bankruptcy bar and the high degree of interdependency among the few bankruptcy attorneys. See Sullivan, Warren and Westbrook, above n 38, at 848–9; Whitford, above n 39, at 409–10.

[45] A random sample of 213 bankruptcy files of individuals was selected, analysed and coded. The schedules found in the bankruptcy files included extensive information on the debtors' financial condition. Also in the bankruptcy files, copies of the Official Receiver's detailed investigatory reports and related documents provided valuable insight of the bankruptcy process. The sample was composed exclusively of individuals who voluntarily filed for bankruptcy between September 1996 and July 1998. The sample of 213 files constitutes 38% of the average annualised number of actual filings during the sample period. For further detail on the methodology of that study, see Efrat, above n 37.

[46] After a petitioner files an application for the commencement of bankruptcy protection, a court must decide whether to issue a commencement order (sometimes referred to as a receiving order). Under the bankruptcy legislation, a petitioner's application for commencing bankruptcy protection should be granted by a judge as long as: (a) the petitioner has debts that amount to no less than 10,000 NIS (approximately $2,500); (b) the petitioner attached to her application a detailed financial report relating to her family's assets, liabilities, income and expenses; and (c) the petitioner attached a written waiver allowing the Official Receiver to obtain from any source any confidential data on the petitioner's financial affairs. In addition, the petitioner must allege in the application that she is unable to repay her debts. See § 17(a) & (b) of The 1980 Bankruptcy Ordinance, as amended in 1560 SH 60, (1996). However, a court may deny a debtor's application where it determines that the debtor is able to repay her debts or for any other sufficient cause. See *ibid* at § 14.

a stay order, an adjudication order[47] or even a discharge order, are conditional on the debtors making some kind of monthly repayments to their creditors. Interestingly, despite inferior household earnings reported by petitioners in the creditor-camp as compared to the debtor-camp, courts in the two camps issue orders with similar repayment amounts. The gross monthly household income of petitioners in the debtor-oriented camp was more than two-third's higher than in the creditor-oriented camp. Nonetheless, the amount of monthly repayment was approximately the same in the two camps.

These differences apparently are the product of diametrically opposed approaches to calculating the amount the debtor should pay as a condition of commencing bankruptcy protection or as a condition of being adjudicated bankrupt. Under the bankruptcy law, a judge is given unfettered discretion to determine the amount of monthly repayments a debtor must pay as a condition of commencing bankruptcy protection or as a condition of being adjudicated as bankrupt.[48] In the debtor-friendly camp, judges generally issued monthly repayment orders that were principally based on the debtor's ability to pay. In contrast, in the creditor-oriented camp, judges tended to issue monthly repayment orders that were weighted heavily by the amount of the debtor's debts. As a result, the inferior earnings of the petitioners in districts belonging to the creditor-oriented camp seem to have played a limited role in affecting the amount the debtors were ordered to pay to creditors.

When compared to petitioners in the debtor-friendly district, petitioners filing for bankruptcy protection in the creditor-friendly districts also face a delayed and bureaucratic process. Under the bankruptcy laws in Israel, before the debtor can be officially declared bankrupt, a court must approve the debtor's petition by issuing a commencement order. While the average time for a court in the debtor-friendly district to issue a commencement order was three weeks, the average time to accomplish the same in the creditor-friendly districts was six times longer. This delay in the creditor-friendly jurisdictions postpones for that much longer the bankruptcy adjudication hearing, which is generally scheduled six months after a court issues the bankruptcy commencement order. Since it is during that bankruptcy adjudication hearing that a court may consider the issue of debt discharge, the delay in issuing a commencement order inevitably delays deliberation on the issue of discharge.[49]

[47] Six months after the issuance of a receiving order, the court must conduct a hearing to determine whether the debtor should be adjudicated and declared bankrupt.A court will generally declare the debtor bankrupt unless it finds that the debtor was acting in bad faith when she applied for bankruptcy protection, or that the debtor can repay her debts. See § 18e(a)(2) of The 1980 Bankruptcy Ordinance, as amended in 1560 SH 60, (1996).

[48] See, eg, *Bar Dror v Kasif* 37(3) PD 729 at 734 (holding that a judge is in charge of a debtor's post-petition earnings and the court has the absolute power to make decisions regarding disposition of said earnings).

[49] Six months after the issuance of a commencement order, a court must conduct a hearing to determine whether the debtor should be adjudicated and declared bankrupt. It is at that hearing that a judge may, for the first time, consider the issue of debtor's discharge. See § 18a(a) & 18e(a)(3) of The 1980 Bankruptcy Ordinance, as amended in 1560 SH 60, (1996).

Not only did it take much longer to obtain a commencement order in the creditor-oriented districts, it was also more cumbersome. For example, petitioners in the debtor-friendly district need not appear for a commencement order hearing. In contrast, petitioners in some of the creditor-friendly districts are required to attend and submit to questioning in a formal hearing for a commencement order.

Other differences between the various geographic regions exist. The four districts in Israel sharply diverge in their approach to debt forgiveness in bankruptcy. Instead of insisting that the debtor initiate an application for debt forgiveness, the 1996 reform enabled a court of its own motion, but no earlier than six months after the bankruptcy petition is filed, to raise that issue of debt forgiveness during the bankruptcy adjudication hearings of certain petitioners.[50] While there was at least a good faith attempt to implement this provision of the reform in the debtor-oriented district, the creditor-oriented districts had by and large ignored it. In the debtor-friendly district, discharge was addressed during the first six months of the case in almost 20 per cent of the cases, whereas in the creditor-oriented district it was raised anywhere from none at all to five per cent during the first six months of the case. Even in the few cases where discharge was raised, the judges in the creditor-oriented districts have always opted to deny such relief. In contrast, the courts in the debtor-friendly district have issued a discharge order at the conclusion of each of such hearings where the issue of discharge was raised.

D. Actors Shaping Legal Culture

While the studies in the United States and Israel have identified similar experiences in the lack of geographic uniformity in the implementation of bankruptcy law, some important differences in the studies' findings have surfaced. First, the studies in the United States have suggested that the influence of the American legal culture on the operations of the bankruptcy system is a product of the perceptions and views held by a number of key repeat players in the bankruptcy system (including attorneys, judges, United States Trustees, Chapter 13 Trustees and the local bar). In contrast, the study in Israel indicates that the influence of the Israeli legal culture is almost exclusively a product of the Official Receiver's attitudes and perceptions about the role of bankruptcy in Israeli society.

The Official Receiver's almost total control in shaping the legal culture in personal bankruptcy in Israel is due to the lack of interest by creditors, the lack of sophistication and representation by the petitioners and the unmatched deference given to the Official Receiver by judges. Creditors are rarely involved in the Israeli bankruptcy process.[51] The average bankruptcy petitioner has 17

[50] See § 18e(a)(3) of The 1980 Bankruptcy Ordinance, as amended in 1560 SH 60, (1996).

[51] While creditors generally take a passive role in asserting their rights in any given personal bankruptcy case, representatives of the banking industry have taken an active role in influencing the

creditors, but on average only one creditor attends the creditors' meeting. Creditors have opted not only to stay away from the creditors' meeting, but also the vast majority of them do not file a proof of claim, only a few of them attend the important hearing on debtor's bankruptcy adjudication and only a handful of them ever voice their views when debtors move to reduce monthly payments. In fact, the Official Receiver indirectly discourages creditors from getting too involved in the process as it does most of the work for them.

Just as creditors are passive players in the Israeli bankruptcy system, so are the debtors. Debtors in Israel are not influential actors in the bankruptcy system as most of them are unsophisticated individuals who are not represented by counsel. Most petitioners do not hire attorneys for the entire duration of the bankruptcy process primarily because of the prohibitive costs of representation. As a result, bankruptcy petitioners in Israel are largely uninformed about their rights and rarely assert them. The Israeli petitioners seem to rely primarily on the Official Receiver for advice and direction throughout the bankruptcy process.

Despite being repeat players in the bankruptcy process, judges do not seem to have significant influence over the legal culture in the Israeli bankruptcy system. Unlike bankruptcy judges in the United States who deal exclusively with bankruptcy matters, there are no judges in Israel that specialise in bankruptcy matters. Hence, most judges in Israel seem to have limited expertise in that obscure area of law. As a result, judges, who have only limited expertise and limited time to devote to each case, tend to defer, to a great extent, to the Official Receiver's recommendations relating to a debtor's bankruptcy petition. For example, one study found that the judges strictly followed the Official Receiver's recommendation in 97 per cent of the cases on whether to grant the debtor's application for commencing bankruptcy protection. Also, judges usually followed the Official Receiver's position relating to a debtor's application for reduction in the amount of monthly payments due. Similarly, the judges adopted most of the Official Receiver's recommendations regarding a debtor's adjudication as bankrupt. Lastly, the judges followed in most cases the Official Receiver's recommendation whether to grant the debtor a discharge.

Hence, the apathy of creditors, the powerlessness and ignorance of the petitioners, and the deference exercised by the judiciary have all helped the Official Receiver to become the dominant actor in the Israeli bankruptcy scene. By becoming the only prominent player in the Israeli bankruptcy system, the Official Receiver has been enjoying almost the exclusive power to influence and shape the legal culture in the Israeli bankruptcy regime.

The attitudes, perceptions and views of the Official Receiver in Israel help to explain the regional disparities in bankruptcy practices. The results from the empirical study indicate that the relatively autonomous directors of the regional divisions of the Official Receiver coupled with the deeply rooted historical pro-

legislative process affecting bankruptcy. See, eg, *Proposed Amendment of the Bankruptcy Ordinance: Hearings Before the Subcomm. on Bankruptcy Reform of the Judiciary Comm.*, 13th Knesset 1 (30 May 1995).

creditor institutionalised sentiments in the regional offices of the Official Receiver have contributed to the said disparities. Apparently, the leadership at the highest level of the Official Receiver in Israel, including the Chief Administrator and regional directors, has historically been exceedingly suspicious of the fresh-start policy in bankruptcy. However, with the 1994 appointment to the Official Receiver of a new chief, who was favourably predisposed towards the plight of debtors, one judicial district has embraced a pro-debtor philosophy. Nonetheless, despite the pro-debtor orientation of the new Chief Administrator of the Official Receiver, the continued pro-creditor environment in a number of regional districts of the Official Receiver was made possible by the decentralised functioning of the Official Receiver institution.

Even the pro-debtor orientation of the Jerusalem District seems to be a function of the favourable predisposition of the head of that regional district towards the fresh-start policy in bankruptcy. Indeed, the regional head's firm personal support for the early discharge provision of the bankruptcy reform was manifested in one of the cases in the sample of the study where he made a rare personal appearance before a judge to support the Official Receiver's application for an unconditional discharge of the debtor's debts.

In contrast, the pro-creditor orientation of the Northern, Southern and Central Districts seems to be a function of the firm personal views (as manifested in letters and interviews) held by the three directors of those regional districts against an expansive fresh-start policy in bankruptcy. Underlying the suspicion and, at times, resentment held by the three regional directors of the Official Receiver in the creditor-oriented camp towards the liberalised fresh-start policy is a firm belief that bankruptcy should primarily serve the interests of creditors. The regional directors of the Official Receiver in these three districts have pursued various practices that condition valuable bankruptcy-related debtor's relief on either the debtor furthering the creditors' interests or the debtor obtaining creditors' consent.

For example, the Official Receivers in these three districts have opposed, on many occasions, the debtor's request to reduce the monthly payments the debtor is required to make, reasoning that such relief would impair the creditors' interests in obtaining a meaningful repayment. Also, the Official Receiver in the Central District generally withholds its support for debtor's adjudication as bankrupt unless the few creditors who participate in the process consent. Similarly, the Official Receiver in the Southern and Northern District have withheld their support for debtor's adjudication as bankrupt when they were convinced that the debtor had failed to exert maximum efforts to repay his creditors prior to and during bankruptcy. Lastly, the Official Receiver in the Northern District has an unofficial policy of opposing the debtor's discharge unless he has made payments for a number of years that have reduced the principal balance owed to creditors by at least half.[52]

[52] See Interview with L Bar-Oz, Director of the Northern District's Official Receiver, in Haifa, Israel (9 July 1998).

Also, underlying the distrust and, at times, bitterness of these three regional heads of the Official Receiver towards the liberalised fresh-start policy is an unyielding belief that most petitioners are abusing the system and only a number of deserving debtors should be entitled to bankruptcy relief. To be regarded as a deserving petitioner, the regional heads of the Official Receiver in the pro-creditor camp generally must be convinced that the petitioner's current lifestyle and standard of living are modest. To that extent, the Official Receiver's investigative unit routinely conducts surprise visits to petitioners' homes to ascertain whether their standard of living is sufficiently low to justify adjudication as bankrupt or a reduction in monthly payments. The investigative unit also conducts the following: a comprehensive search and valuation of the debtor's assets; one-on-one questioning sessions with the debtor; interviews of third parties to ascertain the debtor's good faith in becoming insolvent; a thorough inquiry into the causes of the debtor's bankruptcy; and a review of the debtor's historical financial performance.

Lastly, to be regarded as a deserving petitioner, the debtor must not have engaged in what the regional heads of the Official Receiver in the pro-creditor camps deem to be irresponsible conduct. In one case, a pro-creditor regional head of the Official Receiver opposed the debtor's discharge application partly because the debtor 'irresponsibly' invested in the stock market. In another case, a pro-creditor regional head of the Official Receiver opposed the debtor's bankruptcy adjudication because the debtor acted 'irresponsibly' when he previously got involved in a number of business ventures that have had failed or that were poorly managed.

V. CONCLUSION

Modern western legal institutions have generally followed the trend of liberalising their approach to dealing with financially troubled individuals in the bankruptcy setting. In contrast, the legal institutions in various Jewish communities in the Diaspora and now in Israel have followed a somewhat different trend. While initially the Jewish tradition was largely obsessed with promoting the dignity and freedom of the financially troubled individual debtor, it has gradually adopted more restrictions, limitations and penalties against such an individual. Unfortunately, this trend has been reinforced and vigorously pursued in Israel during most of its first 50 years.

To a large extent, this evolution of the fresh-start policy in Israel has been shaped by the Israeli government's paternalistic orientation.[53] This attitude is

[53] Others have also referred to the Israeli government policies as paternalistic. See Y Aharoni, 'The Israeli Economy: Dreams & Realities' (London, Routledge, 1991) 328; SN Lehman-Wilzig, 'Wildfire: Grassroots Revolts in Israel in the Post-Socialist Era' (Albany, State University of New York Press, 1992) 22–31; L Sebba, 'Sanctioning Policy in Israel—An Historical Overview' (1996) 30 *Israel Law Review* 234 at 249–56 (describing the penal system in Israel as both welfarist and paternalistic).

reflected in the bankruptcy context by the system's heavy-handed and punitive approach of treating the bankrupt, while at the same time providing a broad level of property exemptions, and, whether or not bankrupt, generous welfare benefits. The government's paternalistic orientation is also reflected in the rationale the government advanced historically for restricting debtors' access to bankruptcy. On several occasions, legislative opponents of a more liberal fresh-start policy contended that it would not be in the debtors' best interests to file for bankruptcy and that the limited access offered to bankruptcy was justified as a way of preventing the debtors from harming themselves.

Moreover, the government's paternalistic orientation is manifested in the active role it has traditionally taken in the debtor-creditor relationship. To that end, the government has undertaken the de facto responsibility of collecting unpaid debts in the market place even on behalf of private creditors. This stems from the government's belief that it must collect these debts as a way of instilling morality and integrity in the country's commercial system. To accomplish those goals, the government has traditionally subsidised and continues to date to subsidise the costs of the debtors' prison system for defaulting debtors and fully finances the costs of the Official Receiver in bankruptcy. The Official Receiver is the governmental agency engaged in what one would expect the creditors to do: investigate the reasons for the financial failure of the bankrupt and vigorously search for his or her concealed assets.

While government officials continuously complain about the rising costs of administrating the bankruptcy system, they have not considered turning over the enforcement role to the creditors. Instead, they have placed the blame of cost overruns on the bankrupts by severely curtailing their access to the system. Moreover, by assuming the role of debt collector, the government has not only committed valuable public funds to this endeavour, but has also indirectly contributed to an environment whereby the creditors have passively sat on the sideline while they have delightfully accepted the bankruptcy estate's distributions generated primarily through the government's labour-intensive work.

The 1996 reform of the bankruptcy laws clearly marked an important departure from the traditionally conservative approach to the fresh-start policy in Israel. Regrettably, the groundbreaking 1996 bankruptcy reform has not been uniformly implemented. This chapter summarises evidence that supports the proposition that the internal legal culture has contributed to the wide disparities in bankruptcy practices followed by the various judicial districts in Israel. Indeed, the values, attitudes and beliefs shared by key government officials from the Official Receiver's administrative office seem to be playing the critical role in shaping practices in the Israeli personal bankruptcy system.

In addition to demonstrating the dramatic impact of the Official Receiver institution on the legal culture in the Israeli bankruptcy system, the chapter calls into question the present role of the Official Receiver in the bankruptcy regime. As stated earlier, like its counterpart in the United States and Canada, the Official Receiver in Israel has a facilitative role in the bankruptcy process. It serves as a depository of bankruptcy documents and as a liaison between the debtor, the creditors and the court. However, in stark contrast to its counterpart in the United States and Canada, the Official Receiver in Israel has assumed an investigatory role in the bankruptcy process. In that capacity, the Official Receiver routinely conducts an exhaustive investigation of the debtor's financial condition and the causes of bankruptcy.

These painstaking investigative efforts by the Official Receiver not only unduly infringe on the debtor's privacy, but also are inefficient and only marginally effective. The Official Receiver's sweeping investigatory efforts unduly infringe on the debtor's privacy because they are highly intrusive. Admittedly, most of the Official Receiver's investigatory efforts are aimed at promoting the creditors' legitimate collection interest. Nonetheless, invasion of privacy inevitably results when a government agent from the Official Receiver conducts surprise inspections of a debtor's home to ascertain whether the debtor possesses any consumer goods that are deemed luxuries, such as brand name appliances, a personal home computer or a relatively new car. Infringement of the debtor's privacy also results when an Official Receiver's agent suggests to the court that the debtor's request for bankruptcy relief should be denied because the debtor has incurred certain 'unnecessary expenses,' such as television cable fees or newspaper subscription fees.

Beyond privacy concerns, the current role of the Official Receiver raises some efficiency concerns. Since creditors are arguably the more efficient risk bearers in a credit transaction,[54] it is the duty of legislators to provide creditors with incentives to engage in due diligence when extending credit. However, when a government assures creditors that it will undertake and finance investigation and collection activities for the creditors' bad debt, it provides little incentive for creditors to engage in the necessary level of due diligence. By handling and paying for most of the collection costs in bankruptcy, the government in Israel has reduced the costs of bad loans to creditors, and thereby made the need for creditors' due diligence less apparent. Further, by agreeing to finance investigative costs in bankruptcy, the government has assumed a role that presumably can be handled just as effectively but with more efficiency by creditors, who are in the business of lending and collecting money.[55] The efficiency argument against a government role in investigating insolvencies is particularly compelling in the Israeli bankruptcy system since relatively sophisticated creditors—primarily financial institutions—are by far the largest creditors in the pool of bankruptcy

[54] See SL Harris, 'A Reply to Theodore Eisenberg's Bankruptcy Law in Perspective' (1982) 30 *UCLA Law Review* 327 at 362; M Howard, 'A Theory of Discharge in Consumer Bankruptcy' (1987) 48 *Ohio State Law Journal* 1047 at 1063–4; TH Jackson, 'The Fresh-Start Policy in Bankruptcy Law' (1985) 98 *Harvard Law Review* 1393 at 1399.

[55] To address the collective action problem, whereby some creditors may be reluctant to undertake collection costs and then have to share with other creditors the benefits derived from such efforts, reform legislation may consider the establishment of a creditors' committee feature, whereby costs of the committee will be borne by the bankruptcy estate.

creditors.[56] Lastly, from an overall public policy consideration, it seems unnecessary and unwise to use scarce public resources to subsidise the enormous investigation and collection efforts relating to bad credit extended largely by sophisticated, private creditors.

Finally, the current role of the Official Receiver in Israel is not cost effective. While no exact figures are available, the expanded role of the Official Receiver in the Israeli bankruptcy system is costly.[57] The fixed, as well as the marginal costs associated with retaining a staff of investigators, financial analysts, attorneys and administrators who are expected to vigorously lead the investigative efforts relating to each bankruptcy petition must be significant. The costs seem to be especially unjustifiable in light of the small potential returns to creditors in most cases. While no published data is available on the actual bankruptcy repayment rate, the repayment rate in the parallel system of civil judgment execution, where the government is equally involved in the collection process, is a dismal five per cent of total debts.[58] Similar concerns about the cost effectiveness of an expansive government role in the bankruptcy system were voiced in England in the early 1980s, before it abandoned the discretionary discharge regime.[59] Scholars in the United States have also expressed uneasiness about the cost effectiveness of proposed legislation that would have mandated a larger governmental role in personal bankruptcy.[60]

A reconceptualisation of the Official Receiver's role in the Israeli bankruptcy system should take the burden and expense of investigation away from the Official Receiver. Such a move might prompt creditors to extend credit more efficiently, and assume the role and costs of bad-debt investigation. This shift would eliminate unnecessary public expenditure and make the creditors bear the collection costs arising out of defaults. This would place the burden of default on the party presumably able to absorb the costs most efficiently.

In addition to reducing the government's role in bankruptcy, there is an urgent need to give debtors more power. As suggested earlier, due to lack of representation, bankruptcy petitioners in Israel are largely uninformed about their rights and hence they rarely assert them. Instead they tend to rely on the Official

[56] More than 50% of the debtors' average total debts are owed to relatively sophisticated financial institutions. The average debt owed by the bankrupt population to financial institutions was 562,642 NIS. The average total debt owed by the bankrupt population was 1,120,942 NIS. A similar finding was reported in a Canadian bankruptcy sample. See I Ramsay, 'Individual Bankruptcy: Preliminary Findings of Socio-Legal Analysis' (1999) 37 *Osgoode Hall Law Journal* 15 at 53–4 ('Debts owed to financial institutions represent over two-thirds of total debt outstanding.').

[57] See A Shaharabani-Bomgertan *et al*, 'The Reform in Bankruptcy Law' (1996) 7 *Haglima* 14 at 14.

[58] See R Harris, 'From Imprisonment to Discharge: Setting an Agenda for Reform in Debtor-Creditor Law' (2000) 23 *Tel-Aviv University Law Review* 641 at 641, quoting a newspaper article that reported that only 5% of debts submitted for collection in the Israeli judgment execution system are collected despite the substantial public resources expended on the collection undertaking.

[59] See DG Boshkoff, 'Limited, Conditional, and Suspended Discharges in Anglo-American Bankruptcy Proceedings' (1982) 131 *University of Pennsylvania Law Review* 69 at 102.

[60] See E Warren, 'The Bankruptcy Crisis' (1998) 73 *Indiana Law Journal* 1079 at 1090–1.

Receiver for advice. Since the Official Receiver does not generally view itself as an advocate for debtors, the reliance of debtors on the Official Receiver is misplaced.

Debtor empowerment in Israeli bankruptcy practice could be achieved, to an extent, by making it possible for more debtors to be represented by attorneys. An increased rate of representation would result in increased access to available debt relief in bankruptcy, since attorneys would likely assert available rights on behalf of the debtors and as the attorneys would presumably serve as a watchdog against government and creditor overreaching. Recent elimination of prohibitions on attorney advertising[61] should, in the foreseeable future, enhance competition for rendering legal services, reduce the costs of legal representation, and lead to increased affordability and hence to a higher rate of represented and empowered debtors in the Israeli bankruptcy system.[62]

[61] See Attorney Bar ordinances, 2001, KT 6094, 629.

[62] Empirical studies in the US suggest that increased advertising by attorneys reduces the price of legal representation in the long run. See Federal Trade Commission Staff, Improving Consumer Access to Legal Services: The Case for Removing Restrictions on Truthful Advertising (November 1984).

9

Current Trends in Consumer Insolvency in Hong Kong

CHARLES D BOOTH*

I. INTRODUCTION

BANKRUPTCY[1] IS ON the rise in Hong Kong, at levels never before seen in the jurisdiction. The 2,441 petitions filed in November 2002 set a monthly filing record. Even more dramatic is the level of petitions filed by debtors themselves. The following figures, drawn from the Official Receiver's Office website[2] put the overall situation into perspective:

The overall increase in bankruptcy filings over the last decade, from 224 in 1989 to 26,922 in 2002 is astounding. The total number of petitions filed in 2002 represents more than a 120-fold increase from the 224 petitions filed in 1989 and exceeds the combined number of filings from January 1989 through November 2001 (26,526)! The number of monthly filings alone in November 2002 (2,441) is greater than the *total* number of petitions filed from 1989 through 1994 (2,115) or from 1994 through 1996 (1,843).

Even more dramatic is the mammoth increase in annual filings by debtors from a mere 3 in 1994 to 25,138 in 2002. From 1994 to 2002, the percentage of total bankruptcy cases filed by debtors has increased from 0.71 per cent to 93.37 per cent. These statistics demonstrate that there has been a huge cultural change in Hong Kong—from bankruptcy being a procedure that creditors used against

* This chapter is an expanded and updated version of 'Consumer Bankruptcy in Hong Kong: Record Level of Filings is Likely to Continue,' (Aug 2002), *Hong Kong Lawyer* 72. Earlier versions were presented at the Recent Developments in Consumer Bankruptcy Panel Session at the Joint Meetings of the Law and Society Association and Research Committee on the Sociology of Law in Budapest, Hungary, on 6 July 2001, and at the Academics Meeting, INSOL International 6th World Congress, London, England, on 18 July 2001. I am grateful to Ms Wendy Chiu, Senior Research Assistant (AIIFL), for her research assistance in the preparation of this chapter.

[1] In Hong Kong, the insolvency law of individuals is separate from that of companies. The former is called bankruptcy law and is contained in the Bankruptcy Ordinance (cap 6), Laws of Hong Kong (the LHK) [the Bankruptcy Ordinance], and the latter is called liquidation (or winding-up) law and is contained in the Companies Ordinance (cap 32), LHK [the Companies Ordinance].

[2] <http://www.info.gov.hk/oro/statistics/statistics.htm>.

Table 1 Bankruptcy Petitions and Receiving Orders 1994–2002

Year	Number of bankruptcy petitions	Number of petitions filed by debtors	% of overall petitions filed by debtors	Number of receiving/ bankruptcy orders made*
1994	420	3	0.71	306
1995	643	10	1.56	455
1996	780	23	2.95	543
1997	829	39	4.70	639
1998 (Jan–Mar)**	262	19	7.25	165
1998 (Apr–Dec)**	1,100	473	43.0	728
Total 1998	1,362	492	36.12	893
1999	3,876	2,721	70.20	3,071
2000	5,487	3,810	69.44	4,606
2001	13,186	11,089	84.10	9,151
2002	26,922	25,138	93.37	25,328

* The Bankruptcy (Amendment) Ordinance 1996 came into operation on 1 April 1998.

** The data refers to receiving orders prior to 1 April 1998 and to bankruptcy orders on or after that date.

recalcitrant debtors to a mechanism that debtors choose as a solution to their financial problems.

Part II of this chapter will first set out the reasons for the dramatic increase in the number of bankruptcy cases and, in so doing, highlight some important changes recently made to Hong Kong bankruptcy law. Part III will then turn to the new voluntary arrangement ('VA') procedure (a collective debt discharge/ repayment procedure), which thus far has not proved as popular for either debtors or creditors, but which recently is increasing in use. From there, in Part IV the focus will switch to an analysis of the causes of consumer bankruptcy in Hong Kong and then in Part V to the role of credit card debt in consumer bankruptcies. The chapter will conclude by considering where bankruptcy and VA levels are likely to go from here.

II. REASONS FOR THE INCREASE IN BANKRUPTCY CASES

The dramatic increase in the level of the filings results from several factors. Part of the overall increase in the number of cases is due to the fallout from the Asian financial crisis that hit Hong Kong in late 1997 and early 1998 and the poor economic conditions that have remained since then. However, the weak Hong Kong economy cannot fully explain the dramatic increase in the number of self-petitions, which has accounted for the lion's share of the increase in the number of bankruptcy filings. Rather, the factor primarily responsible for the increase in the number of self-petitions is the enactment of the Bankruptcy (Amendment) Ordinance 1996[3] (the 'BAO'), which came into operation on 1 July 1998. This legislation made sweeping changes to Hong Kong bankruptcy law, the first in over a century. These amendments are responsible for the change in the way that debtors (especially consumers) view bankruptcy.

The old Hong Kong bankruptcy law dated back to the late nineteenth century, a time in which bankruptcy was primarily a weapon to be used by creditors against uncooperative merchants. For creditors to commence cases under the old law, they had to prove that the debtor had committed an 'act of bankruptcy,' a concept with origins in early English statutes from the Middle Ages.[4] Most of the acts of bankruptcy contained in the old bankruptcy law were premised on wrongful actions by the debtor, such as making a fraudulent conveyance of one's property[5] or removing one's property from the jurisdiction with the intent to defeat or delay one's creditors.[6] At the heart of the concept of acts of bankruptcy was the notion that a gentleman repays his debts and that a bankruptcy petition was justifiable when a gentleman's actions made it clear that he would not be doing so.

Under the old régime, once a debtor became bankrupt, the norm was for him to remain a bankrupt for the rest of his life.[7] Although discharge was theoretically possible, it was very difficult to achieve in practice. Many years it was not unusual for only one per cent of bankrupts to obtain a discharge.[8] The limited exemption of the property of the estate that a bankrupt was able to retain further contributed to the punitive nature of the procedure (although the trustee in practice usually ignored the limitation[9]). The old section 43 of the Bankruptcy Ordinance enabled a bankrupt to retain only the following:

> The tools (if any) of his trade and the necessary wearing apparel and bedding of himself and his family dependent on and residing with him, to a value, inclusive of tools and apparel and bedding, not exceeding [HK]$3,000 in the whole.

A. Bankruptcy Law Reform[10]

By the late 1980s, it had become clear that many aspects of the old bankruptcy law (such as the old section 43) had become obsolete and were inadequate to

[3] Hong Kong Bankruptcy (Amendment) Ordinance 1996, Ord No 76 of 1996 [the BAO], as incorporated into the Bankruptcy Ordinance.

[4] See Act Against Such As Do Make Bankrupt, 34 and 35 Henry VIII ch 4 (1542); 13 Eliz ch 7 (1571).

[5] Bankruptcy Ordinance, above n 1, old s 3(1)(b).

[6] *Ibid* old s 3(1)(d).

[7] The Law Reform Commission of Hong Kong, *Report on Bankruptcy* (Hong Kong, Government Printer, May 1995), para 17.1, at 156.

[8] For example, during the 10-year period from 1983 to 1992. See *ibid* para 17.8, at 161.

[9] *Ibid* para 13.5, at 121.

[10] For a more detailed discussion of the changes made by the BAO, *see* CD Booth, 'Leaping forward to 1997: Bankruptcy Law Reform in Hong Kong,' (1997) 6 *International Insolvency Review*

address many of the problems that debtors were confronting in Hong Kong's growing consumer credit economy. The bankruptcy law reform effort that ensued was part of an overall review of Hong Kong insolvency law that began in September 1990 when the Law Reform Commission of Hong Kong (the 'Law Reform Commission') appointed a Sub-Committee on Insolvency to conduct a review of bankruptcy and liquidation law and practice in Hong Kong. The Sub-Committee issued its *Consultative Document on Bankruptcy* in August 1993[11] and the Law Reform Commission's *Report on Bankruptcy* followed in May 1995.[12] The Commission's recommendations adopted most of the proposals of the Sub-Committee[13] and were incorporated into the Bankruptcy (Amendment) Bill 1996[14] and then into the BAO, which was enacted in December 1996. However, the legislation did not come into operation until 1 April 1998, in part to provide the government with sufficient time to draft appropriate bankruptcy rules.[15] Thus, it was pure coincidence that the new bankruptcy law was enacted at the time that the effects of the Asian financial crisis were gripping Hong Kong. If the law reform process had been more efficient, the new legislation would have been enacted several years earlier.

The enactment of new insolvency legislation does not necessarily lead to a dramatic increase in case filings. This has certainly been the experience of most Asian jurisdictions that have enacted new corporate insolvency laws in the aftermath of the Asian financial crisis.[16] However, the experience in Hong Kong in relation to personal bankruptcy law has been quite different. Within nine months of the enactment of the new law (the last nine months of 1998), the number of petitions filed by debtors increased more than 12-fold to 473. Since then, the number of self-petitions has continued to increase to record annual levels.

Prior to 1 April 1998, there was little incentive for a debtor to file his own bankruptcy petition. It was more sensible to try to make do and wait to see if one's creditors would eventually file a petition. The statistics set out above show that this is no longer the case. More and more debtors in Hong Kong have come

183. *See also* CD Booth 'Hong Kong Insolvency Law Reform: Preparing for the Next Millenium,' (2001) *Journal of Business Law* 126 at 134–46.

[11] Law Reform Commission of Hong Kong Sub-Committee on Insolvency, *Consultative Document on Bankruptcy* (Hong Kong, Government Printer, Aug 1993).

[12] See *Report on Bankruptcy*, above n 7.

[13] But see the Law Reform Commission's discussion of the jurisdictional criterion involving the presence of assets, *ibid* paras 2.12-.36, at 23–29, and of the relation back doctrine, *ibid*, paras 14.5–14.13, at 134–37.

[14] Bankruptcy (Amendment) Bill 1996, *Legal Supplement No 3 to the Hong Kong Government Gazette*, 1 March 1996.

[15] The Hong Kong Bankruptcy (Amendment) Rules 1998 (LN 77 of 1998) (13 Feb 1998), incorporated into the Hong Kong Bankruptcy Rules, cap 6, sub leg A, LHK [the Bankruptcy Rules]. The Bankruptcy Rules are in the form of subsidiary legislation dealing with procedural aspects of bankruptcy.

[16] See 'Insolvency Law Reforms in the Asian Region—Report of the Office of the General Counsel on TA 5795–Reg: Insolvency Law Reforms' in *Law and Policy Reform at the Asian Development Bank*, Vol 1 (Apr 2000) 70–72.

to view bankruptcy law as a viable option for addressing their financial problems and have filed self-petitions. Some well-known celebrities have also pursued this strategy; the cantopop singer Kenny Bee is a recent high-profile example.

B. Automatic Discharge

The greatest incentive for debtors to use the new bankruptcy law is the ability to benefit from the automatic discharge and achieve a fresh start—to escape from one's financial problems and become free of onerous debt obligations. Under the new section 30A of the Bankruptcy Ordinance, an automatic discharge is available to bankrupts. In the absence of objections by either the trustee or the bankrupt's creditors,[17] a first-time bankrupt will be discharged from bankruptcy four years from the date of the bankruptcy order; and repeat bankrupts will be discharged in five years. Where valid objections are raised, these periods may be extended for up to eight years.[18] For bankrupts who flee Hong Kong pre-or post-commencement (or who fail to return to Hong Kong on a date or within a period specified by the trustee), these periods do not begin to run until the bankrupt returns to Hong Kong and notifies the trustee. Thus, bankrupts who flee Hong Kong and never return can never be discharged.

The overall structure of the discharge provisions is based on the carrot and stick approach. The sticks consist of the possibility of a delayed discharge for up to 8 years, or longer for absconding debtors. A carrot offered to bankrupts is included in the early discharge provision in the new section 30B, which is available to qualifying debtors.[19]

[17] In 2001–2002, objections to discharge were raised in 59 cases and 497 bankrupts were discharged under the automatic discharge procedure. Official Receiver's Office, *2001–2002 Official Receiver's Office Annual Departmental Report* (Hong Kong, Official Receiver's Office, 2002), para 3.14 at 99.

[18] The new s 30A(9) provides that the granting of a discharge may be conditional on a bankrupt continuing to make contributions to his estate for up to 8 years from the date of the bankruptcy order.

[19] The court shall not order an early discharge if the bankrupt has done any of the following: previously entered into a composition, scheme of arrangement or a VA; has unsecured liabilities that exceed 150% of his income (as determined by the trustee) during the year immediately preceding the date of the bankruptcy order; has failed to disclose a beneficial interest in any property; has failed to disclose any liability that existed at the date of the bankruptcy order; has failed to disclose in his statement of affairs income that he expected to receive in the 12 months after filing the statement; has engaged after the making of the bankruptcy order in misleading conduct in relation to a person in respect of an amount or amounts exceeding HK$15,000; has after the making of the bankruptcy order, continued to act as a director or has taken part in the management of a company, except with the leave of the court, contrary to s 156 of the Companies Ordinance; has failed or refused to give his passport or other travel document to the trustee when requested to do so; or has failed to co-operate with the trustee.

C. Exempted Property

Since 1 April 1998, bankrupts have also benefitted from the liberalizsed exemption provisions in the revised section 43 of the Bankruptcy Ordinance. The HK$3,000 cap in the old section 43 had become unworkable and has been abolished. The new section 43(2) does not include a dollar limit on exempted property. Rather, it provides that bankrupts may retain:

> (a) such tools, books, vehicles, and other items of equipment as are necessary to the bankrupt for use personally by him in his employment, business or vocation;
> (b) such clothing, bedding, furniture, household equipment and provisions as are necessary for satisfying the basic domestic needs of the bankrupt and his family.

To prevent abuses, the trustee is permitted by the new section 43B of the Bankruptcy Ordinance to claim items of excess value from the bankrupt. In addition, the bankrupt's creditors may apply to the trustee to include a particular item in the bankrupt's estate.[20] Another change to the law is in section 43A, which provides that property which the bankrupt acquires post-petition does not vest in the trustee unless the trustee serves a notice in writing to claim the property.[21] Lastly, the new section 43E authorises the court, on the application of the trustee, to make 'an income payments order' pursuant to which the bankrupt must pay to his estate a portion of his income for the period in which the order is in effect, which in theory, could continue post-discharge. However, in practice, income payment orders are quite rare. One reason for their infrequent use is that it is not uncommon for bankrupts to make voluntary contributions to creditors on a monthly basis up to the time of discharge.[22]

D. Family Home

A further benefit for bankrupts is included in the new section 43F of the Bankruptcy Ordinance, which enables a bankrupt to continue occupying his family home for a period of six months from the making of the bankruptcy order. The debtor may apply to the court for a further six-month extension, but section 43F(2) provides that 'the court shall assume, unless the circumstances of the case are exceptional, that the interests of the bankrupt's creditors outweigh all other considerations.'

[20] New s 43D.

[21] Previously, all post-petition property vested in the trustee, which proved administratively cumbersome and was difficult to enforce. See Report on Bankruptcy, above n 7, para 13.51, at 130.

[22] It is estimated by the Official Receiver's Office that such voluntary contributions are made in 20–35% of all bankruptcy cases.

E. Abolition of Acts of Bankruptcy

The notion of acts of bankruptcy has been abolished. Although the abolition is not directly relevant to self-petitions by debtors, it is still significant because it demonstrates that the reformed law has moved away from the notion that a debtor's wrongful actions should trigger a bankruptcy filing in favour of the notion that a petition should be based on the debtor's problematic financial condition. The balance has quite clearly shifted in favour of rehabilitating rather than punishing the debtor. This not to say, however, that punitive provisions are no longer contained in the Bankruptcy Ordinance. Many such provisions are listed as bankruptcy offences in Part VIII of the Ordinance.

III. VOLUNTARY ARRANGEMENTS[23]

When considering the high level of bankruptcy cases in Hong Kong, some thought should be given to why more debtors have not pursued the new voluntary arrangement ('VA') procedure as an alternative to filing a bankruptcy petition. The enactment of the VA procedure was intended to address inadequacies under the old bankruptcy law. Under the bankruptcy law prior to 1 April 1998, following the making of a receiving order against a debtor, the debtor's creditors were to decide at their first meeting whether to accept a proposal for a composition or a scheme of arrangement. In theory, this was intended to give the creditors the option of avoiding a liquidation of the debtor's assets. In practice, however, by the time the bankruptcy petition was filed it was usually too late for a debtor to negotiate a settlement with his creditors, so such proposals were rarely accepted.

One of the important reforms included in the BAO was the adoption of a VA procedure that is based on the Individual Voluntary Arrangement ('IVA') procedure contained in Part VIII of the UK Insolvency Act 1986. The VA procedure is available to both bankrupts and non-bankrupts, but most importantly the procedure enables a debtor to seek relief at an earlier stage of his financial difficulties and thereby avoid the stigma attached to the commencement of a bankruptcy case.

The VA procedure is included in the new sections 20–20L of the Bankruptcy Ordinance. New section 20A permits a debtor (or where the debtor is an undischarged bankrupt, the debtor, the trustee, or the Official Receiver) to apply for an interim order. Pursuant to the new section 20(2), the making of an interim order provides the debtor with a moratorium—during the period in which the order is in effect, a bankruptcy petition may not be presented or proceeded with

[23] For further discussion of Voluntary Arrangements, see S Briscoe, 'Personal Insolvency and the Individual Voluntary Arrangement: Theory and Practice,' (2002) 32 *Hong Kong Law Journal* 343.

against the debtor and no other proceedings, execution, legal process or distress may be commenced or continued against the debtor except with the leave of the court.

To initiate the VA procedure, a debtor should contact an insolvency practitioner with a view to gaining advice as to putting a proposal to his creditors and to getting the practitioner to agree to serve as the nominee in relation to the VA.[24] The theory underlying the new procedure is that both the debtor and creditors will benefit. The debtor will be able to avoid the stigma that flows from being an adjudicated bankrupt. The creditors, in turn, will benefit from a higher level of distribution from the debtor's payments out of future cash flow than would be possible if the debtor's assets were liquidated.

Despite the potential advantages of a VA over bankruptcy, the number of VAs in Hong Kong has been quite low. From 1 April 1998 through 31 December 2001 only 12 VAs were approved. In 2002, the number of VAs started to increase, and by year's end an additional 520 VAs were approved.[25] This creates a ratio of roughly one VA for every 50 bankruptcies. This ratio remains far below the level of IVAs in England and Wales—the data from England and Wales shows that in 2000–2001, for every three bankruptcies, there was roughly one IVA.[26] Even at the recent rate of use, the number of VAs in Hong Kong still pales in comparison to the rate of IVAs in England and Wales.

The attitudes of both debtors and creditors have contributed to the low levels of VAs. Debtors have not pursued the procedure in great numbers, and where they have tried to resort to the procedure, their creditors (especially the financial institutions) have (until recently) not been supportive. Some of the factors that are frequently mentioned in Hong Kong as contributing to the low number of VAs are as follows:

i. The morality argument—banks and credit card companies still distrust individuals who do not repay their debts and desire to punish such individuals by forcing them to resort to bankruptcy;
ii. The large number of creditors in many of these cases makes it difficult for an agreement to be reached; and

[24] Prior to 2 Sept 2002, the Official Receiver was also willing to serve as a nominee under a VA. In cases commenced on or after 2 Sept 2002, the Official Receiver only serves in the role of a facilitator. However, the policy change was not retroactive and the Official Receiver continues to serve as nominee in cases commenced prior to 2 Sept 2002.

[25] The monthly number of approved VAs is as follows: Jan—4; Feb—7; Mar—3; Apr—3; May—3; June—18; July—27; Aug—18; Sept—54; Oct—76; Nov— 90; and Dec—217. Figures supplied by the Official Receiver's Office, Jan 2003.

[26] In 2001 there were 6,298 IVAs and 23,477 bankruptcy orders, for a ratio of .27 IVAs per bankruptcy. The equivalent ratio for 2000 was .37. See The Insolvency Service <http://www.insolvency.gov.uk/information/stats/statistics.htm>.

iii. VAs are best suited to cases involving individuals in higher income brackets, which excludes the majority of bankrupts (and certainly all those who are unemployed).[27]

Most financial institutions in Hong Kong appear to have a double standard: institutions that are reluctant to push their corporate customers into liquidation and instead try to structure rehabilitation under the *Guidelines on Corporate Difficulties* issued by the Hong Kong Monetary Authority ('HKMA') and the Hong Kong Association of Banks ('HKAB')[28] nevertheless are reluctant to enter into VAs with individual bankrupts. Perhaps there has been a concern among banks in Hong Kong that their general acceptance of the VA procedure would lead even more debtors to default on their credit card bills. However, with the charge-off rates increasing to all-time highs in 2002, with the year-to-date annualised percentage standing at 13.25 per cent at the end of the fourth quarter of 2002 (in contrast to 5.46 per cent per cent at the end of the fourth quarter of 2001),[29] it is clear that there are thousands of consumers in Hong Kong who currently are unable to pay back their credit card debt. If the banks and finance companies were willing to adopt a more flexible approach to such consumers, it is arguable that the banks would, in many cases, recoup a higher percentage of their debts in VAs than they are receiving in the debtors' bankruptcy proceedings. In fact, this is now starting to happen.

IV. CAUSES OF CONSUMER BANKRUPTCY

One response to the dramatic increase in the number of bankruptcy cases has been the assertion that the current level is too high and should be reduced. For example, legislator Chan Kam-lam was quoted as calling for a review of the bankruptcy law with a view to extending the current four-year period leading to the automatic discharge and thereby providing more of a deterrence.[30] It is also understood that many banks have voiced similar concerns to the Official Receiver's Office.

However, before criticising the high level of bankruptcies, it is first necessary to ascertain the reason for bankruptcy filings and analyse the data in the context of current economic conditions. A high bankruptcy rate may be healthy for

[27] See Arthur Andersen, *Review of the Role of the Official Receiver's Office Consultation Paper* (Hong Kong, Financial Services Bureau, June 2002), para 3.6, at 17.

[28] Hong Kong Monetary Authority (HKMA) & Hong Kong Association of Banks (HKAB), *Hong* 'Hong Kong Approach to Corporate Difficulties (Guidelines on Corporate Difficulties),' (11/99) *HKMA Quarterly Bulletin* 13–16.

[29] The information is available on the HKMA's website at: Media Release (2002), 'Credit Card Lending Survey Results for Fourth Quarter 2002,' HKMA <http://www.info.gov.hk/hkma/eng/press/2003/20030217e3.htm> ['Lending Survey'].

[30] C Lo and S Lee, 'Suspected bankruptcy fraud cases balloon,' *South China Morning Post* (14 June 2001) 7.

society if it provides honest debtors caught in a downward credit spiral[31] with a fresh start, but unhealthy if it creates incentives for dishonest debtors to go on shopping sprees with credit cards that they have no intention of ever repaying.

What does the data say? Who is the typical debtor in Hong Kong? At the outset, it is clear that the number of alleged bankruptcy fraud cases is on the increase. In 2002, 619 suspected bankruptcy fraud cases were lodged by banks, finance companies and the Official Receiver's Office, more than doubling the figure for the whole of 2001 (263 cases) and increasing by more than 56 times the number from 2000 (11 cases).[32] Although such cases are on the increase, the level of fraud remains low when viewed in the overall context of the 26,922 bankruptcy cases commenced in 2002, which amounts to a ratio of 2.3 per cent.

One of the best sources about the causes of bankruptcy is the data collected by the Official Receiver's Office. The data below is drawn from the *2000–2001 Official Receiver's Office Annual Departmental Report*[33] and the *2001–2002 Official Receiver's Office Annual Departmental Report*.[34] (The data included in these *Reports* is based on a reporting year running from 1 April–31 March, in contrast to the data on the Official Receiver's Office website, which is based on actual calendar years.)

For 2000–2001, there was a total of 4,928 bankruptcies in which bankruptcy orders were made. Of this total, 429 (8.7 per cent) were individuals engaged in trading, 4,395 (89.2 per cent) were non-trading individuals (who will be referred to below as consumers), and the remaining 104 (2.1 per cent) were unknown.[35] For 2001–2002, there was a total of 11,764 bankruptcies in which bankruptcy orders were made. Of this total, 443 (3.8 per cent) were individuals engaged in trading, 11,037 (93.8 per cent) were consumers, and the remaining 284 (2.4 per cent) were unknown.[36]

The nature of the major creditor's claim in consumer bankruptcies 2000–2001 and 2001–2002 was as follows as set out in Table 2.[37]

The main causes of failure leading to consumer bankruptcy in 2000–2001 and 2001–2002 were as laid out in Table 3.[38]

The information in Table 3 is quite helpful in getting a sense of the causes of bankruptcy. Loss of employment is by far the most important cause of consumer bankruptcies. The unemployment rate in Hong Kong is one of the

[31] For example, debtors whose financial difficulties are triggered by unemployment, the collapse of property and stock markets, high medical costs or high interest rates on credit cards.

[32] P Moy, 'Alarm as bankruptcy fraud leaps by 135pc,' *South China Morning Post* (9 Feb 2003) 4.

[33] Official Receiver's Office, *2000–2001 Official R eceiver's Office Annual Departmental Report* (Hong Kong, Official Receiver's Office, 2001) [2000–2001 Annual Report].

[34] See *2001–2002 Annual Report*, above n 17.

[35] *2000–2001 Annual Report,* above n 33, Annex 7.

[36] *2001–2002 Annual Report,* above n 17, Annexes 8 and 10.

[37] *2000–2001 Annual Report,* above n 33, Annex 7; *2001–2002 Annual Report,* above n 17, Annex 10.

[38] *Ibid*, Annex 6.

Table 2 Nature of major creditor's claim

Claim	Number and % of cases 2000–2001	Number and % of cases 2001–2002
Consumer Credit	3,501 (79.7%)	9,544 (86.5%)
Guaranteed Debt	620 (14.1%)	804 (7.3%)
Others (including personal loans, rent arrears, etc.)	274 (6.2%)	689 (6.2%)

Table 3 Causes of failure for consumers

Cause	Number and % of cases 2000–2001	Number and % of cases 2001–2002
Lack of gainful employment	1,554 (36.5%)	4,861 (44.3%)
Excessive use of credit facilities	640 (15%)	1,408 (12.8%)
Overspending	488 (11.5%)	1,200 (10.9%)
Loss in investment	482 (11.3%)	1,235 (11.3%)
Personal guarantee liabilities	467 (11%)	621 (5.7%)
Gambling	299 (7%)	613 (5.6%)
Speculation in shares, etc.	98 (2.3%)	141 (1.3%)
Others	230 (5.4%)	888 (8.1%)
Total	4,258	10,967

highest in Asia and remains over 7 per cent.[39] A portion of the cases triggered by the personal guarantee liabilities are possibly also job related, because many of these cases are likely to include calls made on company directors or officers who guaranteed corporate debt that their company was unable to pay back. Thus, up to 45–50 per cent of bankruptcy cases are triggered by the loss of employment or contingent claims resulting from corporate failure.

From Table 2 above, it can be seen that in a whopping 79.7 per cent of cases in 2000–2001 and 86.5 per cent in 2001–2002 the nature of the creditor's major claim was consumer credit. In addition, as shown in Table 3, in roughly a quarter of all cases (combining the excessive use of credit facilities and overspending) consumer spending was the cause of the debtor's failure, with another 11 per cent of cases being caused by investment losses.

Further data profiling of bankrupts in Hong Kong recently released by the Official Receiver's Office further demonstrates the connection between consumers, credit card debt and personal bankruptcy.[40] This data was compiled

[39] After climbing from a seasonally adjusted rate of 4.5% in April–June 2001 to a high of 7.8% in May–July 2002, the rate steadily declined to 7.1% for the period Sept–Nov 2002, and then increased to 7.2% for the period Oct–Dec 2002. See HKMA <http://www.info.gov.hk/censtatd/eng/hkstat/fas/labour/ghs/labour1_index.html>.

[40] Strictly speaking, since the data was drawn from both consumers and non-consumers, some of the conclusions regarding consumers and consumer debt may be slightly skewed.

from a sample of 200 bankruptcy cases (in which bankruptcy orders were issued) for a seven-month period running from 26 November 2001 to 24 June 2002. The Official Receiver's Office claims that this sampling offers a realistic view of the recent bankruptcy caseloads in Hong Kong.

Table 4 Income and Age of Bankrupts

Monthly Income (in HK$)	Age <=30	Age 31–40	Age 41–50	Age >=51	Total	%
0	14	30	23	6	73	36.50
above $0-$ 10,000	21	18	21	5	65	32.50
above $10,000–$20,000	14	19	15	5	53	26.50
above $20,000–$25,0000	0	3	2	0	5	2.50
above $25,000–$30,000	0	0	0	0	0	0.00
above $30,0000	0	1	3	0	4	2.00
Total	49	71	64	16	200	100.00
%	24.5	35.50	32.00	8.0		

Table 5 Types of Residences of Bankrupts

Public Housing	Private Rented Apartment	Charged Self-owned Property	Total
86	98	16	200
43%	49%	8%	100%

Table 6 Total Liabilities of Bankrupts

Liabilities (in HK$)	No. of Bankrupts	%
$200,000 or below	39	19.50
above $200,000–$400,000	85	42.50
above $400,000–$600,000	38	19.00
above $600,000–$800,000	16	8.00
above $800,000–$1,000,000	6	3.00
above $1,000,000–$2,000,000	9	4.50
above $2,000,000–$6,000,000	7	3.50
Total:	200	100.00

In this sampling of bankrupts, the average indebtedness was nearly HK$500,000 (approximately US$64,500). The average number of creditors in the same was 12.3, and the average number of credit cards held was nearly nine.

The data collected by the Official Receiver's Office shows that the majority of bankrupts are at the low end of the salary scale: 36.5 per cent of the sample are unemployed and an additional 59 per cent earn less than HK$20,000 (approximately US$2,600 at the rate of HK$7.75/US$1) per month. The typical bankrupt lives in public housing or a rental dwelling, carries nine credit cards, and has total liabilities of roughly HK$500,000, owed to 12 creditors. For the two-thirds of the sample with a monthly income of HK$10,000 or less, this average debt load would be at least 50 times the monthly income. With the average outstanding indebtedness at such a high level, many bankrupts would face annual interest charges exceeding their annual pay.

The data demonstrates that although a few celebrity bankrupts get much of the publicity, the typical bankrupt has lived in a much more austere economic environment, under severe financial burdens. For such individuals, the ability to file a bankruptcy petition and emerge four years later with a fresh start proves attractive.

The data from the Official Receiver's office provides a helpful profile of Hong Kong bankrupts. To gain an even better understanding of the causes of consumer bankruptcy, it would be helpful if the Official Receiver's Office could increase the size of their sampling of bankrupts and extend the data to include further demographic information including gender, marital status and level of education.

Although the number of bankruptcy cases is increasing, not all debtors in Hong Kong are willing to resort to bankruptcy. A couple of years ago I learned of an individual who found himself in a position in which the monthly payments on his credit cards exceeded his monthly salary. Rather than filing for bankruptcy, he did the same thing that a relative of his had done several years earlier: he quit his job, changed his residence, cancelled his old credit cards, assumed a new name and started afresh—a true fresh start. I have since learned that this debtor's response was not unique. In a society in which shame still attaches to bankruptcy (although, granted, much less than it did in the past) and in which aggressive debt collectors and triads do not consider their claims discharged by bankruptcy, there still remain debtors who are not convinced that bankruptcy will solve their problems.

V. THE ROLE OF CREDIT CARD DEBT IN CONSUMER BANKRUPTCY

It can be seen from the above data that the rising level of credit card debt in Hong Kong is a contributing factor to many Hong Kong consumer bankruptcies. There has been a dramatic increase in credit card debt in Hong Kong. Statistics show that advances on credit cards rose from HK$7 billion 10 years ago[41] to approximately HK$59.7 billion at the end of the third quarter of 2002.[42]

[41] J van der Kamp, Column, *South China Morning Post* (*Business Post* 2) (6 Mar 2002) 1.

[42] See the information available on the HKMA's website, above n 29.

It was reported in 2002 that Hong Kong has the highest default rate in the world on outstanding credit card debt[43] (at a year-to-date annualised rate of 12.75 per cent at the end of the third quarter of 2002[44]) and that the average consumer in default in Hong Kong owes 55 months of his income.[45]

To address the increasing rate of credit card charge-offs, the Hong Kong Association of Banks proposed to the Hong Kong Monetary Authority and the Government that banks be able to share 'positive' consumer credit card information, such as how many credit cards a customer has and approved credit limits and outstanding balances.[46] The Privacy Commissioner decided to implement this policy as of 1 April 2003.[47] It has been argued that in the longer term, sharing positive information will decrease the number of consumer bankruptcy cases. This is a possible result, but only if the banks use the information to decrease their risk and try to cut back on lending to customers who have too many credit cards or large outstanding credit card debts.

V. BANKRUPTCY AND VA LEVELS: WHERE ARE THEY LIKELY TO GO FROM HERE?

One of the costs to society of easing access to consumer credit is an increase in the consumer bankruptcy rate. As the recent data demonstrates, Hong Kong is now experiencing this first-hand. Society needs to inculcate in its members the moral responsibility to repay one's contractual and financial obligations. It also needs to educate its citizenry about how money and consumer credit work and about the dangers of taking on too much debt. On the other hand, society needs to acknowledge that when the point comes at which an honest, good faith debtor is unable to pay back his debts in full, it is better for society as well as the individual if mechanisms are available for giving the debtor a fresh start. A debtor with no foreseeable possibility of becoming solvent does not have the appropriate incentives to act in a thrifty or entrepreneurial way. Society is not likely to reap as much benefit from his labour if he is not granted a discharge.

43 'The New Spendthrifts,' *The Economist* (20 Apr 2002), Economist.com <http://economist.com>.

44 See 'Lending Survey,' above n 29.

45 See 'The New Spendthrifts', above n 43 (quoting John Ott of McKinsey). The data compiled by the Official Receiver's Office from the recent sampling of bankruptcy cases (see Tables 4 and 6 and related text above) is consistent with this claim.

46 For further information and to access a copy of the HKMA's discussion paper on the sharing of positive consumer credit card data, see HKMA <http://www.info.gov.hk/hkma/eng/pos/index.htm>. The Office of the Privacy Commissioner for Personal Data (PCO) issued a consultation paper in August 2002 in relation to the sharing of positive credit data. For further information and to access a copy of the PCO's paper, see PCO <http://www.pco.org.hk/english/ordinance/codes.html>.

47 E Yiu, 'Banks to share more customer data,' *South China Morning Post* (24 Jan 2003) 3. At the request of the banking industry, implementation was delayed to 2 June 2003. There will be a two-year transitional period during which banks may not review the credit information of existing clients unless they apply for new loans or credit restructuring. (*Ibid*).

When reports emerge of individuals taking advantage of the system and running up credit card bills that they have no intention of repaying, there is a certain appeal to making access to bankruptcy more difficult. However, before rushing through legislation that moves in this direction, it is important that the government collect the appropriate empirical data. At this stage, just a few years after enacting a new bankruptcy law, it would be unfortunate if more restrictive legislation enacted to combat the actions of reckless and dishonest debtors also had the effect of adversely affecting good faith, honest debtors. A better approach, as recently proposed by Arthur Andersen in its *Review of the Role of the Official Receiver's Office Consultation Paper*,[48] which was commissioned by the Financial Services Bureau, would be to create a fast-track discharge procedure for selected consumer cases that is linked to 'increased penalties for false declaration of assets'[49] and 'a tougher penalty regime for reckless or deliberate abuse of credit after a fast track discharge.'[50] Thought should also also be given to the creation of a non-judicial bankruptcy process, as is also proposed in the *Consultation Paper*.[51]

One of the best ways to bring down the bankruptcy rate would be to implement education for consumers about credit.[52] Ideally it would be helpful if such classes could be offered at secondary or tertiary education levels and also as part of consumer counselling services. Thought should also be given to mandating that all bankrupts and participants in VAs must attend credit-education seminars.

Hong Kong is in the midst of a difficult period, which has adversely affected hundreds of thousands of families in Hong Kong living at low-income levels. In addition, there are thousands of other middle-income families that have negative equity in their flats. Many of these families have also fallen behind on credit card and other consumer debts with interest rates of 25 to 30 per cent (or even higher). Many of the hundreds of thousands of debtors caught in this downward debt spiral would benefit from bankruptcy, and others might well be but one economic disaster away. Given that Hong Kong's poor economic climate is likely to continue for the near future and that there is an increasing perception among the general population that bankruptcy 'works,' I would expect that the number of bankruptcy cases will continue to increase for several more years before beginning to level off. I would not be surprised if this higher rate then became the norm for Hong Kong.

48 See above n 27.

49 *Ibid* para 3.18, at 20; para 3.34, at 25.

50 *Ibid* para 3.19, at 20. Although a suggested time frame is not proposed in the *Consultation Paper*, there are references to procedures in other jurisdictions in which discharge is available in certain cases within six to 12 months.

51 *Ibid* paras 3.21–3.25, at 21–2.

52 Such an initiative has recently been announced by the Hong Kong Consumer Council. See Media Release, 'Consumer Council Press Release,' (6 Jan 2003), Consumer Council's website <http://www.consumer.org.hk/20030106/030106e.htm>.

The long-term level of bankruptcies in Hong Kong will, in part, be dependent on the popularity of VAs. The number of VAs increased dramatically in 2002, and I expect that this trend will continue as creditors and debtors alike come to appreciate the benefits that VAs offer over bankruptcy. My prediction is that five years from now VAs will constitute 15 to 20 per cent of all insolvency cases in Hong Kong.

Part IV

Changes in and Evaluations of Mature Consumer Bankruptcy Regimes

10

Bankruptcy in Transition: The Case of England and Wales—The Neo-Liberal Cuckoo in the European Bankruptcy Nest?

IAIN RAMSAY*

I. INTRODUCTION

IN 1986 I WROTE that in England and Wales 'there is great hesitation to make bankruptcy a routinised procedure for the ordinary individual debtor.'[1] That statement was made in the light of the recommendations of the Cork Committee[2] which proposed a Debts Arrangement Order rather than bankruptcy as the solution for over-indebted consumers. This order would have replaced the inadequate system of County Court administration orders. The Insolvency Act 1986 did not implement this proposal but introduced the Individual Voluntary Arrangement, designed to be used by small businesses and professionals. During this period, debt advice agencies also did not view bankruptcy as a solution to their clients' problems.[3] Debt problems in the UK were closely connected to issues of poverty and changed circumstances such as unemployment. A national study of credit and debt in the late 1980s by Berthoud and

* This chapter is a preliminary aspect of a comparative study of individual bankruptcy in Canada and England and Wales, funded by the Social Sciences and Humanities Research Council of Canada. I would like to thank those individuals who provided me with valuable information on bankruptcy practice and debt management in England and Wales: officials of the English Insolvency Service and the Lord Chancellor's department; Sue Edwards of Citizens Advice; Pat Conaty, who was also helpful in suggesting individuals to interview; Andrew Buswell, Birmingham Money Advice Centre; Sophie Brookes, National Debtline and Nick Pearson, Federation of Information and Advice Centres. Thanks also to Bill Whitford for comments on an earlier draft.

[1] See I Ramsay, 'Themes and Issues' in I Ramsay (ed), *Debtors and Creditors* (Abingdon, Professional Books, Butterworth, 1986) 1 at 12.

[2] *Insolvency Law and Practice: Report of the Review Committee* (London, HMSO, 1982) at Ch 6 [*Insolvency Law and Practice Report*].

[3] See T Hinton and R Berthoud, *Money Advice Services* (London, Policy Studies Institute, 1988) at 68–72.

Kempson concluded that problems of debt over-commitment were related primarily to poverty rather than consumerism.[4]

In this chapter I take the statements in the previous paragraph as a starting point and explore whether they need to be revised in the light of social and economic changes since the late 1980s. I outline current findings on credit and over-indebtedness in the UK and also the law and practice of bankruptcy and debt adjustment in England and Wales as it existed immediately prior to the insolvency reforms in the Enterprise Act 2002. I then discuss the reforms to personal insolvency enacted by that Act and speculate on the extent to which these reforms may result in significant changes in the role of bankruptcy law as a solution to consumer over-indebtedness.

II. CONSUMER CREDIT AND OVER-INDEBTEDNESS

Although some commentators have noted with concern recent increases in individual bankruptcy, England and Wales has a relatively low rate of individual bankruptcy compared to other common law jurisdictions such as the US, Canada or Australia.[5] In addition, consumer bankruptcies represented only 53 per cent of personal insolvencies in England and Wales in 2000,[6] whereas in North America and Australia the great majority of individual bankruptcies are consumer bankruptcies. There has however been growing concern in the UK in relation to over-indebtedness. The media have reported record-breaking debt-to-disposable income levels of 110 per cent and significant increases in credit card borrowing.[7] Citizens Advice (formerly the National Assocation of Citizens' Advice Bureaux) indicated that in 2001/2002 it dealt with nearly 1.5 million new debt problems and that its caseload in this area had increased by 46 per cent over the past five years.[8] In response to these concerns the government established a Task Force on Over-indebtedness in 2000 which made a variety of recommendations including the development of further research on the causes, effects and extent of over-indebtedness.[9]

[4] R Berthoud and E Kempson, *Credit and Debt: the PSI Report* (London, Policy Studies Institute, 1992). See also J Ford and M Wilson, 'Personal Debt and Insolvency' in H Rajak (ed), *Insolvency Law: Theory and Practice* (London, Sweet and Maxwell, 1993) at 106 'Debt is largely concentrated amongst poorer households.'

[5] See eg A Keay, 'Balancing Interests in Bankruptcy Law' (2001) *Common Law World Review* 206. In 1999 the consumer insolvency rate in England and Wales was 0.55 per 1,000 population. This compares with the US (4.8), Canada (2.72), and Australia (1.44). See *International Consumer Insolvency Statistics* (Ottawa, Office of Superintendent of Bankruptcy, 2001).

[6] See *Insolvency—A Second Chance* (Cm 5234, Department of Trade and Industry, The Insolvency Service) at 1.46.

[7] See H Stewart and C Denny, 'Personal Debt hits record high' *The Guardian* (31 August 2001).

[8] See 'Insolvency—A second Chance. A Response by the CAB Service to the Insolvency Service White Paper', Citizen's Advice Bureau <http://www.citizensadvice.org.uk/polfull.ihtml?table=legl&ai=0000097> (last visited 7 March 2003).

[9] See *First Report by the Task Force on Tackling Overindebtedness* (Department of Trade and Industry, Consumer Affairs Directorate, July 2001) at 4. See also the subsequent *Task Force on Tackling OverIndebtedness: Second Report* (London, Department of Trade and Industry, 2003).

This research conducted by Elaine Kempson[10] found that 75 per cent of households had access to credit facilities although only 50 per cent actually had credit outstanding on these credit facilities. There had been a doubling of unsecured credit outstanding between 1994 and 2001 and the use of credit cards as a source of revolving credit had increased significantly since the Berthoud and Kempson study in 1989, as had outstanding balances on the cards. The average amount owed by individuals carrying a balance was £1,570. However, most households used credit modestly. The heaviest users of credit were two parent families who were buying homes on a mortgage, with low to middle income households and households who had experienced a drop in income in the past 12 months representing the largest sub-groups within this classification. About 25 per cent of households had been in financial difficulties during the past 12 months. Financial difficulties tended to be associated with young families setting up home, households with low and unstable incomes, and those which had experienced a drop in income. These findings may be related to recent research by the Financial Services Authority which indicated that debt difficulties were most concentrated among families with mortgages in the 35 to 44 age group who fall within social grades C1 and C2.[11] In the Kempson study, the largest single cause of financial difficulties was job loss. There was no evidence of young people, still living at home, being heavy credit users. Although there was a significant growth in enquiries to debt advice agencies during the late 1990s, formal measures of arrears such as money plaints in the County Court and mortgage repossessions had decreased during this period. The research also noted a significant increase in private debt management organisations which advertise heavily in the media.

The Kempson study drew attention to the increasing competition in the credit card market and the introduction of many practices first developed in the US such as automatic increases in credit limits, low interest introductory offers, reducing the minimum payment on credit cards, credit card cheques and significant increases in late charges and penalties. It concluded that although the historically high levels of borrowing were problematic for only a small number of people, a far greater number of consumers were at risk in the event of a serious economic downturn or sustained increases in interest rates.

There are currently few restrictions on credit granting in England and Wales, with substantial deregulation of the consumer credit market having occurred in the 1980s at the same time as the introduction of financial services reform.

[10] See E Kempson, *Over-Indebtedness in Britain: A Report to the Department of Trade and Industry* (Bristol, Personal Finance Research Centre, 2002).

[11] See Financial Services Authority, *Financial Risk Outlook 2003* (London, Financial Services Authority, 2003) at 41. Social grade C1 is supervisory or clerical and junior managerial, administrative or professional. C2 are skilled manual workers. Families in social grade DE (semi-skilled and unskilled manual workers, state pensioners or widows (no other earner) casual or lowest grade workers) were more likely than other social grades to have some sort of difficulty meeting debt repayments.

Debt-to-income ratios increased from 25 per cent in 1981 to 68 per cent in 1988.[12] There are no interest rate ceilings on consumer credit. Licensing, disclosures and controls of unfair terms are the primary form of regulation. The courts have recognised only faintly the concept of *social force majeure* as a legal principle in consumer lending[13] (ie adjustment of debts where an individual has suffered an unforeseen change of circumstances) although financial institutions have committed themselves through a code of practice to the concept of 'prudent lending.' There is a flourishing alternative consumer credit market where individuals pay extremely high interest rates and which has attracted criticism. There does exist the possibility of a credit agreement being reopened as an extortionate credit bargain under the Consumer Credit Act 1974,[14] but the open-texture of this standard reduces its general impact on transactions.

III. ALTERNATIVES AVAILABLE TO OVER-INDEBTED CONSUMERS

A. Personal Insolvency Law and Practice (pre Enterprise Act)

Responsibility for the operation of the insolvency system rests with the Insolvency Service, an Executive Agency within the Department of Trade and Industry. The Service administers the system of official receivers throughout England and Wales and authorises and regulates insolvency practitioners.[15] The Insolvency Service is funded through fees charged on insolvent estates and investment income from funds realised in bankruptcy which are required to be deposited in the Insolvency Services Account maintained by the Department of Trade and Industry at the Bank of England. As a consequence of this practice the Service operates at a profit.[16] The traditional role of the official receiver in relation to individual insolvency has been to act as a trustee where no private sector insolvency practitioner is appointed and to investigate the affairs of a bankrupt.

An individual who wishes to use the bankruptcy procedures in the Insolvency Act must petition the court for a bankruptcy order on the grounds that she is unable to pay her debts.[17] She must pay an initial fee of £250 to cover the costs

[12] See I Ramsay, 'Credit, Class and the Normalisation of Debt Default' in G Howells, I Crow, and M Moroney (eds), *Aspects of Credit and Debt* (London, Sweet & Maxwell, 1993) at 65.

[13] See ss 129, 136 Consumer Credit Act 1974 (making of time orders for repayment) and see I Ramsay, 'Consumer Credit Law, Distributive Justice and the Welfare State' (1995) 15 *Oxford Journal of Legal Studies* 177 at 196.

[14] See ss 137–39, Consumer Credit Act 1974. These provisions are currently under review by the Department of Trade and Industry as part of a general review of the Consumer Credit Act 1974.

[15] For a more extensive account of the legal framework of regulation, see I Fletcher, *The Law of Insolvency* 3rd edn (London, Sweet and Maxwell, 2002) at 25–34; F Tolmie, *Introduction to Corporate and Personal Insolvency Law* (London, Sweet and Maxwell, 1998) at 198–211.

[16] For a criticism that these profits are made at the expense of ordinary creditors see Justice, *Insolvency Law An Agenda for Reform* (London, Justice, 1994) at 24.

[17] Insolvency Act 1986 c 45, s 273: 'A debtor's petition may be presented to the court only on the grounds that the debtor is unable to pay his debts.'

of administration and also pay court fees, for a total fee of approximately £370. It is possible for the court to refer a petition to an insolvency practitioner at this stage if there appears to be the possibility of an individual being able to enter an Individual Voluntary Arrangement.[18] Assuming a court makes a bankruptcy order then this may be either for summary or ordinary administration. In a summary administration case (where unsecured creditors represent less than £20,000 and the debtor has not been bankrupt within previous five years[19]) the period of discharge is two rather than three years, there is no meeting of creditors, the official receiver is not under a duty to investigate the circumstances leading up to the bankruptcy,[20] and the official receiver will act as the trustee of the estate. For the first-time bankrupt, discharge is automatic after the running of the two or three year period and only the official receiver may object to discharge.[21] A bankrupt may retain exempt personal property, such as vehicles and tools to the extent that they are necessary for use in her employment, business or vocation, and household furniture and equipment which are necessary to satisfy the basic domestic needs of the bankrupt and his family.[22] There is no real property exemption. A bankrupt may be required to make income payments to the estate only where she is in receipt of income beyond what is necessary to support herself and her family. The trustee may seek an income payments order from the court and it is possible for a court to make an order which will continue to have effect after the discharge.[23] While a bankrupt is undischarged she will be subject to a number of disabilities such as obtaining credit over £250 without disclosing the bankruptcy, and various disqualifications such as sitting as a Member of Parliament or member of a local authority.

There are no systematic empirical analyses of the operation in practice of the insolvency system in England and Wales as it affects consumers. The Association of Business Recovery Professionals, which represents a large number of insolvency professionals, has published data on individuals using private insolvency practitioners but these statistics are of limited value since insolvency practitioners will act as trustee in a minority of consumer bankruptcies.[24] The

[18] *Ibid* s273 (where unsecured liabilities less than £20,000, value of debtor's estate is at least £2,000 and debtor has not been adjudged bankrupt or entered into a composition or scheme of affairs with creditors during the past five years).

[19] *Ibid* ss 275 (1) and (2).

[20] *Ibid* s 289(5).

[21] *Ibid* ss 278, 279 [not automatic where individual adjudged bankrupt under 264(1) (b) or if had been an undischarged bankrupt within 15 years of commencement of bankruptcy]. For a US perspective on the old regime where an individual was required to make application for a discharge, see D Boshkoff, 'Limited, Conditional and Suspended Discharges in Anglo-American Bankruptcy Proceedings' (1982) 131 *University of Pennsylvania Law Review* 69. Fletcher indicates that the reforms to the automatic discharge procedures introduced by the Insolvency Act 1986, which introduces a 'fixed, and relatively short, duration of the condition of bankruptcy for those debtors who respect their legal obligations . . . has undoubtedly marked a fundamental adjustment in prevailing social attitudes towards bankruptcy, and towards those who undergo it.' Fletcher, above n 16, at 11–004.

[22] Insolvency Act 1986, above n 17, s 283.

[23] *Ibid* ss 310(1) (6).

[24] See *9th Survey of Personal Insolvency*, R3 <http://www.r3.org.uk>.

statistics on privately processed bankruptcies do indicate that 80 per cent of individuals using insolvency or IVAs are male, and most are self-employed, semiskilled or unskilled workers. Data maintained by the Insolvency Service indicate that between 20–25 per cent of bankrupts classify themselves as 'no occupation and unemployed' at the time of bankruptcy.

The following observations on the English system are based on interviews and discussions with officials of the Insolvency Service, the Lord Chancellor's Department, debt advisers and the limited empirical data which does exist on the operation of the consumer bankruptcy system. It would appear that the majority of consumer bankruptcies are administered by the Official Receiver (OR), the procedure is relatively straightforward, the court proceedings are generally a formality and in a significant number of cases the Official Receiver will conduct an examination of the debtor by telephone. After this initial interview the debtor will simply wait out the required period until the automatic discharge takes effect. A study of debt advisers in Money Advice Centres in 1999 noted that 'many clients report that the process . . . is not at all onerous and does not cause the problems or embarrassment many feared at the outset.'[25]

Income payment orders are made in about 10 per cent of cases.[26] They are almost always made with the consent of the bankrupt although they must be approved by a county court Registrar. It is rare for a debtor to attend this hearing and it is also rare for such orders to run past discharge.[27] There are internal guidelines within the Official Receiver's Office on when income payments orders should be applied for as well as rules of thumb (eg no orders under £50 a month, payments of half surplus income) but there remains scope for the exercise of discretion here, for example, in relation to differing costs of living within England and Wales. There is also the existence of discretion in relation to property exemptions such as an automobile needed in a trade or calling. The phenomenon of local legal culture—where individual offices or trustees may take different approaches—may therefore be of significance in the administration of English bankruptcies.

The requirement of the initial fee of £250 is viewed by groups such as Citizens Advice as posing a significant barrier to access to bankruptcy for those on low incomes. It has been challenged unsuccessfully under section 6 of the European Convention on Human Rights as restricting a fundamental right of access to the courts.[28] Debt advice workers may be able to obtain the £250 bankruptcy fee from charitable organisations. Citizens Advice reported in 2001 that one trust

[25] See European Project 97/C277/04, 'Overindebtedness of consumers in Europe: Are extra-judicial proceedings the solution?' Country Report/England [Newcastle City Council, Money Advice Association, Money Advice Trust and Federated Credit Ltd] (unpublished study on file with author) at 21.

[26] See *Bankruptcy A Fresh Start* (London, The Insolvency Service, 2000) at 20.

[27] *Ibid* at para 7.7.

[28] *R v Lord Chancellor ex parte Lightfoot* [2000] 2 WLR 318. The European Court of Human Rights rejected an appeal from this decision.

fund had paid over £400,000 since 1999 to help CABx and other advice agency clients to petition for bankruptcy.[29]

B. Individual Voluntary Arrangements

Individual voluntary arrangements were introduced in 1986 as an alternative to bankruptcy, permitting individuals to reach an arrangement with their creditors. The Cork Committee envisaged that this mechanism would be used by company directors who had guaranteed debts of a company, professionals who would lose their status if they resorted to bankruptcy and self-employed business persons.[30]

An IVA permits a debtor to make a binding composition with her creditors.[31] It may involve the sale of assets or income repayments. Under an IVA, a debtor will normally obtain a qualified private insolvency practitioner to act as nominee and supervisor of the arrangement. The role of the nominee is to submit a report to the court as to whether a meeting of creditors should be held to consider the proposal. Approval of a proposal requires a majority in excess of 75 per cent in value of unsecured creditors present or voting by proxy. The rights of secured or preferential creditors cannot be affected without the consent of these creditors. The arrangement is registered with the Insolvency Service. The great majority of IVAs are made before bankruptcy but it is possible for an undischarged bankrupt to enter into an IVA and to have her bankruptcy annulled. In recent years IVAs have represented 20–25 per cent of all personal insolvency cases.

The IVA was not designed for use by consumers and the costs of an IVA would make it prohibitive for many consumers. Research by the Insolvency Service indicates that the average nominee fee in small cases is £1500 and the supervisor's fee is £2500. The costs in these cases often represent more than 50 per cent of the receipts.[32] However, there is anecdotal evidence of attempts by some insolvency practitioners to market IVAs on a relatively routinised and presumably lower cost basis to individuals who might be unwilling to file for bankruptcy because of their professional status. There have also been allegations that some private debt advice agencies act as 'ambulance chasers' for a small number of Insolvency Practitioners who then charge consumers high fees

[29] See NACAB Briefing, Enterprise Bill Standing Committee Amendment Number C9, Citizen's Advice Bureau <http://www.citizensadvice.org.uk/polfull.ihtml?table=bref&id=0000071> (last visited: 7 March 2003).

[30] *Insolvency Law and Practice Report*, above n 2, at para 365.

[31] See Part VIII, Insolvency Act 1986 and Fletcher and Tolmie, above n 15, at paras 4–002 –4–044 and 67–81 respectively.

[32] See *Regulatory Impact Assessment for Insolvency Provisions in Enterprise Bill as introduced to House of Lords*, 19 June 2002 at 10.

for IVAs which subsequently fail. The relatively profitable nature of IVAs does mean that there is a professional intermediary with an interest in the maintenance and expansion of these arrangements.[33]

A survey of IVAs commenced in the late 1980s found that the great majority of IVAs lasted for three years,[34] the period of the automatic discharge. This study concluded that they were relatively successful in achieving a higher rate of return for creditors and permitting individuals to avoid bankruptcy. However, 33 per cent of arrangements ran into difficulties and the majority of those which failed were cases where individuals were required to make income payments rather than realise assets. A more recent study indicates that many arrangements (44 per cent) now last for over three years and that there has been an increase in their use in consumer cases.[35]

C. County Court Administration Order

The administration order has been described as the 'poor person's bankruptcy' since its introduction in the Bankruptcy Act of 1883. It was intended to avoid the difficulties of recovering small debts in the 'wage earning classes' in cases where it would be too costly to apply the machinery of the Bankruptcy Act, and to provide a middle way between immunity from liability for the debtor and imprisonment for debt.[36] During the next 80 years it seems to have been used very modestly and the committal procedure which resulted in imprisonment for debt continued in England and Wales into the mid-twentieth century with debtors constituting 14 per cent of the prison population in the early 1960s.[37] On the recommendation of the Payne Committee,[38] committal to imprisonment for non-payment of debts was abolished in 1970.[39] Both the Payne Committee and the Cork Committee[40] envisaged a significant role for a modified form of administration order which would address the needs of the consumer debtor who would be provided with the opportunity to repay all or a portion of their debts over a period of three years.

[33] See Insolvency Practices Council, *Annual Report* (2001) at 7, ICP <http://www.insolvency practices.org.uk>.

[34] See K Pond, 'The Individual Voluntary Arrangement Experience' (1995) *Journal of Business Law* 118.

[35] See K Pond, 'An Insolvent Decade: the changing nature of the IVA 1987–1997 at 8–9, SSRN Working Paper Series available at <http://papers.ssrn.com/so/3/results.ctm>.

[36] 'The system we are trying to improve is an attempt to avoid the present difficulties attending the recovery of small debts in the wage earning classes. By applying the principles of the Bankruptcy Law to cases which are too small and too poor to pay for the machinery of that law, and in this way to escape from the alternatives of immunity from liability on the one hand, and imprisonment for debt on the other' quoted in J Davies, 'Delegalisation of Debt Recovery Proceedings: A Socio-Legal Study of Money Advice Centres and Administration Orders' in I Ramsay, above n 1, at 189.

[37] OR McGregor, *Social History and Law Reform* (London, Stevens, 1981) at 38.

[38] See *Report of the Committee on the Enforcement of Judgement Debts* (The Payne Committee) (London, HMSO, Cmnd 309, 1969).

[39] See Administration of Justice Act 1970.

[40] *Insolvency Law and Practice Report*, above n 2, at Ch 6.

The current structure of administration orders is that where an individual has a judgment against her which she is unable to pay immediately and a total indebtedness of less than £5000 the court may, on application by the debtor, make an administration order. This may be for full or partial repayment of the debts and there is no limitation on the time period for which an administration order may be made.[41] Creditors included in the order are prevented from taking proceedings against a debtor while the order is in force. There are approximately 6–7,000 administration orders made annually. In contrast to bankruptcy, there is no entry fee payable by a debtor for an administration order and court fees for the implementation of the order, which may not exceed ten per cent of the total amount of the debts, are deducted from the repayments.

In response to criticisms of the operation in practice of administration orders the Civil Justice Review in 1988 made several recommendations to make the administration order more widely available. These included dropping the requirement of a judgment debt as a condition for granting an order, raising the monetary limit, restricting the period of an order to three years with the balance of the debts being written off, and the introduction of an enforcement restriction order where a debtor has no realisable assets or income.[42] These reforms, intended to provide a 'mini-bankruptcy' for individuals and an opportunity for rehabilitation[43] were enacted in section 13 of the Courts and Legal Services Act 1990.[44] However, they have not yet been brought into force by successive governments. The ostensible reason for this failure is that the definition of 'debt' in the amendments could include secured debts and would permit a debtor to compromise large secured debts, given the three year limit. However, since this could have been changed by a simple amendment, a more plausible explanation is that creditor pressure and concerns about the costs of increased numbers of administration orders have been primary reasons for failure to implement this section.

There are many anecdotal criticisms of the current regime of administration orders and it is probably fair to state that many observers believe that they are currently an unsatisfactory alternative for both debtors and creditors. The debt ceiling of £5000 (established in 1981) is unrealistic. Most orders are unsuccessful with debtors not maintaining repayments, orders are made for long periods of time such as six or seven years with small repayments, and courts don't monitor them closely. There seems also to be evidence of local legal culture with some courts compounding debts while others do not, and some restricting repayments to three years while others do not. The Lord Chancellor's Department has commissioned research to provide systematic information on the operation of administration orders.

[41] See County Court Act 1984, ss 112–17and Order 39 of the County Court Rules, 1981.

[42] See *Civil Justice Review* (London, Cmnd 394, HMSO) para 645.

[43] *Ibid.*

[44] Courts and Legal Services Act 1990 c 41, s 13.

D. Alternatives to Formal Debt Repayment Procedures and the Role of Debt Advice Agencies

Individuals who experience problems with debts may turn to a variety of publicly supported and private debt advice agencies which offer informal repayment alternatives as well as channelling individuals to more formal procedures. According to a recent article 'debt advice is Britain's new growth industry.'[45] The significance of these informal alternatives to a discussion of insolvency is illustrated by a survey of debt advice agencies in 1999 concerning their treatment of multiple debt cases.[46] The income and liability profile of debtors who were surveyed did not differ greatly from those of Canadian consumer bankrupts.[47] Debtors had an average of eight unsecured creditors totalling £13,000. Eighteen per cent were unemployed and thirteen per cent were unable to work. Thirty nine per cent received means tested benefits (an indicator of low income) and forty four per cent were homeowners. Forty eight per cent of debtors were female. The reasons given for the debtor's financial position are indicated in Table 1.

Table 1 Reason(s) given for debtor's financial position

	%
Business Failure	9.7
Unemployment	19.0
Sickness/Disability	23.0
Relationship Breakdown	25.4
Addition to Family	8.1
Increased Housing Costs	2.4
Insufficient Income	32.3
Bereavement	2.4
Overcommittment	36.3
Other	6.5

Source: European Project 97/C277/04 Overindebtedness of consumers in Europe: are extra-judicial proceedings the solution? Country Report/England at 36.

45 'Jobs and Money' *The Guardian* (21 September,2002) 3. See also C Whyley and S Collard, *Fee or Free? The role of fee-charging debt advice companies in money advice provision* (London, Federation of Independent Advice Agencies, 1999) at 5.

46 Above n 25.

47 See S Schwartz, 'The Empirical Dimensions of Consumer Bankruptcy: Results from a Survey of Canadian Bankrupts' (1999) 37 *Osgoode Hall LawJournal* 83 (Median of eight debts, median liability $26,016, more than 25 per cent unemployed, 57 per cent had received government transfer payment in two years preceding bankruptcy protection). I Ramsay 'Individual Bankruptcy: Preliminary Findings of a Socio-Legal Analysis' (1999) 37 *Osgoode Hall Law Journal* 15 (median liability $32,649, 31 per cent unemployed).

Table 2 Outcome of Advice

	%
Informal pro-rata for all creditors	37
Informal pro-rata & Instalment Orders	10.9
General Moratorium	15.7
Administration Order	7.8
Individual Voluntary Arrangement	7.4
Bankruptcy under £20,000	10.9
Bankruptcy over £20,000	10.4

Source: European Project 97/C277/04 Overindebtedness of Consumers in Europe: are extrajudicial proceedings the solution? Country Report/England.

Table 2 indicates the variety of approaches adopted to resolve the individuals' debt problems with bankruptcy only being used by approximately 20 per cent of clients notwithstanding the fact that a larger percentage of these clients may be insolvent. Some of the alternative procedures such as a general moratorium on debt repayment are 'informal bankruptcies' where debtors are not repaying their creditors notwithstanding the fact that they have not declared bankruptcy.

Free money advice centres developed in the early 1970s in England when legal advice workers recognised that their clients increasingly required financial advice which was 'time consuming and required expertise not necessarily associated with lawyers.'[48] An influential model of free independent money advice was developed by the Birmingham Settlement Money Advice Centre. This model uses specialist lay advisers to advise debtors, represent them in court and negotiate with creditors on their behalf.[49] The adviser will attempt to maximise the income and benefits of the client, address priority debts (such as mortgage and fuel arrears) and then deal with consumer credit obligations. This is sometimes described as a holistic approach to debt problems.

This model of debt advice is followed by Citizens Advice which, with 2,000 outlets, claims to be the largest independent network of free advice centres in Europe. Established as a voluntary agency at the beginning of the Second World War in 1939, CABx have grown to become a primary source of legal advice to consumers, particularly those living on modest incomes who have problems with public services and safety net benefits. The majority of its offices provide specialist money advice. Citizens Advice has also been influential in keeping the issue of over-indebtedness on the public agenda and in lobbying for a reduction in financial barriers to access to bankruptcy. The individual CABx are

[48] See Hinton and Berthoud, above n 3, at 6. See also generally P Conaty, 'Credit, Debt and Financial Control in Great Britain' and P Conaty, J Ford, S Johnson, J Kruse and P Woodall, 'Private and Public Concerns—Unemployment, Credit and Debt in Britain: An Overview' in J Ford and U Reifner (eds), *Banking for People* (Berlin, Walter de Gruyter, 1992) at 72–73 and 558–59.

[49] See Hinton and Berthoud, above n 3, at 6.

independent charities, relying on funding from local authorities, local businesses and individuals. 82 per cent of the people working for CABx are volunteers. National standards are established and monitored by Citizens Advice which receives two-thirds of its annual funding of approximately £25m from the Department of Trade and Industry.

A survey of their debt clients in 2001 indicated that most individuals who seek advice from the CABx are poorer than the general population with an average household income less than half the national average. One third were claiming safety net benefits and 60 per cent were renting their home compared with a national owner-occupier rate of 70 per cent. Their average level of debt was £10,700 with the majority of debts related to consumer credit. Approximately half indicated that the reason for being over-indebted was change of circumstance and less than a quarter cited over commitment or money management. The top three reasons cited were job loss, poverty and over commitment.[50]

It would appear that CABx often have limited and insecure funding. Not all bureaux have specialist money advisers so that a significant amount of advice is provided by volunteers. There are also problems of accessibility in relation to CABx. A recent study concluded that a common experience and expectation among individuals with justiciable problems was that obtaining free advice from a CAB is extremely difficult with prospective clients discouraged because of limited opening hours, unanswered telephones, full offices and queues.[51] These pressures on funding and the high resource costs of individualised debt management and advice might create increased incentives for CABx to channel more over-indebted individuals into bankruptcy rather than extended repayments plans. In addition to the CABx, there are approximately 1000 independent advice centres associated with Advice UK. About 300 of these centres provide free debt advice to clients with a similar demographic profile to CABx clients. Reviews of publicly funded money advice centres have been generally favourable in terms of the quality of advice but also draw attention to the limited resources devoted to this resource-intensive work.[52]

A different approach to debt advice is found in the Consumer Credit Counselling Service (CCCS), a credit counselling service based on the North American model of credit counselling. Funded through donations by creditors it provides free advice and runs debt management plans. It receives approximately 100,000 calls annually from individuals who have an average debt of £24,000. About 10 per cent of these individuals will undertake repayment plans. The service advertises that it is able to help consumers avoid bankruptcy and therefore may channel individuals away from the bankruptcy alternative. I was informed by debt advice workers that it serves greater numbers of middle class and more

[50] See NACAB, 'Advice Week: 2001 Debt Briefing', Citizen's Advice Bureau <http://www.citizensadvice.org.uk/polfull.ihtml?table=legl&id=0000096> (last visited: 7 March 2003).

[51] See H Genn *et al*, *Paths to Justice; What People Do and Think About Going to Law* (Oxford, Hart Publishing, 1999) at 78.

[52] See S Collard, J Steele, and E Kempson, *Quality Assured? An Assessment of the Quality of Independent Money Advice* (Bristol, Personal Finance Research Centre, 2000).

affluent debtors than the CABx. The government has also funded expansion of free telephone advice through National Debtline, a service developed originally in the late 1980s. It provides advice and assists in establishing debt management plans which are run with CCCS. The average unsecured debts of individuals being provided with advice by National Debtline is £25,000. A further alternative is Federated Credit Limited which operates Payplan, an on-line repayment programme financed by creditors, and offers also IVAs to consumers through in-house insolvency practitioners. The company finances this latter alternative by getting lenders rather than consumers to pay the fees associated with the arrangement.

Finally, there has grown up a significant number (over 100) of private debt management companies which charge consumers a fee for managing their debts. The industry is dominated by three large providers and they focus on providing standardised debt management plans primarily for unsecured debts, rather than the holistic approach to money advice adopted by the free money advice sector. These companies also do not present clients with the alternative of personal bankruptcy. These companies have been criticised for charging high fees and misleading consumers concerning their ability to solve a consumer's problems.[53] A review of their services indicated that they served a more middle class client base than Citizens Advice Bureaux and that individuals who consulted them had problems with credit cards and unsecured debts rather than housing costs or utilities. Most clients appeared satisfied with the agencies and although the report called for greater regulation, it concluded that 'these companies are part of an increasingly mixed economy of advice provision for people with financial difficulties and debt problems.'[54]

E. Insolvency Practitioners

Insolvency practitioners are accountants or lawyers who are authorised either by professional bodies such as the Institute of Chartered Accountants or by direct application to the Department of Trade and Industry.[55] There are approximately 2,000 authorised insolvency practitioners of whom about half are chartered accountants. Traditionally private insolvency practitioners have not been involved with consumer debtors since it was assumed that this was an unprofitable market. However, IVAs have been promoted to individuals by insolvency firms that have seen a profit in this market. In addition, the Insolvency Service uses private insolvency practitioners to administer aspects of consumer bankruptcy work such as the administration of income payment orders.

[53] See eg Press Release, Consumers' Association, 'Debt management companies slated' 09/01/2003, Consumers' Association Media Centre <http://www.which.net/media/pr/jan03/which/debtmgmt.html> (last visited 23 January 2003).

[54] C Whyley and S Collard, *Fee or Free? The role of fee-charging debt advice companies in money advice provision* (London, Federation of Independent Advice Agencies, 1999).

[55] Insolvency Act 1986, above n 17, s390.

F. Summary

I noted at the outset that England has a relatively low rate of consumer bankruptcy compared with Canada and Australia. Even including the approximately 7,000 administration orders within the umbrella of insolvency, the English rate is lower than these countries. Nor does the difference seem to be accounted for solely by differences in consumer credit levels or welfare state protections. The earlier sections of the chapter have outlined some of the potential reasons for this difference. There is the cost of the English process which requires a substantial initial fee. Unlike Canada, individuals may not spread the costs of bankruptcy by making instalment payments. There appear to be many individuals in England who might benefit from bankruptcy[56] but for whom it is not accessible. Some of these individuals may be in a state of insolvency with no capacity to repay debts or making token payments on repayment plans. The significance of the cost hurdle is illustrated by the contrast with Scotland where there was a very large rise in personal bankruptcies during the late 1980s when the state subsidised private trustees' handling of small estates.

It is also possible that individuals are channelled by intermediaries such as CABx, credit counselling services and debt-management companies into other alternatives. Because most consumer bankruptcies continue to be administered by a public institution, there are no private intermediaries such as lawyers or accountants with a financial interest in promoting the availability of bankruptcy as a solution to consumer debt problems.

IV. CONSUMER BANKRUPTCY AND THE ENTERPRISE ACT

There are a number of reforms to personal insolvency law in the Enterprise Act that are intended to reduce the severity and stigma of bankruptcy for the honest but unfortunate debtor.[57] The discharge period is reduced to a maximum of 12 months. An earlier discharge is possible if the Official Receiver concludes that the affairs of the bankrupt do not require further investigation.[58] This will probably result in a discharge within two or three months for the majority of consumer bankrupts. Many of the existing disqualifications which currently apply to discharged bankrupts are abolished.[59] The Official Receiver's discretion not to investigate a bankruptcy will be extended from summary administration cases to include all cases.[60] Individuals with discretionary income may be sub-

[56] See *9th Survey of Personal Insolvency*, above n 24, at 24–27. Ford and Wilson, writing in the early 1990s, drew attention to many individuals who were in fact insolvent but without the resources to take advantage of insolvency relief. See above n 4, at 97.

[57] It is expected that the individual insolvency proposals will come into effect in 2004.

[58] Enterprise Act 2002 c 40, s256 (amending Insolvency Act 1986, above n 17, ss 279 (1) and (2)).

[59] *Ibid* ss 266–68.

[60] *Ibid* s 258 (amending Insolvency Act 1986, above n17, s289).

ject to a contribution order of up to three years and the OR may enter into an income payments agreement for up to three years with a bankrupt without the necessity of a court application.[61] The Bill also envisages that the Official Receiver may act as the nominee and supervisor of a post bankruptcy IVA under a 'fast track' procedure.[62] The assumption is that the public agency, which will already have information on a debtor, will be able to deliver this service in many small cases in a more cost-effective manner than private practitioners.

There is also the possibility of a bankruptcy restriction order which may last from two to 15 years.[63] The introduction of this order responds partly to the practical difficulties which the OR encountered in instituting criminal actions against practices such as credit card fraud and is intended to provide a lower cost and more effective method of sanctioning reckless, irresponsible and fraudulent debtors. This Order may be applied for by the Official Receiver where, for example, an individual had incurred a bankruptcy debt without reasonable expectation of being able to pay it, demonstrated unjustifiable extravagance in living, or had filed a previous bankruptcy within six years.[64] An individual who has abused credit cards could be caught within this section and it is expected that this will be a significant focus for these orders. The effect of the BRO would include the prevention of an individual obtaining credit more than £500 without revealing that a bankruptcy restriction order is in force and disqualification from acting as director of a company. A primary sanction is the publicity from the existence of a public register of these orders which is intended to provide a signal to creditors so that they can distinguish between the honest but unfortunate debtor and the irresponsible debtor.

The insolvency provisions of the Act were preceded by a Consultation Paper[65] and a White Paper.[66] These documents indicate that the primary objective of the reforms is to encourage 'responsible risk taking.' The Consultation Paper, which originated within the Insolvency Service, included both consumers and business within this objective and outlined the possibility of a broad review of the various mechanisms, public and private, used by consumers to address problems of over-indebtedness.[67] However, because the insolvency reforms were folded into an Enterprise Bill, the focus by the government in the White Paper and Parliamentary debates was on the role of bankruptcy in promoting entrepreneurialism. By reducing the fear of failure the government claims that bankruptcy reform will encourage the type of entrepreneurialism believed to exist in the US, and facilitate British competitiveness with other countries in the

[61] *Ibid* s 310A (amending Insolvency Act 1986, above n 17, s310).

[62] *Ibid* s264 and Schedule 22.

[63] *Ibid* s 257 and Schedule 20 (amending Insolvency Act 1986, above n 17, Schedule 4A)

[64] *Ibid* Schedule 20 s2.

[65] *Bankruptcy—A Fresh Start*, above n 26.

[66] *Insolvency—A Second Chance*, above n 6.

[67] It seems also to have been influenced by the report published by The Council of Justice in 1994. See above n 16.

EU.[68] This belief that the US model of bankruptcy promotes entrepreneurialism was a significant influence in the development of the proposals.[69] The focus was not therefore on consumer debtors and any benefits to consumers are a sidewind of these entrepreneurial objectives. However, the White Paper recognised that the increase in the percentage of consumer bankruptcies foreshadowed the fact that England was moving towards a situation similar to the US, Canada and Australia where consumer bankruptcies form a very significant majority of cases. It also speculated that during the last 15 years the growth in the availability of personal credit had led to a 'fundamental change in society's view of both personal debt and personal insolvency' with the likelihood 'that such changes will accelerate in the future'.[70] The solution for this problem was further investigation of the role of income repayment orders and County Court administration orders within a rationalised scheme of income repayment alternatives for over-indebted individuals.

These documents emphasised also the importance of the 'can pay should pay' principle which is embodied in the provision for income payments agreements, and Individual Voluntary Arrangements. This reflects the idea that those who have disposable income should make a repayment contribution. The Consultation Paper had also raised the possibility of creating a home exemption (up to £20,000) to provide some protection for small businesses which had capitalised homes, and the introduction of financial counselling for bankrupts. The home exemption was based on the US homestead allowance with the modification that it would only be available if an individual could demonstrate that it had been used to raise capital for a business. Both these reforms received little support in consultations and the Government did not include them in the Enterprise Bill.

Since the reforms in the Act apply to individual bankrupts and do not distinguish between business and consumer bankrupts, a significant topic during the Parliamentary debates was the impact of reform on the rate of consumer bankruptcies. Once again the US model was appealed to, but on this occasion it was held up as a recipe for social disaster. Opposition members, briefed by credit granters, claimed that the reduction in stigma and the short discharge period would result in an 'explosion' of consumer bankruptcies. They drew on stories of US bankruptcy such as the following example: '[M]ost commentators would agree that notions of responsibility in the USA have been eroded simply by the ease with which bankruptcy can occur. It has also been estimated that the aver-

[68] 'In the UK 31.5 per cent of people say that fear of failure would prevent them from starting a business. In the United States, that level is only 21 per cent' (Global Entrepreneurship Monitor 2001Executive Report) quoted by Melanie Johnson, Parliamentary Under Secretary of State for Competition, Consumers and Markets in speech to Insolvency Lawyers' Association, Department of Industry Homepage <http://www.dti.gov.uk/ministers/speeches/MJohnson131102.html>.

[69] See eg the earlier White Paper, *Opportunity for All in a World of Change: A White Paper on Enterprise, Skills and Innovation* (London, DTI, 1999), Department of Industry Home Page <www.dti.gov.uk/opportunity for all/pdf/whitepaper.pdf>.[70] Above n 6, at para. 1.45.

age American family pays $400 a year for the cost of bankruptcy.'[71] Although the $400 figure has been discredited in the US,[72] it has been transplanted to the UK to be placed among other stories of US excessiveness.

In contrast, other MPs, briefed by Citizens Advice, argued that the Bill did not adequately meet over-indebted individuals' needs because of the absence of financial counselling and drew attention to the problems of access to bankruptcy for poor debtors who are unable to pay the £250 bankruptcy fee.

The response of the relevant Minister to these issues reveals the approach of the current government to consumer bankruptcy.

> [A] person's entry into bankruptcy is not a right and should be considered very much a last resort . . . bankruptcy is not the only method of dealing with debts . . . There are several other routes available to individuals with financial problems . . . Many individuals can, and do, apply to county court for administration orders and discharge their liabilities through monthly payments, which are set at a level that the individual can afford. Additionally, growing numbers of individuals with debt problems seek advice and assistance from organisations in the voluntary sector such as the Consumer Credit Counselling Service and Paylink . . . Several of them offer repayment plans of as little as a £1 per week.[73]

In addition, the Minister stated that the introduction of bankruptcy restriction orders and the requirement of income payment orders for those who can pay distinguished the English approach from the US, although it was also noted that current US reform proposals would move the US system closer to the English model.

The Minister's comments reflect an unwillingness to make bankruptcy widely available to ordinary consumers. While this might be explicable by concerns over costs, there may also be historical continuity here. Paul Johnson, in his study of nineteenth century debt enforcement, noted the discrimination which existed between the treatment of working class debtors who suffered from draconian repayment orders and the threat of imprisonment and those traders who were able to take advantage of the bankruptcy laws. He attributed this distinction to class prejudice by judges, who were influential in reform discussions and who viewed male manual workers as feckless individuals for whom the threat of imprisonment was necessary in contrast to traders 'who may have missed success by the merest chance.'[74] The reluctance to view bankruptcy as a consumer remedy might reflect the contemporary replacement of the spectre of the feckless worker by the irresponsible credit card user.

[71] UK HC Parliamentary Debates Standing Committee Enterprise Bill Col 645 (M Waterson), The United Kindom Website <http://www.publications.parliament.uk/pa/cm200102/cmstand/b/st020514/am/20514s07.htm>.

[72] See E Warren, 'The Market for Data: The Changing Role of Social Sciences in Shaping the Law' (2002) *Wisconsin Law Review* 1 at 13. Warren concludes at 15 that the basic maths behind the $400 figure is 'absurd.'[73] UK HC Parliamentary Debates Col. 61 (17 June, 2002) (Ms Melanie Johnson).

[74] See P Johnson, 'Creditors, Debtors and the Law in Victorian and Edwardian England' in W Steinmetz (ed), *Private Law and Social Inequality in the Industrial Age* (Oxford, Oxford University Press, 2000) at 503.

A more benign interpretation is that the above comments are premature. The Lord Chancellor's Department and the Insolvency Service have commissioned research into administration orders and individual insolvency.[75] This research is intended to provide a basis for developing a coordinated response to the development of the role of repayment orders and insolvency for individual consumers as well as situating this within policies addressing over-indebtedness and social exclusion. The research is therefore part of the commitment to 'joined-up government,' which refers to the current Labour government's objective of integrating government services so that they work together to achieve common goals. One possible strategy is that the Insolvency Service might become the central gatekeeper for determining an appropriate solution for debtors seeking relief from multiple debts.

A. The Impact of the Enterprise Act

It is difficult to predict the future course of personal insolvency administration in England but I hazard the following comments. The reduction in the discharge period may result in greater use of bankruptcy by consumers, although it must be added that the government intends to maintain the existing cost regime for bankruptcy which will restrict accessibility to individuals unable to pay the initial fees. The trade-off for creditors is the bankruptcy restriction order which re-introduces in a new guise the concept of the conditional discharge order. The view of professionals as reported in the media is that bankruptcies will increase significantly with one insolvency practitioner predicing that:

> the number of people becoming bankrupt would continue to snowball as credit card debt rises and the new 'soft touch' personal insolvency legislation made it easier to get out of bankruptcy unscathed.[76]

However, it would be dangerous to draw broad conclusions from an increase in the bankruptcy statistics, for example, that bankruptcy reform had changed morality, reduced stigma or resulted in individuals recklessly using credit cards and then discharging their debts. Unfortunately this may occur and the following is not untypical of current media reporting on credit and bankruptcy:

> We're going bust but we don't care. Personal bankruptcies are on the increase and a leading expert on insolvency believes a rising number of people may be choosing to go bust officially as a way to deal with debt . . . [x] says the stigma of bankruptcy may be starting to evaporate in a culture increasingly comfortable with debt.[77]

[75] The parameters of the research and its relationship to policy development are outlined in the document 'Who Uses County Court Administration Orders and Personal Bankruptcy and How Successful are They?' (unpublished document, Lord Chancellor's Office, on file with author).

[76] See A Zea, 'Bankruptcy Flood Warning' *Accountancy Age* (14 November 2002) 3.

[77] *The Observer* (10 February 2002).

These dire warnings are not substantiated by the empirical research outlined at the beginning of this chapter which indicates that significant causes of financial difficulties remain changes of circumstances and low or unstable income. I discuss at greater length in Chapter 1 the role of credit cards in bankruptcy which suggests that we should be sceptical of claims that credit cards undermine the morality of debt repayment. It is true that reducing the overall price of bankruptcy will, *ceteris paribus*, result in greater use but a significant part of this increase in use might be explained by situations where over-indebted individuals substitute bankruptcy for other existing alternatives, such as repayments of £1 a week over a long period of time or an informal general moratorium on debt repayment. This substitution might be regarded as beneficial in terms of providing a 'fresh start' rather than a lingering, continuing battle with debt. Changes in bankruptcy statistics measure only whether individuals use a particular legal procedure. They do not measure over-indebtedness which should be a primary focus of concern for social policy, and they are a crude form of social indicator. There are undoubtedly costs and benefits from a liberalisation of bankruptcy. The costs to creditors are not easy to measure since we cannot assume that, in the absence of bankruptcy, lenders would have made significant recovery from a borrower.

V. CONCLUSION

The recent reform of insolvency law in England was not introduced as a response to consumer concerns that access to bankruptcy be made a solution to over-indebtedness. It resulted partly from the interest of the Insolvency Service in reducing the costs of processing no-asset bankruptcies which raised no issues for investigation and a belief by the government that a liberalised bankruptcy law would promote entrepreneurialism. Concerns about costs also influenced the refusal by the government to alter the cost structure for individual bankruptcy. Liberalisation was not a functional response to concerns about consumer credit or the decline of the welfare state. The continuing evidence of over-indebtedness among those on means-tested benefits suggests that the existence of the welfare state had not prevented problems of over-indebtedness among individuals in England.

Johanna Niemi-Kiesiläinen has noted that the reforms to Continental European debt adjustment laws during the 1990s emphasised three features which distinguish them from the US approach to bankruptcy. These are: (1) the absence of open access to bankruptcy with moral judgements conditioning access; (2) the insistence on a mandatory payment plan for all debtors as a condition of a discharge; (3) a strong emphasis on debt counselling services as an integral part of the debt adjustment procedure.[78] She also posits ideal type

[78] See J Niemi-Kiesilainen, 'Consumer Bankruptcy in Comparison: Do we Cure a Market Failure or a Social Problem?' (1999) 37 *Osgoode Hall Law Journal* 473 at 475.

models of bankruptcy regimes based on liberal and welfare models of law. The former model, associated with the US approach to bankruptcy, constructs the citizen as a risk-taking consumer who should be provided with a swift re-entry to the credit market, whereas the latter welfare model constructs the debtor as a citizen to be rehabilitated and reintegrated into society.

The reforms to English personal insolvency law raise the question of relating England to these models. The English reforms do not incorporate directly any of the features of the European model such as counselling, a moral judgement as a condition of entry to bankruptcy, or the requirement of payments as a condition of discharge. However, moral judgements are reflected through the introduction of the bankruptcy restriction order, the emphasis on income repayment orders, and the 'can pay should pay' principle, which are all intended to signal that the reforms will not make bankruptcy an easy option. The unwillingness to include counselling as part of the bankruptcy process may relate once again to issues of costs and perhaps an unwillingness to view the bankruptcy process as part of a social welfare response to problems of over-indebtedness.

The Welfare State has been subject to the winds of privatisation, for example, in housing and pensions, and higher education is financed through loans rather than state grants. In 1991, 28 per cent of students financed further education through loans whereas 77 per cent did so in 1999. These changes may be viewed as suggesting that the social citizenship of the Keynesian welfare state is being replaced by a situation where individuals are increasingly required to be self-reliant risk-takers who plan their own biography.[79] The 'Third Way'[80] has become influential as a model for the UK government. According to Anthony Giddens, this model embraces entrepreneurialism and greater individual responsibility within a framework which promotes human and social capital and recognises that both government and the market need to be limited in the interests of social solidarity and justice.[81] Applying this approach to issues of credit and debt management, the Minister responsible for this area has stated that:

> [w]e want to build a generation of empowered consumers who can manage their credit effectively . . . Ultimately, individuals have the responsibility to manage their own finances effectively.

Increasing individualisation of responsibility may result in debt problems being attributed more frequently to individual failings and is reflected also in the currently popular policy of financial literacy as a potential solution to issues of

[79] See 'The United Kingdom: Rolling Back the Welfare State?' in P Alcock and G Craig, *International Social Policy: Welfare Regimes in the Developed World* (Basingstoke, Palgrave, 2001) Ch 7.

[80] See A Giddens, *The Third Way and its Critics* (London, Polity, 2000).

[81] *Ibid* at 50–54.

over-indebtedness.[82] There has also been a growth of governmental interest in the concept of economic and social exclusion, which describes circumstances which prevent individuals from participating effectively in economic, social and cultural life. This policy is clearly relevant to low income and unemployed debtors who may be clients of CABx and subjects of administration orders in the County Court. Financial literacy, micro-finance and access to mainstream financial services are viewed as important policies to combat financial exclusion. These general observations should be set against the background of significant inequality in income and wealth in the UK which has a higher level of income inequality than most other European countries.

Returning to my opening comments to this chapter, there continues to be an absence of broad support in England and Wales for the idea of bankruptcy as a routinised procedure for the over-indebted consumer. The comment in 1994 by an influential group that the use of bankruptcy by many small consumer debtors was 'a most disturbing phenomenon', representing an 'abuse of the system', continues to resonate among decision makers.[83] Although individual consumers are increasingly constructed as responsible risk-takers the government would prefer not to conceptualise bankruptcy as a consumer remedy and consequently part of a regime of consumer protection. Consumer bankruptcy is inconsistent with the values of personal responsibility emphasised by the 'Third Way.' It would seem therefore that at first sight England does not fit within the liberal model of bankruptcy evidenced by the US approach. However, in practice, if an individual is able to afford the fee then bankruptcy may increasingly provide a solution for over-indebted consumers. In addition, it is tempting to suggest that the UK is edging towards the US model of a 'Consumers' Republic' with citizens conceptualised as responsible risk-taking consumers within a residual welfare state. Defenders of these developments may characterise them as part of the 'Third Way' but critics have suggested that much of the 'Third Way' is a repackaging of late nineteenth century liberalism.[84] Hence the neo-liberal cuckoo in the European bankruptcy nest.

[82] See Melanie Johnson MP, 'Financial Education and Personal Debt: the Role of the State, the Market and the Individual' and see also 'Over-indebtedness Fact or Fiction?', Department of Industry <http://www.dti.gov.uk/ministers/speeches/MJohnson051102.html> and <http://www.dti.gov.uk/ministers/speeches/MJohnson271102.html> respectively.

[83] See Justice, above n 16, at 15.

[84] See eg A Ryan, 'Britain: Recycling the Third Way' (1999) 46 *Dissent* 77.

11

Developments in Consumer Bankruptcy in Australia

ROSALIND MASON AND JOHN DUNS*

I. INTRODUCTION

IN KEEPING WITH developments in common law countries such as Canada and the United States, bankruptcy numbers in Australia have been steadily increasing since the 1980s. In 2001–02, 24,109 persons[1] in Australia became bankrupt,[2] in effect approximately 1.2 persons per 1000 head of population. This upward trend persists despite the introduction in December 1996 of a new low cost alternative to bankruptcy, debt agreements, which low income debtors can propose to their creditors.

The vast majority of bankruptcies in the past two decades have resulted from 'consumer debts', that is debts incurred in the consumption of goods and services as distinct from those directly related to a proprietary interest in a business or company. The proportion of consumer bankruptcies to all bankruptcies has been steadily increasing over the last decade, rising to 83.1 per cent in 2000–01.[3] The consequences of this rising trend in consumer bankruptcy are of concern for financial institutions, insolvency administrators, regulators, legislators and the wider community.[4]

There is a lack of hard data on consumer insolvency in Australia. While significant studies have been conducted in other jurisdictions,[5] the absence of

* The authors acknowledge the research assistance of Tiani Robertson and Melanie Lewis (USQ Faculty of Business, Class of 2002) in the preparation of this chapter.

[1] Unverified figures available at the time of writing at Insolvency and Trustee Services Australia <http://www.itsa. gov.au/>. Verified figures are included in the Annual Report, normally available in October. Given that the Annual Reports contain verified figures and greater detail than interim statistics available on the ITSA website, this chapter is based on the 2000–01 publication being the latest available at the time of writing.

[2] That is, they became subject to a collective administration of their available estate by a trustee on behalf of creditors and in accordance with statutory distribution rules.

[3] Insolvency and Trustee Service Australia, *Annual Report of the Inspector General in Bankruptcy on the Operation of the Bankruptcy Act 2000–2001* (Canberra, Commonwealth of Australia, 2001) [*Operation of Bankruptcy Act*].

[4] J Kumar, R Mason and D Ralston, 'Consumer Bankruptcies: Causes and Implications for the Credit Industry' (1998) 17 (3) *Economic Papers* 18.

[5] See in particular Symposium (1999) 37 *Osgoode Hall Law Journal* (special issue).

Chart 1 Business and Non-business Bankruptcy Rates

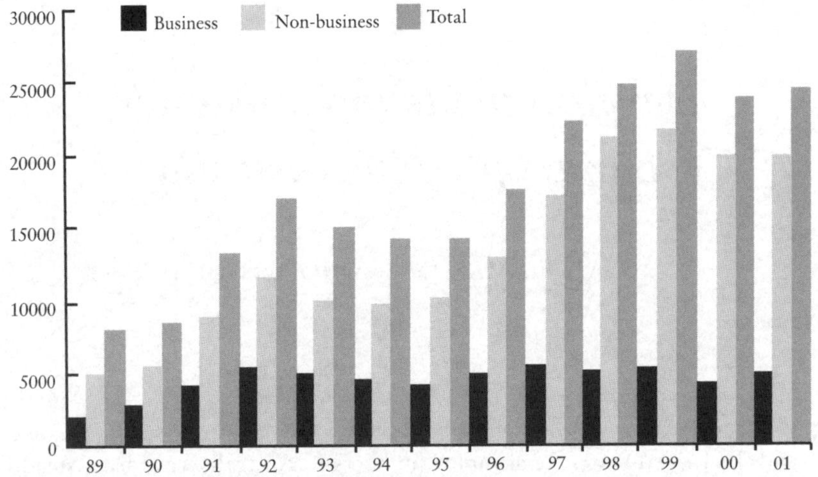

Source: Annual Report by Inspector General in Bankruptcy on the Operation of the Bankruptcy Act 1966, 1 July 2000 to 30 June 2001, Figure 1, p 6. http://www.itsa.gov.au/aghome/commaff/itsa/frame_pubs.html->Annual Reports->2000/2001

such an Australian study is striking. Nevertheless, prompt quarterly and annual statistical data are being made available by the Insolvency and Trustee Service Australia (ITSA).[6] Such data as there is suggests that bankruptcy is generally only resorted to by consumers who are critically insolvent.

In 1989, a sample of undischarged consumer bankrupts and others involved in the bankruptcy process were interviewed in a study in Melbourne. This study found that bankrupts were largely victims of low income, changes in circumstance and the questionable lending practices of finance companies rather than poor debt management or dishonesty.[7] A link was also found between excessive creditor harassment and the decision by the over-committed debtors to petition for their own bankruptcy.[8]

A recent ITSA study of the statement of affairs of all the debtors who became bankrupt or entered into debt agreements in 2001–02 concluded that bankrupts 'are at the lower end of the socio-economic scale.'[9] The median income level was AUD 15,000 while 61 per cent had an income below AUD 20,000. This com-

[6] <http://www.itsa.gov.au/> Statistics.

[7] M Ryan, 'Consumer Bankrupts in Melbourne' (1993) 28 *Australian Journal of Social Issues* 34. See also M Ryan, *The Last Resort: A Study of Consumer Bankrupts* (Aldershot, Avebury, 1995).

[8] M Ryan, 'Consumer Bankruptcy: Is there a link between creditor harassment and consumer bankruptcy?' (1993) 18 (4) *Alternative Law Journal* 158.

[9] Insolvency and Trustee Service Australia, *Profiles of Debtors who became Bankrupt or Entered into Debt Agreements in 2001/2002* (Canberra, Insolvency and Trustee Service Australia, 2002) at 22 [ITSA Debtors Profile].

pares to a poverty line income level for a single unemployed adult with no dependants for the March quarter 2001 of $14,458, rising to $18,561 for a single parent with one dependant child.[10] Unemployment was the largest single attributed cause of bankruptcy and 61 per cent of the bankrupts were not employed.

The Annual Reports of the Inspector-General in Bankruptcy list the most common causes of bankruptcy, as described by the bankrupts themselves. These statistics are compiled by ITSA officials who collate the bankrupts' responses from their statements of affairs[11] according to present categories.[12] For non-business bankruptcies, the 2000–01 Annual Report notes that unemployment was the main cause attributed, followed by excessive credit card use and domestic discord.[13]

Table 1 Major Causes of Bankruptcies in Australia

Business Bankruptcies		Consumer Bankruptcies	
Major Causes	Percent	Major Causes	Percent
Economic conditions	40	Unemployment	40
Personal reasons	20	Excessive use of credit	21
Lack of capital	15	Domestic discord	16
Lack of business ability	11	Ill-health	9
Excessive interest	6	Adverse litigation	6
Total	92%		92%

Source: Annual Report by Inspector General in Bankruptcy on the Operation of the Bankruptcy Act 1966, 1 July 2000 to 30 June 2001, pp 15–17

Despite this evidence, debtor abuse of the bankruptcy system has been identified by Australian policy-makers as a major cause of the increased bankruptcies and, as a result, has been targeted for reform. In March 2002, announcing that a bankruptcy reform bill would be re-introduced into federal Parliament,[14] the Attorney-General in a press release entitled 'Bankruptcy Crackdown'[15] stated that:

[10] As cited by the ITSA Debtors Profile, the Henderson Poverty Line income level reported by the *Melbourne Institute of Applied Economics and Social Research—Poverty Lines* <http://www.melbourneinstitute.com> Research Programs → Labour, Social And Fiscal Studies → Others: Poverty Lines < http://wff2.ecom.unimelb.edu.au/iaesrwww/miesi/PovertyLines.pdf>.

[11] From 03 Statement of Affairs Q 2: 'List what you believe is the primary cause of your insolvency.'

[12] For non-business related bankruptcies, the options are: Unemployment or loss of income; Adverse legal action; Liabilities due to guarantees; Gambling, speculation & extravagance in living; Ill health or absence of health insurance; Domestic discord or relationship breakdowns; Excessive use of credit facilities including losses on repossessions, high interest payments and pressure selling.

[13] The ITSA Debtors Profile (see above n 9) also confirms these as the three main causes for 2001–02.

[14] An earlier similar Bill had lapsed upon the calling of a general election.

[15] Media Release (2002), The Attorney-General, The Hon Daryl Williams, 'Bankruptcy Crackdown', 21 March, ITSA <http://www.itsa.gov.au/aghome/commaff/itsa/frame_bankreforms.html>.

> Bankruptcy should be a last resort for people who have overwhelming debts and need a fresh start. However, some people see it as a way to get out of paying debts they can afford to pay. The new bankruptcy laws will make it harder for these people to abuse Australia's bankruptcy system. . . . These amendments are designed to stop abuses of the bankruptcy system and to encourage people to consider alternatives to bankruptcy such as debt agreements. They address concerns that bankruptcy is 'too easy' and better balance the interests of debtors and creditors.

These amendments have been passed by the lower House; however, the government does not have a majority in the upper House and so amendments are a possibility. Current opposition party proposals include amending, rather than repealing, the early discharge provisions and amending the procedures underpinning formal arrangements with creditors to address perceived related party abuses.[16]

This paper has three major parts. First, it introduces the various administrations available for insolvent individuals in Australia. Next, it elaborates on particular issues surrounding individuals whose estates are sequestrated in bankruptcy; discharge from bankruptcy (including the discontinued cooling-off period amendments), exempt property and income contributions during bankruptcy. Finally, it examines debt agreements, including information surrounding their use and developments in the regulation of administrators.

II. AUSTRALIAN PERSONAL INSOLVENCY ADMINISTRATIONS

While Australian bankruptcy law does not explicitly differentiate between consumer and business insolvency, Australian law distinguishes between the insolvency of personal and corporate debtors.[17] Although there has been occasional debate on a merged regulatory framework for personal and corporate insolvencies,[18] there is little indication at present that the policy-makers intend to change the current regimes.

[16] The Commonwealth government has announced a comprehensive review of Part X to investigate concerns that some debtors are abusing the arrangements. See Issues Papers 'Review of Part X of the Bankruptcy Act 1966', ITSA<http://www.itsa.gov.au/aghome/commaff/itsa/frame_bankreforms.html> Issues Papers 'Review of Part X of the Bankruptcy Act 1966'. It is to be conducted by ITSA and the Attorney-General's Department, in consultation with the Bankruptcy Reform Consultative Forum: Media Release (2002), The Attorney-General, The Hon. Daryl Williams, 'Review of Part X of the Bankruptcy Act', 20 September, <http://www.law.gov.au/aghome/agnews/2002newsag/98_02.htm>.

[17] Corporate insolvency had been regulated by state laws, albeit largely uniform laws in recent decades, until the states referred corporate powers to the Commonwealth, which enabled federal corporations laws which include the corporate insolvency provisions, to be enacted in *Corporations Act 2001* (Cth).

[18] Australian Law Reform Commission, *Report No 45, General Insolvency Inquiry* by Mr R W Harmer, Commissioner-in-Charge, (Canberra, Australian Government Publishing Service, 1998) at para 933. A Keay, 'The Unity of Insolvency Legislation: Time for a Re-think?' (1999) 7 *Insolvency Law Journal* 4. In 2003, see http://www.aph.gov.au/senate/committee/corporations_ctte/ail/issuespaper.doc.

The federal Parliament has constitutional power to make laws with respect to 'bankruptcy and insolvency'[19] and while colonial, then state, bankruptcy laws continued in place following federation in 1901, they became obsolete when the Commonwealth Parliament enacted federal bankruptcy laws effective from 1928. The laws dealing with personal bankruptcies and alternative arrangements with creditors are largely to be found in the *Bankruptcy Act 1966* (Cth).[20]

Individual insolvency is regulated (and many bankruptcies are administered) by the Insolvency and Trustee Service Australia (ITSA). This is an Executive Agency within the Attorney General's Department portfolio. The organisation reports directly to the Attorney General.[21] Personal insolvency administrations are conducted by both the public and private sector. Bankruptcies may be administered by trustees from either sector although the vast majority is administered by the public sector.[22] Formal arrangements with creditors may be administered by Official Receivers as well as by private registered trustees, although in practice they remain in the domain of the private sector.[23]

Proposals for less formal arrangements by low income debtors are processed by the public sector, whereas the agreements once approved may be administered by the public or private sector, although not necessarily a registered bankruptcy trustee. When debt agreements were introduced, they were to be 'a low cost, simple process under which a debt agreement administrator could be any person, such as a debtor's friend or family member, and need hold no formal qualifications.'[24]

Where a person is insolvent and is unable to pay his or her debts as and when they become due and payable,[25] a number of options is available. In addition to informal action taken outside the regulatory framework, debtors may have their estates administered in bankruptcy under Part IV of the Act or, in the less common case of deceased estates, Part XI (93.5 per cent of new administrations for 2000–01).[26] Alternatively, they may enter into binding arrangements with cred-

[19] S 51 (xvii) *Commonwealth Constitution.*

[20] Also see *Bankruptcy (Estate Charges) Act 1997* (Cth); *Bankruptcy (Registration Charges) Act 1997* (Cth). Unless otherwise advised, all statutory references in this chapter are to the *Bankruptcy Act 1966* (Cth).

[21] 'Action Plan—Strategic Overview of ITSA', ITSA <http://www.itsa.gov.au/aghome/comaff/itsa/frame_actionplan.html>.

[22] In 2000–01, 27,324 new bankruptcy administrations were received by the Official Trustee and 2,312 by private registered trustees: above n 3, at 13–4. The Official Trustee, a corporation sole with perpetual succession (s 18), is the trustee of any estate for which no private registered trustee is appointed. In practice, the Official Trustee acts through the Official Receivers for each (state/territory) bankruptcy district who conduct the administration of estates.

[23] House of Representatives, *Bankruptcy Legislation Amendment Bill 1996: Explanatory Memorandum* (Canberra, Australian Government Publishing Service, 1996) at para 137.2 [*1996 Explanatory Memorandum*].

[24] House of Representatives, *Bankruptcy Legislation Amendment Bill 2002: Explanatory Memorandum* (Canberra, Australian Government Publishing Service, 2002) at para 207 [*2002 Explanatory Memorandum*].

[25] S 5.

[26] In 2000–01 of 25,565 new administrations reported in the Annual Report, 23,097 were under Part IV and Part XI, 424 under Part X, and 1234 under Part IX. *Operation of Bankruptcy Act*, above n 3.

itors to satisfy their debts in part or in full under Part X arrangements (1.7 per cent for 2000–01) or Part IX debt agreements (4.8 per cent for 2000–01). Part X arrangements are somewhat more complex than debt agreements and hence more costly. Accordingly, they are not dealt with in this chapter, which concentrates on non-business or consumer debtors.[27]

III. BANKRUPTCY

Voluntary bankruptcies constitute the overwhelming majority of all bankruptcies in Australia. In 2000–01, almost 95 per cent of bankruptcies were initiated by debtor's petition.[28] In most cases, a debtor enters voluntary bankruptcy simply by presenting a petition to the Official Receiver together with a statement[29] of the debtor's financial affairs.[30] No fee is payable for filing the debtor's petition.[31] If the debtor wishes to appoint a registered trustee to administer his or her bankrupt estate, rather than have it administered by the Official Trustee, the trustee's consent to act must also be submitted.[32] In practice, it is rare for a debtor to appoint a registered trustee, mainly because a large proportion of voluntary bankruptcies are assetless.

If the documentation appears to be in order, the Official Receiver, after giving the debtor certain prescribed information about sources of financial advice, alternatives to bankruptcy and the consequences of bankruptcy,[33] must accept and endorse the petition. The debtor is thereupon deemed to have become bankrupt at the beginning of that day.[34]

The Bankruptcy Legislation Amendment Bill 2002 (the 2002 Bill) proposes to introduce a discretion for Official Receivers to reject debtors' petitions where it appears that, within a reasonable time, the debtor could pay all the debts listed in the debtors statement of affairs and that the debtor's petition is an abuse of the bankruptcy system.[35]

The ITSA commentary on the proposed reforms suggests that some debtors are choosing bankruptcy for reasons such as to avoid paying for goods or

[27] For a discussion of this form of administration, see R Mason, 'Consumer Bankruptcies: An Australian Perspective' (1999) 37 *Osgoode Hall Law Journal* 449 at 455.

[28] *Operation of Bankruptcy Act*, above n 3, at ix.

[29] Section 6A & ITSA Approved Form 3, ITSA: Statutory Forms <http://www.itsa.gov.au/aghome/commaff/itsa/index.html>

[30] S 55.

[31] According to ITSA's prescribed information on Bankruptcy and Alternatives under reg 4.11 dated November 2001 (see ITSA <http://www.itsa.gov.au/aghome/commaff/itsa/frame_bankruptcy.html>), ITSA's fees for administering an estate are set by law and are normally a minimum of $4,000, plus goods and services tax, but it is paid only if money is received in the estate.

[32] Bankruptcy Regulation 4.12.

[33] S 55(3A). The information is prescribed under Bankruptcy Regulation 4.11, above n 31. The information is available on the ITSA web site: Bankruptcy & Alternatives <http://www.itsa.gov.au/>.

[34] S 57A.

[35] *2002 Explanatory Memorandum*, above n 24, at para 3.

services received or to deny their spouse marriage property settlements;[36] however, lack of empirical evidence makes it difficult to substantiate this. An alleged misuse of bankruptcy, which has attracted much community and political interest, is that of voluntary bankruptcy by high-income bankrupts, such as barristers and other professionals, who were thereby released from substantial taxation debts.[37] In 2001, amendments were made to the New South Wales legislation regulating the legal profession, in particular requiring a legal practitioner who has committed an act of bankruptcy or a taxation offence to show cause why he or she is a 'fit and proper person' to hold a practising certificate.[38]

In his second reading speech on the 2002 Bill in the lower House, the Attorney-General referred to a task force established in March 2001 to report on whether any changes were needed to the bankruptcy and taxation laws to ensure that bankruptcy law could not be used to avoid tax obligations.[39] While the government is yet to respond to the task force's report, the Attorney General noted that this proposed amendment will permit the court, on application by a creditor such as the Australian Taxation Office, to annul the bankruptcy of a high-income professional who is technically insolvent but who could have chosen to meet unpaid taxation obligations. This amendment is intended to address only the most blatant abuses of the system and ITSA does not envisage 'that any petition will be rejected under this proposed measure without personal or telephone contact first being made with the debtor by senior, experienced ITSA staff.'[40]

Thus, the Official Receiver would be able to reject a petition where it appears from information in the statement of affairs or otherwise supplied by the debtor that, if the debtor did not become a bankrupt, the debtor would be solvent; and either it is evident to the Official Receiver that the debtor is petitioning because of an unwillingness (and not an incapacity) to pay; or the debtor has been bankrupt previously, on his or her own petition, either at least three times or at least once in the last five years.[41]

Compulsory bankruptcy results from a creditor's petition presented at a Federal Court or Federal Magistrates Court Registry. The prerequisites include a liquidated sum of AUD 2,000 owing by the debtor to the creditor.[42] Initially

[36] Media Release (2002), The Attorney-General, 'Bankruptcy Legislation Amendment Act 2002—Reforms to the Bankruptcy Act', 10 December, ITSA <http://www.itsa.gov.au/aghome/commaff/itsa/frame_bankreforms.html>.

[37] Media Release (2001), The Attorney-General, The Hon Daryl Williams, 'Attorneys-General to consider compulsory reporting of bankruptcy for barristers', 28 February, Australian Law Online <http://www.1aw.gov.au/aghome/agnews/200lnewsag/926_0l.htm>.

[38] *Legal Profession Amendment (Disciplinary Provisions) Act 2001* (NSW).

[39] Commonwealth, House of Representatives *Parliamentary Debates Second Reading Speech* (30 May 2002) at 2825 (Mr Williams).

[40] D Costello, 'Bankruptcy Reforms Package' (2001) 11 (1) *New Direction in Bankruptcy* 14 at 16.

[41] Above n 24, at para 89.

[42] Ss 43–44.

all creditors' petitions are heard by a Registrar exercising delegated powers.[43] The potential outcomes are adjournment, dismissal, withdrawal of the petition or a sequestration order.[44]

A. Discharge from Bankruptcy

The Australian approach to a 'fresh start' policy can be characterised as reasonably generous to bankrupts, although changes are proposed to the discharge provisions. There is currently an automatic administrative discharge from bankruptcy three years from the date of filing of the debtor's statement of affairs.[45] However, there are avenues for this period to be decreased through early discharge or extended through an objection to discharge by the trustee or the Official Receiver.

Discharge generally releases the former bankrupt from all provable debts.[46] A creditor is nevertheless entitled to receive a dividend from the bankrupt estate after discharge. Debts released include secured debts,[47] however, the secured creditor may still deal with the security,[48] to the extent that the creditor has not proved in the bankruptcy.[49] That is, they can only prove if they surrender their security or prove to the extent that the security is inadequate.[50] Thus secured creditors are free to exercise their proprietary rights over relevant property.

There are a number of exceptions to this scheme of release from provable debts.[51] For example, the bankrupt is not released from a liability under the Act to make an income contribution, a liability under a maintenance agreement or order[52] or a debt or liability incurred in the context of fraud.[53]

1. *Early Discharge*

Currently, a bankrupt may make written application to the trustee for early discharge from bankruptcy at any time after six months from the date of filing the

[43] Federal Court Rules Order 77 r 7; Federal Magistrates Court (Delegation to Registrars) Rules 2000 r 1.4(1).

[44] A Keay and M Murray, *Insolvency: Personal and Corporate Law and Practice*, 4th edn (Sydney, Lawbook Co, 2002) at 60.

[45] S 149.

[46] S 153.

[47] Whether or not the secured creditor has surrendered the security for the benefit of creditors generally: s 153(1).

[48] The creation of securities is invalidated in some situations, under the relation back (s 115) or voidable transaction provisions (s 120–122). Also the trustee in bankruptcy may disclaim property that is subject to a security in the creditor's favour: s 133.

[49] S 153(3).

[50] That is, to the extent that they are in fact unsecured: ss 90–94.

[51] S 153(2). The reference to 'debts' includes liabilities: s 5(1).

[52] Except to the extent that the court has ordered a release from liability to pay arrears under such an agreement or order: ss l53(2)(c); 153(2A).

[53] S 1 53(2)(b). See *Cornelius v Barewa Oil & Mining NL (in liq)* (1982) 42 Australian Law Reports 83; *Chittick v Maxwell* (1993) 118 Australian Law Reports 728; *Re Sharp; Ex Parte Tietyens Investments Pty Ltd (in liq)* [1998] 1367 FCA (26 October 1998).

statement of affairs.[54] However, only a small proportion of bankrupts who are eligible for discharge apply. During 2000–01, 5,964 applications for early discharge were granted.[55] This represents approximately 25 per cent of new bankruptcies for 2000–01, although applications may well have been made by people who were made bankrupt in a previous financial year.[56]

A bankrupt is eligible for early discharge only if there is not enough money available to pay the remuneration and expenses of the trustee or to pay a dividend to creditors. Even those bankrupts who meet the eligibility criteria for early discharge may nevertheless be disqualified.[57] In the Explanatory Memorandum to the 2002 Bill's proposed repeal of early discharge, it is noted that:

> These provisions are most often cited as the cause of concern that bankruptcy is too easy. The reduced period of bankruptcy is seen to discourage debtors from trying to enter formal or informal arrangements with their creditors to settle debts, and provides little opportunity for debtors to become better financial managers.
>
> Also, when introduced, early discharge was described as applying to those whose bankruptcy was brought about by misfortune rather than misdeed. The provisions were targeted at a new category of bankrupt consumer debtors with low asset-backing who over-extend and then cannot repay their debts. However, they have not achieved their stated intent. There is no evidence that qualifying for early discharge is a sound measure of whether a bankruptcy has been due to misfortune rather than misdeed.
>
> There is no intrinsic reason why bankrupts who have assets available for distribution or income sufficient to make a contribution to the estate (which disqualifies them for early discharge) are less worthy of early discharge than those who do not. In addition, allowing only those whose debts exceed 150 per cent of income to apply, discriminates against women who have joint debts with, and generally a lower income than, their spouse. In other words, the provisions operate in quite discriminatory ways.[58]

However, there has been some opposition to this move. The Australian Financial Counselling & Credit Reform Association has reservations about the abolition of early discharge.[59] When the 2001 Bill was before Parliament, the Senate recommended it be referred to the Senate Legal and Constitutional

[54] S 149S(1).

[55] *Operation of Bankruptcy Act*, above n 3, Table 21.

[56] The total number of bankrupts as at 30 June 2001, based on new bankruptcies since 1993, less annulments and discharges, has been estimated at approximately 68,000: Telephone conversation with Peter Lowe, Executive Director, ITSA, Canberra, 25 September 2002.

[57] Ss 149X–149ZE.

[58] *2002 Explanatory Memorandum*, above n 24, at paras 42–44.

[59] Commonwealth, Senate Legal and Constitutional Legislation Committee 2001, *Inquiry into the Provisions of the Bankruptcy Legislation Amendment Bill 2001 and the Bankruptcy (Estate Charges) Amendment Bill 2001* (Canberra, Senate Printing Unit, 2001) at para 2.10 [Senate Committee Inquiry]. Also see J Pentland, 'Bankruptcy Legislation Amendment Bill 2002' (2002) 3(2) *Credit Line Financial Counselling Services Sharkwatch*, <http://www.wesleymission.org.au/centres creditline/sharkwatch0206.asp#3>.

Legislation Committee and drew particular attention to the impact on low-income earners of the Bill's abolition of the early discharge provisions.[60] During its inquiry, the Committee received submissions to retain the early discharge provisions from community legal services,[61] whereas the Law Council of Australia expressed the view that the provisions had never operated as intended.[62] The body representing credit unions was of the opinion that they actually disadvantaged low income earners, who were led thereby to believe 'it was all over' after six months, whereas bankruptcy still showed up on a debtor's credit advantage file and so affected the availability of credit for seven years.[63] During the 2002 Bill's passage through the federal Parliament, the opposition party has proposed an amendment such that early discharge might be applied for after two years rather than six months.[64]

2. *Objections to Discharge*

At any time before the bankrupt is automatically discharged from bankruptcy the trustee may file with the Official Receiver, or the Official Receiver on his or her own initiative may file, a written notice of objection to the discharge.[65] The trustee must file a notice of objection to the discharge if he or she believes that this is the only way to make the bankrupt perform a duty that the bankrupt has not done.[66] In 2000–01, only a small number of objections to automatic discharge were filed.[67]

An objection takes effect from the beginning of the day on which details of the notice of objection are entered in the register, the National Personal Insolvency Index.[68] Its effect is to extend the period of bankruptcy either to five or eight years from the date of filing of the statement of affairs depending on the grounds specified.[69] Case law has established that an objection can only be lodged to advance the administration of the bankruptcy, not to punish the bankrupt.[70]

60 Senate Committee Inquiry, above n 59, at para 1.2. <http://www.aph.gov.au/Senate/committee/legcon_ctte/bankruptcybills01/Bankruptcy.pdf>.

61 Wesley Community Legal Service (Senate Committee Inquiry, *ibid* at para 3.8) and West Heidelberg Community Legal Service (Senate Committee Inquiry, *ibid* at para 3.9).

62 Senate Committee Inquiry, *ibid* at para 3.12.

63 Senate Committee Inquiry, *ibid* at para 3.11.

64 Amendment to Bankruptcy Legislation Amendment Bill 2002, Schedule 1, item 127, at 29 (lines 19 and 20), in s 149S(1) omit 'six months', substitute 'two years' proposed by Mr McClelland.

65 S 149B(1).

66 S 149B(2).

67 Objections to automatic discharge totalled 301, which is approximately 0.4% of all new bankruptcies for the three-year period (normal length of a bankruptcy) of 1998–99, 1999–2000 and 2000–01. Obviously this is an estimate given the lack of data about the financial year in which the 301 bankrupts entered bankruptcy. On objections, see *Operation of Bankruptcy Act*, above n 3, Table 22.

68 Section 149G.

69 Section 149A(2).

70 *2002 Explanatory Memorandum*, above n 24, at para 164; *Inspector-General in Bankruptcy v Nelson* (1998) 168 Australian Law Reports 340.

Examples of bankrupts' non-compliance with their statutory obligations, which may ground an objection, include failure to comply with a trustee's written request for information about property or income or to disclose liabilities existing at the date of bankruptcy. It can also include failure to pay an income contribution, to sign a document or to attend a creditors meeting or an examination.[71]

The 2002 Bill proposes to strengthen the provisions which allow trustees to lodge objections to discharge.[72] It is proposed that trustee objections will fall into one of two groups, those which specify a 'special ground' and those which specify none. In the first group, the trustee's notice of objection will have to set out the ground(s) of objection and the evidence relied on to establish it or them. These special grounds include where the bankrupt, when requested in writing by the trustee to provide written information about the bankrupt's property, income, or expected income, failed to comply with the request, and where the bankrupt failed to pay to the trustee an amount that the bankrupt was liable to pay under the contribution scheme. In the second group, where no 'special ground' is specified, the trustee will be obliged to provide in the notice his or her reasons for lodging an objection. Additional new grounds for objection include types of intentional behaviour by bankrupts which can disrupt a trustee's administration as well as transfers of property with the intention of defeating creditors.

3. 30 Day Cooling Off Period

One of the most controversial proposed amendments in the Bankruptcy Legislation Amendment Bill 2001 was the introduction of a mandatory 30-day cooling-off period following acceptance of a debtor's petition. This proposal has been removed from the 2002 Bill.[73]

The earlier proposal was aimed at allowing debtors who have acted too hastily in petitioning for bankruptcy to reconsider their decision. If they were satisfied that bankruptcy would not be the best option for them, they would have been able to withdraw their petition by giving written notice to the Official Receiver. The cooling-off period was also intended to allow the creditors the opportunity to consider whether a debtor's bankruptcy would be in the creditors' best interests.

This cooling-off period was the subject of adverse comment during the consultation process. Even before the 2001 Bill was finalised, the proposal was changed to restrict access, for example if a debtor sought to abuse the system

[71] Ss 149C – 149D.

[72] *2002 Explanatory Memorandum*, above n 24, at paras 45–54, 159–179.

[73] Therefore it will not repeal the current seven-day moratorium procedure: 'Declaration of Intention to Present a Debtor's Petition' (ss 54A–54L). This procedure 'freezes' the debts of an individual debtor for up to 7 days, allowing a brief opportunity for him or her to consider alternatives to bankruptcy. See House of Representatives, *Bankruptcy Amendment Bill 1987: Explanatory Memorandum* (Canberra, Australian Government Publishing Service, 1987) at paras 5, 127.

through repeated presentation and withdrawal of petitions or if a debtor had been in business in the 30 days before presenting a petition. The concern with the latter situation was the need for an immediate appointment of a trustee to prevent dissipation of assets and to facilitate the business being sold as a going concern. Nevertheless, serious concerns were still being raised about the administrative complexity of the 2001 proposal.

In his speech to Parliament when introducing the 2002 Bill, the Attorney General announced the government's decision not to proceed with this initiative after re-canvassing the views of stakeholders, the majority of whom doubted that many creditors would change their mind during the cooling-off period. Financial counsellors were also concerned that undesirable pressure might be placed on the debtor by creditors during the 30 days.

The Attorney-General also noted the recent sharp rise in the number of debt agreements. This latter development was seen as evidence that people in financial difficulty are considering and choosing debt agreements as an alternative to bankruptcy, thus indicating the extended cooling-off period was unnecessary. This trend would be supported by the 2002 Bill's increase in the income threshold for debt agreements and thus enhanced availability.[74]

B. Exempt Property

The *Bankruptcy Act* provides for an automatic vesting of a debtor's property on bankruptcy.[75] When a debtor becomes bankrupt 'the property of the bankrupt' vests automatically in the Official Trustee or, where one has been appointed, the registered trustee.[76] Property subsequently acquired by (or which devolves upon) the bankrupt also vests automatically in the trustee. The term 'the property of the bankrupt' is defined as that property which is 'divisible among the bankrupt's creditors,' together with rights and powers in relation to such property.[77]

The Act then allows the bankrupt to keep certain property by providing that it is not divisible among creditors and thus exempting it from this vesting process. The exemptions[78] include property, often up to a defined amount, which comprises household property, property which is used to earn income by person exertion,[79] property used primarily as a means for transport,[80] and life assurance, superannuation and retirement savings accounts.

[74] Commonwealth, House of Representatives, Parliamentary Debates Second Reading Speech (21 March 2002) at 1844 (Mr Williams).

[75] S 58.

[76] Where legislation requires that the transmission of property be registered, equitable title only in the property vests in the trustee until the registration requirements have been met: s 58(2).

[77] S 5(1).

[78] S 116(2).

[79] The relevant amount is prescribed by Bankruptcy Regulation 6.04 and allows for adjustments for CPI increases from 1 July 1997. At the time of writing, the amount is AUD 2,800.

[80] The maximum amount currently prescribed by Bankruptcy Regulation 6.04 is AUD 5,500. If the car or motorcycle is realised by the trustee an amount up to the maximum is given to the

A bankrupt's 'household property' is exempted if, according to Bankruptcy Regulation 6.03, it 'is reasonably necessary for the domestic use of the bankrupt's household, having regard to current social standards,' taking into account factors such as the particular requirements of the bankrupt's household and the practicability of selling the property. The Regulation also specifies particular items, such as various types of kitchen equipment, 'sufficient beds for members of the household', educational, sporting or recreational items for the use of children or students, a television, video recorder, stereo equipment, washing machine and drier, refrigerator and freezer and telephone. The 2002 Bill proposes to introduce a provision allowing creditors, by special resolution, to permit a bankrupt to retain sentimental property of a prescribed kind. It is proposed to prescribe items such as sporting medals, trophies, and civil and military awards, but not jewellery.[81] Property is also exempted if creditors pass an ordinary resolution exempting certain household property identified for the purpose.[82]

A bankrupt's interests in and payments made after the date of bankruptcy from: (a) life or endowment assurance policies (b) regulated superannuation funds[83] and (c) a retirement savings account[84] other than a payment in the form of a pension or annuity. There is a limit on the amount of this exemption,[85] which is, in general terms, up to the 'reasonable benefit limit' (RBL) as defined in taxation legislation.[86] Opponents to bankruptcy have argued that this limit is relatively generous. For the 2001–02 financial year, it is AUD 1,058,742.

A bankrupt also retains any right he or she might have to recover damages or compensation for 'personal injury or wrong' done to the bankrupt (including defamation), the bankrupt's spouse or a member of the bankrupt's family, or in respect of the death of the spouse or family member.[87]

C. Income Contributions

In principle, income earned by a bankrupt after the commencement of bankruptcy would fall within a bankrupt's after-acquired property and so be available to creditors. However, the policy of the legislation has been to treat

bankrupt and any balance is available for distribution. Creditors may resolve to increase the amount: s 116(2B).

81 *2002 Explanatory Memorandum*, above n 24, at para 133.

82 S 116(2B). This can only be done if the property has not already been realised by the trustee. If such a resolution is passed, the property then revests in the bankrupt.

83 Within the meaning of the *Superannuation Industry (Supervision) Act 1993* (Cth).

84 As defined in the *Retirement Savings Accounts Act 1997* (Cth).

85 Sub-ss 116(5)—(8). See also Bankruptcy Regulations 6.06–6.08.

86 *Income Tax Assessment Act 1936* (Cth).

87 Damages or compensation recovered can be retained by the bankrupt whether recovered before or after the date of bankruptcy. The exemption also extends to property purchased, or the principal of a loan repaid, from all or substantially all of the damages or compensation recovered by the bankrupt.

income as a special case, on the basis that bankrupts should be encouraged, as part of the rehabilitation process, to earn income during bankruptcy.

There is an administrative procedure, without the need to apply to the court, for a trustee to assess income contributions by a bankrupt.[88] The amount of the contribution is half the difference between the bankrupt's income and a threshold amount specified by the Act. This threshold amount is linked to pension rates under the *Social Security Act 1991*(Cth), which in turn are based on a proportion of average male weekly earnings.[89] The trustee must make an assessment of the income that is likely to be derived by the bankrupt.[90] The bankrupt is required to provide evidence of his or her income together with relevant books.[91] The trustee also has power to estimate income where there are reasonable grounds to believe that income has been derived by the bankrupt.[92] The income of the bankrupt includes income according to ordinary usages and concepts but is also significantly extended to overcome devices for avoiding contributions, such as the use of loans or payments to associated trust or corporate entities.[93]

A mere 1,662 bankrupts were liable to contribute income as at 30 June 2001,[94] only 2.4 per cent of the approximate total number of bankrupts at that date.[95] The total contributions collected during 2000–01 amounted to AUD 6,303,067. The contributions outstanding as at 30 June 2001, and considered by the trustee to be recoverable, amounted to AUD 2,856,397.[96]

Where the bankrupt believes that he or she will suffer hardship as a result of having to make an income contribution, the bankrupt may apply to the Official Receiver to increase the threshold amount and so reduce the bankrupt's contribution.[97] The grounds[98] are limited to certain medical, child day-care, and

[88] Bankrupts may also make voluntary donations from their income and in 2000–2001, they voluntarily contributed AUD 241,102. *Operation of Bankruptcy Act*, above n 3, at 18.

[89] For example, part of the calculation of a single person's pension is that it must be at least 25% of male total earnings (See Australian Bureau of Statistics 2002, *6302.0 Average Weekly Earnings Australia, Table3 Average Weekly Earnings of Employees Australia (Dollars)—Original*, Australian Bureau of Statistics <http://www.abs.gov.au>). The threshold amount is determined by upward movements in the consumer price index on the relevant pension rate. It also increases if the bankrupt has dependants: s 139K. For example, with one dependant, it increases by 18% and with four or more, it increases by 36%.

[90] Derivation of income is determined on a receipts basis so that income is derived during an assessment period even if received for work done or services performed before or after that period: s 139M(3). See *Re Sharpe* [1998] FCA 6 (16 January 1998); (1998) 80 FCR 536, where fees rendered and not paid by the date of bankruptcy are to be treated as income rather than debts owing to the estate.

[91] S 139U. If the trustee has reasonable grounds to suspect that particulars given by the bankrupt are false or misleading in a material respect, or that a material particular has been omitted, the trustee can require such information or books: s 139V.

[92] S 139Z.

[93] Ss 139L, 139N, 139Y.

[94] *Operation of Bankruptcy Act*, above n 3, at 18.

[95] That is 68,000: see telephone conversation with Peter Lowe, above n 56.

[96] That is AUD 634,728 for the Official Trustee and AUD 2,221,669 for the registered trustees. *Operation of Bankruptcy Act*, above n 3, at 18.

[97] S 139T.

[98] S 139T.

rental costs and substantial travelling expenses to and from work. The bankrupt may also apply on the basis of inability, through unemployment, illness or injury, of the bankrupt's spouse, or another person who resides with the bankrupt, to continue to contribute to the costs of maintaining the bankrupt's household.[99] Only 32 applications to appeal assessments were made on grounds of hardship during the 2000–01 financial year, 13 of which were successful.[100]

The 2002 Bill proposes to fine-tune the income contribution scheme. For example, dependants will be allowed to earn up to a prescribed amount and still qualify as dependants. (Currently there is a 'zero income' test.) Trustees, rather than the Official Receiver, will be allowed to determine a higher income threshold if the bankrupt is suffering hardship.

IV. PART IX DEBT AGREEMENTS

While the unverified figures for people filing for bankruptcy in 2001–02 show a small increase after two years of relative stability, in the same financial year, there was a significant increase, more than 200 per cent, in the number of debt agreements, which number had already been almost doubling in each previous financial year. While there does not appear to be any research to explain the reasons for this exponential growth, anecdotal evidence, such as increased advertising, would seem to suggest that a new niche market has been identified by business with an interest in the debt collection area.

This increase raises the question of whether there may be insolvent individuals who, until debt agreements were introduced, remained outside the insolvency 'system,' neither entering bankruptcy nor the more formal (and expensive) collective arrangements with their creditors.[101] A recent report on the household sector by the Australian Bureau of Statistics (ABS) indicates a worsening debt service ability for households since 1995, both from the perspective of debt to income ratio and the debt to liquid assets ratio. Since 2000, both ABS and Reserve Bank of Australia data indicates that more than one year's income is required to repay a household's debt. However, the ratio of debt to liquidated assets ratio remains at less than 100 per cent, indicating a capability to meet debt commitments out of available resources.[102]

[99] Bankruptcy Regulation 6.16 prescribes an additional reason for variation where a circumstance has occurred in relation to a bankrupt or a bankrupt's dependant that in the Official Receiver's opinion is of an exceptional nature and imposes an excessive financial burden on the bankrupt.

[100] *Operation of Bankruptcy Act*, above n 3, at 19.

[101] The number of more formal and expensive Part X arrangements with creditors, for which there is no minimum income and balance sheet test, has remained relatively steady over the past five years. That is, between approximately 400–450 arrangements across Australia.

[102] According to the ABS, this lends support to 'wealth effects' being an influence on households' demand for debt: Australian Bureau of Statistics 2002, 'Australian National Accounts: Financial Accounts: Household sector data in the financial accounts (March Quarter 2002)', at paras 12–13. Note, however, that because of data availability, the household sector is deemed to include persons

A government paper entitled 'The household balance sheet in Australia' includes the following chart which shows that since consistent data became available in mid-1995, increases in the aggregate value of household financial and non-financial assets have coincided with rises in household debt.

Chart 2 Household sector balance sheet (a)

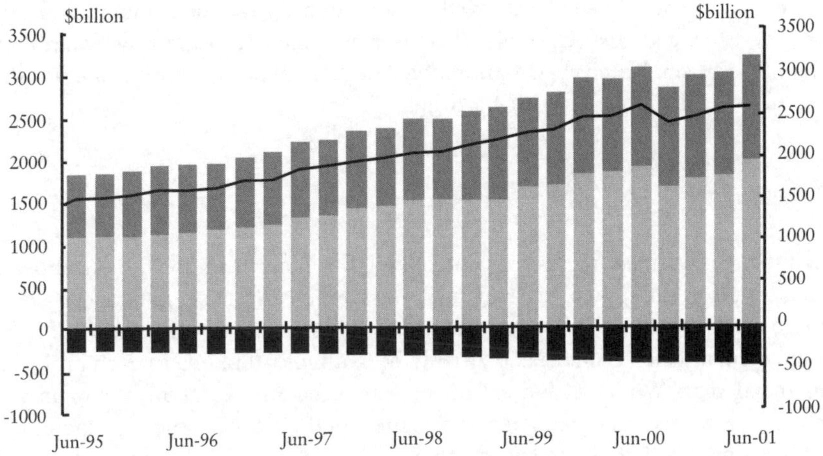

(a) Consistent data are not available prior to the June quarter 1995.
This is based on ABS Cat No 5232.0 and RBA Statement on Monetary Policy.
Source: http://www.treasury.gov.au/documents/108/HTML/docshell.asp?URL=6 house.asp

The paper notes the concern by some commentators about the rising debt levels of households, yet argues that it is misleading to consider household debt in isolation. During the period 1996–2001, the higher debt levels have been offset by the growth on the asset side of the household balance sheet and the net wealth of households has grown by an average of 10 per cent annually in nominal terms.[103]

Under the debt agreement procedure, the debtor submits a proposal and a statement of affairs to the Official Trustee, who determines whether the debtor meets the eligibility requirements under Part IX.[104] ITSA then advises the creditors of the proposal as well as providing a summary of the debtor's statement

in their capacity as consumers; unincorporated businesses whose activities are mixed with personal activities; and non-profit institutions serving households (churches, charities, political parties, trades unions for example).

[103] Australia, Commonwealth, Department of Treasury, *The Household Balance Sheet in Australia* (Canberra, 2001) at 1. Find this at The Commonwealth Treasury <http://www.treasury.gov.au/documents/108/HTML/docshell.asp?URL=6 house.asp>.

[104] Ss 185C–185E.

of affairs and allows the creditors to vote on the proposal either at a meeting or by post.[105] Debt agreements may include payment by instalments, payment of a lump sum or transfer of an asset to the creditors.[106]

While the proposal is being processed, a moratorium applies to creditors proceeding against the debtor in respect of frozen debts.[107] If a majority of the creditors accept the proposal, details of the agreement are recorded on the National Personal Insolvency Index, which generally effects a release of debts which would have been provable in the event of the debtor's bankruptcy[108] and a moratorium on creditor action.[109]

Part IX debt agreements are intended to be:

> a viable low cost alternative to bankruptcy for low income debtors with little or no property, with few creditors and with low levels of liability, for whom entry into a Part X administration is not possible because of set up costs.[110]

They provide debtors and creditors with a simple form of administration to enable them to come to a legally binding arrangement for the settlement of debt.

To be eligible, a debtor must have limited assets and liabilities (less than AUD 65,225) and an annual after-tax income of less than AUD 32,614. These sums are linked to pension rates as well as movements in the consumer price index.[111] It is noted in the Explanatory Memorandum to the 2002 Bill that debtors who were 'too poor' to be required to make income contributions were nevertheless invited under Part IX to make a debt agreement proposal.[112] The 2002 Bill proposes to increase the income threshold amount by 50 per cent so that debtors who earn approximately AUD 48,000 after tax (around AUD 68,500 before tax) may consider this option. The ITSA Debtors Profile shows that the average gross income of debt agreement debtors in 2001–02 was AUD 24,200.[113] This is less than half the average total earnings of full time adult employees in May 2002 of approximately AUD 47, 150 per annum.[114]

Debt agreements are promoted as providing a better alternative to creditors who would be likely to receive very little through a bankruptcy of a debtor with the relatively few assets and low income required to be eligible for the scheme.

[105] Ss 185C, 185E.

[106] *Operation of Bankruptcy Act*, above n 3, at 36.

[107] S 185F. This does not apply to debts arising under a maintenance agreement or maintenance order (s185).

[108] S 185J.

[109] S 185K.

[110] *1996 Explanatory Memorandum*, above n 23, at para 135.16.

[111] For current amounts and information on how they are calculated, see <http://www.itsa.gov.au -> Trustees -> Current Amounts. Also a debtor is disqualified where during the past 10 years he or she has been a bankrupt, a debtor under a Part IX debt agreement or has given an authority to commence a Part X arrangement.

[112] *2002 Explanatory Memorandum*, above n 24, at para 58.

[113] The median income was AUD 24,946. ITSA Debtors Profile, above n 9, at 18.

[114] 6302.0 Average Weekly Earnings, States and Australia, Australian Bureau of Statistics 2002 <http://www.abs.gov.au> Main Features -> 63 Earnings, hours and employment conditions -> 6302.0—Average Weekly Earnings, Australia.

It is less costly to establish than a formal Part X arrangement, however it relies on the debtor disclosing full particulars as no independent trustee is appointed during the proposal stage.

The provisional figures on the number of debt agreements entered during 2001–02 show more than a 200 per cent increase to 3,287.[115] The verified figures for the 2000–01 financial year disclose that while 1,234 were accepted, 2,320 were proposed by debtors; 2,240 were accepted by ITSA for processing; and 597 were rejected by creditors.

Chart 3 Debt Agreements

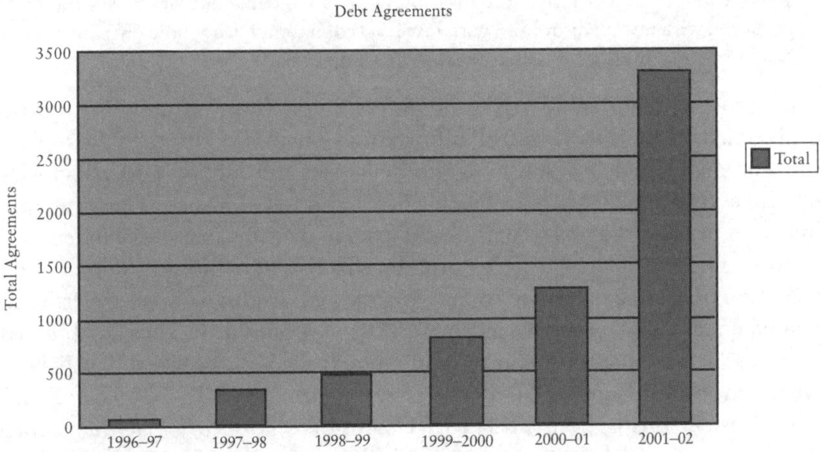

Source: ITSA Provisional Statistics, Financial Year ended 30 June 2002 http://www.itsa.gov.au/aghome/commaff/itsa/frame_statistics.html

Because of the substantial number of debt agreements which were lodged in a bankruptcy district other than that in which the debtor resided, figures on the interstate distribution has since January 2000 been reported on the basis of the state in which the debtor resides. Nevertheless, there is still an interstate variation in the rates of debt agreement per 1000 head of population. In 2001–02, they range from .32 in Queensland, .25 in Tasmania, .14 in Victoria, .13 in New South Wales, .12 in South Australia and .09 in Western Australia. This also largely reflects the interstate variation in bankruptcy rates per 1000 head of (approximate) population in that Queensland and Tasmania lead the field: 2 in Tasmania, 1.8 in Queensland, 1.6 in South Australia, 1.2 in Western Australia, 1 in New South Wales and 1 in Victoria.[116]

[115] ITSA: Bankruptcy Statistics—Annual Statistics <http://www.itsa.gov.au/aghome/commaff/itsa/frame_statistics.html>.

[116] <http://www.itsa.gov.au/aghome/commaff/itsa/frame_statistics.html> and Australian Bureau of Statistics population figures.

The ITSA Debtors Profile for 2001–02 shows that the average age of debtors subject to debt agreements was 35, the median age being 33, which was only slightly younger than bankrupts, 39 and 37 years of age respectively. A greater difference between the two groups was their employment status: 73 per cent of debt agreement debtors were employed compared to only 39 per cent of bankrupts. Also, the proportion of debtors under agreement who were either home owners or purchasing their own home was almost three times that of the bankrupts.[117] Secured creditors, such as lenders for home mortgages, may rely on their proprietary interest and not participate in the debt agreement procedure.[118] In theory, one would expect that debtors entering these agreements would offer a proposal to their unsecured creditors that was calculated to enable them to meet their home mortgage commitments.

Although debt agreements may be administered by the debtor or any other party nominated in a debt agreement proposal accepted by the creditors, there are an increasing number administered by remunerated debt agreement administrators. During 2000–2001, an evaluation of the operation of the debt agreement provisions was undertaken by ITSA. This process included consultation with interest groups including financial counsellors, creditor representatives, registered trustees and debt agreement administrators. It found that debt agreements are largely being administered by professionals who have identified a niche market and that the activities of some operators indicated a need for regulation. The ITSA Debtors Profile confirms this as almost all debt agreements entered in 2001–02 are administered by professional administrators, that is, not by the debtor, family friend or creditor. Of those who entered into debt agreements, 83 per cent nominated their source of information as a debt agreement administrator.[119]

The 2002 Bill proposes to introduce regulation of this sector. As the Explanatory Memorandum states:

> Whilst it is desirable, as far as possible, to continue [the] informal approach, the vast majority of debt agreements are administered by persons who do so as a business. It therefore is appropriate for a regulatory regime—but less detailed than that provided in the Act in relation to registered trustees—to be established. It is proposed that the regulations will provide criteria under which certain persons will be ineligible to be nominated as debt agreement administrators in debt agreement proposals.[120]

It is proposed to allow the Inspector-General to inquire into the activities of debt agreement administrators[121] and to require an Official Receiver to refuse

[117] 16% of debtors subject to debt agreements compared to 5% of bankrupts. Nevertheless both figures are significantly lower than the general population. According to the 2001 Census, 66.2% of the private dwellings in Australia were either fully owned or being purchased: ITSA Debtors Profile, above n 9, at 22.

[118] S 185(1) 'provable debt' and see above n 46–50.

[119] ITSA Debtors Profile, above n 9, at 16.

[120] *2002 Explanatory Memorandum*, above n 24, at para 208.

[121] Proposed new sub-s 12(1)(bb).

to accept a debt agreement proposal for processing if the nominated administrator is ineligible, under the regulations, so to act.[122] Evidence to support concern about this new 'industry' of debt agreement administrators is the poor success rate of agreements. The introduction to the ITSA Debtors Profile indicates that around 40 per cent of debt agreements are terminated before their term is completed.[123]

V. CONCLUSION

Despite the fact that Australia makes no explicit provision for consumer debts in its Bankruptcy Act, there are number of features of this Act that impact primarily on consumer debtors. In some respects Australia's fresh start policy is a reasonably vigorous one. The range of claims discharged on bankruptcy is quite comprehensive. On the other hand, the early discharge provision is subject to proposed repeal. Another noteworthy aspect to Australia's consumer bankruptcy procedures is that a person may file for voluntary bankruptcy without any upfront payment fee. In addition, the public sector essentially handles the asset-less administrations. This is to be viewed in the context of an 8 per cent realisations charge being payable to the Commonwealth by registered trustees on realisations in bankrupt estates.[124] The debt agreement procedure is an innovative feature of the Australian approach to consumer insolvency. This allows debtors and creditors to avoid the consequences of bankruptcy with the minimum of fuss. Policymakers appear keen to extend this scheme, albeit with some increased regulatory oversight of the intermediaries. However, during the process leading up to the current reforms, comment has been made that, as with a number of previous reforms, the proposals appear to be based more on political than empirical grounds. This criticism has been noted in the Senate Legal and Constitutional Legislation Committee Report on the Bankruptcy Legislation Amendment Bill 2001[125] and by the opposition in its debate in the House of Representatives,[126] particularly in respect of the repeal of the early discharge provisions. Ultimately, the Upper House debate on the 2002 Bill did not continue the call for more empirical data to justify some of the proposed changes to the Australian bankruptcy system. In fact, the 2002 Bill was passed during the last week of the 2002 Parliamentary session without amendment. The new legislative provisions commenced their effect on 5 May 2003.[127]

122 Proposed new sub-s 185E(2A).

123 ITSA Debtors Profile, above n 9, at 5.

124 *Bankruptcy (Estate Charges) Act 1997* (Cth). Registration charges are also payable by registered trustees under *Bankruptcy (Registration Charges) Act 1997* (Cth).

125 <http://www.aph.gov.au/senate/committee/legcon_ctte/bankruptcybills01/Bankruptcy.pdf>.

126 Commonwealth, House of Representatives, *Parliamentary Debates Second Reading Speech* 30 May 2002) at 2816 (Mr McClelland).

127 Notably early discharge has been repealed. See http://www.itsa.gov.au -> About us -> Reforms.

12

New Zealand Bankruptcy Law Reform: The New Role of the Official Assignee and the Prospects for a No-Asset Regime

THOMAS G W TELFER*

I. INTRODUCTION

THE LAW GOVERNING the bankruptcy of individuals in New Zealand has largely remained unchanged since Parliament enacted the Insolvency Act 1967. The Act provides for a court supervised discretionary discharge regime that permits debtors to obtain a release of debts after a three-year period. In addition, the Act establishes two mechanisms that enable a debtor to enter into a repayment plan with creditors. Insolvent debtors, however, do not frequently rely upon these two alternatives and increasingly opt for bankruptcy.

In 1999, the Labour-Alliance government announced the first comprehensive review of insolvency law since the mid 1960s.[1] Although New Zealand has enacted comprehensive consumer law reforms regulating the supply of goods and services, consumer credit law and consumer bankruptcy law have not kept pace with the new consumer credit marketplace that has emerged in New Zealand since 1984.[2] In the first half of 2001, the Ministry of Economic Development and the New Zealand Law Commission released discussion papers that contained wide-ranging proposals on the administration of bankruptcy and formal alternative procedures.[3] After public consultation on these

* Research support was provided by the Chapman Tripp Research Scholar Programme at the University of Auckland Faculty of Law. I would like to thank Iain Ramsay and William Whitford for their helpful comments on earlier versions of this paper.

[1] The Labour Alliance coalition can be broadly characterised as centre-left. The Ministry of Justice briefly considered reform options in 1988. See N.Z., Law Reform Division, *Insolvency Law Reform: A Discussion Paper* (Wellington, Department of Justice, 1988).

[2] The government introduced a new Consumer Credit Bill (2002 No 2–1) on 17 September 2002. See also Ministry of Consumer Affairs, 'Consumer Credit Laws to be Overhauled' (8 August 2001), online: Ministry of Economic Development <http://www.med.govt.nz/consumer/index.html>.

[3] N.Z., Ministry of Economic Development, *Insolvency Law Review: Tier One Discussion Documents* (Wellington, Ministry of Economic Development, January 2001) [MED, *Tier One*];

two major reports, the government has announced several key policy decisions on the shape of future insolvency reforms. It is anticipated that these decisions will form the basis of an Insolvency Bill.[4] This chapter examines two key aspects of the reform proposals: the expanded role of the Official Assignee (OA) and the new No Asset Procedure.

Ironically, the privatisation and deregulation movement that swept through New Zealand from the mid 1980s to the early 1990s did not alter the institutions governing the administration of bankruptcies. Personal bankruptcies continue to be the responsibility of the public sector through the office of the Official Assignee. However, the formal alternative procedures fall outside the responsibility of the Official Assignee. Under the current regime, there is no common intermediary that provides information and advice to debtors on bankruptcy and the formal alternatives. Many debtors simply do not know of Part XV or Part XVI of the Act, which permit repayment plans.

The reforms propose to expand the role of the Official Assignee and make bankruptcy an administrative procedure. The reforms provide for a common and state-funded initial point of contact for debtors wishing to pursue bankruptcy or make a proposal to creditors. All debtors will be required to first consult with an Official Assignee before invoking any of the proceedings. The office of the Official Assignee will not only retain its monopoly over bankruptcy administration, but it will also assume responsibility for several matters that currently fall under the jurisdiction of the courts, including adjudication of debtors' petitions and proposals. The consolidation of the numerous proceedings in the office of the Official Assignee will reduce costs and potentially increase accessibility. However, in this chapter I focus on the issue of potential conflicts of interest raised by the consolidation since the Official Assignee will play the role of fact finder, adjudicator and creditor representative, as well as a counsellor to the debtor.

This chapter also considers the recommendation to create a separate No Asset Procedure for low-income debtors. In addition to the roles mentioned above, the Assignee will also be responsible for screening candidates for this new No Asset Procedure. Rather than focus on the potentially small pool of debtors with surplus income, the Ministry has proposed to create a new and streamlined procedure for the much larger group of no asset debtors. A No Asset Procedure would enable qualifying debtors to obtain a discharge within the shorter period of 12 months. I argue that the difference between the three-year straight bankruptcy regime and the more attractive 12-month No Asset

New Zealand Law Commission, *Insolvency Law Reform: Promoting Trust and Confidence: An Advisory Report to the Ministry of Economic Development* (Wellington, N.Z.: Law Commission, Study Paper 11, June 2001) [NZLC, *Promoting Trust and Confidence*]. For a full list, see <http://www.med.govt.nz/ri/insolvency/review-docs.html>.

[4] Hon Laila Harré, 'Tier One Decisions and Where to From Here' (Speech to Business Law Forum on Insolvency Review, November 2001); Hon Lalia Harré, 'Keynote Speech to Butterworth's Insolvency Law Conference' (February 2002). See <http://www.med.govt.nz/ri/insolvency/review-docs.html>.

Procedure may require the Official Assignee to devote resources to a screening function to ensure that only truly qualified debtors use the No Asset Procedure. Thus the benefits to be gained by a separate, streamlined procedure may well be outweighed by the costs involved in the screening for qualified debtors.

Part II of the chapter provides an overview of the economic changes that have occurred in New Zealand since the mid-1980s. Part III examines the existing framework of the Insolvency Act 1967 and some possible institutional reasons why debtors do not rely upon the two proposal regimes. The chapter concludes with an examination in Part IV of the key reform proposals and offers a suggestion as to why the shift to an administrative model may well succeed in New Zealand.

II. THE ECONOMIC CONTEXT

The proposed reforms take into account the significant changes to the New Zealand economy that have occurred since the original Act was passed in 1967. In 2001, the Ministry of Economic Development concluded that the:

> changing make-up of a 'typical bankrupt' means that the regime is no longer providing an effective solution to the majority of debtors and creditors.[5]

The vast majority of individual bankrupts can now be classified as consumer bankrupts rather than sole-traders.[6]

The rise in the number of bankruptcies and the emergence of a consumer bankrupt ('[s]uch a person was unknown in New Zealand in 1967')[7] cannot be separated from the dramatic changes to the New Zealand economy in the mid-1980s.[8] The New Zealand Law Commission in its report, *Promoting Trust and Confidence*, noted that in the nine months that followed the election of the Labour government in 1984:

> [A] series of events occurred which transformed New Zealand from one of the most heavily regulated economies in the western world to one of the least regulated economies.[9]

Prior to 1984, the Economic Stabilisation Act 1948 had been used to 'regulate most sectors of the New Zealand economy by executive order.'[10] Until the

[5] MED, *Tier One*, above n 3, at 21.

[6] N.Z., Office of the Associate Minister of Commerce, 'Insolvency Law Review: Bankruptcy Administration' FIN (01) 131 (August 2001) (Cabinet Finance, Infrastructure and Environment Committee, Chair) at 2 ['Bankruptcy Administration'].

[7] P Heath, 'Consumer Bankruptcies: A New Zealand Perspective' (1999) 37 *Osgoode Hall Law Journal* 427 at 436.

[8] *Ibid* at 436. See also A Sawyer, 'Passing the Century Mark: The Urgent Need for Reform of Insolvency Law and Policy in New Zealand' (1999) 3 *The Flinders Journal of Law Reform* 183.

[9] NZLC, *Promoting Trust and Confidence*, above n 3, at 20–21.

[10] *Ibid* at 21. See also, N Quigley, 'Monetary Policy and the New Zealand Financial System: An Historical Perspective' in Reserve Bank of New Zealand, *Monetary Policy and the New Zealand Financial System* (Wellington, Reserve Bank of New Zealand, 1992) at 204.

changes in 1984, the 'government . . . actively controlled the provision of credit as part of microeconomic management.'[11] The banking and finance industry was 'one of the most highly regulated sectors of the economy when the Government took office in 1984.'[12] The Insolvency Act 1967 was passed in an 'era of almost no unemployment and limited access to credit.'[13]

The Labour Government in 1984 took dramatic steps to alter the way New Zealand was governed. The freeze of interest rates was removed, along with controls on wages, prices and rents. In 1987, the Economic Stabilisation Act was repealed.[14] While credit cards were introduced in New Zealand in 1981,[15] the deregulation of the banking industry that followed in the mid-1980s significantly increased the level of consumer choice in the credit market.[16] The removal of restrictions on the types of business particular financial institutions could undertake, the growth in the number of registered banks, and the privatisation of public financial institutions changed the financial landscape of New Zealand 'beyond recognition'.[17] These policy changes 'released a suppressed demand for consumer credit, while leading to major structural changes in supply.'[18] The Ministry of Consumer Affairs noted in a 1999 report that most New Zealanders have 'easy access to consumer credit through a housing loan, credit card or hire purchase agreement.'[19]

The suppressed demand for consumer credit inevitably led to rising levels of personal indebtedness and bankruptcies.[20] The level of bankruptcies increased from 402 in 1971, the year the Insolvency Act 1967 came into force, to an all time high of 3224 in 1998.[21] Since 1998, the numbers have fluctuated, dipping to 2746 in 2000 and rising slightly in 2001 to 2985.[22] In 1998, consumer bankruptcies represented 55 per cent of all individual bankruptcies while in 1999 the rate was 63 per cent.[23]

[11] N.Z., Ministry of Consumer Affairs, *Consumer Credit Law Review: Part 3 Transparency in Consumer Credit: Interest, Fees and Disclosure* (Wellington, Ministry of Consumer Affairs, 2000) at 11.

[12] N.Z., Ministry of Consumer Affairs, *Consumers and Credit* (Wellington, Ministry of Consumer Affairs, 1988) at 8.

[13] 'Bankruptcy Administration', above n 6, at 2.

[14] Economic Stabilisation Act Repeal Act 1987. See NZLC, *Promoting Trust and Confidence,* above n 3 at 21.

[15] Heath, above n 7, at 428.

[16] N.Z., Ministry of Consumer Affairs, *Consumers and Credit* (Wellington, Ministry of Consumer Affairs 1988) at 8.

[17] C Thorp and B Ung, 'Trends in Household Assets and Liabilities since 1978' (2000) 63 *Reserve Bank of New Zealand Bulletin* 17 at 21.

[18] N.Z., Ministry of Consumer Affairs, *Consumer Credit Law Review: Part 1 Setting the Scene* (Wellington, Ministry of Consumer Affairs, 1999) at 16.

[19] *Ibid.*

[20] N.Z., Ministry of Consumer Affairs, *Consumer Credit Law Review: Part 4 Overindebtedness, Insurance and E-Credit* (Wellington, Ministry of Consumer Affairs, 2000) at 4.

[21] Prior to 1988, statistics are drawn from the Statistics New Zealand, *New Zealand Official Yearbook*. After 1988, see Ministry of Economic Development, New Zealand Insolvency and Trustee Service Statistics at <http://www.med.govt.nz/ri/insolvency/statistics.html>.

[22] In 2002 there were 2,672 bankruptcies. *Ibid.*

[23] MED, *Tier One*, above n 3, at 30.

Although the total number of bankruptcies has risen dramatically between 1971 and the present day, a recent comparative study illustrates that in New Zealand the rate of bankruptcy, when measured on a population basis, does not match the levels in other jurisdictions. For example, in 1997 there were approximately 0.7 bankruptcies per 1000 individuals in New Zealand. In that same year, Australia had a filing rate of 1.7 per 1000 while Canada had a rate of 3 bankruptcies per 1000. In the United States, the 1997 rate was approximately 5 filings per 1000 individuals.[24]

While the deregulation movement had a significant impact upon consumer credit and consumer bankruptcy rates, it is equally important to point out that during 1980s and 1990s the Official Assignee's office was not privatised. The continuing monopoly of the Official Assignee's office over bankruptcy administration and the absence of private trustees or lawyers advertising for bankruptcy work in part explains New Zealand's lower bankruptcy rate. More importantly, for the purposes of this chapter, the absence of an established association of private trustees has enabled the government in 2001 and 2002 to propose an administrative model for bankruptcy without significant opposition.

The changed economic context of bankruptcies and the emergence of consumer bankrupts led the government to conclude in 2001 that 'the personal insolvency regime is no longer providing an effective solution for the majority of debtors and creditors.'[25] As Part III will demonstrate, the Insolvency Act 1967 falls short of providing an adequate means of redressing the problem of consumer indebtedness.

III. THE INSOLVENCY ACT 1967: THE BASIC FRAMEWORK AND INSTITUTIONAL DESIGN

The Insolvency Act 1967, which came into force on 1 January 1971,[26] purported to modernise what was perceived to be an out of date statute.[27] The 1967 Act replaced the Bankruptcy Act of 1908,[28] which had largely been modelled on the landmark English reforms of 1883.[29] The 1967 Act made substantial changes to the discharge provisions and introduced two new repayment schemes as alternatives to bankruptcy. Writing in 1968, one author claimed that New Zealand bankruptcy legislation had always emphasised rehabilitation, but that the

[24] See R Efrat, 'Global Trends in Personal Bankruptcy' (2002) 76 *American Bankruptcy Law Journal* 81 at 100–101.

[25] 'Bankruptcy Administration', above n 6, at 2.

[26] Heath, above n 7, at 428.

[27] N.Z., *Hansard*, Debate-Draft: Insolvency Bill (vol 345 at 3903) 28 October 1965 (Hon JR Hanan). For an overview of the 1967 Act, see P McKenzie, 'Insolvency Act 1967' (1968) 3 *New Zealand Universities Law Review* 210.

[28] I Hansen, *Bankruptcy: In the Beginning: An Historical Survey of the Laws of Bankruptcy* (Wellington, New Zealand Institute of Credit and Financial Management, 1980) at 13,14.

[29] V Lester, *Victorian Insolvency: Bankruptcy, Imprisonment for Debt and Company Winding Up in Nineteenth Century England* (Oxford, Clarendon Press, 1995) at 170.

Insolvency Act of 1967 pays 'particular attention to this aspect of bankruptcy.'[30] The author optimistically noted that 'the new Act goes a long way toward allowing and encouraging rehabilitation without prejudicing the rights of creditors.'[31]

A. Bankruptcy and the Discharge

The 1967 Act retained the basic framework of requiring the publicly funded office of the Official Assignee to administer all bankruptcies.[32] However, the Act introduced several important changes. First, the Act removed the obligation of the debtor to apply for a discharge. The legislation permitted a debtor to obtain an automatic discharge, unless opposed by a creditor or Official Assignee, after a period of three years.[33] Second, Parliament widened the court's discretion on the granting of a discharge. Whereas the Bankruptcy Act 1908 specified the circumstances in which an unconditional order of discharge would not be granted (eg guilty of misconduct or gross negligence in the conduct of business),[34] the Insolvency Act 1967 created a broad discretionary jurisdiction for the courts to grant an immediate order of discharge or, in appropriate circumstances, to refuse, suspend or issue a conditional order of discharge.[35] In *Re Anderson*, Justice Pennlington concluded that in comparison to the 'restricted approach' under the 1908 Act, the discretion under the Insolvency Act 1967 is 'completely unfettered.'[36]

B. Alternatives to Bankruptcy: Part XV and Part XVI

Parliament also created Part XV and Part XVI as alternatives to bankruptcy. Under these two separate mechanisms, a debtor can make a formal proposal to his or her creditors and avoid the bankruptcy regime altogether.[37] Parliament designed the two regimes with different classes of debtors in mind. Parliament intended Part XV as a mechanism 'to enable a person in trade or business who is unable to pay his debts to offer his creditors a compromise.'[38] In contrast, Part XVI was designed for wage earners.

[30] E Flitton, 'The Insolvency Act, 1967' [1968] *New Zealand Law Journal* 394.

[31] *Ibid* at 396.

[32] NZLC, *Promoting Trust and Confidence*, above n 3, at 37.

[33] Insolvency Act 1967 s 107. Under the 1908 Act, the cost of discharge applications 'was beyond the resources of many bankrupts.' See Hansen, above n 28, at 15.

[34] Bankruptcy Act 1908 s 127.

[35] Insolvency Act 1967 s 110.

[36] *Re Anderson* (HC Hamilton, B.213/89, 14 April 1992, Pennlington J) at 20. See also *ASB v Hogg* [1993] 3 NZLR 156 (CA) at 157,158.

[37] Heath, above n 7, at 435.

[38] N.Z., *Hansard*, Debate-Second Reading: Insolvency Bill (vol 352 at 2072) 20 July 1967 (Hon JR Hanan).

Under Part XV, a debtor may offer to compromise his or her debts through a proposal requiring approval by creditors and the court. Proposals may include an offer to pay debts by instalments or to compromise the insolvent's debts at less than 100 cents on the dollar.[39] Debtors must obtain approval from a majority in number and a three-fourths in value of the creditors voting, as well as court approval.[40] After court approval, no creditor may file a creditor's petition against the debtor while the proposal remains in force. In addition, no creditor may take civil proceedings against the debtor in respect of a debt subject to the proposal.[41]

Part XV is said to offer the debtor the protection 'from the social stigma and restrictions of bankruptcy.'[42] It encourages a separate regime for the distribution of the debtor's assets without the requirement of a bankruptcy and the consequent administration costs that would otherwise fall upon the office of the Official Assignee.[43] Private insolvency practitioners may act as a trustee of the proposal. However, as discussed below, Part XV proposals have not been widely utilised and are not providing a viable alternative to bankruptcy.

Part XVI Summary Instalment Orders (SIO) are more limited in their scope and offer the 'small non-commercial insolvent . . . that is, the wage earner'[44] a mechanism to pay off debts over time out of future earnings.[45] Speaking in Parliament in 1967, the Minister responsible for the bill claimed that SIOs represented 'a bold, and, as far as New Zealand is concerned, a completely fresh approach to a very real problem.'[46] Originally limited to debtors whose total unsecured debts did not exceed $1000 (the current threshold is $12,000),[47] the scheme was:

> designed to give practical assistance and guidance to people who find themselves in financial difficulties and are unable to meet their debts as they become due.[48]

In Parliament it was noted that once debts became overwhelming, there was 'evidence to suggest that in such cases the debtor becomes apathetic' and 'feels hopeless.' The Bankruptcy Act of 1908 gave the debtor little incentive to pay off his or her debts.[49] The SIO regime was established so that a debtor could 'short

[39] Insolvency Act 1967, s 140(2).

[40] Insolvency Act 1967, ss 142, 143. See P Heath, 'Proposals under Part XV Insolvency Act: Is the Public Interest Relevant?' [1991] *New Zealand Law Journal* 52; A Sawyer, 'Proposing an Alternative to Bankruptcy: Part XV in Retrospect' (1995) 6 *Canterbury Law Review* 175.

[41] Insolvency Act 1967 s 144.

[42] *Guest v Duffy* [1991] 1 NZLR 183 (CA) at 184.

[43] Heath, above n 40.

[44] N.Z., *Hansard*, Debate-Draft: Insolvency Bill (vol 345 at 3903) 28 October 1965 (Hon JR Hanan).

[45] R Sutton, *The Law of Creditors' Remedies in New Zealand* (Wellington, Butterworths, 1978) at 36.

[46] N.Z., *Hansard*, Debate-Second Reading: Insolvency Bill (vol 352 at 2190) 9 August 1967 (Hon JR Hanan).

[47] The Insolvency Amendment Act 1990 (1990 No 7), s 6(3).

[48] *Summary Instalment Orders (Magistrates' Courts) Rules 1970* (N.Z.), 1970/271, Form 6 Explanatory Note.

[49] N.Z., *Hansard*, Debate-Draft: Insolvency Bill (vol 345 at 3903) 28 October 1965 (Hon JR Hanan).

circuit the bankruptcy proceedings, so that step . . . need not necessarily be taken.'[50]

Under Part XVI, a debtor may obtain an order of the District Court, which provides for the payment of debts by instalments and either in full 'or to such extent as the court considers practicable.'[51] Orders are limited to three years in duration[52] and the Court, in directing that the debtor make payments by instalments, may also make orders requiring an employer to make wage payments to the supervisor of the Part XVI order.[53] Part XVI operates as a stay of any proceedings in the District Court and also provides a statutory ground to stay or dismiss a bankruptcy petition.[54] It thus provides a 'breathing space' in which to meet the debtor's obligations.[55]

If an order is made a 'supervisor is usually appointed by the Court to assist the debtor in the management of his financial affairs.'[56] The summary instalment supervisor has the responsibility of distributing moneys collected to the individual creditors.[57] Parliament intended that such an approved person, acting as a supervisor of the order, have 'welfare experience.' This scheme, however, contemplated that a pool of such experienced people would be freely available for all debtors in New Zealand. The desired welfare experience of the Part XVI orders 'will give firm backing to budgetary and advisory schemes that are operated already by welfare organisations throughout the country.'[58] Part XVI has never measured up to these expectations.

The Ministry of Economic Development concludes that the two alternatives to bankruptcy 'are not widely used in New Zealand.'[59] In a recent Cabinet paper, it is acknowledged that Part XV proposals are hardly ever used 'because the process is more complex than it needs to be.' Similarly, Cabinet acknowledged the low use of the SIO regime and suggested that the $12,000 limit set in 1990 'does not reflect contemporary needs.'[60] However, a more complete explanation for the failure may be found in the institutional framework for the delivery of these two regimes.

[50] N.Z., *Hansard*, Debate-General: Insolvency Bill (vol 350 at 739) 23 May 1967 (Hon JR Hanan).

[51] *Re Sturdee (a debtor)* [1985] 2 NZLR 627 at 632.

[52] Insolvency Act 1967, s 146(12).

[53] Insolvency Act 1967, s 146(9).

[54] Insolvency Act 1967, s 148, s 26(3). See *Re Sturdee (a debtor)* [1985] 2 NZLR 627.

[55] R Sutton, *The Law of Creditors' Remedies in New Zealand* (Wellington, Butterworths, 1978) at 36.

[56] *Re Sturdee (a debtor)* [1985] 2 NZLR 627 at 632.

[57] See P McKenzie (ed), *Spratt and McKenzie's Law of Insolvency*, 2nd edn (Wellington, Butterworths, 1972) at 316.

[58] N.Z., *Hansard*, Debate-Second Reading: Insolvency Bill (vol 352 at 2190) 9 August 1967 (Hon JR Hanan); P McKenzie (ed), *Spratt and McKenzie's Law of Insolvency*, 2nd edn (Wellington, Butterworths, 1972) at 316.

[59] MED, *Tier One*, above n 3, at 38. See also N.Z., Commercial Affairs Division, *Proposal for Alternative Processes to Bankruptcy* (Discussion Paper prepared for consultation with the NZLS and the NZSA Joint Committee on Insolvency Law Reform, 1994) at 6.

[60] 'Bankruptcy Administration', above n 6, at 11.

C. Institutional Explanations for Low Levels of Proposal Use

Iain Ramsay notes that individuals burdened with debts 'must often make important choices such as whom to consult concerning their problem, and what route to choose as a method of dealing with their debt.' Ramsay concludes that debtors must 'depend on intermediaries to help them appraise the alternatives.'[61]

> 'If legislation provides a number of complex alternatives for debtors in order to provide a variety of choices for differently situated debtors, it is possible that the rise in decision-making costs for the consumer may result in the disempowerment of the consumer rather than the maximisation of individual choice.'[62]

In New Zealand, the lack of a common forum (the High Court has jurisdiction over bankruptcies and Part XV, while Part XVI must be pursued in the District Court) is compounded by the variety of intermediaries that are available with whom a debtor might consult. Debtors may consult with the Official Assignee, a budget advisory office or a private insolvency practitioner. Each of these intermediaries is constrained in that none can provide a service that encompasses all of the debtor's options. While the Official Assignee has a monopoly on the administration of bankrupts' estates, the Official Assignee does not administer SIOs and private practitioners may act as a trustee under a formal Part XV proposal.

More importantly, there is no required initial point of contact for debtors to receive advice. Under a voluntary bankruptcy proceeding, adjudication in bankruptcy is automatic on the filing of a debtor's petition.[63] It is only after the Official Assignee receives notice of adjudication that the bankrupt is asked to complete a statement of affairs setting out the debtor's financial position.[64] Thus, in many instances, a debtor may file a petition in the High Court 'without being provided with any advice on the consequences of bankruptcy, or the alternatives available to them.'[65]

Even if a debtor is aware of the possibility of pursuing a Part XV or Part XVI application, there is little institutional support given to these two options. Part XV proposals require creditor and court approval, and private practitioners may act as trustees of the proposal. A major drawback of the Part XV proposal option, beyond the expense of court proceedings, is that it does not 'deliver adequate supervision, administrative support and punitive provisions for breach of agreements to ensure creditor agreement.'[66] There is no identifiable pool of

[61] I Ramsay, 'Models of Consumer Bankruptcy: Implications for Research and Policy' (1997) 20 *Journal of Consumer Policy* 269 at 277 ['Models of Consumer Bankruptcy'].

[62] *Ibid* at 277–78.

[63] Insolvency Act 1967 s 21.

[64] Insolvency Act 1967 s 33.

[65] Hon Laila Harré, 'Tier One Decisions and Where to From Here' (Speech to Business Law Forum on Insolvency Review, November 2001) at 4.

[66] MED, *Tier One*, above n 3, at 38.

trustees available to administer the proposals and many insolvents are often unaware of the proposal procedure.[67]

Part XVI SIOs are administered by a court-appointed supervisor. The original drafters of the 1967 Act contemplated that debtors would not only avoid bankruptcy but that they would also receive budgeting assistance from the supervisor.[68] Clearly Parliament intended debtors to learn from their experience. The original Explanatory Note to Form 6 of the Summary Instalment Orders Rules provides as follows:

> At the end of the period of the order your financial affairs should be restored to a sound basis and you will have had experience in family budgeting to assist you from then on.[69]

There is no national database kept on the use of SIOs. Whether a debtor has access to a SIO regime may be affected by a debtor's location. SIOs require the appointment of a supervisor, ideally a person with budgeting experience. This experience may not be available in all regions of the country.[70] There is a shortage of qualified supervisors of SIOs as they only receive a nominal remuneration.[71] Creditors are largely unaware of the procedure and the staff in the District Court do not actively promote it.[72] Many debtors 'do not know about [Part XV and Part XVI] until after they are adjudged bankrupt.'[73] The existing New Zealand regime does little to fulfil the goal of 'informed consumer choice.'[74]

IV. THE REFORM PROPOSALS

A. The New Role of the Official Assignee

The government proposes to address the institutional flaws in the existing regime by introducing sweeping changes to the role of the Official Assignee. Under the new model, many bankruptcy and proposal procedures would be

[67] N.Z., Commercial Affairs Division, *Proposal for Alternative Processes to Bankruptcy* (Discussion Paper prepared for consultation with the NZLS and the NZSA Joint Committee on Insolvency Law Reform, 1994) at 6.

[68] *Summary Instalment Orders (Magistrates' Courts) Rules 1970* (N.Z.), 1970/271, Form 6 Explanatory Note. See also *Re Sturdee (a debtor)* [1985] 2 NZLR 627 at 632.

[69] *Summary Instalment Orders (Magistrates' Courts) Rules 1970* (N.Z.), 1970/271, Form 6 Explanatory Note.

[70] Telephone interview 18 and 23 June 2001 with Jannette Brown, Summary Instalment Supervisor for Auckland, Wellington, Blenheim, Rotorua and Taupo. See also Hansen, above n 28, at 15.

[71] N.Z., Commercial Affairs Division, *Proposal for Alternative Processes to Bankruptcy* (Discussion Paper prepared for consultation with the NZLS and the NZSA Joint Committee on Insolvency Law Reform, 1994) at 5.

[72] *Ibid.*

[73] MED, *Tier One*, above n 3, at 38.

[74] 'Models of Consumer Bankruptcy', above n 61, at 277.

administrative functions of the Official Assignee. As a starting point, under the proposed new regime a debtor will be required to file a financial statement of affairs with the Official Assignee before pursuing the bankruptcy option. Under the existing bankruptcy regime, there is no preliminary financial audit prior to the debtor filing for bankruptcy, commencing a SIO or initiating a Part XV proposal. The new pre-bankruptcy audit will allow a debtor 'to receive advice from the Official Assignee, to be made aware of the available options and to make an informed decision of what option might produce the best result for them.'[75] The Official Assignee could thus offer information on the implications of bankruptcy, but also provide advice on other alternatives such as Part XV proposals and Part XVI summary administration orders.

The cabinet policy paper emphasised the 'importance of debtor education and the need for information regarding the availability of alternatives to be readily accessible.' According to this policy document, the proposed reforms address this issue by the following: opening up an avenue for communication between the Official Assignee and the debtor by requiring the debtor to contact the Official Assignee to file a debtor's petition; requiring the Official Assignee to provide information on options to the debtor.[76]

However, the proposed reforms to the role of the Official Assignee go well beyond improving the flow of information to debtors. The recommendations would fundamentally alter the role and nature of the office of the Official Assignee. The government recommends the transfer of three services from the courts to the Official Assignee. Under the new regime, the Official Assignee would assume responsibility for receiving debtors' petitions and deciding Part XV and Part XVI applications. These are 'administrative processes and the court does not need to be involved.'[77] The Official Assignee would not only provide advice and information on the best possible option, it would also make substantive decisions on the option pursued.

Fundamental to these proposed reforms is the government's decision to maintain the monopoly of the Official Assignee over bankruptcy administration. As Bruce Carruthers and Terence Halliday have demonstrated, the decision over the 'institutional locus of bankruptcy work' has significant implications for all parties as it determines the relative influence of public and private interests in the bankruptcy proceedings.[78] In New Zealand, Official Assignees are salaried public servants and have a statutory responsibility for, and monopoly over, the administration of bankruptcies under the Insolvency Act 1967.[79] The Law

[75] Hon Laila Harré, 'Tier One Decisions and Where to From Here' (Speech to Business Law Forum on Insolvency Review, November 2001) at 4.

[76] 'Bankruptcy Administration', above n 6, at 6.

[77] *Ibid* at 3.

[78] B Carruthers and T Halliday, *Rescuing Business: The Making of Corporate Bankruptcy Law in England and the United States* (Oxford, Clarendon Press, 1998) at 375.

[79] NZLC, *Promoting Trust and Confidence,* above n 3, at 48.

Commission's report included a recommendation to permit private practitioners to act as a trustee of a bankrupt estate.[80]

Cabinet, however, in early 2002, decided to retain the state's current monopoly over bankruptcy administration. In February 2002, the Associate Minister of Justice's speech claimed that the 'interests of debtors are better observed by the state than by the private sector, primarily because the Official Assignee is not profit driven.'[81] The Insolvency Act 1967 gives a great deal of power and discretion to Official Assignees in the management and distribution of the estate. This wide discretion and power in the hands of the Official Assignee was not troubling to the government. However, it was feared that this wide discretion in the hands of private practitioners motivated by financial incentives would create the 'real risk that some practitioners would act more harshly towards debtors and even exceed their statutory authority.'[82]

In Canada, where private practitioners operate as trustees in bankruptcy, criticisms have been raised of the market model of bankruptcy administration.[83] The criticisms have in part focused on the possible conflicts that a private trustee faces. A conflict may arise at the time the debtor first approaches a private insolvency practitioner. If bankruptcy is the recommended solution, the practitioner will inevitably nominate himself or herself or a member of the firm to act as the trustee.[84] However, the potential for conflict goes beyond the trustee's initial appointment and financial motivations may play a part in the trustee's advice on whether to pursue bankruptcy or a proposal. Iain Ramsay's study of the Canadian regime notes that 'debtors who have a genuine choice between declaring bankruptcy and making a consumer proposal may be influenced by advice which reflects a trustee's financial incentives and perception of the value of the proposal.'[85] However, a broader criticism has been made of the Canadian regime. Jacob Ziegel notes that in Canada the trustee has multiple roles and serves the consumer, the bankruptcy court, the Superintendent of Bankruptcy and the consumer's creditors. He argues that a consumer debtor may not be able to distinguish between the trustee's initial role of providing advice and coun-

[80] NZLC, *Promoting Trust and Confidence,* above n 3, at 58–59.

[81] Hon Laila Harré, 'Keynote Speech to Butterworths Insolvency Law Conference' (February 2002). The Minister was a member of the Alliance party and part of the coalition government. This was the position taken by an Official Assignee operating under the 1892 Act. 'The impartial administration of the Act . . . by Officials who are under government control and perfectly audited is regarded by the commercial community at large as the best safeguard against fraud.' See *New Zealand Official Yearbook* (1894) at 275, cited in Hansen, above n 28, at 17.

[82] N.Z., Office of the Associate Minister of Commerce, 'Insolvency Law Review: Role of the State' (undated) (Cabinet Finance, Infrastructure and Environment Committee, Chair) at 3.

[83] For a discussion of trustees fees in Canada, see J Ziegel, 'Financing Consumer Bankruptcies, *Re Berthelette*, and Public Policy' (2000) 33 *Canadian Business Law Journal* 294.

[84] See also J Ziegel, *Comparative Consumer Insolvency Regimes From a Canadian Perspective: A Report for Industry Canada* (Ottawa, Industry Canada, April 2000) at 178, 179.

[85] I Ramsay, 'Market Imperatives, Professional Discretion and the Role of Intermediaries in Consumer Bankruptcy: A Comparative Study of the Canadian Trustee in Bankruptcy' (2000) 74 *American Bankruptcy Law Journal* 399 at 454 ['Market Imperatives'].

selling, and the trustee's subsequent role in administering the bankrupt's estate where the interests of the creditors and the bankruptcy court are also to be served.[86]

In New Zealand, the retention of the Official Assignees' monopoly over bankruptcy administration may well avoid some of the potential problems associated with a private trustee regime. The government seems to have concluded that the office of the Official Assignee is more independent and capable of providing a better level of service to consumer debtors than privately motivated trustees.[87] While the courts in New Zealand have traditionally viewed the office of the Official Assignee as the 'guardian of the public interest,'[88] it remains to be seen to what extent the debtor's interests will be served, given the multiple roles that the Official Assignee would have to fulfill under the proposed reforms.

In addition to providing information on debtor's options (a debtor may perceive this as the informal counselling or advice phase), the Official Assignee will also administer the bankruptcy, where the interests of the creditors must also be served and adjudicate on debtor proposals. Making bankruptcy and its two alternatives more of an administrative process offers certain advantages over the court-driven structure of the current regime. However, can the Official Assignee fulfill the role of fact-finder and decision-maker and, at the same time, represent creditor interests and be a counsellor to the debtor? Under the new regime, will the Official Assignee develop interests that ultimately serve the objectives of the state bureaucracy rather than that of the bankruptcy administration process and the debtor?[89] One should not lose sight of the fact that there will be certain budgetary constraints on public office holders that will ultimately limit the amount of investigation and administration that can be carried out.[90]

Given that the Official Assignee will be responsible for making decisions on debtors' petitions and applications under Part XV and Part XVI, will debtors be channelled into repayment plans such that the Official Assignee will be able to report that the total number of bankruptcies has dropped? It remains to be seen whether the reforms will alter the mix of bankruptcies and Part XV and Part XVI procedures. Making information available about various options at an

[86] J Ziegel, 'The Philosophy and Design of Contemporary Consumer Bankruptcy Systems: A Canada-United States Comparison' (1999) 37 *Osgoode Hall Law Journal* 205 at 256; J Ziegel, *Comparative Consumer Insolvency Regimes From a Canadian Perspective: A Report for Industry Canada* (Ottawa, Industry Canada, April 2000) at 178, 179.

[87] Ramsay notes that all intermediaries or mediators have interests and values that might shape the debtor's decision. 'Market Imperatives', above n 85, at 457.

[88] NZLC, *Promoting Trust and Confidence,* above n 3, at 48.

[89] Carruthers and Halliday, above n 78, at 412, in the United States context, discuss objections to an administrative solution including the criticism of the overlapping roles of counselling, fact finding and decision-making. Carruthers and Halliday note that bureaucracies do develop interests that may compete with their ostensible purposes. This issue arose in the context of a proposal in the United States to, in effect, nationalise bankruptcy administration. The struggle between the private bar and those favouring public administration is described in great detail by Carruthers and Halliday, above n 78, at 412.

[90] Heath, above n 7, at 447. See also NZLC, *Promoting Trust and Confidence*, above n 3, at 42–49 for the Law Commission's criticisms of the Official Assignee's enforcement function.

earlier stage, reducing court involvement and raising the cap on SIOs from $12,000 to $40,000 may increase the usage of these two alternative procedures. Indeed, this appears to be the explicit aim of the reform proposals.

Improving the alternatives to bankruptcy, it is argued, 'will increase debtors' and creditors' access to and use of them.' According to the Ministry, '[t]his should . . . decrease the number of debtors in bankruptcy that could have explored other options'.[91] Under the current regime:

> estates that would be better suited to the alternatives end up in formal bankruptcy proceedings. When debtors become bankrupt, their ability to participate in the marketplace, contributing to the economy as a whole, is removed.[92]

That may be true, but a regime that unnecessarily encourages debtors into repayment plans may also inhibit a debtor's ability to fully participate in the marketplace.[93]

The renewed emphasis upon repayment plans is consistent with trends in other jurisdictions, such as Canada and the United States, that have in the past embraced varying forms of the discharge as a means of a fresh start. Canadian reforms, for example, have moved away from the notion that a discharge offers a means of debtor rehabilitation towards the concept that debtor repayment plans offer a more responsible way to rehabilitate.[94] In the context of American reform proposals, William Whitford illustrates what he calls the 'lessened public commitment to the core values that have historically justified a fresh start in consumer bankruptcy.'[95] The new emphasis on debt repayment from future income suggests that there has been a 'paradigm shift' in the 'collective public assumptions concerning the opportunity to discharge individual debts in bankruptcy.'[96]

Although the fresh start in New Zealand has never guaranteed a debtor the right to an absolute discharge, the existing regime, in appropriate circumstances, does offer the bankrupt relief from the burdens of debt and an opportunity to start anew. It remains to be seen whether the increase in information about repayment plans and easier accessibility to the alternative procedures will divert debtors away from bankruptcy. Finally, given the expanded powers of the Official Assignee, Parliament will have to ensure that realistic appeal or even mediation options are available to a debtor who is unhappy with the recommendation or decision of an Official Assignee.

[91] MED, *Tier One,* above n 3, at 44.

[92] *Ibid* at 38.

[93] T Telfer, 'Access to the Discharge in Canadian Bankruptcy Law and the New Role of Surplus Income: An Historical Perspective' in C Rickett and T Telfer (ed), *International Perspectives on Consumers' Access to Justice* (Cambridge University Press, 2003).

[94] *Ibid.*

[95] W Whitford, 'Changing Definitions of Fresh Start in US Bankruptcy Law' (1997) 20 *Journal of Consumer Policy* 179 at 191; C Tabb, 'The Death of Consumer Bankruptcy in the United States?' in C Rickett and T Telfer (eds), *International Perspectives on Consumers' Access to Justice* (Cambridge University Press, 2003).

[96] R Coulson, 'Consumer Abuse of Bankruptcy: An Evolving Philosophy of Debtor Qualification for Bankruptcy Discharge' (1998) 62 *Albany Law Review* 467 at 499. See also T Jackson, 'The Fresh Start Policy in Bankruptcy Law' (1985) 98 *Harvard Law Review* 1393 at 1432.

B. Surplus Income and the No Asset Procedure

The initial Ministry discussion papers echoed many of the concerns expressed in Canada and the United States that bankrupts were not paying enough and that bankruptcy was therefore too easy an option. The Ministry proposal to capture surplus income post-discharge through the establishment of an Income Payment Order (IPO) regime would have fundamentally altered the basic principle of the fresh start offered by the discharge. Fortunately, the Ministry has decided not to pursue this option and has instead focused its efforts on the establishment of a No Asset Procedure.[97] Before considering the details of the No Asset Procedure, this part will briefly examine the IPO procedure and its shortcomings as a policy initiative.

1. *The IPO Regime*

The IPO regime would have required debtors to provide the Official Assignee with information on their financial position for a period of 12 months after discharge. The regime required a debtor to file a signed declaration once every three months indicating that the debtor's financial position had not altered or a signed declaration within 14 days of the financial change. During the one-year period after discharge, an IPO order could be made for a period not exceeding 12 months.[98]

The IPO regime, if it had been pursued as a policy option, would have radically altered the nature of the discharge. Under the Insolvency Act 1967, if an unconditional discharge is granted, the order releases the bankrupt from 'all debts provable in the bankruptcy.'[99] New Zealand courts have long had the ability to impose conditions upon a discharge including a requirement that a debtor make payments over time out of future income. Thus, a debtor may receive a discharge conditional upon making specified payments to the Official Assignee for a fixed period. However, an assessment of the factors leading to the conditional order is made at the time of the discharge hearing and not afterwards.[100]

The IPO regime would also have revolutionised the current provisions that deal with surplus income. Under New Zealand law, a bankrupt's income earned after adjudication is prima facie part of the estate. However, it is subject to the

[97] The original version of this paper was presented at the Law and Society conference in Budapest in July 2001. The original paper contained an extensive review and critique of the IPO regime. The author forwarded a copy of the original version of the paper to the Ministry of Economic Development in July 2001 as a submission on the discussion paper.

[98] MED, *Tier One*, above n 3, at 47–48.

[99] Insolvency Act 1967, s 114.

[100] Section 112 of the Insolvency Act permits a court to reverse any absolute or conditional order of discharge within 2 years. However, such a reversal is not to take place unless facts are established, which had they been known to the court at the time of the order, would have justified the court in making a different order.

common law rule that a bankrupt may retain those earnings that are sufficient to maintain the bankrupt and his or her family.[101] The common law rule has now been supplemented by section 45.[102] Under this provision, the Official Assignee has the statutory power to require the bankrupt to pay any amount or periodic payments to the Assignee.[103] Section 45 is 'intended to provide a satisfactory method of enabling the Official Assignee to obtain some control over moneys coming into the bankrupt's possession during bankruptcy.'[104] A discharge does not affect a section 45 order and thus surplus income payments required under section 45 survive a discharge. However, under the existing regime there is no evaluation or re-evaluation of the debtor's circumstances post-discharge. In other words, once a discharge has been granted, an Official Assignee will not be able to demand section 45 contributions.[105]

The short one-year period of the IPO regime might suggest that there would have been few adverse consequences if the government had decided to pursue the idea. Indeed, one might interpret the IPO as a type of mandatory deferred proposal or repayment regime following the three-year period of bankruptcy. Such a regime might be viewed as a possible trade-off for an absolute discharge. On the other hand, the reporting requirements post discharge may have encouraged deception and dishonesty with respect to a debtor's change in circumstances.[106] The original form of the discharge was introduced in England in 1705 to encourage co-operation on the part of the debtor and to deter fraudulent activity.[107] Imposing reporting requirements post-discharge lessens the incentives for co-operation. The requirement to file post discharge audit reports and possibly pay over new-found sources of income undermines

[101] *Re Burney, ex parte Official Assignee* [1955] NZLR 1071.

[102] Insolvency Act s 45 as amended by Insolvency Amendment Act 2001, 2001–22, s 3. The amendment significantly added to the Official Assignee's powers by removing the need for court approval of s 45 orders.

[103] While no court approval is required for the initial order, the bankrupt may apply to the court to vary, suspend, or cancel the obligation to make a s 45 contribution.

[104] *Re Bertrand* [1980] 2 NZLR 72 (CA) at 77. Judicial commentary on the prior version of s 45 suggested that contribution orders should not be excessive and should realistically assess the debtor's financial means. See eg *Re Dransfield* (HC Auckland, B1540–1/90, 26 August 1993, Anderson J); *Re Burney* [1955] NZLR 1071.

[105] Justice Anderson in *Re Dransfield* (HC Hamilton, B1540–1/90, 26 August 1993), at 2, held that s 45 of the Insolvency Act 1967 'envisage the making of original orders under that section only during the period of bankruptcy.'

[106] For criticisms of mandatory repayment plans and the importance of the fresh start policy, see eg M Howard, 'A Theory of Discharge in Consumer Bankruptcy' (1987) 48 *Ohio State Law Journal* 1047 at 1085; R Coulson, 'Consumer Abuse of Bankruptcy: An Evolving Philosophy of Debtor Qualification for Bankruptcy Discharge' (1998) 62 *Albany Law Review* 467 at 523; W Whitford, 'Changing Definitions of Fresh Start in U.S. Bankruptcy Law' (1997) 20 *Journal of Consumer Policy* 179 at 191; J Czarnetzky, 'The Individual and Failure: A Theory of the Bankruptcy Discharge' (2000) 32 *Arizona State Law Journal* 393 at 463; N Georgakopoulos, 'Bankruptcy Law for Productivity' (2002) 37 *Wake Forest Law Review* 51 at 58.

[107] On the origins of the discharge, see eg C Tabb, 'The Historical Evolution of the Bankruptcy Discharge' (1991) 65 *American Bankruptcy Law Journal* 325.

the rehabilitative function of the discharge which has long been recognised in New Zealand.[108]

2. *No Asset Procedure*

Perhaps the most important issue to be raised in the context of an IPO regime is whether there are a significant numbers of debtors that actually have surplus income. Empirical studies in other jurisdictions illustrate that few bankrupts have surplus income.[109] The little empirical evidence available on New Zealand bankrupts suggests that a similar conclusion can be drawn. A study of a small sample of bankrupts during the period of 1 July 1997 to 30 June 1998 revealed that 'almost 80 percent of bankrupt estates do not return a dividend to creditors.' The study further revealed that 'half the bankrupts are receiving income support, so have no income with which to pay creditors.'[110] The Ministry's analysis of bankruptcy statistics for the period of 1 July 2000 to 30 June 2001 paints an even more dismal picture of the financial situation of many New Zealand bankrupts:

> Available statistics show that a large number of these consumer bankrupts are beneficiaries or on a low income and tread a fine line between solvency and insolvency. These individuals often do not earn enough money to repay debt and do not have any realisable assets. Based on current bankruptcy figures, this analysis would apply to approximately 40% of current bankrupts.[111]

In a significant shift in policy, the Ministry has abandoned its plans to introduce an IPO regime and has announced its intention to introduce a No Asset Procedure. Requiring all debtors to advise of a change in circumstances when few will have the means to make surplus income payments is not sound public policy.[112] However, tailoring a separate procedure for the large number of consumer bankrupts with no assets and little prospect of making income contributions is a welcome initiative. Further, the Ministry has recognised that the traditional straight bankruptcy procedure, with all of its consequent restrictions for a three-year period, is no longer appropriate for a large number of debtors.

The current bankruptcy regime is designed to deter individuals from becoming insolvent and bankrupt. However, consumer bankrupts who receive state

[108] *Re Jones* [1926] NZLR 318 at 320. Cf *Re Atwill* [1958] NZLR 873. The link between rehabilitation and the discharge was also raised during the Parliamentary debates in 1967. N.Z., *Hansard*, Debate-Second Reading: Insolvency Bill (vol 352 at 2069) 20 July 1967 (Hon JR Hanan).

[109] In Canada, see I Ramsay, 'Individual Bankruptcy: Preliminary Findings of a Socio-Legal Analysis' (1999) 37 *Osgoode Hall Law Journal* 15 ['Individual Bankruptcy]; S Schwartz, 'The Empirical Dimensions of Consumer Bankruptcy: Results from a Survey of Canadian Bankrupts' (1999) 37 *Osgoode Hall Law Journal* 83.

[110] MED, *Tier One*, above n 3, at 30, 31.

[111] N.Z., Ministry of Economic Development, *No Asset Procedure Paper* (Wellington, Ministry of Economic Development, April 2002) at 2 [*No Asset Procedure*].

[112] See eg J Ziegel, 'The Philosophy and Design of Contemporary Consumer Bankruptcy Systems: A Canada-United States Comparison' (1999) 37 *Osgoode Hall Law Journal* 205 at 228.

assistance or are on low incomes 'have a very limited ability to repay any debts' and there is 'very little action they can take to avoid bankruptcy.' The level of fault of this particular type of debtor 'is not commensurate with the punishment' found in the current regime.[113] The No Asset Procedure is being developed 'as an alternative to bankruptcy for consumer debtors with low income, no assets and for whom other alternatives are unavailable.'[114] A debtor that qualifies for the No Asset Procedure would be entitled to a discharge after 12 months rather than the traditional three-year period.

The Ministry has established draft entry criteria in an attempt to screen out debtors that do not fit the aims of the No Asset Procedure. However, defining such a suitable debtor is problematic. As a starting point there is difficulty in coming up with an appropriate definition of the larger category of all consumer bankrupts. There is disagreement over whether an arbitrary dollar amount of liabilities captures the essence of a consumer bankrupt.[115] The New Zealand No Asset Procedure seeks to take a subset of the elusive category of consumer bankrupt out of the straight bankruptcy regime by screening for no asset debtors.

Only debtors who are unable to utilise the formal alternatives found in Part XV and Part XVI would be eligible for the No Asset Procedure. In addition, a debtor must also meet other entry criteria. The entry criteria are designed to 'safeguard the process against abuse and ensure that only those debtors who meet the policy objectives gain entry to the procedure.' The proposed entry criteria include:

i) no business-related debts;
ii) no realisable assets (other than exempt property);
ii) no previous use of the procedure;
iv) no use of a trust to conceal assets;
v) no evidence of conduct that would constitute an offence in the event of bankruptcy;
vi) a maximum liability threshold (this could be $10,000, $20,000, $40,000 or $100,000);
vii) a net disposable income of no more than $50 per week (guidelines are to be developed which would assist the OA in determining the appropriate level of disposable income that qualifies);
viii) little or no likelihood that the debtor's circumstances will change in the near future to enable the re-payment of debt.

In addition, unsecured creditors would be able to object to the use of the No Asset Procedure.[116]

113 *No Asset Procedure,* above n 111, at 2.

114 *Ibid* at 3.

115 Heath, above n 7, at 443–444.

116 *No Asset Procedure,* above n 111, at 3–5. An objecting creditor must provide evidence of the debtor concealing assets or income or provide evidence of a bankruptcy offence. Alternatively the creditor must satisfy the Official Assignee that there is an intention to commence bankruptcy proceedings and that bankruptcy is a more appropriate remedy.

The final form of these entry criteria will ultimately determine how many debtors will be able to use the new procedure. The entry criteria combine fixed rules with some general standards that will give the Official Assignee some discretion to determine whether a particular debtor qualifies. However, it is unclear how the criteria will ultimately balance the need for easy identification of qualified debtors through clear rules and the need to guard against abuse through the creation of more open-ended discretion-based standards.[117] While many of the criteria might be quickly analysed, other matters, such as the whether the debtor meets the maximum level of disposable income or whether the debtor's circumstances are likely to change, will require more investigation and inquiry. The Ministry acknowledges that these latter two criteria will 'involve the OA making a judgement about the debtor's situation.' The debtor's situation will 'require close examination by NZITS staff at the time when debtors initiate formal insolvency proceedings with the OA.'[118] Again the Official Assignee will assume a multiple role in providing initial guidance, gathering the relevant facts and adjudicating on the entry criteria. This regime will also have to include a well-balanced appeal or mediation process to enable debtors to challenge the Official Assignee's decision on the entry criteria.[119]

Iain Ramsay has argued that there is a need to simplify and routinise bankruptcy administration so as to reduce the use of costly intermediaries. He claims that routinisation and the transformation of bankruptcy proceedings into an administrative process has appeal given that the vast majority of consumer bankruptcies are no asset cases. He suggests that the 'benefits of routinization include a swifter process than individualized scrutiny, an entitlement not subject to the discretion of a professional intermediary, and the reduction of stigma.'[120] The New Zealand No Asset Procedure may not go as far as Ramsay suggests in that the Official Assignee will still play an important gate-keeping function through the control of access to the regime.

As debtors come to realise that there are two tracks to a discharge, it is possible that the No Asset Procedure will come under pressure as the preferred option to pursue, whether or not debtors legitimately qualify for entry. The challenge in designing such a scheme, given the shorter 12-month period, 'is to avoid misuse of the process by those who should go into formal bankruptcy.'[121] To some extent, the procedure for objecting creditors may prevent some misuse. In addition, the Ministry has placed its hopes on the efforts of the Official

[117] On the importance of the choice between rules and standards, see T Janger, 'Crystals and Mud in Bankruptcy Law: Judicial Competence and Statutory Design' (2001) 43 *Arizona Law Review* 559.

[118] *No Asset Procedure,* above n 111, at 4.

[119] S 86 of the Insolvency Act enables a debtor or creditor to appeal to the court if aggrieved by a decision of the Official Assignee. Janger notes that in a consumer bankruptcy context few cases will be litigated and thus evidentiary presumptions become a key factor in statutory design. Janger, above n 117, at 601.

[120] 'Market Imperatives', above n 85 at 459.

[121] 'Bankruptcy Administration', above n 6, at 6.

Assignee to carefully measure the qualifications of the debtor. There will also be sanctions against debtors who falsify documentation. However, the greater the disparity between the No Asset Procedure and the regular bankruptcy track, the greater the resources that will have to be devoted to ensuring that misuse of the procedure does not become a problem.

Beyond offering the possibility of a streamlined and routinised scheme, the No Asset Procedure may signal an important shift in bankruptcy policy on the issue of access to the discharge. Bankruptcy law has traditionally tried to offer different levels of access to the discharge based upon some notions of fault.[122] However, legislative drafters have never quite managed to distinguish the honest but unfortunate from the irresponsible.[123] Achieving this distinction in the form of statutory language has been difficult, given the inherent value judgements that come into play when one has to determine how the debtor became insolvent. On that issue, there will always be those who will raise the spectre of fault or the debtor's lack of responsibility.[124]

The Ministry has, in fact, abandoned its earlier proposal to return to a fault-based statutory test to determine access to the discharge. Under this earlier recommendation, debtors who had not engaged in 'commercial misconduct' would be entitled to an earlier discharge after a period of only one year.[125] The boundaries of commercial misconduct would have proven too elusive.[126] Under the current recommendations, any eligibility for an earlier discharge will depend upon a debtor's application to the court or possible qualification for the No Asset Procedure.

The creation of the No Asset Procedure will move bankruptcy further away from the notion of debtor as a deviant[127] to a regime that encompasses the realistic financial situation of numerous low-income debtors. The No Asset Procedure will in effect create a separate tier of bankruptcy administration with a shorter discharge period for financially qualified debtors. However, as details of the No Asset Procedure become known and the entry criteria are refined through submissions and debate, there will no doubt be suggestions that mat-

[122] See eg Bankruptcy Act 1908, s 127. A court was not permitted to grant a discharge if it appeared that the bankrupt had committed an offence or where the court was of the opinion that the bankrupt had been 'guilty of misconduct or gross negligence in the conduct of his business.'

[123] In 1849, England attempted to create three 'moral categories' of discharge. Legislation permitted the courts to grant discharges in either the first, second, or third degree. The regime was ultimately abandoned. B Weiss, '*The Hell of the English: Bankruptcy and the Victorian Novel*' (Lewisburg, Bucknell University Press, 1986) at 43–45.

[124] A Keay, 'Bankruptcy Law Reform and Distinguishing Between the Kinds of Debtors who Enter Bankruptcy' (2000) 8 *Insolvency Law Journal* 63. See also 'Individual Bankruptcy' above n 109, at 17; N Huls, 'Overindebtedness and Overlegalization: Consumer Bankruptcy as a Field for Alternative Dispute Resolution' (1997) 20 *Journal of Consumer Policy* 143.

[125] The Ministry did not have any firm views on whether the shorter period should be one or two years and sought input on this issue. I have used one year as an illustrative example. Repeat bankrupts and fraudulent bankrupts would not be entitled to a discharge before three years.

[126] An extended critique of this proposal appears in the original conference paper and was submitted to the Ministry of Economic Development.

[127] 'Models of Consumer Bankruptcy' above n 61, at 271.

ters of fault and responsibility be taken into account as a means to further limit the shorter route to the discharge.[128]

V. CONCLUSION

Perhaps the most important recommendation to come out of the discussion papers is the suggestion that information collected from debtors be utilised to ensure that future policy decisions can be better informed by empirical data. This will be a significant improvement upon the current state of affairs. There is very little existing empirical information available on New Zealand consumer bankrupts.[129] The requirement that all debtors complete a statement of affairs prior to commencing any of the formal proceedings offers the opportunity to collect and collate electronic data on New Zealand debtors. This data will play an important role in assessing the impact of legislative change and act as an important input into future reforms.

The current proposals aim to strengthen and expand the role of the Official Assignee in an attempt to improve upon the weak institutional design of the current regime. The use of the Official Assignee's office as a gatekeeper to bankruptcy, the two proposal regimes and the No Asset Procedure will mean that debtors will have more information about the four procedures. However, given the new multiple roles that the Official Assignee will assume, Parliament may wish to consider a formal separation of function to ensure that the overlapping Official Assignee roles of counsellor, fact-finder and decision-maker are kept distinct through the creation of a separate official to act as a debtor adviser on the various options available.

Perhaps concerns about possible conflicts and overlapping roles of the Official Assignee may be alleviated by the significant numbers of consumer bankrupts who may well utilise the No Asset Procedure. If this new alternative becomes a streamlined procedure, this will significantly reduce the role of the Official Assignee as an intermediary who guides choice. For many debtors, the No Asset Procedure will be the only choice available. However, if Parliament attempts to control access to the No Asset Procedure by incorporating a

[128] Debtors that commit a bankruptcy offence will be screened out. However, apart from future ability to repay, the regime does not appear to distinguish between a debtor who, for example, experienced financial difficulty due to illness and a debtor that mismanaged credit card debt. On this issue in the American context, see M Jacoby, 'Collecting Debts from the Ill and Injured: The Rhetorical Significance, but Practical Irrelevance, of Culpability and Ability to Pay' (2001) 51 *American University Law Review* 229.

[129] NZLC, *Promoting Trust and Confidence,* above n 3, at 63. On the importance of empirical evidence to support bankruptcy law reform see K Bennetts, 'Bankruptcy Reform: The Significance of Systematic Data and Consultative Processes in Developing Our Bankruptcy Law' (1997) 1 *The Flinders Journal of Law Reform* 199 at 201; S Schwartz, 'The Empirical Dimensions of Consumer Bankruptcy: Results from a Survey of Canadian Bankrupts' (1999) 37 *Osgoode Hall Law Journal* 83 at 120.

number of subjective standards as entry criteria, the benefits of a streamlined no fault bankruptcy procedure will be lost.

As the reform suggestions have only been recently released, there has been little debate over the future direction of consumer bankruptcies in New Zealand. Because the scope of the insolvency reform project is comprehensive and also includes corporate insolvencies, the issue of consumer bankruptcy reform will have to compete with other insolvency topics for attention in the public eye. Topics of greater interest to insolvency practitioners, such as the introduction of a reorganisation regime, will likely dominate the debate over insolvency reform. Further, given the long-standing monopoly of the Official Assignee and the absence of established private bankruptcy assignees, the expansion of the Official Assignee's powers may attract little attention among the accounting or legal profession. The shift to an administrative model may well occur because there are few private practitioners, either accountants or lawyers, that currently derive much work from the personal bankruptcy regime. Indeed, one might speculate that if the privatisation movement of the 1980s and early 1990s had abolished the office of the Official Assignee as a public servant, the shift to an administrative model that the government now proposes would not be possible.

13

*Who Uses Chapter 13?**

TERESA A SULLIVAN, ELIZABETH WARREN,
JAY LAWRENCE WESTBROOK

I. INTRODUCTION

BANKRUPTCY IN THE United States is reserved by the constitution to federal courts, and Congress makes bankruptcy laws. An administered payment option in bankruptcy has been available officially for over 60 years, and is now called Chapter 13. This option did not originate with Congress, however; instead, the administered payment choice in bankruptcy developed through the extra-statutory actions of a bankruptcy judge (then called a referee) in Northern Alabama. In its history the administered payment plan has evolved from a judicial improvisation to the preferred policy of congressional legislators.

In the impoverished South of the early 20th century, indebtedness was the common lot of many ordinary folks.[1] 'Straight' bankruptcy, or a liquidation bankruptcy (now called Chapter 7), required giving up all non-exempt property to be sold and divided pro rata among creditors. Seeing that many debtors had no assets worth selling for the benefit of their creditors, but did have steady paychecks, a special bankruptcy referee in Birmingham, Alabama developed a technique whereby a fixed amount of the debtor's paycheck would be paid to a trustee each month until creditors had received all or an acceptable part of their debts back.[2] This approach was informally called a wage-earner plan. Alternatively, debtors such as farmers, who did have assets, could not afford to sell their assets if they were to continue to have a livelihood, and so the

* An earlier version of this paper was presented at the annual meeting of the Law and Society Association, Budapest, 5 July 2001. The data presented here come from three projects to collect data on consumer bankruptcy. The 1981 study was sponsored by National Science Foundation grant SES–8310173. The 1991 study was sponsored by the Education Endowment of the National Conference of Bankruptcy Judges. The 1999 study was financed by Harvard Law School and The University of Texas School of Law. More information about these studies appears at nn 22–24 and accompanying text. Any opinions, findings, conclusions and recommendations expressed in this paper are those of the authors and do not necessarily reflect the views of the National Science Foundation or of any other sponsor. We express our thanks to research assistant Tracey Kyckelhahn.

[1] G Jaynes, *Branches Without Roots: Genesis of the Black Working Class in the American South, 1862–1882* (New York, Oxford University Press, 1986).

[2] See generally TW Dixon and DG Epstein, 'Where Did Chapter 13 Come From and Where Should It Go?' (2002) 10 *American Bankruptcy Institute Law Review* 741.

wage-earner plan also provided them with a means of keeping their property while they repaid their debts. The new system spread to Tennessee, parts of Mississippi and Georgia, and North Carolina.[3]

The wage-earner approach became national when Congress recognised the wage-earner plan as Chapter XIII in the Bankruptcy Code of 1938. In succeeding legislation, the terminology was changed to Chapter 13. An important part of the history of bankruptcy reform legislation since that date has been tinkering with Chapter 13. In the course of this tinkering, Congress apparently became convinced that Chapter 13 was a more responsible way for consumers to handle their debt than a liquidation in Chapter 7, and each successive iteration of legislation appeared to be designed to encourage or coerce more debtors to enter the programme.

All forms of bankruptcy require the debtor to provide the court, under penalty of perjury, with detailed information concerning the debtors' income, assets and debts, together with a list of creditors and the answers to numerous questions (for example, 'Have any financial records been lost?'). In a Chapter 13 bankruptcy, a debtor must also present to the court a personal budget that lists all necessary expenses and monthly income, and a plan that specifies the amount of money that must be paid every month to a court-appointed trustee.[4] This sum is supposed to equal the disposable income of the debtor, or that portion of income that is not required to meet basic necessities of food, shelter, clothing and job-related expenses. The trustee is entitled to a percentage of the monthly payment as compensation for administrative expenses. If the court approves ('confirms') the plan, the trustee receives the payment every month and makes repayments to the creditors as specified by the plan. If a debtor has paid the court-ordered sum for every month in the confirmed plan, then any remaining unsecured debt is discharged (that is, forgiven.)

Given its informal origin, the original wage-earner plan was subject to some potential abuses. The first was the length of the plan, a potential abuse of the debtor. The earliest wage-earner plans did not necessarily have a set term of

[3] These states also had historically low levels of property exemptions, so that creditors in a Chapter 7 could take most of what a debtor owned. An interesting fact in the evolution of Chapter 13 was its widespread acceptance in states such as Texas, which have historically had generous exemptions. The fact that Chapter 13 flourishes in both low-exemption and high-exemption states suggests that exemption levels alone are not the most important determinant of the debtor's choice to use Chapter 13. There is also a private equivalent to Chapter 13 offered through consumer credit counselling agencies. Credit counsellors, with the voluntary consent of the creditors, help debtors devise repayment plans. The costs are usually borne by both the creditors and the debtors, and sometimes the local unified charitable campaign also contributes some of the costs of running the agency. We have not found credible information on trends in the use of consumer credit counselling or in the establishment of private repayment plans, nor do we know the success of these plans. That there is a high volume of work is evident in most cities; individual counsellors tell us that the agencies have been overworked for at least a decade. It is conceivable that the volume of these private Chapter 13s has grown to such an extent that the data in Table 1 are potentially misleading.

[4] Chapter 13 is limited to natural persons. Because the Chapter 13 debtors might have been in business, some bankruptcy filings are classified as 'business 13s,' but this terminology does not imply that the debtor is a corporate entity.

months or years, and stories were circulated about debtors (usually African American) who had been 'on the trustee' for many years. When Congress reformed bankruptcy in 1978, Chapter 13 was limited to a period of 36 to 60 months, and the court specified the time period when it confirmed the plan.

A second potential abuse was the amount that had to be repaid, a potential abuse of the creditors. According to the 1978 legislation, the amount repaid was supposed to be more than the unsecured creditors would get from a liquidation from the sale of assets (that is, a Chapter 7 bankruptcy). Because many debtors have no assets worth selling, meeting the positive dividend requirement required very little repayment. In our 1981 study we found a wide range of acceptable repayment practices, from 100 cents repaid on every dollar of debt to only one or two cents repaid on the dollar. Local judges and the local bar played a major role in deciding how much repayment was enough. Congress moved to close this loophole in 1984, when additional legislation specified that the amount to be repaid every month must be the debtors' disposable income—that is, the amount of income left over after all necessary expenses have been met.[5] Although this provision ensures that creditors will receive at least some repayment on the dollars owed if the minimal budget permits it, it also means that the debtor will have no income left over for savings, emergencies or any non-essential purchase. Even with this provision, there are some zero-payment plans for the unsecured creditors.

Besides closing loopholes, however, Congress has seemed intent on persuading more debtors to enter Chapter 13. As early as 1978, Congress tried to make Chapter 13 more attractive by broadening the discharge available in it. Some debts that could not be discharged in Chapter 7 could be discharged in Chapter 13.[6] By 1984, Congress had made the law still more insistent, and debtors' attorneys were required to explain to debtors the difference between Chapter 7 and Chapter 13. Substantial abuse provisions were also added to Chapter 7,[7] with the intent of forcing some debtors either into Chapter 13 or out of bankruptcy altogether.

In the 1990s, there was an explosion in consumer bankruptcies, with the number of annual filings increasing from about 330,000 at the beginning of the decade to 1.3 million by the end of the decade. Given the sustained economic prosperity of the same period, many legislators and pundits concluded that consumers must be abusing bankruptcy.[8] The demand for new bankruptcy regulations grew, fueled by a well-organised—and well-financed—campaign by the creditor community. In 1994, Congress put off the credit community with a few minor changes, including a provision to establish a blue-ribbon review

[5] 11 USC §1325(b).

[6] 11 USC §1328 (a).

[7] 11 U.S.C. §707(b).

[8] But see T Sullivan, E Warren, and JL Westbrook, *Fragile Middle Class: Americans in Debt* (Yale University Press, New Haven, CT, 2000) [Fragile Middle Class]; E Warren, 'The Bankruptcy Crisis' (1998) 73 *Indiana Law Journal* 1079 (for the proposition that the increase in filings is not due to abuse).

commission for which the credit industry had lobbied. The industry sought a 'means test' that would screen debtors' access to Chapter 7, along with a host of smaller changes that would make access to the bankruptcy system more difficult. The National Bankruptcy Review Commission accepted the premise that debtors should be encouraged to file for Chapter 13 if they were able to repay, but it did not support the industry's demands since it also found that the vast majority of debtors could pay little and that there was scant evidence of system-wide abuse in Chapter 7 filings. The credit industry has carried its fight to Congress, where its proposals are still pending.[9]

Over the years, the congressional strategy has been to increase the relative proportion of filings in Chapter 13 while nevertheless making the Chapter 13 experience fairly unpleasant. At the present time, a debtor in Chapter 13 faces an austerity programme for up to five years, in which only necessary expenses are allowed and all additional income is paid to the Chapter 13 trustee.[10]

II. PREVIOUS RESEARCH

Two sets of findings dominate the previous research on Chapter 13. The first finding is that there remains a pronounced geographic skew in the use of Chapter 13.[11] Despite efforts by Congress over the past 23 years, the use of Chapter 13 remains concentrated in the southern states, where it began, and in a few districts elsewhere. This geographic concentration manifests a local legal culture, in that certain local judges and attorneys appear to favour the use of Chapter 13. Strong evidence that local legal culture influences chapter choice is that the use of Chapter 13 varies *within* states as much as it does *between* states. In Ohio, for example, the use of Chapter 13 is much more prevalent in the Southern District than in the Northern. With a single state, there is no variance in the formal law applicable to the case that could explain this variation. These patterns of geographic variation have persisted for at least 20 years.[12]

[9] For a fuller discussion of the Commission and subsequent congressional debate, see MB Jacoby, 'Generosity *v* Accessibility: Bankruptcy, Consumer Credit, and Health Care Finance in the US' in this volume.

[10] The extra-statutory aspects of Chapter 13 persist, however, in some additional local efforts at 'debtor rehabilitation.' In some districts, the debtor is required to attend adult education programmes on personal finance and budgeting. At least one judicial district has begun a formal programme to reintroduce debtors to the credit community at the successful completion of their Chapter 13 plan. For a fuller discussion, see J Braucher, 'Debtor Education in Bankruptcy: The Perspective of Interest Analysis' in this volume.

[11] See T Sullivan, E Warren and JL Westbrook, 'The Persistence of Local Legal Culture: Twenty Years of Evidence from the Federal Bankruptcy Courts' (1994) 17 *Harvard Journal of Law & Public Policy* 801 [Persistence of Local Legal Culture]; E Flynn and G Bermant, 'Measuring Projected Performance in Chapter 13: Comparisons Across the States' (2000) 6 *American Bankruptcy Journal* 22; E Flynn and G Bermant, 'Sources of Variability in Chapter 13 Performance' (2001) 3 *American Bankruptcy Institute Journal* 20.

[12] Persistence of Local Legal Culture, *ibid*; WC Whitford, 'Has the Time Come to Repeal Chapter 13?' (1989) 65 *Indiana Law Journal* 85.

The second finding is that the operation of Chapter 13 does not appear to work as Congress intended. The ideological marketing of Chapter 13 appears to be in sharp contrast with the practical realities facing the debtors. Several studies have shown that only one-third of debtors who initially file in Chapter 13 eventually complete their plan and receive a discharge.[13] Although there is substantial concurrence concerning the one-third success rate, there are disagreements about whether this fraction is high or low and whether it represents a high level of success or a dismal record of failure. The argument for success is that it was better for the debtor to have attempted the honourable act of repayment than not even to try, and the limited period of repayment may nevertheless have offered enough time to cure mortgage arrears and receive some respite from bill collectors through the automatic stay. The argument for failure is that the debtor expends too many resources for too little benefit.[14] Further, many Chapter 13s were doomed from their initiation. Many plans were predictably unsuccessful because the budget presented to the court implicitly assumes both that income will not fall and that expenses will not rise, assumptions that are rarely correct.

During the 1990s, in particular, as much as one-fifth of the US labour market found itself in contingent employment. By 2000, one-fourth of all US workers had been with their current employers for less than 12 months.[15] Numerous rounds of downsizing, 'job shedding,' industrial restructuring and plant closures affected workers in firms of all size. Both white-collar and blue-collar workers were affected. As many as two-thirds of all bankrupt debtors report a job problem—layoff, cutback or unemployment—as a factor in the decision to file bankruptcy.[16] The unpredictability of employment situations led inevitably to income fluctuations that could wreck any tight budget, but especially a Chapter 13 budget that does not leave so much as a dollar of flexibility.

[13] See T Sullivan, E Warren and JL Westbrook, *As We Forgive Our Debtors: Bankruptcy and Consumer Credit in America* (New York, Oxford University Press, 1989) at 216 [As We Forgive Our Debtors]; J Wannamaker, 'The Washington Beat' (Oct. 1993) 6 *National Association of Chapter Thirteen Trustees Newsletter* 7; SF Norberg, 'Consumer Bankruptcy's New Clothes: An Empirical Study of Discharge and Debt Collection in Chapter 13 Cases' (1999) 76 *American Bankruptcy Institute Law Review* 415 [Consumer Bankruptcy's New Clothes] . But see ML Girth, 'The Role of Empirical Data in Developing Bankruptcy Legislation for Individuals' (1989) 65 *Indiana Law Journal* 17. Girth studied only post-confirmation cases. Our earlier study, As We Forgive Our Debtors, showed that about one-third of the cases failed before confirmation. If Girth studied a population in which one-third of the initial filings had already been removed from the sample because they failed early, then her data falls right into line with all other studies. In addition to these studies, two unpublished working papers by Bork and Turk address the geographic differences in filing rates and the termination states of Chapter 13 cases. See M Bork and SD Turk, Bankruptcy Statistical Trends, Chapter 13 Dispositions (unpublished working paper, on file with the Administrative Office of the US Courts in Washington).

[14] WC Whitford, 'The Ideal of Individualized Justice: Consumer Bankruptcy as Consumer Protection, and Consumer Protection in Consumer Bankruptcy' 68 (1994) *American Bankruptcy Law Journal* 397 [Ideal of Individualized Justice].

[15] United States Bureau of Labor Statistics, United States Department of Labor 00–245, 'Employee Tenure in 2000' (News release of 29 August 2000).

[16] Fragile Middle Class, above n 8.

Moreover, the Chapter 13 budgets may not take into account contingencies such as increased expenditures. The normal ageing of a family, especially a family with small children, means that over a period of five years expenses are likely to increase. For a family of relatively low income—below $36,800—annual expenditures for raising a child rise from $6,080 annually for a toddler under the age of two to $7,150 for a child aged 12–14.[17] Bankruptcy judges find themselves trying to decide whether orthodontia or college tuition constitute necessary expenses. A Chapter 13 debtor who finds herself without medical insurance may discover that an automobile accident or an illness produces unanticipated medical expenses. Even if she has medical insurance, the time off from work may result in lower wages.[18] In addition, one might suppose that debtors who find themselves in bankruptcy are probably not sophisticated in developing and using budgets, let alone austerity budgets.[19] There is no reason to believe that problems such as employment instability, rising family costs, extended health care risks and financial naiveté have been solved simply because the debtor declared bankruptcy.

As a result of these difficulties of the debtors, the need to repay secured creditors, and the tightness of the budgets to begin with, the amount of money paid to unsecured creditors is relatively small.[20] The frequent charge that debtors abuse bankruptcy by filing again and again is partially explained by the fact that debtors who fail in Chapter 13 often file again in Chapter 7 still seeking relief from the same debts.[21] They may have been better advised to file Chapter 7 initially. Others try Chapter 13 multiple times, dropping out when their incomes fall or their expenses jump, but re-filing when their finances seem steadier or their creditors have pressed them harder.

III. RESEARCH QUESTION AND HYPOTHESIS

The fraction of all non-business bankruptcy filings that are in Chapter 13 has changed relatively little since 1981, but the absolute number of Chapter 13 filings has risen nearly five-fold since 1981. Given the implicit Congressional policy directive to increase the use of Chapter 13, we want to know whether any part of this increase represents debtors who would have filed in Chapter 7 were it not for encouragement to use Chapter 13. One way to test for such a shift to

[17] United States Bureau of the Census. *Statistical Abstract of the United States* 120th edn (Government Printing Office, Washington, 2000) at 462.

[18] M Jacoby, TA Sullivan and E Warren, 'Rethinking the Debates Over Health Care Financing: Evidence from the Bankruptcy Courts' (2001) 76 *New York University Law Review* 375 [Rethinking the Debates].

[19] To make matters worse, we have discovered in our studies that judges sometimes approve budgets that show more expenses than income, thus making it clear from the outset that the plan cannot be completed.

[20] Ideal of Individualized Justice, above n 14; Consumer Bankruptcy's New Clothes, above n 13.

[21] As We Forgive Our Debtors, above n 13, at 191; SL DeJarnett, 'Once is Not Enough: Preserving Consumers' Rights to Bankruptcy Protection' (1999) 74 *Indiana Law Journal* 455.

Chapter 13 is to ask whether the characteristics of debtors choosing Chapter 13 have changed over time? Any effect of the encouragement to file in Chapter 13 is not likely to be distributed evenly across different demographic groups. A finding of substantial differences in Chapter 13 filing rates over time within particular demographic groups would suggest that the effort to encourage filing in Chapter 13 has had some effect. A finding of little demographic change in Chapter 13 filing rates would suggest that the considerations for choosing Chapter 13 have remained static over time. Those considerations will be discussed later and are hereinafter referred to as the 'legal' criteria or variables.

Table 1 shows the proportion of filings in Chapter 13 for 19 years. At the beginning of this time period, the 1978 reforms to encourage the use of Chapter 13 had just taken effect. By the end of this time period, the encouragement and threatened coercion to use Chapter 13 were in full bloom. The remarkable story of this table is simply its stability; in every year, the proportion of cases filed in Chapter 13 varies narrowly between 27 and 32 per cent. There is no evident trend. The fact that there were many more Chapter 13 cases in 1999 than there

Table 1 Chapter 13 Cases, Non-Business and Business, with Proportion of all Non-Business Cases that are Chapter 13, 1981–2001

Year	Non-business Chapter 13's	Business Chapter 13's	Total non-Business Cases	Non-business Chapter 13's as a % of all non-business cases
1981	81,913	4,865	312,914	26.2%
1982	92,689	6,016	311,443	29.8
1983	94,455	7,746	304,916	31.0
1984	84,535	6,823	282,105	30.0
1985	91,328	7,124	297,885	30.7
1986	112,772	7,954	401,575	28.1
1987	130,189	11,999	495,567	26.3
1988	148,338	7,607	549,612	27.0
1989	175,139	8,089	616,753	28.4
1990	208,666	8,802	718,107	29.1
1991	251,883	10,123	872,438	28.9
1992	254,138	11,439	900,874	28.2
1993	241,464	10,309	812,898	29.7
1994	240,639	9,238	780,455	30.8
1995	276,225	10,363	874,642	31.6
1996	344,092	11,031	1,125,006	30.6
1997	391,930	11,095	1,350,118	29.0
1998	389,398	8,221	1,398,182	27.9
1999	376,311	5,903	1,281,581	29.4
2000	378,400	5,903	1,217,927	31.1
2001	419,750	5,542	1,452,030	28.9

Source: Administrative Office of the US Courts, Annual Reports, 1981–2001

had been in 1981 was a function of the overall increase in bankruptcies alone, and not an evident shift in debtor preferences.

The stability indicated in Table 1 provides initial evidence for the alternative hypothesis: the factors influencing the choice of chapter have changed little over time, and the demographic composition of Chapter 13 will therefore be stable. In this paper, we will go behind this basic data to examine in more detail the characteristics of bankrupt debtors choosing Chapter 13 in 1981, 1991 and 1999. We are looking for evidence of demographic change in the population of Chapter 13 filers.

IV. DATA AND METHODS

The data reported here come from three studies of consumer bankruptcy that we have conducted. Our original study, drawn from cases filed in 1981, consisted of systematic samples of debtors in the 10 federal judicial districts located in Illinois, Pennsylvania and Texas. The data were limited to variables that could be collected from the records filed with the court. The court asks for little demographic information, and so one limitation on the present paper is the availability of variables from 1981.[22]

The 1991 study used questionnaires answered by bankrupt debtors at the time that they appeared at the bankruptcy court for the required meeting with creditors. The same districts in Illinois, Pennsylvania and Texas were used, but the states of California and Tennessee were added. For one district in each state, the questionnaire data were enriched with data from the court files.[23]

The 1999 study was based solely on questionnaires that were collected at the time of the required meeting with creditors. One district in each of the previous states was used, and additional districts in Ohio, Kentucky and Wisconsin were added. The questionnaire itself was closely modelled on the 1991 questionnaire, with some additional questions concerning household composition and reason for bankruptcy.[24]

The advantages of these three studies are that they represent the best available multi-district, multi-state repeated analyses of consumer bankruptcies. The reuse of a core group of five districts in each study helps provide a rough control for the operation of a local legal culture. We eliminated outliers in each sample by using the outlier characteristics identified in 1981 and then inflating them by the Consumer Price Index to eliminate cases with similar, extreme values in 1991 and 1999.[25]

[22] See T Sullivan, E Warren and JL Westbrook, 'Laws, Models, and Real People: Choice of Chapter in Personal Bankruptcy' (1989b) 13 *Law & Social Inquiry* 661 at 342ff (for details about this data set) [Laws, Models, and Real People].

[23] See Fragile Middle Class, above n 8 at 262ff, for details about this study.

[24] See Rethinking the Debates, above n 18, for a more detailed discussion about this study.

[25] See Laws, Models, and Real People, above n 22, at 77 (n 2) for details.

There are, however, also some difficulties.[26] The three studies are not perfect replicates. Although some variables appear in each year of the study, other interesting variables are available only for one or two of the studies. We can identify Hispanics in all three studies, but we can identify African-Americans only in the second and third studies. Moreover, the measurement of the variables is not necessarily the same from year to year. Hispanic identification in 1981 was done by coding surnames from the Census Bureau's list of Spanish surnames, one of several techniques that was used in the 1980 census. In the two subsequent studies, we used self-identification of ethnicity, with the result that we had substantial item non-response but more close approximation with the method currently used by the Census Bureau.

Because of item non-response, the sample sizes reported below may not correspond to the sample sizes we have reported in earlier studies. Unless otherwise noted, we have used pair-wise deletion to handle missing values.

V. INDEPENDENT VARIABLES

This analysis uses seven variables that are available in all three studies and that are believed relevant to chapter choice. The dependent variable is chapter choice, with filing in Chapter 13 coded 1 and filing in Chapter 7 coded 0.[27] Four of the independent variables are demographic: joint filing, current marital status, gender if filing alone (coded 1 for women, 0 for men), and Hispanic ethnicity (coded 1 for yes, 0 otherwise). Two variables are potentially relevant from a legal point of view: total debt, coded in nominal dollars, and homeownership. The final variable is included as a measure of local legal culture; filers in Texas receive a code of 1, and filers in other states receive a code of 0.

Joint filing is available to any married couple, and is believed to be relevant to chapter choice because married couples are more likely to be stable (and thus able to complete the plan) and to have two earners. Thus, we expect a positive correlation with chapter choice. We also included marital status, which is coded

[26] The first is somewhat technical: there may be a design effect resulting from the use of three somewhat different data collection techniques. The 1981 sample was a systematic sample drawn from the court docket. Sampling error for this study can be reliably modelled and is unlikely to affect the results significantly; more importantly, inferential statistics are suitable for analysis. The 1991 study was a sample from a very large set of questionnaires that were themselves subject to non-response bias. We have previously analysed the non-response bias and do not believe that it affects the major variables of interest, but nevertheless the 1991 data bring an additional source of potential error. Inferential statistics are probably still appropriate. In 1999, we used a quota design in collecting questionnaires, but the days on which the data were collected were randomised. By looking at the sex composition (inferred from first names) of a sample of the docket compared with the sample we obtained, we found a negligible non-response bias, at least for this variable. Some purists might object that this third design violates the assumptions for inferential statistics, but there is the protection offered by a relatively large sample size. One possible result of these three differing designs is a design effect that we have not detected.

[27] The skew of 70/30 in the dependent variable is suitable for ordinary least squares analysis.

1 if married and 0 otherwise. Although all joint filers are married, not all married people file jointly.[28] We would also expect married filers to be more likely to file in Chapter 13, even if they do not file jointly.[29]

We expect that women filing alone will be more likely to file in Chapter 7, so that there will be a negative correlation with filing in Chapter 13. We base this expectation on the fact that women in bankruptcy are more likely to give family reasons for their bankruptcy than to give economic reasons, and thus their expectations for an economic recovery and repayment possibilities may be lower.

Lawyers have told us that their Hispanic clients prefer to file in Chapter 13 because they see it as the more honourable route in bankruptcy. Although our 1981 study did not support this hypothesis, we have not to date tested the hypothesis for 1991 and 1999.

We anticipate that total debt will make a debtor less likely to file in Chapter 13, because the likelihood of repayment is lower, and we also anticipate that owning a home will make a debtor more likely to enter Chapter 13 to try to keep that valuable asset.[30]

Finally, because Texas debtors have a long history of disproportionately choosing Chapter 13, especially in the districts we have studied in 1991 and 1999, we have hypothesised that there will be a positive correlation between living in Texas and filing in Chapter 13.

VI. FINDINGS

Table 2 shows the zero-order Pearson correlation coefficients between filing in Chapter 13 and the preceding variables. In this table, a positive value indicates that the variable is associated with filing in Chapter 13, while a negative value indicates that the variable is associated with filing in Chapter 7. An initial evaluation of Table 2 suggests that our preceding expectations were correct and that demographic variables are useful in predicting chapter choice. As we will see below, however, this initial evaluation is fundamentally misleading and the data contain several hidden surprises.

In 1981, all of the variables are in the predicted direction and only total debt fails to achieve significance. (Joint filing is barely significant at $p = 0.054$.) By 1991, joint filing had changed direction so that it was negatively associated with filing in Chapter 13, and the coefficients for female and Hispanic had gained

[28] J Braucher, 'Lawyers and Consumer Bankruptcy: One Code, Many Cultures?' (1993) 67 *American Bankruptcy Law Journal* 501.

[29] Surprisingly, these two variables are not collinear, even though they might seem to be measuring the same concept; the zero-order correlations between being married and joint filing decline from .798 in 1981 to .756 in 1991 to .718 in 1999.

[30] Homeownership, although positively correlated with total debt ($r=0.34$ in 1981, $r=0.36$ in 1991, $r = 0.30$ in 1999) is nevertheless not collinear with total debt.

Table 2 Zero-order Correlation Coefficients between Chapter and Specified Variables 1981, 1991 and 1999 (Dependent variable is Chapter choice, where Chapter 13 = 1)

Variable	1981	1991	1999
Joint	.050+	–.105**	.028
Married	.077**	.113**	.063*
Female	–.044+	–.131***	.002
Total debt	–.005	–.062	–.041
Owns home	.235***	.341***	.243***
Hispanic	.054*	.104**	.015
Texan	.097***	.180***	.200***

Source: Consumer Bankruptcy Projects. See text. Outliers removed.
Significance:
+ = $.05<p\leq.10$
* = $.01<p\leq.05$
** = $.001<p\leq.01$
*** = $p\leq.001$

greater significance. In general, however, the correlations for 1991 looked fairly similar to those of 1981.

The large changes came between 1991 and 1999. In particular, three of the four demographic variables had lost significance. By 1999, joint filing was again positive but no longer significant. The significance of married status had declined. Being female lost significance and had become positive. Being Hispanic lost significance.

In all three years, the legal variable total debt was negatively correlated but not significant, and homeownership was strongly significant and positive. The local legal culture variable was also positive and strongly significant. Table 2 seems to suggest, then, that the demographic characteristics of the debtors might have broadened a bit but remained less important than the other variables.

Table 3 shows the standardised regression coefficients for ordinary least squares (OLS) regression equations in which the chapter of filing is the dependent variable. Because this dependent variable is not very skewed in our samples, we have used OLS rather than logistic regression for clarity of exposition. The standardised coefficients may be compared with one another in magnitude for an indication of how strong the influence of each variable is once all the other variables in the equation have been taken into account. The positive coefficients indicate a tendency to file in Chapter 13, controlling for all the other variables, and a negative coefficient indicates a tendency to file in Chapter 7, controlling for all the other variables. The value of Table 3, compared with Table 2, is that Table 3 can isolate the effect of each variable while controlling for the effect of the others.

The F tests indicate that each of the models is significant, or to put it differently, each model is a 'good fit' for the data analysed. The R-squared coefficient

Table 3 Predicting Chapter Choice: Standardised Regression Coefficients for 1981, 1991 and 1999 (Dependent variable is Chapter choice, where Chapter 13 = 1)

Variable	1981	1991	1999
Joint	–.071+	.076	–.056
Married	.041	.054	.061
Female	–.043	–.065	.007
Total debt	–.137***	–.098**	–.101**
Owns home	.264***	.311***	.221***
Hispanic	.026	–.087*	–.016
Texan	.101***	.125**	.166***
R**2	.08	.15	.09
F	20.1***	16.67***	16.12**
N	1539	2452	1506

Source: Consumer Bankruptcy Projects. See text. Outliers removed.
Significance:
+ = $.05<p\leq.10$
* = $.01<p\leq.05$
** = $.001<p\leq.01$
*** = $p\leq.001$

indicates that relatively little of the choice of chapter is explained by these seven variables—only 15 per cent in 1991, for example, is explained by these seven variables.

As we might have suspected from Table 2, the largest single effect is homeownership, which is strongly positive and very significant in every year. Regardless of other influences, homeowners choose Chapter 13, very likely because the home is an asset that they are eager to keep. The second greatest influence is being a Texan, our proxy for local legal culture. Even controlling for homeownership, Hispanic identity and so on, the Texas filers are significantly more likely to file in Chapter 13. The third strongest indicator is the remaining legal indicator, total debt, which is negatively associated with Chapter 13, although it loses some of its significance in 1991 and 1999 compared with 1981. On the other hand, considering that total debt is *never* significant in Table 2, it is surprising that it has now become the third strongest predictor of chapter of filing. In the case of this total debt, the predictive value is negative: a debtor is less likely to file in Chapter 13, and thus more likely to file in Chapter 7, the greater the total debt. Again, total debt is considered here once homeownership has already been taken into account.

Once we have controlled for all of the legal variables, the demographic variables lose their significance. Joint filing is only barely significant in 1981, and in the wrong direction from the hypothesis (that is, more likely to file in Chapter 7). Hispanic ethnicity attains significance only in 1991, and again not in the hypothesised direction. Once residence, homeownership and debt are controlled, Hispanics are more likely to file in Chapter 7. Demonstrating that marital status and joint filing are not the same thing, the two variables take on different directions in both 1981 and 1999, with joint filing negatively associated and being married positively associated with Chapter 13, but marital status never attains significance. Gender never attains significance either, although its direction becomes weakly positive in 1999, indicating a somewhat greater (but statistically insignificant) likelihood for women to file in Chapter 13 when all other variables are taken into account.

So despite the fact that every demographic variable was significantly associated with the choice of Chapter 13 in Table 2, these effects are completely washed out by the more legally significant variables of total debt, homeownership, and residence (our proxy value for local legal culture).

VII. DISCUSSION

How did the demographic variables that were significant in Table 2 become *insignificant* once the legal variables were controlled? One answer is that the demographic variables are associated with the legal variables in some fairly predictable ways. Women have less total debt, they are less likely to own homes and they are less represented in our Texas samples. Hispanics have less total debt and are more likely to be homeowners.[31] Married people have more total debt, are more likely to own homes and are more likely to be in our Texas samples.

The legal variables are substantively more significant and better predictors of the choice of bankruptcy, and this has been true consistently over time. From the point of view of how the bankruptcy system works, this finding indicates that attorneys are using reasonable criteria of saving assets (homes) and reasonable repayment possibilities (total debt) in advising their clients to choose Chapter 13. There is little evidence of demographic profiling. The local legal culture appears to be alive and well, with Chapter 13 more attractive in some jurisdictions even when assets and debt have been controlled.

To go a bit further, however, the data could refute the speculation that the recent increases in filings were due to abuse. The data indicate that the debtors not choosing Chapter 13 are realistically less likely to be able to pay, and thus they are not good candidates for Chapter 13. This conclusion comes from the negative effect of total debt—those with greater debt are less likely to be able to pay, and they are entering Chapter 7. Similarly, those with lower levels of debt and therefore more capable of repayment are entering Chapter 13.[32]

[31] Texas residence was not collinear with Hispanic ethnicity; in fact, in 1991 there was a negative correlation between filing in Texas and self-reporting Hispanic identity. In both 1981 and 1999, the correlation between filing in Texas and being Hispanic was positive.

[32] There is good evidence that the debtors filing in Chapter 7 have little ability to repay. See M B Culhane M White, 'Taking the New Consumer Bankruptcy Model for a Test Drive: Means-Testing for Chapter 7 Debtors' (1999) 7 *American Bankruptcy Institute Law Review* 27.

Realistically, if members of Congress want to increase the proportions of debtors filing voluntarily in Chapter 13, the number of options appears limited.

1. Require debtors who enter bankruptcy to file in Chapter 13 at lower levels of total debt than they do customarily. The effect of this effort might be to increase the fraction of Chapter 13 filings, but it would probably discourage the total number of bankruptcy filings.
2. Encourage more Americans to become homeowners, recognising that those who have a greater stake in the community are more likely to stay engaged, including the long-term engagement required to repay creditors.
3. Seek to spread the local legal culture that encourages Chapter 13.

It is not clear how one would best enact the third option. Perhaps the current chorus of exhortation and the threat of future coercion is designed to do just that. In the absence of such an effort, it appears that those who choose Chapter 13 will continue do so on the basis of what we have called legally relevant variables.

Finally, it is worth asking whether the goal of placing an ever-increasing number of bankrupt debtors into Chapter 13 repayment plans is desirable. The two-thirds failure rate in Chapter 13 suggests that too many families with too many problems are already trying plans that have no hope of success. If the goal of the consumer bankruptcy system was restated to focus on successful sorting between those who can repay and those who cannot and sorting them in Chapter 13 repayment plans and Chapter 7 liquidations respectively, then the ideal proportion of Chapter 13 filings might be lower—not higher. At a minimum, these data suggest that a serious re-examination of the current efforts to press more debtors into Chapter 13 should be undertaken before consideration of the plan in the proposed legislation to spend significant court resources to try to drive even more debtors out of Chapter 7. In any case, these data confirm that in nearly 20 years of pressure from Washington, the mix of Chapter 13 debtors has not changed appreciably, suggesting that both the operation of the system and the influences that can be exercised from Washington are both poorly understood and ineffectively implemented.

14

Generosity Versus Accessibility: Bankruptcy, Consumer Credit, and Health Care Finance in the US

MELISSA B JACOBY*

I. INTRODUCTION

FOR INDIVIDUALS AND families in the United States, health problems and financial problems go hand in hand. Like many Americans, ill or injured individuals are active users not only of widely-available consumer credit products, but of the US bankruptcy system. In its current form, the US bankruptcy system is not only 'the most generous in the world,'[1] but it is quite accessible to potential users as compared to traditional social welfare programmes in the US. The US Congress has been considering legislation that, under the guise of weeding out a small handful of system abusers, bureaucratises the bankruptcy system in ways likely to keep out legitimate users, with little-considered effects on medical-related bankruptcies.

In this chapter, I first provide a brief overview of the very complex US health care finance system. This overview reveals why it is not surprising to find many Americans with both medical problems and financial problems. From there, I explore the private sector safety net of consumer credit as well as the federal bankruptcy system in its current and potentially reformed states. Both consumer credit and bankruptcy functionally have become part of the health care finance system. Based on this discussion, I will suggest that it would be a mistake to

* Thanks to Johanna Niemi-Kiesiläinen, Iain Ramsay and William Whitford for inviting me to participate and for helpful comments on a presentation and earlier drafts of this paper. I also appreciate Elizabeth Dennis' capable research assistance, the efforts of the law librarians at Temple, and the financial support of Temple University School of Law. I also am grateful to Elizabeth Warren and Teresa Sullivan, with whom I had the opportunity to study bankruptcy filers in 1999, which produced some of the thought-provoking findings about medical-related financial problems discussed herein.

[1] J Niemi-Kiesiläinen, 'Consumer Bankruptcy In Comparison: Do We Cure a Market Failure or a Social Problem' (1999) 37 *Osgoode Hall Law Journal* 473 at 475; R Efrat, 'Global Trends in Personal Bankruptcy' (2002) 76 *American Bankruptcy Law Journal* 81 at 87.

bureaucratise bankruptcy unless the government desires under-utilisation of bankruptcy as a redress for failures of the health care finance system.

II. HEALTH CARE FINANCE

A. The US Health Care Finance System

By a traditional account, health care in the US is financed principally through private insurance (often, but not always, employment-based) and a variety of government programmes such as Medicare (principally for those over 65), Medicaid (categories of low income), or State Children's Health Insurance Program (children in low-income households).[2] Complicating matters, '[e]ach system has its own complex regulatory and eligibility mechanisms that are governed at the state, federal, and local levels, as well as by the private market.'[3] Some individuals rely on a combination of coverage; others lack coverage and receive care on an ad hoc basis, if at all.[4] People espouse widely diverging theories regarding the causes of the gaps, complexity and cost, and offer markedly different solutions.[5] All should be able to agree, however, that some individuals experience considerable financial pressures under the health system as it currently exists.

Health coverage in the US, whether private or governmental, cannot be equated with having low-cost or no-cost health care. Covered individuals often pay part or all of rising insurance premiums, share the cost of some medical services, and bear total financial responsibility for other services or medications.[6] Individuals may not know in advance how much their plans will cover, nor can they always evaluate the relevance of coverage gaps until an unexpected illness or injury arises.

[2] LG Trubek, 'Barriers To Access To Health Care: Working On the Puzzle: Health Care Coverage For Low-Wage Workers' (2002) 12 *Health Matrix* 157 at 157; O Carrasquillo *et al*, 'Private Employers' Role in Providing Health Insurance: A Reappraisal' (1999) 340 *New England Journal of Medicine* 109 at 110, 113.

[3] Trubek, above n 2 at 157.

[4] HF Daly III *et al*, 'Barriers To Access To Health Care: Into the Red To Stay in the Pink: The Hidden Cost of Being Uninsured' (2002) 12 *Health Matrix* 39.

[5] Compare TM Jost, 'Private or Public Approaches To Insuring the Uninsured: Lessons From International Experience With Private Insurance' (2001) 76 *New York University Law Review* 419; DJ Besharov, 'Creating a Marketplace For Social Welfare Services' (2002) 16 *Notre Dame Journal of Law, Ethics, and Public Policy* 519, 519.

[6] See, eg J Gabel *et al*, 'Individual Insurance: How Much Financial Protection Does it Provide' (April 2002) 21 *Health Affairs* 18; S Maxwell, M Moon and M Segal, 'Growth in Medicare and Out-Of-Pocket Spending: Impact On Vulnerable Beneficiaries', The Urban Institute <http://www.urban.org/health/growth-in-medicare.html> (24 July 2002); FM McClellan, 'Is Managed Care Good For What Ails You? Ruminations on Race, Age and Class' (1999) 44 *Villanova Law Review* 227 at 230, n 10 (discussing cost consequences of options in Medicare programme).

Millions of individuals are not enrolled in any private insurance or government programmes.[7] Un-covered individuals are sometimes charged higher fees for health care services than those charged for services covered by insurance providers.[8] For those who lack insurance due to inability to pay,[9] medical services themselves may be unaffordable. Physicians may refuse to serve uninsured patients who cannot pay cash or have outstanding balances for previous services, perhaps leaving only the possibility of emergency room care when health problems have escalated.[10] Un-covered individuals may forgo health care, and ultimately may develop illness or injury that is expensive to treat.[11]

Some uninsured and underinsured individuals are actually eligible for, but are not enrolled in, government benefits.[12] Under-enrolment in US social welfare programmes is a widespread phenomenon.[13] Many factors may explain this situation, such as out-of-pocket costs notwithstanding coverage,[14] stigma associated with low income programmes or lack of interest,[15] but the complexity of eligibility standards and enrolment procedures should not be overlooked. One study of under-enrolment in Medicaid describes a variety of barriers that might explain low take-up rates, including changing eligibility status over time,

[7] RJ Mills, 'People At Risk: Health Insurance Coverage, 2000', US Census Bureau <http://www.census.gov/population/pop-profile/2000/chap15.pdf> (8 February 2003) (reporting that 14% of the population was without insurance coverage during the entire year in 2000).

[8] Daly III *et al*, above n 4, at 45; I Wielawski, 'Gouging the Medically Uninsured: A Tale of Two Bills' (2000) 19 *Health Affairs* 180, 180; BR Furrow, 'Regulating the Managed Care Revolution: Private Accreditation and a New System Ethos' (1998) 43 *Villanova Law Review* 361 at 362.

[9] R Kronick and T Gilmer, 'Explaining the Decline in Health Insurance Coverage 1979–1995' (1999) 18 *Health Affairs* 30 at 45.

[10] Daly III *et al*, above n 4, at 43, 45. For a more historical and technical perspective on uncompensated care, see LE Fishman and JD Bentley, 'The Evolution of Support For Safety-Net Hospitals' (1997) 16 *Health Affairs* 30 at 31.

[11] KJ Bauman, 'Extended Measures of Well-Being: Meeting Basic Needs In 1995', US Census Bureau <www.census.gov/prod/99pubs/p70–67.pdf> (12 July 2002) at 5 (reporting that 'lack of health insurance strongly affected the probability that there would be a person in the household who needed to see the doctor but did not go.').

[12] See, eg L Dubay, J Haley and G Kenney, 'Children's Eligibility For Medicaid and SCHIP: A View From 2000', The Urban Institute <http://www.urban.org/UploadedPDF/310435.pdf> (24 July 2002) at 5.

[13] DK Remler, JE Rachlin and SA Glied, 'What Can the Take-Up of Other Programs Teach Us About How To Improve Take-Up of Health Insurance Programs' (Working Paper No 8185, National Bureau of Economic Research, 2001); M Laschober *et al*, 'Final Report On Review of the Literature On Evaluations of Outreach for Public Health Insurance and Selected Other Programs', Barents Group <http://www.cms.hhs.gov/schip/outreach/rpt33100.pdf> (24 July 2002); LA Hall, G Hampton and D Bhargava, 'Bringing Down the Barriers: Low-Income Leaders Address Obstacles To Enrollment In Federal Programs', National Housing Institute <http://www.nhi.org.online/issues/114/organize.html> (3 February 2003); AS Hart, 'Book Review: America's Health Care Safety Net: Intact But Endangered' (2000) 284 *Journal of the American Medical Association* 2117; AS Hart, 'New Online Service Helps Seniors, Caregivers Access Hundreds of Public Benefits Programs', The National Council on the Aging <www.ncoa.org/press/bcu/> (12 July 2002).

[14] See, eg AS Hart, 'Research Shows the Negative Impact of Out-of-Pocket Costs On Low-Income People', Families USA <http://www.familiesusa.org/html/medicaid/Costsharing2.pdf> (3 February 2003); AS Hart, 'Medicare at a Glance', Kaiser Family Foundation (October 2002) <http://www.kff.org/content/archive/1066/1066–04v2 (3 February 2003).

[15] Remler, Rachlin and Glied, above n 13; L Dubay, J Haley and G Kenney, above n 12.

confusion over eligibility and attributes of the actual enrolment process.[16] Some researchers have concluded that, among other factors, automatic enrolment in a programme 'has an enormous effect on take-up.'[17]

In addition to those who do not try to enrol, some eligible individuals try to enrol but encounter obstacles that prevent receipt of the benefit. As one example, the Social Security Administration acknowledges that its high rejection rate of disability benefit applications is error-ridden, and yet it can take years to exhaust the process of seeking to reverse that initial denial of benefits.[18]

Therefore, it is not surprising that many individuals become financially vulnerable when they confront medical problems. Putting aside whether the US' current approach is sufficiently generous, bureaucracy may be deterring access by eligible applicants and enjoyment of full benefits even by those who are enrolled.

B. An Expanded View of the US Health Care Finance System: Consumer Credit

Recourse to consumer credit is one possible response when an individual confronts significant financial difficulties under the complex US health care and related social welfare system. Consumer credit is offered in generous amounts in very short order, with little paperwork or delay. This is increasingly true even among low income families, although the price and the terms vary considerably.[19] American consumers accept a fraction of the credit that lenders offer them, but their debt-income ratios are record-setting.[20]

Like those facing difficulties in obtaining other needed goods and services, some consumers use third party financing to obtain health services and products, satisfy unpaid health bills, and deal with the indirect costs of health problems. Credit cards provide one method.[21] Individuals have reported to the news media that they use credit cards to pay for expensive medications for seri-

[16] MJ Perry, E Stark and RB Valdez, 'Barriers To Medi-Cal Enrollment and Ideas for Improving Enrollment: Findings From Eight Focus Groups In California With Parents of Potentially Eligible Children', Kaiser Family Foundation Publication #1436 (September 1998). See also Dubay, Haley, and Kenney, above n 13.

[17] Remler, Rachlin and Glied, above n 13, at 3, 11, 13.

[18] 'Social Security and Supplemental Security Income Disability Programs: Managing For Today Planning For Tomorrow', Social Security Administration (11 March 1999) <http://www.ssa.gov/policy/pubs/dibreport.html> (3 February 2003) at 6.

[19] MS Barr, 'Access To Financial Services in the 21st Century: Five Opportunities For the Bush Administration and the 107th Congress' (2002) 16 *Notre Dame Journal of Law, Ethics and Public Policy* 447, 447, 456.

[20] See generally DM Maki 'The Growth of Consumer Credit and the Household Debt Service Burden', The Federal Reserve Board <http://www.federalreserve.gov//pubs/feds/2000/200012/200012abs.html> (15 July 2002).

[21] MB Jacoby, TA Sullivan and E Warren, 'Rethinking the Debates Over Health Care Financing: Evidence From the Bankruptcy Courts' (2001) 76 *New York University Law Review* 375.

ous diseases when private insurance will not pay, to finance the construction of a ramp into a home for a wheelchair-ridden spouse, and for food and general necessities when illness results in loss of income.[22] Others incur secured debt to finance their health problems by borrowing against the equity in their homes for medical related purposes.[23]

Third party credit may perform an important public health function to the extent it enables ill or injured individuals to obtain health care, medications, or other health-maximising goods, such as healthy food. Yet, this credit does not come cheap. The credit card borrower who stretches repayment over time does not merely repay the principal, of course, but also the compounding interest, late payment charges, annual or membership fees and/or over-the-limit fees. In addition, the resulting indebtedness itself could adversely affect health. The large debt load incurred to obtain access to health care ultimately may impede access to future health care.[24] Further, indebtedness can induce stress, which, as discussed below, is often associated with illness.

Empirical research suggests a correlation between indebtedness and health problems. In a 1997 study of credit card debt in Ohio, for example, Patricia Drentea and Paul Lavrakas found that debt-related stress was associated with worse health, that the debt-income ratio was significantly associated with worse physical health and self-reported health and that 'the financial strain of a high debt/income ratio clearly is the stressor affecting health.'[25] David Caplovitz reached similar conclusions in his earlier study of indebted individuals in four major US cities.[26] Nearly half of the debtors in his study reported debt troubles had affected their health, and possible health impairment seemed to correlate with the amount of indebtedness. Caplovitz posited that debt problems might undermine health by producing symptoms associated with anxiety and worry, and noted that debt problems lead debtors to skimp on budgets and correspondingly neglect their health needs. Robert Havlik, Allexander Vukasin and Stephan Ariyan studied the incidence of financial crises of bankruptcy, unemployment and family break-up among patients with melanoma and found a

[22] See, eg S Hansell 'The Debt Trap—A Special Report: Personal Bankruptcies Surging as Economy Hums' *New York Times* (25 August 1996); DL Bartlett and JB Steele, 'Soaked By Congress' *Time* (15 May 2000) 64 at 64–66, 74.

[23] GB Canner, TA Durkin and CA Luckett, 'Recent Developments In Home Equity Lending' (2000) 84 *Federal Reserve Bulletin* 241, 248 Tbl 8 (finding increase in borrowers indicating medical expenses as use for home equity lines of credit and loans); Daly III *et al*, above n 4, at 45 (reporting on Access Project Community Access Monitoring Survey); TA Sullivan, E Warren and JL Westbrook, *The Fragile Middle Class: Americans In Debt* (New Haven, Yale, 2000) (discussing 1970s survey reporting 'the number-one reason for taking out personal loans other than for durable goods was to pay medical costs').

[24] See generally MB Jacoby, 'Does Indebtedness Influence Health? A Preliminary Inquiry' (2002) 30 *Journal of Law, Medicine and Ethics* 560 (2002).

[25] P Drentea and PJ Lavrakas, 'Over the Limit: The Association Among Health, Race, and Debt' (2000) 50 *Social Science and Medicine* 517 at 518.

[26] D Caplovitz, *Consumers in Trouble; A Study of Debtors in Default* (New York, The Free Press, 1974).

significantly higher occurrence of bankruptcy or unemployment in the melanoma group than in the control group.[27]

Whether people with health problems acquire considerable debt in the absence of a viable health care financing alternative, or debt itself exacerbates health problems (or some combination of these non-exclusive explanations), health care policy-makers should recognise the significance of the consumer credit system.

C. Further Expansion of the Health Care Finance System: Bankruptcy

Health problems reveal themselves in bankruptcy in multiple ways. First, medical debt has a measurable presence in the US bankruptcy system. Government researchers Gordon Bermant and Ed Flynn found in a study of bankruptcy filers in 2000 that 56.2 per cent of joint bankruptcy filers had some medical debt. Of those who had medical debt, 11.1 per cent reported US$5,000 or more, and in 4.4 per cent of the cases, medical debt comprised one half or more of total unsecured debt.[28] In the study of bankruptcy filers in 1999 by Teresa Sullivan, Elizabeth Warren and Melissa Jacoby, 33.8 per cent of the filers reported that they incurred medical bills not covered by insurance in excess of US$1,000 during the two years preceding bankruptcy.[29] The Legal Aid Society of Greater Cincinnati (Ohio) studied clients who sought assistance with bankruptcy filings in 2000–2001 and found that 47 per cent had substantial medical debt, and the average medical debt was US$5,028.50.[30] In her study of a narrower subset of Tennessee debtors—those who were judgment-proof—in the mid-1980s, Susan Kovac observed that 80 per cent of the debtors owed some medical debt and that medical debt was 42 per cent of total unsecured debt.[31] Ian Domowitz and Robert Sartain evaluated Survey of Consumer Finance data and 1980 bankruptcy case data, and found that medical debt had the 'single greatest impact of any household condition variable in raising the conditional probability of bankruptcy.'[32]

[27] See, eg RJ Havlik, AP Vukasin and S Ariyan, 'The Impact of Stress On the Clinical Presentation of Melanoma' (July 1992) 90 (1) *Plastic and Reconstructive Surgery* 57 at 59–60. See also RJ Genco *et al*, 'Relationship of Stress, Disease, and Inadequate Coping Behaviors to Periodontal Disease' (1999) 70 (7) *Journal of Periodontology* 711, 715–717. For European studies considering the debt-health correlation, see, eg G Parker, *Getting and Spending; Credit and Debt In Britain*, (Aldershot, Avebury, 1990); S Weyerer and A Wiedenmann, 'Economic Factors and the Rates of Suicide In Germany Between 1881 and 1989' (June 1995) 76 (3) *Psychological Reports* 1331.

[28] E Flynn and G Bermant, 'The Class of 2000' [October 2001] *American Bankruptcy Institute Journal* 20. See also P Shuchman, 'The Average Bankrupt: A Description and Analysis of 753 Personal Bankruptcy Filings in Nine States' (1983) 88 *Commercial Law Journal* 288; P Shuchman, 'New Jersey Debtors 1982–1983: An Empirical Study' (1985) 15 *Seton Hall Law Review* 541.

[29] Jacoby, Sullivan and Warren, above n 21, at 387, 389.

[30] Daly III *et al*, above n 5, at 56.

[31] SD Kovac, 'Judgment-Proof Debtors In Bankruptcy' (1991) 65 *American Bankruptcy Law Journal* 675 at 684, 751.

[32] I Domowitz and RL Sartain, 'Determinants of the Consumer Bankruptcy Decision' (1999) 54 *Journal of Finance* 403.

SMR Research Corporation also has identified medical debt as a central problem in bankruptcy based on a comparison of bankruptcy filing rates and health insurance coverage rates at the state level.[33] Where bankruptcy petition and schedule data have been the main source of information, these studies may be conservative estimates of medical debts' presence in bankruptcy. If consumers incur debt to third party lenders for medical-related purposes, the bankruptcy schedules may not reveal the medical obligations financed with consumer credit.[34] In addition, due to fears of losing future medical services, debtors may not always list their medical providers on their bankruptcy schedules in an effort to hide their financial condition from these providers.[35]

The bankruptcy studies also reinforce the suggestion made in Section IIA that health insurance coverage does not immunise individuals from medical-related financial problems. In the 1999 study by Sullivan, Warren and Jacoby, for example, those with insurance were prominently among those reporting medical-related financial difficulties. Although one in five filers in the sample reported being uninsured, there was no clear association between identifying a medical-related financial problem and being uninsured [36]

Medical problems feature prominently in debtors' own explanations of why they sought bankruptcy relief. In the 1999 study, for example, about one in every four families in the sample (25.2 per cent) identified illness or injury as a reason (although not necessarily the only reason) for seeking bankruptcy relief.[37] In addition, 6.6 per cent of the debtors listed 'addition of a family member,' and 4.4 per cent listed 'death of a family member' as a reason for their bankruptcy filings, both of which may have a medical component. Sullivan, Warren and Jay Lawrence Westbrook found 19 per cent of filings were medical-related in their 1991 study based on debtors' open-ended responses about why they filed for bankruptcy.[38] Adding those who indicated birth and death reasons for bankruptcy increased the percentage to about 37 per cent. The written results of a VISA USA survey report that 16.5 per cent of the debtors identified health and medical reasons, and 14.3 per cent identified medical problems as the last straw that led to bankruptcy.[39]

These studies do not prove that medical problems, by themselves, 'cause' particular people to file for bankruptcy. Even if medical problems are prominent features of some bankruptcy cases, the debt-health literature explored in Part B above supports an alternative (or co-existing) explanation, namely that indebtedness may be making people ill due to stress or deprivation. In addition, it is

[33] SMR Research Corp., *The Personal Bankruptcy Crisis, 1997: Demographics, Causes, Implications and Solutions* (1997) at 94–95.

[34] Jacoby, Sullivan, and Warren, above n 21, at 389.

[35] Sullivan, Warren, and Westbrook,above n 23, at 153.

[36] Jacoby, Sullivan and Warren, above n 21, at 399–400.

[37] *Ibid* at 387, 390.

[38] Sullivan, Warren and Westbrook, above n 23.

[39] 'Consumer Bankruptcy: Bankruptcy Debtor Survey', Visa, Inc. <www.abiworld.org/stats/visa/96debtor.html> (12 July 2002).

possible that some debtors who listed medical problems as reasons for filing were seeking a socially more acceptable explanation for their bankruptcies.[40] Likewise, these data are not being presented to attribute to medical problems the dramatic increase in US bankruptcy filings in recent years.[41] The medical-related bankruptcy data do help demonstrate, however, that bankruptcy is functionally part of the US health care finance system, and changes to bankruptcy law and practice should be considered with this overlap in mind. What ill or injured debtors might expect from bankruptcy is addressed in Section III.

III. THE CURRENT US CONSUMER BANKRUPTCY SYSTEM AND ITS EFFECTS ON THE ILL AND INJURED.

A. The System

A considerable number of American households seek refuge in the US bankruptcy system. Warren estimates that in 2001, one in every 123 adults filed for bankruptcy, and 1 in every 51 children was a dependant in a household that filed.[42] Relative to other US social welfare systems and to other nations' bankruptcy laws, the US bankruptcy system is generous and has few barriers to access. Comparatively, the entry fees are modest,[43] the amount of information initially required is minimal and the grounds for rejecting the filing of a bankruptcy petition, at least at the outset, are practically non-existent.[44] Upon the filing of the petition, bankruptcy relief begins instantaneously, triggering an injunction ('automatic stay') against collection efforts of creditors—including secured creditors—without requiring that the debtor justify the need for this protection.[45]

Chapter 7 relief is notable for its discharge of indebtedness that is largely unconditional. The discharge does not depend on creditor consent, efforts to

[40] Jacoby, Sullivan and Warren, above n 21 at 384–385, fn 51–54.

[41] S Fay, E Hurst and M White 'The Bankruptcy Decision: Does Stigma Matter?' (Working Paper 98–01, University of Michigan Department of Economics, Jan 1998) (concluding from analysis of Panel Survey of Income Dynamics data that health problems for head of household or spouse did not have a statistically significant effect on bankruptcy rates) <http://www.econ.lsa.umich.edu/wpweb/fhw.pdf> (7 May 2002); EH Jones and TJ Zywicki, 'Its Time for Means Testing' [1999] *Brigham Young Law Review* 177 at 244 n274 (noting lack of correlation between cost of health care and bankruptcy filing rates, although acknowledging that medical problems may be a factor in some bankruptcy filings).

[42] E Warren, 'Bankrupt Children' (2002) 86 *Minnesota Law Review* 1003, 1009–1011.

[43] R Efrat, 'Global Trends in Personal Bankruptcy' (2002) 76 *American Bankruptcy Law Journal* 81 at 107–108.

[44] Federal Rules of Bankruptcy Procedure 5005(a)(1).

[45] 11 USC s 362(a) (1994). Compare JS Ziegel, 'The Philosophy and Design of Contemporary Consumer Bankruptcy Systems: A Canada-United States Comparison' (1999) 37 *Osgoode Hall Law Journal* 205 at 221; TM Buckwold, 'Holding the High Ground: The Position of Secured Creditors in Consumer Bankruptcies and Proposals' (1999) 37 *Osgoode Hall Law Journal* 277.

repay or a showing of insolvency.[46] The discharge does not affect a secured creditor's interest in any collateral; if the debtor wishes to retain that collateral, he must make some arrangement with the secured creditor. Moreover, a debtor must forfeit all unencumbered non-exempt interests in property; most individual debtors claim to have few or none.[47] The fact that most Chapter 7 debtors receive a discharge so readily diverges from not only other nations' systems, but from other aspects of US law. For example, US contract law rarely excuses parties of contractual obligations and does so only in highly circumscribed instances that involve detailed factual inquiries.[48] The US's approach to bankruptcy and the discharge is justified, some believe, by the societal benefits of allowing individuals to overcome the productivity dampening effects of insolvency.[49]

Debtor access to a Chapter 7 discharge is sometimes limited by section 707(b). Section 707(b) authorises dismissal of a Chapter 7 case if relief would be a 'substantial abuse' of the bankruptcy system.[50] Some courts have found substantial abuse whenever the debtor has an ability to pay debts out of future income; interpreted this way, section 707(b) provides an eligibility test. However, other courts have not been willing to dismiss a case under section 707(b) solely on the basis of ability to pay.[51] In addition, only the court or a United States Trustee may initiate a section 707(b) challenge; in the past, US Trustee offices have not been uniform in their policing of cases,[52] although the current director of the Executive Office for US Trustees, Lawrence Friedman, has tried to move the programme toward screening cases for substantial abuse in all districts. According to a recent report of the US Trustee programme, US Trustees filed 1,950 substantial abuse motions in fiscal year 2001, 660 were granted by courts and 600 led to voluntary conversion to Chapter 13.[53] In addition, in more than 3,000 additional cases, informal investigations led debtors to either convert to Chapter 13 voluntarily or to provide additional information to support their

[46] Compare J Niemi-Kiesiläinen, 'Consumer Bankruptcy in Comparison: Do We Cure A Market Failure or a Social Problem' (1999) 37 *Osgoode Hall Law Journal* 473 at 491 (describing Finland's Law on Consumer Debt Adjustment).

[47] See, eg J Niemi-Kiesiläinen, 'Bankruptcy Administration: Case Receipts Paid to Creditors and Professionals', United States General Accounting Office GAO/GGD–94–173 (13 July 1994).

[48] RA Hillman, 'Contract Excuse and Bankruptcy' (1990) 43 *Stanford Law Review* 99 at 100–102 ('contract law suggests that bankruptcy discharge should better contemplate individual contract expectancies'); I Ramsay, 'Models of Consumer Bankruptcy: Implications for Research and Policy' (1997) 20 *Journal of Consumer Policy* 269 at 280.

[49] See generally NL Georgakopoulos, 'Bankruptcy Law For Productivity' (2002) 37 *Wake Forest Law Review* 51 at 52, 58.

[50] 11 USC s 707(b) (1994).

[51] See, eg *In re Green* 934 F 2d 568 (4th Cir 1991) (considering factors such as the reason for the bankruptcy filing, pre-petition financial behavior, whether the debtor was forthcoming in the bankruptcy case, and the debtor's projected future financial behaviour).

[52] WR Wells, JM Kurtz and RJ Calhoun, 'The Implementation of Bankruptcy Code Section 707(b): The Law and Reality' (1991) 39 *Cleveland State Law Review* 15 at 21.

[53] United States Trustee Program Annual Report of Significant Accomplishments Fiscal Year 2001 (US Department of Justice 2002) at 8.

Chapter 7 filings.[54] The Assistant United States Trustee in the District of Nebraska reports that 100 per cent of Chapter 7 cases are reviewed there for fraud or abuse.[55]

Pragmatic factors also limit systematic scrutiny of the debtor in the bankruptcy system. The private trustee, chosen by the US Trustee to oversee and administer Chapter 7 cases, spends very little time on most cases.[56] Trustees get paid very little for administering the vast majority of cases in which the debtor has no significant non-exempt assets to be liquidated for creditors.[57]

The Chapter 7 discharge is not devoid of conditions or limits. Debtor wrongdoing can prevent the discharge,[58] and potentially give rise to criminal sanctions,[59] although this rarely happens. More importantly, a significant number of unsecured debts are not dischargeable at all.[60] In addition, debtors can remain personally liable to certain creditors through reaffirmation agreements with those creditors, and many do.[61] Notably, debtors must continue to pay their secured creditors if they want to keep the property that continues to secure those debts. The 'fresh start' of American bankruptcy is rarely a completely new start; some debts usually remain collectible.

Chapter 13, which provides for a repayment plan of a three to five year period, is the other common bankruptcy option for individuals in the US.[62] Chapter 13 has eligibility requirements but they are not onerous.[63] The Bankruptcy Code

[54] United States Trustee Program Annual Report of Significant Accomplishments Fiscal Year 2001 (US Department of Justice 2002) at 8.

[55] *Ibid.*

[56] WC McDow, Jr 'Protecting the Integrity of the Bankruptcy System In Chapter 7 No-Asset Cases', <http://www.usdoj.gov/ust/press/articles/nabtalkfall2001.htm> (2 July 2002); J Braucher, 'Options In Consumer Bankruptcy: An American Perspective' (1999) 37 *Osgoode Hall Law Journal* 155 at 168. See also LM LoPucki, 'Reforming Consumer Bankruptcy Law: Four Proposals: Common Sense Consumer Bankruptcy' (1997) 71 *American Bankruptcy Law Journal* 461 at 467–70 (discussing trustees' disincentives to pursue statutory objections).

[57] United States Trustee Program Annual Report of Significant Accomplishments Fiscal Year 2001 (US Department of Justice 2002) 33, 46 (reporting that approximately 5% of all cases filed under or converted to Chapter 7 are asset cases, and more than 50% of all asset cases involve total receipts of less than US$5,000); 'Bankruptcy Administration: Case Receipts Paid to Creditors and Professionals', United States General Accounting Office GAO/GGD–94–173 (13 July 1994). When there are significant non-exempt assets to be liquidated for creditors, trustees receive a percentage of the assets recovered.

[58] 11 USC s 727 (1994).

[59] 18 USC s 151–57 (1994).

[60] 11 USC s 523 (1994).

[61] See MB Culhane and MM White, 'Debt After Discharge, An Empirical Study of Reaffirmation' (1999) 73 *American Bankruptcy Law Journal* 709 at 713.

[62] Unlike other nations' debt adjustment systems, Chapter 13 is considered 'bankruptcy' even though it involves a repayment plan. Compare JS Ziegel, 'The Philosophy and Design of Contemporary Consumer Bankruptcy Systems: A Canada-United States Comparison' (1999) 37 *Osgoode Hall Law Journal* 205 at 251–52.

[63] A Chapter 13 debtor must have less than US$290,525 in unsecured debts and US$871,550 in secured debts and must have 'regular income': 11 USC s 109(e) (1994). Chapter 13 does not have a direct counterpart to 11 USC s 727(a)(8) (1994), which limits a Chapter 7 debtor's entitlement to a discharge if she received a discharge in a case commenced within six years before the filing of the instant case.

imposes very nominal limits on multiple Chapter 13 filings, whereas a six-year interval must pass between Chapter 7 discharges. Chapter 13 also is generous. A Chapter 13 debtor need not forfeit non-exempt assets and is protected against pre-petition creditor collection efforts for the duration of the multi-year plan. If a debtor does complete the plan, her discharge includes certain types of debts that would have been non-dischargeable in Chapter 7, such as debts based on wilful and malicious injury or fraud.[64]

Creditors in Chapter 13 do not vote on the debtor's proposed repayment plan. To voice dissent, they must raise and litigate the available statutory objections. Over a lender's strenuous objections, a Chapter 13 debtor can cure a default on a home mortgage and continue paying the loan.[65] Even more significantly, the Chapter 13 debtor can modify and restructure loans secured by cars and other property. If the debt is greater than the value of the collateral, the car lender is entitled to receive only the value of its collateral in instalments, plus interest.[66]

General unsecured creditors have even fewer meaningful entitlements in Chapter 13 than secured creditors. They must receive as least as much as they would had the debtor liquidated in Chapter 7,[67] but that is usually nothing. Creditors also are entitled to demand that the debtor dedicate all projected disposable income for a three-year period to the plan.[68] Yet, if the debtor claims to have little or no disposable income, the plan is confirmable nonetheless. The disposable income that is contributed to the plan may be largely committed to the payment of secured creditors, leaving little on the table for unsecured creditors.[69] Finally, even if a plan promises to pay substantial amounts, the debtor may never follow through on those promises. Empirical research suggests that the majority of Chapter 13 filers do not complete plans.[70] A failed Chapter 13 can be converted to a Chapter 7, but this does not happen routinely.

64 11 USC s 1328 (1994).
65 11 USC s 1322(b)(2), (b)(5) (1994).
66 11 USC s 1322(b)(2), 1325(a)(5) (1994).
67 11 USC s 1325(a)(4) (1994).
68 11 USC s 1325(b) (1994).
69 See, eg *In re Greer* 60 BR 547 (Bankr CD Cal 1986).
70 For data on Chapter 13 plan completion suggesting that the majority of Chapter 13 filings do not result in completed plans, see G Bermant and E Flynn, 'Measuring Projected Performance in Chapter 13: Comparisons Across the States' (July–Aug 2000) 19 *American Bankruptcy Institute Journal* 22; M Bork and SD Tuck, 'Bankruptcy Statistical Trends: Chapter 13: Dispositions' 5 (Working Paper No 2, Admin Off of the US Courts, Oct 1994); SF Norberg, 'Consumer Bankruptcy's New Clothes: An Empirical Study of Discharge and Debt Collection in Chapter 13' (1999) 7 *American Bankruptcy Institute Law Review* 415 at 440; HE Hildebrand III, 'Administering Chapter 13—At What Price?' (Aug. 1994) *American Bankruptcy Institute Journal* at 16; TA Sullivan, E Warren and JL Westbrook, 'Consumer Debtors Ten Years Later: A Financial Comparison of Consumer Bankrupts 1981–1991' (1994) 68 *American Bankruptcy Law Journal* 121 at 145; TA Sullivan, E Warren and JL Westbrook, *As We Forgive Our Debtors: Bankruptcy and Consumer Credit in America* (Oxford University Press, Oxford, 1989) at 215–17. Professor Girth found a higher completion rate, but was looking only at confirmed plans. ML Girth, 'The Role of Empirical Data in Developing Bankruptcy Legislation for Individuals' (1989) 65 *Indiana Law Journal* 17 at 42 (1989).

B. What Bankruptcy Might Do for the Ill or Injured

The accessibility of the current system allows ill or injured debtors to obtain some relief under either chapter with relative ease; it is not as simple as filling out a pre-approved credit card application, but it is more straightforward than learning about, navigating the eligibility standards of, and enrolling in various other social welfare programmes. As noted above, medical-related filers are well-represented in both Chapter 7 and Chapter 13. In the 1999 study by Sullivan, Warren and Jacoby, for example, nearly half the debtors in the Chapter 13 sample, as well as the Chapter 7 sample, indicated medical-related bankruptcy (eg, either substantial medical debt or listed medical problems as a cause of filing).[71]

In addition to immediately stopping collection efforts, Chapter 7 may relieve an ill or injured person of personal liability for unmanageable medical-related debts, which would stabilise her financial circumstances and perhaps permit her to adjust to a lifestyle of higher medical expenses and lower income. The absence of complex gatekeepers for Chapter 7 permits the individual to file and proceed quickly through the system, receiving a discharge of debt in a few months. Yet, US bankruptcy laws provide very limited anti-discrimination protection and creditors are relatively free to deny future credit. Thus, the debtor runs the risk of being denied medical care in the future if treatment is not covered by insurance and she cannot pay cash.

Chapter 13 also stops collection efforts, but in addition, helps an ill or injured debtor save a home or car over secured lenders' objections if she is in default. Medical-related financial problems can take many forms, and the loss of income due to health problems certainly can lead to default on car or home loans. Alternatively, a debtor seeking to repay her medical provider to prevent the loss of future credit for medical services might attempt a Chapter 13 plan. The pitfalls of Chapter 13 for a filer with medical problems include the high probability of plan failure and the fact that Chapter 13 does not necessarily lead to a better credit rating.

IV. US BANKRUPTCY REFORM EFFORTS, BUREAUCRATISATION, AND POTENTIAL EFFECTS ON THE ILL OR INJURED

A. National Bankruptcy Review Commission

The US Bankruptcy Code has been in its current form since 1978, but Congress has occasionally amended it. In 1994, Congress passed some modest amend-

[71] MB Jacoby, 'Collecting Debts From the Ill and Injured: The Rhetorical Significance, But Practical Irrelevance, of Culpability and Ability To Pay' (2001) 51 *American University Law Review* 229.

ments and established the National Bankruptcy Review Commission, charged with studying the bankruptcy system and submitting a report to the Chief Justice of the US, the President and Congress two years thereafter. Congress explicitly instructed the Commission as follows:

> The Commission should be aware that Congress is generally satisfied with the basic framework established in the current Bankruptcy Code. Therefore, the work of the Commission should be based upon reviewing, improving, and updating the Code in ways which do not disturb the fundamental tenets of current law.[72]

The Commission was studying the system while the annual filing rate surpassed one million filings for the first time (in 1996). The consumer credit industry, an active participant in the Commission proceedings, cited the rising bankruptcy filing rate as evidence of an overly available bankruptcy system and urged the Commission to propose a Chapter 7 eligibility test.

In the fall of 1997, the Commission submitted a report containing 172 specific recommendations, including several dozen that would affect consumer bankruptcy, but the Commission did not propose Chapter 7 eligibility requirements based on ability to pay.[73]

The consumer credit industry characterised the Commission's report as controversial and pro-debtor.[74] News reports highlighted the fact that only a bare majority of the commissioners—5 out of 9—ultimately endorsed the package of consumer amendments,[75] although areas of disagreement leading to this 5–4 split were actually narrow.[76] These reports suggested that the Commission rejected changing Chapter 7 eligibility by a 5–4 margin. In reality, no member of the Commission requested a vote on Chapter 7 eligibility and, in the final report, only two members of the nine-person Commission endorsed the concept of systematically scrutinising Chapter 7 debtors for ability to pay.

B. Reduced Accessibility and Generosity: 'Bankruptcy Abuse Prevention and Consumer Protection Act'

Legislation that has been on the brink of enactment for several years deviates from Congress' earlier statement of satisfaction with the existing US bankruptcy system. Although the legislation implements some of the Commission's

[72] HR Rep No 103–835 at 59 (1994).

[73] 'Bankruptcy: The Next Twenty Years', National Bankruptcy Review Commission <http://govinfo.library.unt.edu/nbrc/report/01title.html> (21 June 2002) at 62.

[74] See, eg M Derus 'Bankruptcy Revisions Unveiled' *Milwaukee Journal Sentinel* (21 October 1997); D Foust and D Sparks, 'Bankruptcy Reform: Everybody's Mad—And That's Fine' *Business Week* (3 November 1997) 154.

[75] See, eg Foust and Sparks, above n 75; S Singer 'Panel Proposes Bankrupt Reforms; Legislators Divided Over Exemptions' *Sun-Sentinel* (22 October 1997).

[76] Above n 73, at 80 (listing proposals with support among commission members). The most divisive consumer bankruptcy issue was the proper level of regulation of agreements to reaffirm debt.

proposals,[77] the consumer credit industry proposed most of the controversial consumer bankruptcy amendments.[78] The amendments do not dismantle the basic structure of Chapter 7 and Chapter 13. They do, however, bureaucratise the system, substantially increasing the cost and complexity of bankruptcy for all debtors, not just the abusers.

1. *Eligibility*

i. Presumed Abuse of Chapter 7 Based on Ability to Pay

The legislation adds an explicit ability to pay test to the aforementioned section 707(b). To implement the test, it requires a wide range of calculations and paperwork to be submitted by all Chapter 7 individual debtors, even those who are immune from challenge of their petitions on this basis due to their low incomes.[79] Ability to pay according to the statutory formula constitutes 'presumed abuse' and lead to conversion to Chapter 13 or dismissal, unless the debtor could rebut the presumption under narrow circumstances. The legislation requires that the US Trustee review cases for presumed abuse, but creditors, trustees, and the court would be authorised to act as well.

A Chapter 7 filing is presumed abusive by the legislation if the debtor's net monthly income,[80] multiplied by 60 (ie, five years), is at least US$10,000.[81] If the debtor's cumulated net monthly income is less than US$10,000 but more than US$6,000, the debtor's case is still presumed abusive if the calculation suggests she could pay at least 25 per cent of her allowed unsecured claims over the five year period. The presumption of abuse is rebuttable only if additional expenses or an income change reduced the debtor's remaining monthly income to below the statutory thresholds, and if the debtor successfully explains that there is no reasonable alternative to these changes or deductions.

[77] Examples include amendments relating to repeat filings, in rem orders, data collection, creditors' meetings in pre-packaged bankruptcy cases, continuation of solicitation in pre-packaged bankruptcy cases, small business Chapter 11 cases, Chapter 12 for family farmers, and Chapter 9 for municipalities. These proposals are described in: above n 74.

[78] See, eg B Rehfeld 'Top Creditor Lobbyist Tassey Goes For Broke' *American Banker* (17 May 2001). See also VF Nourse and JS Schacter, 'The Politics of Legislative Drafting: A Congressional Case Study' (2002) 77 *New York University Law Review* 575 at 587 (noting extensive use of lobbyists for drafting for Judiciary Committee issues such as bankruptcy).

[79] See HR 333, 107th Congress, s 102 (2001). All references are to the published version as passed by the Senate during the 107th Congress, which differs in minor respects from the version passed by the House of Representatives.

[80] To calculate net monthly income, one first determines the debtor's 'current monthly income,' which is the debtor's average monthly income over the prior six month period (not the debtor's actual current income). One then deducts expenses according to Internal Revenue Service (IRS) collection allowances for delinquent taxpayers. Some IRS allowances vary by region, some vary by family size, and some are national standards. The allowances periodically change, but not on a set schedule and the IRS appears to have full discretion over the changes. One also deducts secured debt payments contractually due over the 60 months following the bankruptcy filing, priority debts (such as child support and taxes) due over the same period, and certain other expenses, such as the hypothetical administrative costs of Chapter 13.

[81] HR 333, above n 79, s 102.

Well-advised debtors will be able to manipulate the outcome of this test by taking on more debt, particularly secured debt, or by timing their filings to occur after a period of reduced income.[82] In addition, the test may not even apply to Chapter 7 filers with large business debts; section 707(b) applies only to individuals with 'primarily consumer debts.'

The formula does not permit consideration of reasons for financial trouble. A debtor whose financial problems were precipitated by serious medical problems may have her case dismissed for abuse, while a profligate spender may get Chapter 7 relief if he cannot pay the requisite amount. The cause of the indebtedness—unavoidable illness versus overuse of consumer credit—is deemed irrelevant in this legislation.

ii. Credit Counselling Eligibility Requirement

Implementing a concept that bankruptcy should truly be a last resort in ways consonant with other nations' bankruptcy laws,[83] the legislation makes an individual ineligible for bankruptcy unless she received consumer credit counselling from an approved agency, if any, within 180 days preceding the bankruptcy filing.[84] A debtor with no counselling could petition the court for access if she presents a 'certification' to the court describing exigent circumstances and satisfactorily explaining the unsuccessful efforts made to obtain services for a five day period. If the court grants permission, the debtor would have a limited period in which to obtain credit counselling after filing.

iii. Heightened Informational Requirements

In addition to the presumed abuse calculations and existing informational requirements of the Bankruptcy Code and Federal Rules of Bankruptcy Procedure, the legislation requires that the debtor compile and produce a variety of other pieces of information and documentation at various times during the bankruptcy case. The typical penalty for failure to comply with each requirement is automatic dismissal.[85]

iv. Deterrence of Chapter 7 Legal Representation

The legislation heightens the responsibilities of debtors' attorneys, under the threat of financial sanctions, to investigate all of the debtor's factual assertions and the circumstances giving rise to the need for bankruptcy.[86] In addition,

[82] MB Culhane and MM White, 'Taking the New Consumer Bankruptcy Model For a Test Drive: Means-Testing Real Chapter 7 Debtors' (1999) 7 *American Bankruptcy Institute Law Review* 27.

[83] See, eg HP Graver, 'Consumer Bankruptcy: A Right or a Privilege? The Role of the Courts In Establishing Moral Standards of Economic Conduct' (1997) 20 *Journal of Consumer Policy* 16 at 165; R Mason, 'Consumer Bankruptcies: An Australian Perspective' (1999) 37 *Osgoode Hall Law Journal* 449 at 455–57.

[84] HR 333, above n 79, s 106.

[85] HR 333, above n 79, s 316.

[86] HR 333, above n 79, s 102, 319.

lawyers who represent individual debtors will be considered 'debt relief agencies,' and will be subject to a new and untested layer of detailed regulations and sanctions.[87] The extra work and risk of sanctions will inevitably increase debtor attorney fees, affecting access to bankruptcy by otherwise eligible debtors who are least able to pay.[88]

2. *Reduced Generosity*

i. Less Automatic Stay Protection

As noted earlier, all bankruptcy filings trigger a stay preventing creditors from commencing or continuing efforts to collect pre-bankruptcy debts. The automatic stay has exceptions to make clear, for example, that police and regulatory functions must go forward even though a debt is somehow involved.[89] The legislation adds several new exceptions to the automatic stay, such as one allowing residential landlords to maintain eviction actions for non-payment of rent.[90] Repeat filers would have even less automatic stay protection.[91]

ii. More Restricted Discharge

The bill's provisions weaken the discharge that a debtor can receive at the end of a bankruptcy case. The legislation expands exceptions to discharge for credit card debts and cash advances incurred within two to three months prior to the bankruptcy filing.[92] A wider range of student loans[93] and more debts to an ex-spouse[94] are non-dischargeable. The legislation also reduces the Chapter 13 discharge so that it more closely resembles the discharge available in Chapter 7.[95] At the same time, the legislation does not seriously address concerns that debtors are being pressured to reaffirm personal liability on otherwise-dischargeable debts.[96] Minimal scrutiny of reaffirmations, coupled with more exceptions to discharge, narrows the bankruptcy discharge as a practical matter.

[87] HR 333, above n 79, s 227–229.

[88] 'Letters To the 107th Congress', American Bar Association <http://www.abanet.org/poladv/letters/107th/bankruptcy042202.html> (24 July 2002); G Klein and M Spade, *Self-Representation in Bankruptcy Court: The Massachusetts Experience* (typescript, Boston, National Consumer Law Center, undated) (finding that pro se debtors are less likely to receive discharges) as cited in Sullivan, Warren and Westbrook, above n 24, at 293, appendix 2.

[89] See, eg 11 USC s 362(b)(1), (b)(4).

[90] HR 333, above n 79, s 311.

[91] HR 333, above n 79, s 302, 303.

[92] See, eg HR, above n 79, 333 s 310.

[93] HR 333, above n 79, s 220.

[94] HR 333, above n 79, s 215.

[95] HR 333, above n 79, s 314.

[96] HR 333, above n 79, s 203 (adding extensive boilerplate language for reaffirmation agreements).

iii. Reduced Secured Debt Modification in Chapter 13

The legislation minimises the circumstances in which secured loans can be modified in Chapter 13. As mentioned previously, current law permits a debtor to retain a vehicle if she pays the value of the car in instalments with interest. So, for example, if a debtor's outstanding car loan is $10,000 but the car is worth $8,000, the debtor must pay $8,000 over time plus interest, and the remaining $2,000 is treated as an unsecured claim. The legislation makes the entire $10,000 payable in many instances.[97] This change will make some Chapter 13 plans non-confirmable, and will encourage longer plans in other circumstances, which further decreases the likelihood of plan completion.[98] Further, secured creditors will enjoy a greater share of debtors' payments under plans that are confirmed and completed.

C. Effects on Ill or Injured Filers

Proponents of the bankruptcy legislation often say that the amendments are targeted toward a small percentage of abusive filers. Yet, the scope and nature of the changes, such as the new eligibility and informational requirements, coupled with attorney financial sanctions, will make bankruptcy substantially more difficult and expensive for all debtors, including those who are ill or injured. In addition, because the Chapter 7 eligibility screens preclude considering a debtor's culpability for her debt problems, it is possible that a legitimate filer with serious health problems could be deemed ineligible for Chapter 7 relief under the presumed abuse test, while a profligate spender who has planned well may be permitted to proceed.

Whatever its merits in theory, the pre-bankruptcy credit counselling requirement further increases the cost and complexity of accessing bankruptcy, even for those who cannot be helped by counselling. The service might entail an additional fee, and may produce additional delay and bureaucracy. Yet, consumer credit counselling may do little or nothing for a person whose major financial problems stem primarily from a significant injury.

The reduced generosity of the system also may affect filers with medical-related financial problems. The expanded non-dischargeability for cash advances and credit card charges could affect medical-related filers to the extent that they use third party credit to finance their health needs. In addition, to the extent that the high number of medical-related Chapter 13 cases found in the 1999 study can be explained in part by the need to deal with secured debts, the tools for dealing with those debts will be much reduced.

[97] HR 333, above n 79, s 306.

[98] H Hildebrand, 'Survey Shows Big Impact of Anti-Lienstripping Provision in S. 625', <http://www.abiworld.org/legis/bills/99mayhildebrandsurvey.html> (17 October 2001).

V. CONCLUSION

The traditional components of the US health care system leave some households seeking ways to deal with unexpected expense, which is often accompanied by income reduction. Principal shortcomings of the traditional system are bureaucracy, complexity and cost. Readily-available consumer credit and bankruptcy by no means offer perfect alternatives, but they both are accessible in ways that the traditional system is not, and functionally have become part of the health care finance system.

Developments in bankruptcy and consumer credit policy therefore should be followed closely not only by those interested in debtor-creditor issues, but also those concerned about health and other socio-economic issues. The bankruptcy system as contemplated by the reform legislation would remain more generous than most other nations' systems, but the reformed system's bureaucracy will reduce access and raise costs for legitimate users, and it is reasonable to conclude that many ill or injured filers will be among them.

Part V

Debtor Education and Debtor Counselling

15

Can Voluntary Debt Settlement and Consumer Bankruptcy Coexist? The Development of Dutch Insolvency Law

NICK HULS, NADJA JUNGMANN, BERT NIEMEIJER

I. INTRODUCTION

THE NETHERLANDS HAS a tradition of voluntary debt settlement that goes back to the end of the seventies. For decades debt management agencies have been quite successful at negotiating voluntary debt settlements between debtors and their creditors. These agencies are funded by municipalities and adhere to a code of practice that lays down guidelines that the agencies should follow when carrying out their functions. The success rate of debt management agencies dropped steadily in the late eighties and early nineties. In response, the legislator enacted the Consumer Bankruptcy Act (*Wet schuldsanering natuurlijke personen* or *Wsnp, in force 1 December 1998*) as a subtitle of the Dutch Bankruptcy Act.

The aims of the Act are to offer a fresh start to the over-indebted debtors who acted in good faith and to encourage more voluntary debt settlements by making judicial debt adjustment financially less attractive to creditors. By preserving the voluntary process and introducing judicial adjustment for those cases in which creditors do not agree, debtors would be empowered vis-à-vis creditors and enabled to assert their 'right' to a fresh start. The Act would be advantageous to debtors because creditors, aware that the judicial procedure would be less favourable to them financially, could be expected to consent to voluntary debt settlement more often. The trade-off was that the odd debtor who unexpectedly opted for judicial debt adjustment would fall under a more stringent regime.

Now, nearly four years later, it is clear that the number of voluntary settlements has not increased. In this chapter, we analyse the reasons for the failure to reach this goal.[1] We will first describe the background of the Act and the legal

[1] For this article, we use findings from a large evaluation survey concerning operation of the *Wsnp*. This survey was conducted by the Research and Documentation Centre (WODC) of the Ministry of Justice: N Jungmann, E Niemeijer and MJ ter Voert, *Van Schuld naar schone*

changes it brought about. Next, we will describe the effects of the Act on voluntary debt settlement.[2] We will then examine judicial debt adjustment and the role of the judiciary.[3] Finally, we will draw some conclusions.

II. CONTEXT OF THE ACT

In the Netherlands, approximately 250,000 of the country's 6.8 million households are over-indebted. A debtor seeking assistance for over-indebtedness is expected to apply to a debt management agency for voluntary debt settlement. If the agency is unable to negotiate a settlement, for instance because all the creditors do not agree to the proposed payment plan, the debtor can file for judicial debt adjustment. In the following paragraph, we will outline the Dutch approach to consumer bankruptcy.

In the Netherlands, debt management is a local responsibility. Municipalities are free to organise it any way they wish. Because no law prescribes how debt counsellors are to work, there are significant differences among the organisations that offer debt management[4] and the service packages they provide. Even though no law regulates debt management, most agencies adhere to a code of practice developed by the Dutch Association of Municipal Banks (NVVK).[5] This code outlines good practice for voluntary debt settlement. Agencies that work in accordance with the code can be expected to offer creditors payment plans that oblige the debtor to pay as much as possible over a three-year period. If the debtor complies, the creditors agree to remission of the remaining amount of the debt.

Many debt management agencies oblige debtors to meet other obligations in addition to the monthly payments. Debtors can be required to cut back unnecessary recurring expenses, sell their car, seek counselling for concomitant problems such as addiction, or take a course in family financial management that will teach them how to put money aside for yearly and unforeseen expenses. Debt management agencies sometimes require debtors to deposit their income

lei. Evaluatie Wet schuldsanering natuurljke personen [From debt to clean slate. Evaluation of the Dutch Consumer Bankruptcy Act] (The Hague, WODC, Ministry of Justice, 2001). The principal source of information on the voluntary debt settlement procedure is the PhD research done by N Jungmann. The research concerning judges has been published as a separate book: N Huls and V Schellekens, *Je ziet de gaten in hun handen. De eerste ervaringen van rechtbanken en gerechtshoven met de toepassing van de Wsnp* [You can see the holes in their hands. Initial experiences of the courts with the *Wsnp*] (Utrecht, Lemma, 2001).

[2] Our findings are based on a comparison of 1,200 debt management files dating from 1997, with 700 files from 2000, and interviews with 35 municipal officials, 27 debt management agency workers and 4 creditors.

[3] The findings are based on research using 580 *Wsnp* files and interviews with 34 trustees and 24 judges.

[4] Usually debt management is offered by municipal banks, social services and private organisations.

[5] This code of practice dates from 1979.

in an agency account. The agency then pays the rent, the utilities, etc, giving the debtor an allowance each week to cover food and personal necessities. The biggest differences in the service packages offered by debt management agencies lie in the obligations they impose, such as requiring clients to seek help for personal problems or to sign up for a family budgeting course.

While the number of applications for debt management has risen over the last 10 years, the percentage of people for whom a voluntary debt settlement could be negotiated has decreased. In 1992, voluntary debt settlement was reached for about 50 per cent of the nearly 40,000 debtors who applied for settlement. In 1996, voluntary settlement was reached for about 40 per cent of the nearly 55,000 applicants. The Consumer Bankruptcy Act, which entered into effect 1 December 1998, aimed to halt the downward trend in voluntary debt settlement as well as to ensure a fresh start for debtors who acted in good faith.

The Act makes it possible under certain conditions for debtors to ask the court to impose debt adjustment. Failure of a debt management agency to negotiate a voluntary settlement is one precondition. To explain to the court why voluntary settlement negotiation failed, the written application for debt adjustment must provide information about the applicant's personal financial situation and give the reasons for failure to reach voluntary settlement. The application for debt adjustment is issued by the municipality or a body authorised to do so. The application is used by the court to determine whether reasonable grounds exist to assume that the debtor will not attempt to evade obligations arising from the scheme and whether he acted in good faith. If the court is satisfied, it will impose debt adjustment. The judge then decides on the length of the payment period, the amount to be discharged and goods accruing to the estate. Debtors must make an effort to pay off as much of the debt as possible. Their entire capital and income above the legal minimum subsistence level are deposited in an estate account. At the end of about three years, as much of the debt as possible will be paid to the creditors.

When adjustment is ordered by the court, an automatic stay takes effect. This means that creditors may no longer exercise their right to claim the outstanding amount. In court, adjustment debtors are generally required to make the same monthly payments over the same period of time they would have made if voluntary debt settlement had been reached. There are a few differences between judicial debt adjustment and voluntary debt settlement. Judicial debt adjustments are published in the Netherlands Government Gazette ('*Staatscourant*'), the (local) daily papers, and in the National Debt Adjustment Registry ('*Landelijk Register Schuldsaneringen*'). Publication is meant to give unknown creditors an opportunity to come forward. In addition, the court appoints a judge and a trustee to monitor the adjustment process. The trustee is responsible for managing the debtor's assets and for making sure that he meets his obligations. He visits the debtor's home to check that there are no excess assets and receives the debtor's mail to verify that the debtor has no undisclosed income. Mail redirection means that even the postcards sent by the neighbours from their holiday resort are seen by the trustee first. The trustee is obliged to make a progress report on the debt adjustment plan twice a year to keep the court informed. If the trustee reports that the debtor is not meeting his obligations, the judge can terminate adjustment. If this happens, adjustment will end and the debtor will be declared bankrupt.

Financially, there is no difference for the debtor between voluntary debt settlement and judicial debt adjustment. In both cases he pays everything he earns above 95 per cent of the Dutch social minimum. For creditors, however, there is a financial difference. Creditors who agree to voluntary settlement receive the full monthly payment. If creditors do not agree and the debtor files for court adjustment, they receive the monthly payment minus about 25 euro. The legislator hoped that this difference would make settlements financially more appealing to creditors, encouraging them to agree to settlement. This would improve the success rate of debt management agencies as well as prevent overloading the courts with applications for debt adjustment.

III. THE EFFECTS OF THE ACT ON VOLUNTARY DEBT SETTLEMENT

Three years after the Act entered into force we can conclude that the goal of increasing the number of voluntary debt settlements has not been attained. In fact, the success rate has gone down rather than up. As mentioned above, in 1992 debt management agencies were able to help about 50 per cent of the debtors filing for voluntary debt settlement. In 1996 they were able to help about 40 per cent and in 1998, the year the Act came into force, this percentage dropped to 35 per cent. This downward spiral has continued, sinking to 28 per cent in 2000. Indications are that the success rate will slide further every year. While the number of debtors helped has decreased, the number of debtors filing for voluntary debt settlement has increased in the last decade.[6] In 1990, almost 40,000 households filed for voluntary debt settlement. In 2000, this number rose to nearly 60,000. Based on the available figures, it can be concluded that the new Consumer Bankruptcy Act has been unable to break the downward trend in the number of voluntary debt settlements. In fact, every year since the introduction of the Act debt management agencies have reached fewer rather than more settlements. This means that the Act has failed to improve the success rate of debt management agencies. Based on our findings, we conclude that the main explanation for this outcome must be sought in changes in the strategies of debt management agencies and creditors.

[6] Only municipal banks have exact figures on the number of debtors filing for voluntary debt settlement. Other research has indicated that municipal banks help about 50 per cent of the debtors who file for voluntary debt settlement. The other 50 per cent are helped by social services and other (private) organisations. By using the figures of the municipal banks we can estimate the number of people helped by all debt settlement agencies.

Voluntary debt settlement can be realised only if four types of actors co-operate: the debtor, the creditors, the municipalities and the debt management agency. Sections A and B, respectively, will describe how the position of each of these four actors has been altered by the Act and then examine the response of these four actors to the Act.

A. The Actors Involved in Voluntary Debt Settlement

Debtors take the initiative by filing for voluntary debt settlement. They co-operate and comply with the conditions stipulated by the debt management agency in order to receive help in settling their debts. The debt management files examined show that debtors applying for voluntary debt settlement have an average of seven creditors. The major creditors are banks, social services, mail-order companies, tax authorities and housing associations. The Act was particularly intended to overcome awkward creditors such as housing associations and tax authorities that have strong legal preferential positions. Before the Act came into force, the chance that all of a debtor's creditors would agree to voluntary debt settlement was largely dependent on the type of creditors involved. Government creditors are often allowed little legal leeway to collaborate in voluntary debt settlement with full discharge at the end. The code of practice of the Dutch Association of Municipal Banks (NVVK) stipulates that voluntary debt settlement can be reached only if all creditors agree. Many debtors had at least one creditor who did not agree to voluntary settlement.

Creditors have felt the biggest change brought about by the Act. Before this legislation came into effect, creditors could continue to claim the outstanding amount for years. It was attractive for creditors not to co-operate in voluntary debt settlement because they could never be sure of the future financial situation of the debtor. With the introduction of the Act, if creditors refuse to agree to voluntary settlement, they run the risk that debtors will apply for judicial debt adjustment. If the court honours the debtor's request, creditors must co-operate in judicial debt adjustment. Because administrative and certain other costs are paid out of the monthly payments in judicial debt adjustment, the creditors receive less money than they would have if they had agreed to voluntary debt settlement.[7]

Municipalities bear responsibility for the debt management agencies. They finance them and some municipalities also establish debt or guarantee funds to facilitate voluntary debt settlement. Debt settlement agencies can apply to these funds on behalf of debtors. Money from these funds can be used to pay

[7] A trustee is paid about 25 Euro per month. This amounts to 900 euro for a three-year debt adjustment. Publication of a judicial debt adjustment in two or three papers and in the Netherlands Government Gazette costs roughly 500 to 750 Euro. So the difference between a judicial debt settlement and a voluntary debt settlement is approximately 1650 Euro. So on a 36 month base the difference is approximately 45 Euro.

creditors in part, for example to prevent eviction. Local authorities set up such funds because it is more costly to finance replacement housing than to pay off (part of) the outstanding rent. The conditions with which a debtor must comply differ across debt management agencies. Some organisations oblige debtors to hand over their budget management to the agency as soon as they request voluntary debt settlement. Others require debtors first to seek treatment for concomitant problems, such as drug or alcohol addictions.

A striking aspect of such funds is that creditors are paid off with municipal money. There are two types of funds: *debt funds* and *guarantee funds*. A *debt fund* is used to provide a creditor with more money than the debtor is able to pay during voluntary debt settlement. Even if creditors do not receive full payment of their claim, they can sometimes be persuaded to agree to voluntary debt settlement if additional money is provided by the debt fund. The conditions under which such money is given differ across municipalities. Some funds are only used to pay specific types of creditors. For instance, landlords might be paid in order to prevent eviction. Other funds are used only to buy off a sole creditor who refuses to co-operate in voluntary debt settlement. In addition to the conditions governing funding, some municipalities set certain other conditions, for instance regarding the debtor's income. A debtor is never obliged to repay the amount paid to the creditors out of the debt fund.

Guarantee funds provide guarantees to debtors who cannot give a municipal bank sufficient certainty that they will meet their voluntary debt settlement commitments. If, during voluntary debt settlement, the debtor ceases to pay the monthly instalments to the municipal bank for any reason whatsoever, the unpaid part of the debt settlement is paid out of the guarantee fund. Debtors without a fixed income (like freelancers) can obtain voluntary debt settlement owing to the existence of funds of this sort.

The declining success rate for voluntary debt settlement in the late eighties and early nineties prompted many local authorities to create such funds. Local authorities expected debtors for whom no voluntary debt settlement could be reached to turn to them sooner or later. Assistance at a later stage would often be more expensive than buying off the debt to facilitate voluntary settlement.

Debt settlement agencies approach creditors on behalf of debtors to realise voluntary debt settlements. Before the Act came into force, debt management agencies were the last hope for a fresh start for debtors. If no settlement could be negotiated, creditors could seize the debtors' income for years and years to come. For this reason, debt settlement advisers did everything in their power to persuade creditors to agree to voluntary debt settlement. The introduction of the Act gave debt management agencies more leverage in their relationship with creditors, at least in theory. If a creditor does not agree, the debt counsellor can point out that the debtor will then probably apply for judicial debt settlement, an outcome that will be financially less advantageous to the creditor.

B. Reaction of the Actors to the Act

The change in the position of the actors has prompted them to re-evaluate their own position. No research has yet studied the reactions of the most important actor: the debtors. What we do know is that the number of applications for voluntary debt settlement has risen since introduction of the Act. Several comments can be made about this development. First, the increase is in line with the yearly increase in the number of applications since 1990. Secondly, some debtors, who requested voluntary debt settlement in the past but could not be helped at the time, probably try again since the Act can offer them a fresh start. Thirdly, the introduction of the Act has heightened public awareness of the debt problem. This means that more households are familiar with debt management agencies, which may stimulate the number of applications.

Entry of the Act into force has not put debtors in a stronger position. It was expected that creditors would prefer out-of-court settlement to court adjustment and that this would make it easier for debtors to 'pressure' creditors into agreeing to settlements. In practice, however, creditors do not favour voluntary debt settlement to judicial debt adjustment for a variety of reasons (discussed in the next paragraphs). As a result, the debtors' 'power base' has been removed.

Introduction of the Act led many creditors to evaluate the pros and cons of settlement versus adjustment.[8] From our interviews it can be concluded that some creditors deliberately refuse to agree to voluntary debt settlement because they prefer judicial debt adjustment. We have found three reasons for this. First, adjustment can be financially more attractive to the creditors than voluntary settlement.[9] Secondly, some creditors appreciate the element of control and the sanctions included in judicial adjustment. Thirdly, the implementation of voluntary debt settlement is inconsistent and not as favourable to creditors as the legislator assumed.

Some creditors conclude that judicial debt adjustment can be more beneficial to them than voluntary debt settlement in some of the following instances:

—*Increased income for the debtor*. Voluntary debt settlement starts with the calculation of the amount the debtor can pay off in three years. This calculation is based on the debtor's income at the moment the settlement takes effect. With judicial debt adjustment, all the debtor's income is deposited in an estate account during the three-year period. If the debtor's income increases during this term, this (extra) money is also deposited in the estate account and will

[8] Here it should be noted that there is no such thing as 'the creditor.' Creditors such as utility companies and landlords, who cannot simply cease all contact with a debtor, take a different approach from creditors who can do so. Government creditors whose latitude in agreeing with claims is bound by statutory provisions are in a different position than creditors who can agree to what they themselves want. The considerations outlined in this paragraph apply to one type of creditor in some instances, and to another type in other cases, but because a creditor's refusal to agree can impinge on the success of voluntary debt settlement, all the considerations described play a part.

[9] This is exactly the opposite of the second aim of the Consumer Bankruptcy Act.

go to the creditors. If the debtor's income increases more than roughly 1,750 euro (the costs of administration and publication), judicial debt adjustment becomes more attractive to creditors than voluntary debt settlement. [10]

—*Liquidation of excess assets*. When judicial debt adjustment takes effect, the trustee is expected to visit the debtor's house and liquidate any excess assets found. Mail redirection is supposed to enable the trustee to track down unreported assets or money. This is not the case in voluntary debt settlement. If a debtor possesses assets worth more than the fees of the trustee and the publication costs (roughly 1750 euro), judicial debt adjustment is financially more appealing to creditors than voluntary debt settlement.

—*Judicial debt adjustment drop-outs*. It is very difficult for debtors to complete judicial debt adjustment. If a debtor does not meet the conditions imposed by the judge, the court can terminate the adjustment. The debtor is then declared bankrupt and cannot apply for adjustment again during the next 10 years. Creditors can seize the debtors' income (again). Some creditors do not agree to voluntary debt settlement, in anticipation of this possibility.

—*Recidivism*. If a creditor agrees to voluntary debt settlement, a debtor can request another settlement a few years later. If creditors do not wish to co-operate a second time, the debtor can still apply for judicial debt adjustment. By not agreeing to voluntary settlement and counting on judicial adjustment, the creditor is assured of not being forced to write off a claim for a second time in the 10 years following adjustment.

—*Debtor shame*. Judicial debt adjustment includes publishing the name of the debtor in daily papers and in a public registry on the Internet. Some debtors are ashamed of being in debt and do not want their name in the papers or on the Internet.[11] Some creditors do not agree to voluntary debt settlement because they anticipate that certain debtors will not go to court for debt adjustment because of the negative publicity this entails. In this case, by not agreeing to voluntary debt settlement the creditor can seize the debtor's income until the debt has been paid.

—*Punishment*. Creditors perceive adjustment as more 'punitive' than settlement because of mail redirection and the publication of the debtor's name. For this reason, some creditors prefer judicial debt adjustment even though it means they will be less well off financially.

When preparing the Act, the legislator supposed that creditors would most likely prefer voluntary debt settlement since judicial debt adjustment is financially less attractive. Not only would settlement be more advantageous to debtors, but also the improved success rate of debt management agencies would

[10] Fn 7 shows that the difference between a judicial and a voluntary debt settlement is approximately 1650 Euro. So, if thanks to a salary increase during the three-year duration of the debt adjustment arrangement, a debtor earns more than 1650 euro, creditors are better off financially.

[11] N Jungmann, *Niet alle uitvallers zijn afvallers, een onderzoek naar uitval in de integrale schuldhulpverlening* [Not all drop-outs are real drop-outs, a research on people dropping out of debt counselling] (Utrecht, Project Integrale Schuldhulpverlening, 2002).

be a tool for granting debtors a fresh start and for preventing court system overload. The legislative authorities assumed that there was a well functioning debt management network that fitted seamlessly into the court system. Now it is apparent that there are enormous differences in the way in which debt settlement is implemented at the local level. For creditors operating at regional and national levels, this means that the conditions under which voluntary debt settlement is offered sometimes differ considerably across debt management agencies. In particular these creditors find it hard to formulate their debt policy taking into account the local differences. Judicial debt adjustments are executed far more uniformly. This encourages creditors to opt for judicial debt adjustment despite a disadvantage which is on average 1650 Euro.[12]

Due to the introduction of the Act, debt management agencies are no longer the only organisations that can help over-indebted debtors. There is always the option of judicial debt adjustment. The failure of voluntary debt settlement no longer means that a debtor's only alternative would be to turn to the local authority for financial assistance. For this reason, some municipalities no longer consider it necessary to pay off principal creditors and have abolished their debt and guarantee funds. Because judicial debt adjustment is more difficult for debtors than voluntary settlement, some municipalities maintain these funds and still try to reach a settlement for debtors wherever possible.[13]

Municipalities do not receive funds from the national government to finance voluntary debt settlement. Implementation of judicial debt adjustment by trustees, to the contrary, is funded by the state. Consequently, voluntary settlement debtors cost local authorities money while judicial adjustment debtors cost them nothing. It is still unclear just how much this financial difference influences the attitude of municipalities toward debt management agencies, but it seems fair to assume that local authorities take this difference into account.

Debt management agencies lost their monopoly with the advent of the Act. Prior to the Act, they were the only hope for debtors wanting a fresh start. Before the Act entered into force, they invested enormous energy in persuading creditors to agree to debt settlement. Creditors who did not want to co-operate

[12] The evaluation of the Act showed that an average of 11 creditors are represented in a judicial debt adjustment package. Voluntary debt settlements average seven creditors. The financial difference between settlement and adjustment amounts to roughly 1650 euro (see fn 7 for the calculation). If the debt package includes 11 creditors, a creditor receives roughly 160 euro less in judicial debt adjustment (if there are no preferred creditors). By settling for this difference and by steering in the direction of judicial debt adjustment, the financial administration of the creditor that categorically refuses voluntary debt settlement because of the sizeable differences in procedure across debt management agencies need not keep track of precisely which conditions apply to which debt settlement.

[13] Roughly two-thirds of the local authorities had a debt and/or guarantee fund when the Act entered into force. Roughly one third of these abolished the fund because the Act came into effect. N Jungmann, E Niemeijer and M ter Voert, *Van schuld naar schone lei. Evaluatie Wet Schuldsanering natuurlijke personen* [From debt to fresh start. Evaluation of the Consumer Bankruptcy Act] (Den Haag, WODC, 2001) at 33. Research voor Beleid, *De Wet schuldsanering natuurlijke personen; effecten op de minnelijke schuldregelingen en het instrumentarium van gemeenten* [The Consumer Bankruptcy Act; effects on debt counselling and the instruments of municipalities] (Leiden, Research voor Beleid, 2001) at 20–24.

on a proposed payment plan were often approached several times in writing or by phone to see whether they would change their mind. Every possible option was explored. The debt management agencies wrote letters in which they explained in detail how the over-indebtedness arose and sometimes even agreed to negotiate a settlement that spanned more than three years.

The code of practice of the Dutch Association of Municipal Banks (NVVK) describes standards of professional practice and conduct for reaching settlements. These standards are often formulated 'in principle'. By setting forth a number of principles, the code grants debt management agencies wide latitude in negotiating settlements, even if the outcome is not completely in line with the code. Terms like 'in principle' were added to ensure that a debtor for whom a settlement could almost be reached would not be left in the cold. Introduction of the Act made the NVVK reconsider its code of practice. Many provisions have been tightened up so as to bring voluntary debt settlement more in line with judicial debt adjustment. All terms such as 'in principle' or 'the starting point is' were removed. The new code of practice is binding on members of the NVVK and they risk sanctions if they fail to fully comply with the code.

The new tightened code of practice grants debt management agencies less latitude in reaching debt settlements. Debt counsellors also report spending less time on cases since the Act came into force. Prior to the Act, they knew they were the only hope a debtor had of making a fresh start so they tried everything they could to reach settlement. Nowadays debt counsellors advise debtors whose creditors do not want to settle to file immediately for judicial debt adjustment. The waiting lists in most municipalities induce counsellors to invest less energy in individual cases.

Where judicial debt adjustment is not necessarily financially unattractive to creditors, municipalities no longer have debt and guarantee funds, and debt management agencies work according to a more stringent code of practice, no longer trying as hard to reach a settlement in difficult cases, it is not surprising that debt management agencies reach fewer voluntary debt settlements than before the Act.

IV. JUDICIAL DEBT ADJUSTMENT AND THE ROLE OF THE JUDICIARY

In both 1999 and 2000 courts honoured some 8,000 applications for judicial debt adjustment. We do not know how many were successfully completed. Thus, it is still too early to evaluate the end results of judicial debt adjustment.

What we do know is how the judiciary has fulfilled its new tasks. The new procedure calls for an approach that combines legal, economic and social aspects. It is not easy for judges to determine the proper course because they continually face new dilemmas in applying the Consumer Bankruptcy Act. Interviews with all 19 district courts and five courts of appeal have taught us more about their activities. In the following section of this chapter, we will describe four dilemmas perceived by district court judges in application of the Act and show how they resolve them.

A. Four Dilemmas in Applying the Consumer Bankruptcy Act

1. *Variety or Uniformity?*

Uniformity is an ideal, yet so elusive. The judicial profession involves working with people and the Dutch judiciary is not a homogenous community. We spoke to young ambitious bankruptcy judges who had just completed their judicial training and with older judges experienced in banking or business law. Some judges enjoy sitting in bankruptcy cases; others find it a chore.

Judges are not civil servants required to apply rules according to strict instructions. They are independent, thus stubborn arbitrators in dispute resolution. For a judge, no two cases are the same, certainly not under the Consumer Bankruptcy Act where every citizen argues his or her own unique position without legal representation. In the majority of courts, our interviewees plainly admitted that their interpretations of certain parts of the Consumer Bankruptcy Act differ. A certain degree of legal provincialism is unavoidable, certainly in such a new area of law. We expect that creditors and trustees will exert greater pressure in the near future for more equal treatment of debtors. Large professional creditors, but also organisations of trustees operating nationwide, demand equal treatment of their claims. They will (continue) to call (public) attention to examples of undesirable legal inequality.

2. *Specialisation or Rotation?*

Within the judiciary there is debate about whether judges, like the bar, should specialise more or should primarily have a broad vision and be able to work in various court sectors. At present, the court secretary is generally the only person to guarantee consistency in case law because he is the sole professional working on Consumer Bankruptcy Act cases over a long period of time. Judicial appointments should be for at least 5 years so that long-term and professionally sound policy lines can be set out at court level.

On the other hand, the rotation of judicial assignments also has advantages. The input from judges with criminal law experience allowed the legislature to forge a previously neglected link between compensation measures and penal sanctions. The contribution of judges with experience in social security cases is a valuable supplement to the civil law expertise that has traditionally coloured the bankruptcy bench. The broad view of judges is in line with the everyday world of the debtor for whom legal and social aspects are inextricably linked.

3. *Partner in the Chain or Tower of Strength?*

In Consumer Bankruptcy Act cases, the court is only one link in the chain. Our research shows that judges have regular and frequent contact with the other links. They participate in all kinds of networks related to the Act. It is in the interest of the courts to develop and maintain good contact with those partners who play a role in other parts of the chain even though communication with them is not unproblematic. Shortfalls were identified in the co-ordination of the preliminary process, in the action taken by local authorities, and in the subsequent appellate phase. Better use of modern communication tools would improve the situation. It is, however, also important for the judiciary to follow its own course and not to depend too much on co-operation with partners in the chain.

The common sense approach pursued by the judiciary was a rude awakening to the voluntary debt settlement advisers. The municipal banks previously enjoyed a monopoly position, operating under a system of self-regulation.[14] The introduction of the Consumer Bankruptcy Act has changed things fundamentally. The businesslike approach of judges made debt adjustment in court an appealing alternative to voluntary settlement for creditors. In this sense, the Act also presents a challenge to the debt settlement community.

4. *Controller or Social Worker?*

The final dilemma concerns the balance between debtors and creditors. Should judges be merciful to debtors or strict and severe? Judges needed to get used to the new type of citizen that appeared before them after introduction of the Consumer Bankruptcy Act. Our interviews indicate that judges have difficulty finding the proper attitude to people from the underside of society. This group demands an approach that differs from the one judges are accustomed to taking in the event of bankruptcies.

Dealing with debtors from other ethnic and cultural backgrounds is another complex factor. Is taking care of family members in a distant country relevant in determining an individual's financial capacity in the Netherlands? How should Dutch judges deal with property and provisions for old age abroad? Our impression is that judges do not readily give special treatment to foreigners under the Act.

[14] N Huls, 'Alternatives to Personal Bankruptcy. The Dutch Situation' in G Hörmann (ed), *Consumer Credit and Consumer Insolvency. Perspectives from Europe and the USA*, Zentrum für Europaisches Rechtspolitik, (Bremen, Bremen University Press, 1986) 289.

B. Old and New Roles

How have Consumer Bankruptcy Act judges dealt with these dilemmas? The old and still dominant self-image of the judge is that he makes binding decisions in individual disputes presented to him. In Consumer Bankruptcy Act proceedings, this means that the judge must decide during a fifteen-minute hearing whether the applicant should be allowed access to the judicial debt adjustment scheme. Nevertheless, Consumer Bankruptcy Act cases are special. Unlike most other ones, in these cases the judge has direct contact with a citizen asking for assistance in resolving financial problems. The applicant frequently has no legal representation and 'the other party'—the creditor—often does not appear in court. The judge must weigh a combination of factors in arriving at his decision: legal, moral, social and financial.

The time that judges only spoke through their decisions is behind us. One of the positive outcomes of our research is that judges no longer restrict themselves to their traditional roles, but have assumed a number of new roles as well. It appears that judges have addressed their new and largely unfamiliar task very proactively. They have pursued an active policy, introducing the Consumer Bankruptcy Act to their own organisation as well as to the surrounding 'field.'

The judge is responsible for the court process from intake to the closing session. A good judge is a manager, who understands the art of delegation. There are almost no judges concentrating full-time on Consumer Bankruptcy cases. Most courts have a bankruptcy division and the judge is member of a team. In all courts, there is considerable consultation and co-ordination between the judges on implementation of Consumer Bankruptcy policy. In practice, many tasks are left to (experienced) court clerks who, in their turn, are supported by a secretariat.

The world of the judge extends beyond the four walls of the court building. In Consumer Bankruptcy Act cases it is also the duty of the judge to supervise the trustees. In this capacity, the judge not only makes decisions and gives consent to certain actions, but he is also the contact person and coach for the trustee. Our findings indicate that trustees without a legal background often ask the bankruptcy judge both practical and legal questions.

Consumer bankruptcy judges frequently belong to a variety of consultation groups outside the courthouse. Judges meet for regular structured consultations with the bar, trustees and local officials. Consumer bankruptcy judges take part in numerous working groups set up to resolve specific practical problems related to implementation of the legislation, including those in the area of administration and information and communication technology. In addition, judges represent their court in national judicial organisations where national policy guidelines are formulated.

V. CONCLUSION

The aims of the Dutch Consumer Bankruptcy Act are to offer debtors a clean slate and to increase the success rate of debt management agencies. We can conclude that the first aim has been (partially) reached. Debtors who acted in good faith can start anew. This is without doubt an important benefit of the Act, but in view of the scale of the debt problem, relatively few debtors in fact get a fresh start through debt settlement or adjustment. In addition, we do not know how many judicial debt adjustments have been successfully completed. The second aim has not been achieved. The success rate of debt management agencies has dropped further rather than improved since the Act came into force. The question is: how could this have happened? We feel that the consequences of the Act can be explained by the history of the legislation itself and by the strategic behaviour of stakeholders involved in implementation of the Act.

A. The Legislation Itself

The Ministry of Justice was the principal author of the policy. As a consequence, the legal perspective dominated in designing the Act, to the detriment of local, social and financial dimensions.

Only at a very late stage did the Ministry of Justice realise how important municipalities really are in the field of debt management. Throughout the legislative process, municipalities, (financially) responsible for debt management organisations, asked for money. It was difficult to counter the logic of their argument: if you want a sound voluntary debt settlement process, you have to invest in it. Because the Ministry of Justice had no financial resources available, the voluntary process remained financially dependent on municipalities, leaving a weak link between the voluntary and judicial process.

In addition, the local and social dimensions of the debt problems were underexposed. With the introduction of the Act, an aspect of life in society dominated for decades by local debt management organisations became legalised and had to function as the path to judicial debt adjustment.

During the course of preparing and implementing the Act, creditors were not considered. The legislator wrongfully assumed that if the judicial route were made less appealing financially to creditors, they would be more likely to agree to voluntary settlement. As it turns out, the financial differences between the voluntary and judicial process are too minimal to interest creditors. Because creditors showed little interest in preparing the legislation, the legislator wrongly concluded that they endorsed the new Act. Creditors have clearly become far more alert and less flexible since conversion of the informal scheme into a judicial right to debt management. The Act has simply provided creditors with an alternative form of debt collection.

B. Strategic Behaviour

In general, implementation of legislation hinges on the way the various stakeholders react to it and to each other. All stakeholders interpret a new piece of legislation from their own perspective and evaluate how they can optimise their own interests under the new regulatory regime. In this sense, stakeholders act strategically. When the Act came into force, each actor was confronted with a new situation.

—Debtors are in principle given the opportunity of a fresh start and are no longer fully dependent on the whims of their creditors for a debt-free future.
—Creditors can be forced into judicial debt settlement if they do not agree to voluntary debt settlement. The legislator expected that creditors would, for financial reasons, prefer settlement to adjustment. In practice, creditors seem to see settlement merely as a forum that precedes, not replaces, the court. Creditors have clear reasons for this: judicial adjustment can be financially more attractive for them, they favour the most drastic option in order to 'punish' debtors for not paying the debt in full, and they have more faith in the uniform implementation of adjustments.
—For municipal and debt management agencies, the pressure to reach settlement diminished.
—And, finally, judges had to perform a new task for a new type of client. The judges have demonstrated engagement in the debt issue and are not afraid of taking unconventional measures to exercise their duties properly. They have taken an active approach to fulfilling the tasks arising from the Consumer Bankruptcy Act and are making every effort to process the flow of cases as quickly and effectively as possible. However, because judges performed their roles so well, they contributed to the failure of the very process they were deemed to strengthen: voluntary debt settlement! This is an unintended consequence of the new Act.

To adapt to the new circumstances, the parties concerned made strategic choices about how to best secure their own objectives, interests and position. Each actor reacted in their own way. The combination of these adjustments and the wrongly assumed causal suppositions of the legislature that creditors will always agree to the kind of debt settlement that is most attractive financially, resulted unexpectedly in a downturn in the success rate of debt management agencies.

The effects of the Act make clear just how hard it is to guide the strategic behaviour of key actors. Despite praise for the consensual nature of Dutch legal culture, the fact that an actor's interests play a role is unavoidable. Legislators that do not take this sufficiently into account will see that the effects of an Act will either fail to occur or run counter to expectations. Despite all criticism of the formal, expensive and bureaucratic work of the courts in the Netherlands, preference was given to formal legislation while a flexible, informal alternative acceptable to all parties involved was already in place. In our opinion, this is one of the major riddles of the new Act. Why did stakeholders withdraw their support for the code of practice, a system of self-regulation that people had been committed to for 20 years without complaint? Debt remission is an exception to the principle of civil law. In this regard, the code of practice was an informal form of *tolerance*. By legalising this exception in the Act, the legislature has put the cat among the pigeons and all parties involved have reconsidered their position. Every debtor who acted in good faith can start anew now, but they pay a high price. The question is whether debtors have benefited in practice from this professionalisation and legalisation.

16

Debtor Education in Bankruptcy: The Perspective of Interest Analysis

JEAN BRAUCHER

I. INTRODUCTION AND OVERVIEW

TWO THEORIES, EMPOWERMENT and social control of debtors, have traditionally been used to explain debtor education in bankruptcy. The rationales of these theories—in bland form—are usually given for existing or proposed programmes. Thus, education is seen as empowering debtors by teaching them new financial management skills to avoid debt problems and to plan to achieve financial goals. Similarly, using a version of social control theory no stronger than what lies behind most consumer protection regulation, education encourages debtors to pay more attention to information about credit transactions, to resist manipulations of sales and marketing techniques, and to exercise more self-control in the marketplace. Whether debtor education in fact achieves the goals of these two theories has yet to be shown.

A stronger and more critical version of empowerment might involve providing debtors with an opportunity to voice concerns about how consumer culture encourages over-indebtedness, perhaps leading to major changes in lifestyle or even demands for systemic change. A stronger version of social control sees the heavily indebted as deviants likely to have other problems that arise from compulsive or impulsive behaviour, such as substance abuse and unstable family situations, but this view lacks empirical support.[1]

My objectives in this chapter are to describe existing US debtor education initiatives and to introduce a third theoretical perspective derived from the school of social science thought known as 'institutionalism.'[2] I will call this perspective

[1] See CA Curnock, 'Insolvency Counselling—Innovation Based on the Fourteenth Century' (1999) 37 *Osgoode Hall Law Journal* 387 for a criticism of required Canadian counselling for debtors that involves exploring psycho-social causes of debt problems as not grounded by good studies.

[2] See JR Sutton, 'Rethinking Social Control' (1996) 21 *Law & Social Inquiry* 943 for a review of WW Powell and PJ DiMaggio (eds), *The New Institutionalism in Organizational Analysis* (Chicago, University of Chicago Press, 1991) [*The New Institutionalism*] and a discussion of the institutional theories of socio-legal systems.

'interest analysis' because it involves identifying how debtor education serves the interests of the various players in consumer bankruptcy.

From most perspectives, education as part of the response to consumer over-indebtedness and bankruptcy seems to make sense. It is hard not to be in favour of education, particularly at a high level of abstraction.[3] But despite the wide appeal of the idea of education in and through bankruptcy, skepticism and critique are appropriate for a number of reasons. Education is not costless. Requiring it in bankruptcy would reduce access for some debtors by increasing the cost in money and time. Education may be able to address some problems but not others. In order to evaluate any programme, its goals need to be defined before its effectiveness can be measured. Education programmes raise difficult normative issues. For example, should debtors be encouraged to consume and borrow less? How much less?

Education in bankruptcy takes many forms. Debtors may learn from experience by going through the process of proposing and carrying out a repayment plan. Thus, there is an inherent educational potential to Chapter 13 bankruptcy in the US, as there is with debt adjustment proceedings in Europe.[4] Through repayment plans, debtors can take ownership of their debt problems by attempting to pay what they owe, at least in part. A fresh start, or unconditional discharge, form of bankruptcy is not inherently educational in the same way as a repayment plan, although some debtors may learn a lesson in the process about avoiding too much debt in the future. Unfortunately, the educational function of repayment plans may often be more rhetoric than reality. Many Chapter 13 bankruptcies have as their principal objective allowing debtors to keep collateral, with little or no payment made to unsecured creditors,[5] and most plans are not completed.[6]

[3] See Curnock, above n 1, at 399, referring to financial management education and counselling as a 'motherhood' solution. See also *National Bankruptcy Review Commission: The Next Twenty Years, Final Report* (1997) at 114–16 (*NBRC Report*), the report of a US commission recommending increased opportunities for debtors in and out of bankruptcy to participate in voluntary financial education programmes. Despite disagreements on many consumer bankruptcy issues, all nine commissioners supported this recommendation. See *NBRC Report*, *Individual Commissioner Views, Recommendations for Reform of Consumer Bankruptcy Law by Four Dissenting Commissioners* at 3 [*Four Dissenters' Recommendations*], which states that 'The nine Commissioners agree on the need to . . . promote pre- and post-bankruptcy debtor education.'

[4] See J Braucher, 'An Empirical Study of Debtor Education in Bankruptcy: Impact on Chapter 13 Completion Not Shown' (2001) 9 *American Bankruptcy Institute Law Review* 557 at 565 ['Empirical Study of Debtor Education'] for a discussion of the long understanding of Chapter 13 as having a rehabilitative and educational purpose; J Niemi-Kiesilainen, 'The Role of Consumer Counselling as Part of the Bankruptcy Process in Europe' (1999) 37 *Osgoode Hall Law Journal* 409 at 413 ['Consumer Counselling in Europe'], stating, 'In Europe we expect to achieve prevention, rehabilitation, a change in lifestyle, and partial repayment of debt through counselling.'

[5] See J Braucher, 'Lawyers and Consumer Bankruptcy: One Code, Many Cultures' (1993) 67 *American Bankruptcy Law Journal* 501 at 529–31 ['Lawyers and Consumer Bankruptcy'] for lawyers' view that holding on to collateral, despite arrears, is the most common reason to file in Chapter 13; many Chapter 13 bankruptcies involve low percentage plans, with most of the amounts paid going to secured lenders.

[6] See WC Whitford, 'The Ideal of Individualized Justice: Consumer Bankruptcy as Consumer Protection, and Consumer Protection in Consumer Bankruptcy' (1994) 68 *American Bankruptcy Law Journal* 397 at 411, reporting 31 per cent national average completion rate in 1993.

Individual counselling, which is used for different purposes in different countries, may be educational in that it helps consumer debtors to identify the causes of their over- indebtedness, to plan to repay old debt in or out of bankruptcy, and to limit the risk of a future debt crisis. In the US, consumer credit counselling usually aims to keep debtors out of bankruptcy by arranging debt adjustment plans, and it also may involve financial management counselling.[7] Canada's bankruptcy law requires debtors to undergo personal and money management counselling.[8] Alternatively, counselling may be directed to complying with a complex bankruptcy process as opposed to long-term financial management. Counselling concerning the legal administrative process is often predominant as part of debt adjustment proceedings in Europe.[9] In the US, lawyers, or document-preparers, provide counselling about the bankruptcy process. Probably only a small percentage of US lawyers take the time to provide detailed counselling about future financial management.[10]

Group classes in personal financial management are the most explicit, formal type of education. My focus will be on classes given to debtors who have already filed in bankruptcy. Most existing US debtor education programmes of this nature are for Chapter 13 debtors. However, the National Bankruptcy Review Commission recognised in its 1997 report that education could also be important to help debtors in Chapter 7 (the fresh start form of bankruptcy) regain their financial equilibrium and avoid another bankruptcy.[11]

Interest in studying existing US debtor education programmes in bankruptcy has been prompted by a legislative proposal to make financial management education after filing mandatory for all debtors as a condition of discharge in either Chapter 7 or Chapter 13. The proposed legislation would also make consumer credit counselling (and thus consideration of a non-bankruptcy debt repayment plan) mandatory for all debtors prior to filing in bankruptcy. Although this legislation was not enacted in 2002 for complex reasons, it was reintroduced in 2003 with uncertain prospects.[12]

[7] See DA Lander, 'Essay: A Snapshot of Two Systems that are Trying to Help People in Financial Trouble' (1999) 7 *American Bankruptcy Institute Law Review* 161 at 176–84, concerning counselling, debt management plans and educational programmes of US consumer credit counselling agencies.

[8] See RE Berry and SLT McGregor, 'Counselling Consumer Debtors under Canada's Bankruptcy and Insolvency Act' (1999) 37 *Osgoode Hall Law Journal* 369 at 380, 385. See also I Ramsay, 'Mandatory Bankruptcy Counselling: The Canadian Experience' (2002) 7 *Fordham Journal of Corporate and Financial Law* 525 at 529 ['Counselling'], which describes the two required sessions, one on consumer and credit education, followed by an individual counselling session.

[9] See 'Consumer Counselling in Europe', above n 4, at 412 (because of complicated legal requirements, counsellors in practice act as paralegals to the debtor).

[10] See 'Lawyers and Consumer Bankruptcy', above n 5, at 554–55. In an interview study of practices and views of 45 US consumer bankruptcy lawyers, only one mentioned spending substantial time on financial planning for the post-bankruptcy period.

[11] See *NBRC Report*, above n 3, at 114–15; *Four Dissenters' Recommendations*, above n 3, at 21 (stating that 'the policy of the fresh start' is 'furthered if debtors have the chance to learn personal financial management skills.')

[12] The legislative initiative for mandatory counselling and education in the US was part of a credit industry-backed bill to subject all debtors to strict eligibility tests for Chapter 7, attempting

Mandatory education and counselling have also been components of 'get tough' legislation requiring more repayment in Canada.[13] In European countries, under personal debt adjustment laws enacted in the 1990s and not providing an immediate fresh start option, counselling focusses on adjusting lifestyle to enable the debtor to propose a viable repayment plan.[14] Thus, in North America and Europe, education and counselling initiatives have been associated primarily with promotion of repayment forms of bankruptcy, as opposed to immediate discharge forms.

Officials who currently administer US debtor education classes in bankruptcy have not sought evidence that education changes behaviour.[15] Instead, they have asked debtors for subjective reactions on class evaluation forms, a means of evaluation that appears to produce favourable reactions. A study I conducted in 1999–2000, described below in Section II, appears to have been the first in the US to attempt to measure directly behavioural impact.[16] Furthermore, there has been only very limited research concerning attitudinal change, focussing on how education promotes debtors' sense of control over their financial lives.[17] In

to push more debtors into Chapter 13, but in the process making access to bankruptcy more complex and expensive for all. *Bankruptcy Abuse Prevention & Consumer Protection Action of 2002*, HR 333, Conf Rep 107–617. Although the US commission supported optional education for all, see *NBRC Report*, above n 3, the bills considered in Congress would have gone further and made education mandatory. For more information concerning new hurdles that would be imposed by the proposed legislation, see J Braucher, 'Means Testing Consumer Bankruptcy: The Problem of Means' (2002) 7 *Fordham Journal of Corporate & Financial Law* 407 at 433–47 ['Means Testing']. See also MB Jacoby, 'Generosity versus Accessibility: Bankruptcy, Consumer Credit, and Health Care Finance in the US' in this volume.

[13] See JS Ziegel, 'The Philosophy and Design of Contemporary Consumer Bankruptcy Systems: A Canada-United States Comparison' (1999) 37 *Osgoode Hall Law Journal* 205.

[14] See J Niemi-Kiesilainen, 'Consumer Bankruptcy in Comparison: Do We Cure a Market Failure or a Social Problem?' (1999) 37 *Osgoode Hall Law Journal* 473 at 475 ['Bankruptcy in Comparison'], which notes that mandatory payment and mandatory counselling are key features of the European debt adjustment laws of the 1990s.

[15] Administrators have asked debtors in the programmes to fill out evaluation forms distributed at the end of classes, but they have not sought evidence of changes in behaviour. See 'Empirical Study of Debtor Education', above n 4, at 585–86. In contrast to the programmes run by bankruptcy trustees, a temporary programme has been established specifically for the purpose of evaluation and programme development. This programme is not run by officials in the bankruptcy system; it is optional and is for both Chapter 7 and Chapter 13 debtors. The programme is described in K Gross, 'Establishing Financial Literacy Programmes for Consumer Debtors: Complex Issues On the Platter' in this volume. See also S Block-Lieb *et al*, 'Lessons from the Trenches: Debtor Education in Theory and Practice' (2002) 7 *Fordham Journal of Corporate & Financial Law* 503.

[16] See 'Empirical Study of Debtor Education', above n 4.

[17] See P Stokes and S Polansky, 'Shifting the Economic Locus of Control: Improving Financial Decision-Making in High-Risk Populations' (1999) 3 *Academic Accounting Financial Studies Journal* 95 where in a one-district survey study of sample 58 debtors who filled out survey instruments before a class and 61 debtors who did so one to 12 months after a class, shifts in attitudes from external to more internal locus of control were shown. Stokes earlier conducted a two-survey study of the same district, in which debtors indicated positive reactions to education classes immediately after them and also reported in follow-up survey later using techniques taught in the classes. See P Stokes, 'Moving from Bankruptcy to Solvency: An Educational Experience that Works' (1995) 97 *Business Credit* 20. The follow-up survey thus is indirect evidence of behavioural change, as self-reported by debtors.

short, US policy-makers have supported expanding debtor education and making it mandatory with little evidence of effect.[18]

This drive to expand and make mandatory education for US debtors in bankruptcy suggests the need for the interest analysis developed in Section III below. Education may or may not be an effective means of empowerment or social control of debtors, but it more obviously serves the self-interested purposes of administrators to expand and justify their roles, of creditors to create hurdles in the way of discharge, and even of debtors to explain themselves in socially acceptable ways. The perspective of interest analysis may supplement rather than necessarily displace empowerment and social control theories, depending on what empirical study eventually reveals about the effects of education. Finally, Section IV suggests that interest analysis helps to explain aspects of consumer insolvency systems in other countries as well.

II. A FOCUS ON EXISTING PROGRAMMES IN THE US

Before exploring theoretical perspectives on debtor education, it may be helpful to have in mind some concrete examples. This section summarises findings in my study concerning some of the existing programmes in the US.

A. Mandatory Chapter 13 Programmes

Three long-standing programmes in the American South. Although US bankruptcy law currently does not explicitly provide for debtor education,[19] some Chapter 13 trustees have required classes for many years and other trustees have added programmes more recently.[20] The focus of my study was on the three trusteeships, all in the American South, that have mandatory debtor education programmes dating back to the 1970s. As a result of cooperation over some years, these three programmes have many similarities. Located in Greensboro, North Carolina, and Forth Worth and San Antonio, Texas, these programmes have a distinct cultural style that includes motivational fervour and belief in personal renewal through the acknowledgement of error or weakness and rededication to straightforward tenets of right and wrong. For example, the San

[18] The proposed legislation provided for a limited study of education only after implementation, apparently using debtor satisfaction surveys. See HR 333, above n 12, ss 105–6.

[19] See 11 USC § 1302(b)(4)(1994) (providing that trustees in Chapter 13 'shall . . . advise, other than on legal matters, and assist the debtor in performance under the plan.') This general language can be used as authority for debtor education, but the National Bankruptcy Review Commission noted that the authority of Chapter 13 trustees to use funds for education has been challenged. See *NBRC Report*, above n 3, at 115.

[20] The three longstanding mandatory programmes formed the Trustees Education Network, Inc (TEN), a non-profit-making organisation that has helped other trustees start programmes. The mandatory nature of the programmes has been achieved by means of judicial support and acquiescence of the debtor bar. See 'Empirical Study of Debtor Education', above n 4, at 580–81.

Antonio trustee has explained his philosophy as, 'There's right and wrong—you owe it, you should pay it.'[21] A motivational video used in these programmes states, 'Yesterday ended last night. Today is the first day of the rest of your life.'[22] These educational programmes thus adopt a secular self-improvement ethos that mimics religious evangelism. The style is used without any explicit religious references or content. Central bankruptcy officials from the Executive Office of the US Trustees in the Department of Justice in Washington, DC who have observed these programmes have raised the question whether this cultural style would work in northern or western settings.[23]

Quantitative finding: Impact on Chapter 13 completion not shown. My study, conducted in 1999–2000,[24] had both quantitative and qualitative features. In the quantitative part, I gathered information from Chapter 13 accounting records on completion of plans in the three longstanding programmes and compared them to completion rates in two Chapter 13 trusteeships (in Charlotte, North Carolina, and Sacramento, California) that did not provide education. The study found that a majority of debtors in both groups did not complete their plans, findings that are generally consistent with earlier research showing high failure rates for Chapter 13 plans.[25] The completion rate for the debtors who received education was 41.9 per cent, while for those who did not receive education it was 29.6 per cent.[26] Some of the reasons for studying completion rates were that the trusteeships with education programmes had explicitly set increasing completion as a goal and that completion of a plan is an objective, behavioural measure of the impact of education.

Although the debtors in trusteeships that provided education completed their plans at a higher rate than those who were not in such programmes, it was not possible to conclude that debtor education contributes to plan completion.[27] Chapter 13 trustees have adopted other local practices that may contribute more to plan completion than education. The trusteeships with education programmes have hands-on trustees who are committed to making Chapter 13 work and who have experimented in a search for the best practices to maximise plan success. For example, one strategy some of these trustees have adopted is using wage orders, requiring debtors to have their plan payments made directly to the trustee by their employers. Where wage orders are not used, debtors must remember to write a monthly check and send it to the trustee. Wage orders seem to be a key way to improve completion rates.

[21] See 'Lawyers and Consumer Bankruptcy', above n 5, at 557.

[22] See *Goal Setting by Zig Ziglar* (Video produced by VISA, USA, as part of its 'Personal Financial Choices' curriculum).

[23] I heard this point made in interviews I conducted in Washington, DC, in June 1999.

[24] 'Empirical Study of Debtor Education', above n 4, at 568, 580–86.

[25] *Ibid* at 557. See also Whitford, above n 6.

[26] 'Empirical Study of Debtor Education', above n 4, at 557, 568–72 (reporting completion rates for cases filed in 1994).

[27] *Ibid* at 557–58, 572–79.

Interestingly, the trusteeship in the study with the highest completion rate (54.9 per cent), in Charlotte, North Carolina, did not offer education, demonstrating that it is not crucial to a relatively high rate of plan success.[28] This trusteeship did, however, adopt the practice of requiring wage orders once debtors default on making payments themselves. It also set a relatively low fee for attorneys that it would routinely approve, and it delayed full payment of attorneys until three years into the plan. These practices reduced the incentive of attorneys to steer clients into unsustainable Chapter 13 plans to get higher fees. In short, it appears that this trusteeship hit upon a relatively successful formula in the combination of administrative practices adopted.

Because of the nature of the accounting records used as a source of data, my study did not include demographic information on individual debtors or information about the problems that drove them into bankruptcy.[29] It is also possible that the debtors in some districts were more likely to succeed with or without education. Moreover, my study could not answer the important question whether education benefits some sorts of debtors more than others.

Qualitative investigation: Trustees' strong commitment to education. The qualitative part of the study involved interviewing Chapter 13 trustees and staff about the methods, content and goals of debtor education classes in four programmes, the three studied quantitatively plus the programme in Columbus, Ohio.[30] I also observed classes in three cities, San Antonio, Fort Worth and Columbus. The Columbus trusteeship was not included in the quantitative part of the study because, among other reasons, it did not use the same computer accounting system, the source of the completion data. Also, the Columbus programme differs from the other three in that it is not mandatory and it is offered near the end of debtors' plans, rather than at the beginning. It is described separately below.

The Chapter 13 trustees in the three locations with mandatory education all have had classes since the 1970s and all have a strong commitment to education. They have started and continued programmes without a legal mandate and in the face of resistance by supervisory officials who must approve education budgets (resistance that has turned to support as Congress has considered making debtor education mandatory). In candid moments, several of these trustees and their staff members said they were committed to education even if no systematic behavioural benefit could be proved. They believe that reaching even a small number of people is worth the expense and effort.

Class evaluations. All of the programmes have asked the debtor-students to fill out evaluation forms at the end of classes, and all report that they get very good evaluations on these forms.[31] The survey forms record the debtors'

[28] *Ibid* at 558–59, 576.

[29] See *ibid* at 590–91 and n 215 (concerning limits of data set, in particular that the accounting records used lacked demographic information).

[30] *Ibid* at 580–90 for a description of programmes based on qualitative research involving interviews of trustees and their staff and visiting classes.

[31] *Ibid* at 585–86.

immediate subjective responses to the classes. They are not designed to determine attitude changes, let alone impact on later behaviour. The day that I visited the class in San Antonio, for example, the survey forms submitted by debtors rated the class as follows: great—12; good—9, ok—4, not ok—0. Several persons did not fill out the survey. One debtor who rated the programme 'great' also wrote, 'I've never looked on how to manage money and budget until your lesson today.' This is the kind of comment that heartens the instructors. A debtor who rated the class merely 'ok,' said, 'I was already aware of most of the stuff that was covered. My financial problems arose because of an ex-husband that refused to spend wisely.' The staff who run the programmes are very proud of their high evaluations from debtors and have responded as much as possible to criticism and suggestions.

Objectives and content. The objectives and content of the mandatory programmes studied are very similar as a result of their collaborative efforts in developing these programmes over the years.[32] Trustees and staff in these programmes all stated that the classes have two sets of related objectives: promoting plan completion and teaching the basics of personal financial management. With the first objective in mind, the trustees and their staff articulate a desire to set up good relations with debtors so as to motivate them to stay in Chapter 13. They treat debtors with respect and sympathy and avoid shaming and blaming. They seek to communicate that they care about the debtors. Instructors speak in the first person plural and use stories from their own lives about spending issues to develop rapport. One administrator explained that debtors 'feel encouraged instead of humiliated.'[33] Trustees and staff congratulate debtors on taking responsibility by filing in Chapter 13.[34]

In addition to spending time trying to motivate debtors to complete their plans, instructors stress the mechanics of doing so. They review the process of Chapter 13 and tell debtors that they need to keep making plan payments. In some of the programmes, a third or more of the time is spent on education to complete Chapter 13 rather than on long-term financial management.

Instructors also talk about how debts listed in bankruptcy schedules are likely to be handled by credit reporting agencies and how to correct erroneous credit reports. One could criticise this discussion as misleading, in that the suggestion is that filing in Chapter 13 will help to re-establish credit worthiness. In fact, creditors are sometimes quicker to offer new credit to Chapter 7 debtors because they get a quick discharge, making them able to handle at least some new credit, and because they cannot get another Chapter 7 discharge for six years.[35] Credit

[32] 'Empirical Study of Debtor Education', above n 4, at 580.

[33] *Ibid* at 586, n 177

[34] *Ibid* at 585, n 169 (concerning a VISA, USA-produced video used in the programmes, in which the announcer states, 'The trustee personally commends you for choosing chapter 13.')

[35] 11 USC §727(a)(8). See *NBRC Report*, above n 3, at 94 about the availability of new credit shortly after discharge in bankruptcy. Chapter 13 debtors typically only get a discharge after completing a three-to-five-year plan.

re-establishment is treated as an important goal and future credit use as inevitable.[36]

The teaching of financial management includes these elements: the technique of tracking and trimming expenses to stay within one's means, awareness—as a buffer against improvident spending—both of sales techniques and of how one uses money to meet emotional needs, the importance of regular savings to provide for unexpected expenses and to achieve goals, and the value of having financial goals as a motivator to stay within one's budget and to save. The financial management part of the classes ranges in length from one to two hours, typically about half of the class time or a little less. Instructors stress that you should 'pay yourself first,' setting aside something for savings from every paycheck. They discuss the difference between needs and wants and how misuse of money can come from using it to show love, anger, power or to cheer one's self up. There is some discussion of how, unless we consciously resist, advertising and sales techniques induce us to buy things we do not need and cannot afford.

The motivational parts of the programmes focus on lining up one's spending with one's values. Although there is an implicit mild critique of prevalent norms and behaviours in this part of the course, the instructors do not heavily stress reducing consumption. An interesting contrast is the video 'Affluenza,' a programme first broadcast by the Public Broadcasting Service in 1998, which makes a strong pitch for reducing consumption and adopts a critical stance toward the values reflected in advertising.[37]

Single session of two to four hours. The programmes in Greensboro, San Antonio and Fort Worth range from two to four hours on a single day.[38] This is probably too short a time to have a good chance of significant behavioural effect, something that the trustees are aware of. Although longer, multiple-class programmes were used some years ago,[39] they have been cut back to the current length as a compromise, to minimise costs and maintain US trustee support.

Optional additional sessions not well attended. Additional optional classes and one-on-one sessions are offered, but only a small percentage of debtors make use of these opportunities.[40] Debtors may be too busy, stressed, or disorganised to do so, but the low voluntary response may also suggest that debtors

[36] See Personal Financial Choices—Setting a New Course, Lesson Six, 6–1 to 6–23 (treatment of 'your credit future' in student workbook used in course and paid for by VISA, USA). In Greensboro, one of the two hours of class is spent on credit re-establishment.

[37] See *Affluenza Video Website* <http://www.pbs.org/kcts/affluenza/show/about.html> (visited: 29 January 2003). The website states, 'Last year, Americans, who make up only five percent of the world's population, used nearly a third of its resources and produced almost half of its hazardous waste. Add overwork, personal stress, the erosion of family and community, skyrocketing debt, and the growing gap between rich and poor, and it's easy to understand why some people say that the American Dream is no bargain. Many are opting out of the consumer chase, redefining the Dream, and making 'voluntary simplicity' one of the top 10 trends of the '90s.' See J De Graaf *et al*, *Affluenza: The All-Consuming Epidemic* (Berrett-Koehler, 2001).

[38] See 'Empirical Study of Debtor Education', above n 4, at 581–82.

[39] *Ibid* at 581 (Fort Worth at one point had a five day programme, with two days mandatory).

[40] *Ibid* at 581 and n 129. For example, Forth Worth optional budgeting class is used by only about 5% of debtors.

do not see education as highly valuable.[41] Even after they go to a mandatory class, have a positive, non-humiliating experience and typically give good to excellent ratings to the class, debtors do not make use of additional voluntary classes at a high rate.

Timing issues. In addition to shortening the programmes to one mandatory class, another compromise made in two of the three trusteeships is conducting the classes on the day that debtors are examined by the trustee about their schedules of debts and expenses and their repayment plans.[42] Although it is convenient for debtors to have the class and the examination on the same day, instructors recognise that the stress of reporting for the examination may interfere with concentration on learning financial management skills.

Another notable aspect of the timing of the classes is that they occur after the debtor has filed and proposed a plan. This means that education comes too late to play a role in chapter choice, or even to help the debtor see the importance of a realistic budget as the basis for a successful Chapter 13 plan. Unfortunately, many debtors commit in their Chapter 13 plans to repay more than they can realistically afford. In theory, debtors might file a modified plan after attending a financial management class, but the classes make no mention of this possibility. Thus, as a result of poor counselling by their lawyers before filing, many debtors are set up for failure. Education is not designed to change this dynamic. The proposed US legislation would require credit counselling before bankruptcy (seemingly to try to deter filing by promotion of non-bankruptcy debt repayment plans) and education after filing,[43] continuing the unfortunate order under current US practices.

Conflict of interest. Education in many settings can involve some conflict of interest for educators, who attempt to socialise students to their goals rather than serving the purely self-defined goals of students. But the conflict seems particularly stark when Chapter 13 trustees provide education to debtors. Trustees are fiduciaries for creditors, with a legal obligation to maximise returns to them, something the trustees and their instructors do not tell debtors in their classes. Although classes give an overview of the law and administration of Chapter 13, they do not—and arguably could not if they were to be consistent with their fiduciary obligations—tell debtors about available legal options that would not be in the interests of the creditors. For example, they do not tell debtors that they might be able to convert to Chapter 7 and get a quick discharge or that they might be able to modify their plans if they have not budgeted all necessary expenses.[44]

[41] See also Block-Lieb, above n 15, at 517–18 concerning the difficulty of getting debtors to attend optional pilot programme.

[42] See 'Empirical Study of Debtor Education', above n 4, at 581–83.

[43] See HR 333, above n 12.

[44] 11 USC § 1307(a) (right of debtor to convert at any time) and s 1329(a) (right to modify plan, including to reduce payments or extend time for them). Trustees cannot provide legal advice to debtors, 11 USC § 1302(b)(4), but they are not prohibited from giving general legal information, something they in fact do when describing the Chapter 13 process.

A similar conflict between allegiance to creditors and debtors is present in the pre-bankruptcy consumer credit counselling that is provided to debtors by agencies that get their funding from creditors. Credit counsellors generally do not mention bankruptcy as an option, or if they do, they may give misinformation to fend off resort to it.[45] Still, credit counsellors as well as Chapter 13 trustees and their staff have a commitment to helping debtors and tend to reconcile conflicts in allegiance in their own minds by believing that it is good for debtors to take responsibility for debts and to learn to deal with the consequences of over-extension as a motivation to avoid it. In short, they elevate the importance of 'credit morality'[46] over the economic benefits of a fresh start and do not empower debtors by giving them full information to make their own choices.

Future use of credit treated as inevitable and unproblematic. There is also a conflict between the allegiance of trustees to creditors and the interests of debtor-students when providing education about future credit use. Although trustees and their instructors tell debtors to use credit responsibly, there is no particular emphasis on reducing credit consumption and avoiding high-interest credit for expenditures that have no durable value. Again, the conflict in the allegiance to both creditors and debtors is avoided by a reconciling perspective; namely, since debtors are going to use credit, they should be told to do so responsibly.

The mandatory programmes do not make a big point about the high cost of credit that debtors are likely to be offered after bankruptcy or the high cost of financing current consumption and the possibility of limiting credit use to homes and cars where secured credit can be obtained and rates will likely be lower. The workbook that the programmes used was consistent with what I observed, which is that future use of credit is treated as inevitable and largely unproblematic. A chapter on 'wise use of credit' states, 'chances are you'll probably need some type of loan in the future.'[47] The workbook, whose original production was funded by VISA, USA, also states, 'Credit is using tomorrow's money to pay for something we get today. Not a bad thing—unless you do not use credit properly. Without credit many of the things we need would be unaffordable to many of us.' Although the workbook advises debtors to pay off as much as possible each month on credit cards and notes that it is cheaper to save

[45] See HB Hoffman, 'Consumer Bankruptcy Filers and Pre-petition Consumer Credit Counseling: Is Congress Trying to Place the Fox in Charge of the Henhouse' (1999) 54 *Business Law* 1629 at 1632. Ordinarily non-profit-making consumer credit counselling agencies get the bulk of their funding from percentage contributions from creditors. See also Lander, above n 7, at 176–77, noting different practices of agencies, with some making bankruptcy referrals and others never doing so. Misrepresentations or failures to disclose important information might be unfair and deceptive practices under state and federal law.

[46] This phrase has been used by creditors at least since the mid–1970s. See DA Skeel Jr, *Debt's Dominion: A History of Bankruptcy Law in America* (Princeton, NJ, Princeton University Press, 2001) at 191 and n 5, which discusses the use of the phrase 'credit morality' by the credit industry during the 1975–6 congressional hearings on bankruptcy reform.

[47] See *Personal Financial Choices—Setting a New Course* at 7–5 (materials used in course and paid for by VISA, USA).

for an item first than to buy it on credit, these possibilities could easily fail to sink in when the main focus is on the bland promotion of vaguely-defined 'wise use.'

Little critical perspective. Classes, as opposed to one-on-one counselling, might seem in theory to offer more potential for having debtors come to see their problems as social and structural and to develop a critique of existing social norms.[48] Increased marketing and use of consumer credit in the face of financial insecurity due to divorce, illness, or unemployment, combined with incomplete social safety nets, inevitably lead to more over-indebtedness and thus the need for bankruptcy.[49] But the classes do not invite this sort of thinking. Although debtors are told that they are in the same boat as a lot of other people,[50] the suggestion is that we all face difficulties avoiding over-indebtedness rather than that there is a possibility of social change. A one-shot class provides little opportunity for informal interaction among debtors that might encourage a social, critical or political perspective on over-indebtedness. Although instructors invite questions and comments from the debtor-students, most stay silent. In addition, the explicit messages are about taking individual responsibility, not possible systemic responses to widespread over-indebtedness. Even unconventional individual responses, such as dramatically decreasing future consumption and use of credit, are not presented.

B. Optional Chapter 13 Programme

Four sessions, later timing. The optional Chapter 13 programme in Columbus, Ohio, provides some interesting contrasts to the mandatory programmes just described. Although only a small percentage of debtors take the course, those who do get a much more elaborate programme, given in four two-hour sessions, spread out once a month over a period of four months.[51] Rather than soon after filing, as in the mandatory programmes, classes are offered to debtors when they are two years from the end of their Chapter 13 plans. Because plans are typically three to five years, this means one to three years after filing.

Assignments and feedback. The topics covered in Columbus, similar to those in the mandatory programmes, are the Chapter 13 process, setting goals and priorities, credit reports and rebuilding credit reputation, budgeting, saving,

[48] See 'Counseling', above n 8, at 539, noting that certain empowerment views of counselling, such as those associated with feminists and minority groups, treat critical perspective as one function of counselling.

[49] See 'Means Testing', above n 12, at 428–30 concerning the deregulation of credit and the expanded supply as creating a need to change demand if over-indebtedness is to be addressed. See also 'Counseling', above n 8, at 540 noting the tendency of counselling not to raise questions about the status quo and to individualise problems rather than raise systemic issues.

[50] See 'Empirical Study of Debtor Education', above n 4, at 585 and n 164 (concerning the opening comments of a San Antonio trustee at a class: 'You are not alone. Millions of people have gone through this.')

[51] *Ibid* at 586–87.

being a smart shopper and wise use of credit. Because there is more time, however, there is more detail given and there are more handouts, exercises, and outside speakers (such as consumer education officials and university extension teachers). Debtors are given assignments between classes and opportunities for feedback from the instructor. Debtors are asked to keep track of their expenses for a month and to bring back the results with a proposed budget. The instructor gives comments to debtors who hand in their budgets, such as ways to trim, and debtors then have an opportunity to revise their budgets. The programme builds to a final session at which creditors talk about how debtors can get credit again and use it wisely.

Goal of credit re-establishment. The primary goal of the programme is credit re-establishment, that is, teaching personal financial management to prepare debtors to be eligible for high-quality credit and its wise use. Those who complete the course get a participant form to take to a meeting with a creditor when applying for a loan. The programme is a reward to successful debtors (most plans do not last long enough for debtors to be eligible for the programme) and gives lawyers something positive to tell clients about the benefits of Chapter 13—that debtors will have an opportunity to learn to rebuild their credit.[52]

Conflict of interest might be a concern about this programme because of its open promotion of using credit again. On the other hand, the Columbus instructor more explicitly distinguishes between types of credit than the instructors in the mandatory programmes. The instructor excludes subprime lenders from the final session, and she urges debtors not to carry a balance on their credit cards or, if they do, to have a written plan as to how to pay them off. Also, goals other than credit re-establishment are discussed, such as retirement planning and saving for children's college education. The advantages of reduced and delayed consumption to long-term financial health seem to be more effectively communicated with the hands-on approach and explicit discussion. Thus, the impact of conflict of interest seems no greater and perhaps less than in the mandatory programmes.

C. Programmes for Chapter 7 Debtors

Lack of administrative infrastructure. Most debtor education in the US has been for Chapter 13 debtors, due in part to the way in which Chapter 7 is administered. Chapter 13 trustees are standing trustees, typically with many employees, who oversee all the cases in an area and are paid up to 10 per cent of distributions to creditors.[53] Chapter 7 trustees are drawn from a panel of trustees, and each one only gets a portion of the cases in a given area. Panel trustees typically

[52] See 'Lawyers and Consumer Bankruptcy', above n 5, at 539.

[53] 28 USC s 586(e) (capping fees at 10% of disbursements). Most trustees charge smaller percentages because they can cover all their expenses with less. See 'Empirical Study of Debtor Education', above n 4, at 588 and n 193.

make $60 per case and only get percentage fees in the small number of cases, mostly not consumer cases, where there are assets to distribute.[54] Thus, Chapter 7 trustees lack the resources to provide classes.

Chapter 13 trustees, as fiduciaries for creditors in cases under their supervision, cannot appropriately finance education for Chapter 7 debtors. Furthermore, the Chapter 13 trustees who currently run most education programmes do not think Chapter 7 debtors should be in the same classes with those in Chapter 13.[55] They do not want Chapter 13 debtors, who are typically undertaking long repayment plans, sitting next to Chapter 7 debtors getting a quick fresh start. A temporary pilot project in the Eastern District of New York, not run by bankruptcy officials, is putting Chapter 7 and Chapter 13 debtors together.[56]

Simple, low-cost programme without instructors. A simple programme in Nashville, Tennessee, involves showing Chapter 7 debtors two 20-minute videos, one on the Chapter 7 process and the other on money management, on the day that the debtors report for examination by a panel trustee.[57] There is no instructor, but debtors are given workbooks, which they can take home. The videos and workbooks have been donated by VISA, USA. A panel trustee who helped set up the programme reported that survey responses for participating debtors have been highly positive. He said that a class with instructors, as in the mandatory Chapter 13 programmes, could be given to Chapter 7 debtors if each one paid $20 to attend. This may be what happens if Congress makes debtor education mandatory. Another possibility is telephone or Internet-based programmes, which might be offered commercially[58] or for free—for example, by university extension services.

Arguably greater need. Chapter 7 debtors arguably have a greater need for education than Chapter 13 debtors because they can get in debt trouble again almost immediately by accepting the high-cost credit they are likely to be offered shortly after discharge.[59] At a minimum, some warnings might therefore be in order. However, if education is provided either by trustees or credit-financed entities, instructors are unlikely to give warnings that creditors would not approve.

[54] 11 USC s 330(b) ($60 trustee fee in no asset Chapter 7 case). See *NBRC Report*, above n 3, at 137 (about 95% of Chapter 7 cases are no asset, and most of the 5% with assets are business liquidations).

[55] See 'Empirical Study of Debtor Education', above n 4, at 589.

[56] See Block-Lieb, above n 15, at 511; Gross, above n 15.

[57] See 'Empirical Study of Debtor Education', above n 4, at 588–90.

[58] See Block-Lieb, above n 15, at 518–19, concerning the risk that commercial providers would engage in predatory practices.

[59] See *NBRC Report*, above n 3, at 94.

III. THEORETICAL PERSPECTIVES

After discussing empowerment and social control perspectives on debtor education in bankruptcy, this section will introduce a third perspective: interest analysis. This perspective contributes insights concerning the ways in which debtor education serves the needs of bankruptcy administrators and policy-makers to defend a flawed bankruptcy system, while also serving the interests of creditors and, to some extent, debtors.

A. Empowerment

Empowerment generally refers to giving individuals tools for self-actualisation in order to realise their full potential and experience a greater sense of personal freedom.[60] The empowerment perspective typically applied to debtor education is that it will enable debtors to function more effectively in the credit economy and to manage their finances. At its most bland and non-threatening, this perspective simply maintains that by learning new financial management skills, debtors will have new capacity to handle their finances successfully. A stronger, more challenging version of empowerment could involve letting debtors fully explore critiques of existing norms concerning consumption and the use of credit.[61] The programmes I have studied mainly embrace the bland version of empowerment. To a limited extent, these programmes suggest a critique of consumer culture, but they avoid an examination of alternative lifestyles that involve dramatic reductions in consumption, and they certainly do not raise issues about the need for systemic change.[62]

A challenge to the empowerment perspective on debtor education is that there is little evidence that lack of financial management skill is what differentiates persons who file in bankruptcy from those who do not. Most Americans probably either do not know or do not use financial management techniques.[63] We do know that debtors in bankruptcy have lower incomes and more debt than the

[60] See 'Counseling', above n 8, at 539. See also Block-Lieb, above n 15, at 504, 509 in reference to setting the goal of education as debtor empowerment to function more effectively in the credit economy.

[61] See 'Counseling', above n 8, at 539 concerning feminist and minority views of counselling as a means to develop a critique of existing social norms.

[62] See n 48–50 and accompanying text. See also Block-Lieb, above n 15, at 510, stating that 'debtor education should also seek to alter debtor attitudes and behavior with respect to money choices'—a goal that seems to go beyond empowerment to at least mild social control.

[63] See, eg *Jumpstart Coalition for Personal Financial Literacy* <www.jumpstart.org> (visited: 29 January 2003). The mission statement of Jumpstart Coalition emphasises the need for financial education programmes for children and young adults. See also LA Vitt *et al*, 'Personal Finance and the Rush to Competence: Financial Literacy Education in the US' (2000), a national US field study commissioned and supported by the Fannie Mae Foundation and conducted by the Institute for Socio-Financial Studies, describing the recent growth of programmes in response to perceived obvious need for greater financial know-how.

rest of the population.[64] It may be that having low income itself contributes more to debt problems and bankruptcy than any deficiencies in financial management skills. Those with higher incomes can more easily cover regular expenses without incurring debt and should also find it easier to save. They may never use budgeting, tracking, and trimming, long-term goal-setting or other techniques recommended in financial management courses, and yet avoid debt problems. In short, training to improve employment opportunities and thus raise incomes might be a more effective way to reduce debt problems than teaching financial management techniques.[65] Higher income employment also would be more broadly empowering than debtor education, by providing more resources with which to pursue personal goals.

On the other hand, raising incomes may be an unrealistic objective. If their incomes are not going to rise, lower-income persons probably need greater financial management skills than higher-income persons. Empirical research suggests that illness, job disruptions and family break-up are frequently precipitating causes of bankruptcy, when combined with carrying a high debt load in relation to income.[66] To reduce bankruptcy filings and other debt problems, education programmes could be designed to convince fewer persons to carry high debt loads and to save as a cushion against income or expense shocks.[67] However, whether the goal is bankruptcy prevention, long-term financial security, or both, education would be more effective if directed to the whole risk pool (all low-income debtors), not just those for whom the risk materialises, leading to default and bankruptcy.

In short, why empower those in bankruptcy but not those at relatively high risk of bankruptcy? One answer that has been given is that bankruptcy is a 'unique opportunity for education.'[68] Mistakes are of course opportunities to learn, but education also could be used to avoid and thus reduce mistakes. For example, the time of credit application is a potential teachable moment—that is the premise of homebuyer education.[69] Alternatively, mandatory education might be better directed to secondary school students, where required programmes could be justified as part of what young people should learn before becoming independent adults. There is a broader financial literacy movement in

[64] See TA Sullivan *et al*, *The Fragile Middle Class: Americans in Debt* (New Haven, CT, Yale University Press, 2000) at 61–63, 70–72.

[65] See 'Counseling', above n 8, at 533, 540–41; AM Dickerson, 'Can Shame, Guilt, or Stigma Be Taught? Why Credit-Focused Debtor Education May Not Work' 32 *Loyola of Los Angeles Law Review* 945 at 948 (noting the lack of marketable job skills as contributing to debt problems).

[66] See Sullivan, above n 64, at 428.

[67] See D Ellis, 'The Effect of Consumer Interest Rate Deregulation on Credit Card Volumes, Charge-Offs, and the Personal Bankruptcy Rate, FDIC: Bank Trends' (1998) <http://www/fdic/gov/bank/analytical/bank/bt_9805.html>, noting the greater propensity of lower income persons to borrow for current consumption, even at high interest rates.

[68] See *NBRC Report*, above n 3, at 114 (reporting this view). See also Block-Lieb, above n 15, at 508.

[69] See EC Yen, 'Current Truth In Lending Issues' (1998) 52 *Consumer Finance Law Quarterly* 25 at 27, discussing the role of homebuyer education and counselling in helping buyers to qualify for high quality mortgage credit and avoid over-indebtedness.

the United States,[70] raising the question whether education early in life or at least before persons take on debt would be a better priority than expanding debtor education in bankruptcy.

B. Social Control

The phrase 'social control' has many connotations, from the inevitably socially-defined nature of the self to the labelling of deviants.[71] The Canadian programme of counselling has been criticised as using a deviance model (because its counselling training materials suggest, without good evidence, that debtors are compulsive and impulsive and thus likely to have substance abuse and family problems along with debt problems).[72] I have not seen anything so loaded in the assumptions behind the US debtor education programmes in Fort Worth, San Antonio, Greensboro and Columbus. The judgements about debtors implicit in the US programmes, that debtors are unskilled in financial management and lacking in self-awareness and self-control, are softened by suggestions that most people have these problems, so that debtors are treated not as deviants but as typical consumers.[73] Thus the degree of social control is not much more pronounced than that behind a great deal of consumer protection regulation, which assumes bounded rationality and will-power on the part of consumers as well as lack of information.

The implicit labelling in US programmes, treating debtors as needing to learn more self-awareness and self-control, can be found in a curriculum that not only teaches budgeting techniques, but also assumes that debtors need to think more about their goals, to use long-term goals to motivate them in the short-term, to be more attuned to the ways in which they use money for emotional reasons, such as to show love, anger or power, and to examine how advertising manipulates them.[74] Teaching techniques of personal financial management is consistent with an empowerment theory of debtor education, but all of the long-standing programmes also have objectives that go beyond providing new skills, to promoting examination of values and changing attitudes. Furthermore, values are treated as subject to rethinking. In short, there is a mild social control purpose that goes hand in hand with empowerment.

[70] Above n 63.

[71] See Sutton, above n 2, at 943–44. Sutton notes, *ibid* at 944, 948–50, that a radical version of the social control thesis can involve an over-simplified portrayal of reformers and policy-makers as 'stooges of a backstage elite,' resulting in a failure to examine why agencies depart from instrumental rationality and adopt practices that are not demonstrably effective.

[72] See Curnock, above n 1, at 392–97.

[73] See I Ramsay, 'Models of Consumer Bankruptcy: Implications for Research and Policy' 20 *Journal of Consumer Policy* 269 at 274–78, concerning the three models of consumer bankruptcy: consumer protection, control of deviant behaviour, or social welfare.

[74] See above text after n 36.

When programmes are mandatory, it is particularly hard to understand them as purely empowering. Even if the programmes only focused on skills such as budgeting, attempting to teach these skills to persons who would not choose to learn them, means that some goal other than self-actualisation is at work. The agenda is that people—at least people who have filed in bankruptcy—should be more careful in their consumption and their use of credit and should save more. This agenda reflects middle-class values of planning, prudence, accumulation and delayed gratification, taught to a lower-income population of adults, who may not be interested in changing their values.[75]

The aim is to change demand for credit by making debtors more prudent, on the assumption that the supply side will be left to do as it pleases. In the US, reimposition of usury or other restrictions on supply seem politically unlikely, but it remains to be seen whether changing demand is any more realistic. Demand for credit to finance current consumption is robust among low-income persons, and creditors often offer new loans to debtors shortly after discharge.[76] Debtor education programmes may serve only the rhetorical purpose of placing blame on debtors.

C. Interest Analysis

The origins of debtor education and counselling programmes in the US suggest a perspective that focuses on how these programmes serve the interests of various players in the institution of consumer bankruptcy, which has been undergoing a crisis of legitimacy.[77] The US bankruptcy system is under attack as permissive and incoherent.[78] Called upon to deal with growing caseloads of persons experiencing complex problems from ambiguous causes, it is not sur-

[75] See 'Counseling', above n 8, at 540, discussing the likelihood that middle class counsellors will convey their values as to what is acceptable behavior.

[76] See Ellis, above n 67, and *NBRC Report*, above n 3, at 94.

[77] The interest analysis perspective is derived from a school of social science thought known as 'institutionalism' or 'neo-institutionalism.' See *The New Institutionalism*, above n 2, at 11–15, 27, tracing the origins of neo-institutionalism to contemporary focus on scripts that institutional actors follow in a process of legitimation. See also two chapters in *The New Institutionalism*, *ibid.*; JW Meyer and B Rowan, 'Institutionalized Organizations: Formal Structure as Myth and Ceremony' 41 at 51–62 (concerning the importance of institutional myths to organisational legitimacy, success and survival, particularly when efficient performance cannot be demonstrated); and WW Powell, 'Expanding the Scope of Institutional Analysis' 183 at 190–92, 200 (concerning institutional responses to political upheaval and processes by which less-than-optimal arrangements are sustained). See also Sutton, above n 2, at 949–55.

[78] For the permissiveness critique, see *NBRC Report*, above n 3; *Four Dissenters' Recommendations*, n 3, at 2 (asserting a 'desperate need for changes in the Bankruptcy Code and its administration' due to 'growing perception that bankruptcy has become a first resort' implying 'that bankruptcy relief is too easy to obtain, that the moral stigma once attached to bankruptcy has eroded. . . .'). For the incoherence critique, see TA Sullivan *et al*, *As We Forgive Our Debtors: Bankruptcy and Consumer Credit in America* (New York, Oxford University Press, 1989) at 239–40, which notes that Chapter 13 debtors are not better off financially than Chapter 7 debtors, so that the two chapters are not doing a good job of sorting debtors according to who can or cannot repay.

prising that bankruptcy administrators have turned to education in their efforts to make sense of a troubled system. By emphasising a process (education) over any particular outcome, they make it hard to evaluate their work, a common institutional response to a difficult and not well thought out assignment. As will be discussed, education also has the benefit of serving certain aims and needs of creditors and debtors, making it a non-controversial way for bankruptcy administrators to expand their domain and gain legitimacy even if there is no measurable impact on debtor behaviour.

US debtor education in bankruptcy began by local initiative in Chapter 13 trusteeships, rather than by any change in national policy. The Chapter 13 trustees are well aware that the debtors in Chapter 13 are overwhelmingly below median income people with a huge amount of debt. Most of these debtors could get a quick discharge in Chapter 7, but instead have signed up—perhaps steered by their lawyers—for an often arduous three- to five-year repayment process. Because most do not complete their plans, they do not get a discharge unless they convert to Chapter 7 or file in Chapter 7 after Chapter 13 dismissal.[79] On a routine basis, Chapter 13 trustees and their staff see debtors who are suffering from the aftermath of various misfortunes, and their repayment plans often obviously stretch them to the limit, making success a long shot. When the inevitable defaults occur, the trustees are typically the ones who seek dismissal of these cases.

To come to terms with working in such a system, the Chapter 13 trustees who created the first education programmes wanted to increase plan completion. The high failure rates in Chapter 13 were and are a challenge to the idea that repayment is feasible, yet the trustees believe strongly in promoting credit morality. In addition to their commitment to making repayment work, the trustees also wanted to do something positive for debtors. These trustees believe that repayment in Chapter 13 is doing the right thing. Doing the right thing might be considered its own reward, but the system seems fairer if there is more concrete benefit. The trustees who started the programmes hoped that education would provide such a benefit by reducing the debtors' risk of future problems, better equipping them to manage their finances, and perhaps even helping them to save for long-term goals—a powerful myth-making package of aspirations.

The programmes did not win immediate acceptance in the sceptical central bankruptcy administrative agency, the Executive Office of the US Trustees. The right of Chapter 13 trustees to spend money on the programmes was challenged by local US trustees who were encouraged by Washington.[80] Creditors did not complain about the programmes, even though they were funded from debtor payments under Chapter 13 plans that would otherwise be distributed to creditors. Rather, the central agency's lack of support stemmed from doubts about a

[79] 11 USC s. 1328(a) (providing for discharge after completion of plan).

[80] See *NBRC Report*, above n 3, at 115, which discussing challenges to the authority of Chapter 13 trustees to spend money on education programmes.

social services approach to bankruptcy.[81] It saw bankruptcy in narrower terms, as a means of discharge in Chapter 7 or collection in Chapter 13. Education costs money to implement and oversee and there was no evidence of increased collections or long-term benefits to debtors from the mandatory education. While the Chapter 13 trustees with education programmes adopted the practice of having debtors fill out forms at the end of classes giving their subjective reactions ('great,' 'ok,' 'not ok'), these evaluations were more helpful in fending off challenges to the legitimacy of the new programmes than in demonstrating effectiveness.[82]

Lacking central administrative backing, local programmes found another source of support: the credit industry, through VISA, USA.[83] The support was not only political, but also financial. VISA invested substantial amounts in videos, workbooks and organisational development for a network of trustees who designed a model programme and promoted it to other trustees.

This was the state of affairs when the National Bankruptcy Review Commission began holding hearings in May of 1996. The thesis of the Commission's 1997 report was that increased supply and resulting use of credit, combined with underlying financial insecurity, caused the increase in bankruptcy over the previous 20 years.[84] The Commission did not recommend a structural change in US bankruptcy law, but instead favoured some modest reform to improve uniformity and fairness.[85] As a result, it proposed to leave in place a system that puts similarly situated debtors into very different bankruptcy options, either a discharge in Chapter 7 or a repayment plan in Chapter 13. Leaving Chapter 13 trustees to defend and make sense of a system lacking coherence, the Commission also gave them support for expanded education. But lacking evidence that bankruptcy is caused by financial mismanagement, the Commission favored voluntary rather than mandatory education.

The recommendations of the Commission were quickly upstaged by creditor supported and drafted legislation.[86] The industry legislation, as first introduced in 1997 and in each of its subsequent versions through 2003, would have required debtor education as a condition of discharge for all debtors. One effect of these bills, passed at various times by large margins in both the House and Senate, was to eliminate central bureaucratic opposition to education, and consequently more Chapter 13 trustees instituted programmes.[87]

[81] I have heard this scepticism expressed by officials in the Executive Office of the US Trustees.

[82] See Sutton, above n 2, at 950 (generally describing institutional avoidance of evaluation by efficiency criteria).

[83] See 'Empirical Study of Debtor Education', above n 4, at 580.

[84] See *NBRC Report*, above n 3, at 82–94.

[85] The Commission noted that it lacked a mandate for structural reforms from Congress, which created it. See *ibid* at iv.

[86] See E Warren, 'The Changing Politics of American Bankruptcy Reform' (1999) 37 *Osgoode Hall Law Journal* 189 at 192–93, describing the huge resources industry poured into backing the legislation and quoting report that bill was drafted by a law firm for the credit industry, Morrison & Forrester of San Francisco.

[87] See 'Empirical Study of Debtor Education', above n 4, at 560–61.

The credit industry's support for mandatory financial management education in bankruptcy, reflected first in VISA's backing and later in the bills it has supported, may seem surprising. Why would creditors want debtor education, particularly without demonstrable effect? First, it should be noted that mandatory education is only one of a long list of new requirements in the industry legislation, which also includes pre-bankruptcy credit counselling, submission of tax returns and preparation of means testing calculations.[88] These requirements would have the benefit, from a credit industry perspective, of making bankruptcy more burdensome and expensive to access. The industry package was designed to allow continued expansion of the volume of credit offered to high-risk debtors, while getting Congress to cut back on access to bankruptcy. This would leave more debtors without protection from collection efforts that would increase returns at the margin. Under the overall plan of the legislation, education that had no effect on behaviour would be ideal. A new hurdle to access to bankruptcy would be created, but one that did not stem the use of high risk credit.

Second, although making debtor education mandatory (and therefore suggesting a need for it) might seem inconsistent with the creditors' thesis that credit immorality caused the recent increase in bankruptcy, the professed aim of the legislation was to keep cheats out of the system so that those in the system could be treated as uneducated rather than bad. Making debtors go through credit counselling before bankruptcy and then take a class in financial management after filing would increase the cost in time and money of filing, thus keeping some debtors out and maintaining the focus on debtor responsibility for over-indebtedness.

One can see the focus on debtor responsibility for over-indebtedness in the response to complaints about expanded credit-card solicitations in 2002 even as bankruptcy filings increased. A spokesperson for the American Bankers Association made this comment, 'Part of the free market is the ability to say no.'[89] However, if debtor education in fact instilled understanding of the advantages of saying no to new and particularly high-cost credit, demand and profits might drop. Given the vigour with which US consumer creditors market new credit to even the most risky borrowers,[90] this was clearly not their goal. Education with no effect on demand would deliver the rhetorical advantage of emphasising debtor responsibility, but without an impact on the bottom line.

While it is easy to see education's advantages to local bankruptcy administrators and to the credit industry, perhaps more surprising is the popularity of mandatory education with debtors, something that has been observed both in

[88] See 'Means Testing', above n 12, at 433–44 (discussing the new burdens of the legislation).

[89] See C Weiser, 'Credit Card Solicitations Keep Coming Despite Debt' *Elmira, NY Star-Gazette* (16 August 2002) 11A. In addition to the quote in the text, the article reported a record volume of credit card solicitations even as bankruptcy filings reached record numbers.

[90] *Ibid*. See also *NBRC Report*, above n 3, at 91–94, concerning the marketing of credit to casino gamblers, to those in high-risk 'sub-prime' pools, to younger and poorer people and to those recently discharged in bankruptcy.

the US and Canada.[91] Why do debtors appreciate education and counselling, even when mandatory? First, it should be noted that the educators in the long-standing US programmes in Chapter 13 have an explicit purpose to establish good rapport with debtors and to motivate them to complete their plans. Debtors appreciate being treated with respect and being given a sense of positive purpose about reordering their financial lives. They also develop a sense that they have greater control over their finances, which makes them feel better. These reactions can be seen as part of a process of cultural accounting that all members of society go through and that is particularly important for those who are undergoing a stigmatising experience—they need to construct reputable self-images.[92] There is value in helping debtors in this way, but the goals of education go beyond short-term hope and good feelings. As yet, there is little evidence of success in improving the financial security of debtors in the long-term. What debtor education in bankruptcy most clearly achieves is a rhetorical function of stressing individual responsibility, while the credit industry continues to expand volume into riskier sectors.

IV. COMPARATIVE PERSPECTIVE AND CONCLUSION

The empowerment, social control and interest analysis perspectives are largely American in their origins, but perhaps they can be translated to other cultures and systems. Certainly the deviance version of social control is already in general currency. For example, the Canadian counselling requirement in bankruptcy has been criticised for treating debtors, without sound empirical research, as deviants in a 'bankruptcy cycle' involving multiple psycho-social problems.[93] Furthermore, this Canadian critique moved seemlessly into interest analysis:

> This [deviance] model was found acceptable, and counselling based on this concept was mandated, because doing so created an ideal situation in which the stakeholders in personal bankruptcy (a category which does not include bankrupt persons) could have their priorities met. There had been Canadian research allegedly proving the need for counselling since the early 1980s. The creditors wanted it. It would allow the Bankruptcy Branch to monitor more closely the way trustees conducted their business, while legitimising a fee increase for going bankrupt. It would create work, or at least a credentialling process, for trustees and credit counsellors. . . . Anyone suggesting it was automatically seen to be 'doing the right thing.' At a time . . . of horror stories

[91] See above n 34 and accompanying text. See also 'Counseling', above n 8, at 536–38 (concerning debtor enthusiasm for Canadian counselling and education).

[92] See Stokes and Polansky, above n 17, concerning the greater sense of control after debtor education. See also 'Counseling', above n 8, at 540–41, concerning the value of being able to tell one's story about a traumatic event.

[93] See Curnock, above n 1, at 398.

> about the escalating rates of bankruptcy, the opportunity to kill that many birds with one stone was too tantalizing to be missed.[94]

One might quibble with the tone of this analysis and also note that Canadian debtors have perhaps been treated as stakeholders in that they have been surveyed about the mandatory counselling provided there, giving it high ratings.[95] But for present purposes, what is striking about this analysis is that it is a clear example of an institutional perspective being used by a scholar in another country than the US.

An institutional interest perspective also seems to have been at work, without that label, in Johanna Niemi-Kiesilainen's analysis of Scandinanvian and continental European consumer debt adjustment proceedings[96] and their counselling components.[97] She describes the adoption of debt adjustment laws in Europe in response to a recession that followed the deregulation of credit and the resulting expansion of the consumer credit market in the 1980s. The institution challenged was the social welfare apparatus, because traditional unemployment benefits were not sufficient for people with excessive debt loads. In this context, as debt adjustment laws were implemented, it seemed obvious to restrict the remedy to persons hit by social risks similar to those for which the welfare state provides, such as unemployment, illness and disability. As Niemi-Kiesiläinen explained, 'Through counselling, the welfare state is given a chance to help.'[98] Europe adopted a social service approach to over-indebtedness and thus protected and extended its social welfare system.

Another important part of the European picture is a weaker commitment to shoring up a culture of consumer credit. Where North American education and counselling in bankruptcy seek to produce better consumers of credit, the European focus in debt adjustment proceedings is on learning to do without credit and to consume less, indeed to live at a subsistence level just to fulfill a plan.[99] Thus, counselling involves coming up with a repayment plan and learning to adjust lifestyle to a minimum social security income level.

Interestingly, while European policy-makers tend to accept the socio-legal analysis that in the US is associated with defending the fresh start, European debt adjustment laws adopt a solution more like that favoured by the credit industry in the US. Europeans see the paradigm case of personal bankruptcy as due to over-indebtedness stemming from causes largely beyond the control of the debtor, yet their new bankruptcy laws of the last 15 years have adopted repayment plans as the central feature, in order to reinforce 'payment morality'

[94] *Ibid* at 399.

[95] See 'Counseling', above n 8, at 536–39, also noting that the reasons for positive response should be further studied and discussing a study in Canada that did not find unambiguous indications of objective benefits from counselling.

[96] See 'Bankruptcy in Comparison', above n 14.

[97] See 'Consumer Counselling in Europe', above n 4, at 409.

[98] 'Bankruptcy in Comparison', above note 14, at 482.

[99] 'Consumer Counselling in Europe', above n 4, at 413.

as well as to provide financial rehabilitation. Immediate discharge is not a feature of these laws. Furthermore, even to qualify for a repayment plan, debtors have to pass through tests designed to ensure that mere imprudent recklessness is not the source of their problems. There is tension and paradox in first requiring that debtors should not have caused their own predicaments, but then requiring them to pay and undergo counselling. Perhaps the key to understanding the paradox is in the difference between the rhetoric of European systems and their results. Those denied access to a debt adjustment form of bankruptcy do not necessarily pay. And neither do those who are given access to the legal process, because if their plans are partial or fail, they do get a discharge after a delay.[100]

The gap between rhetoric and reality is familiar territory to Americans; repayment plans in Chapter 13 are often partial and usually fail, yet there is political support for promoting even more use of Chapter 13. It is unlikely that debtor education could prevent this course of action from resulting in yet more failed plans. With the perspective of interest analysis, one sees more clearly that wishful thinking, myth-making, and raw self-interest cloud the prospects for addressing effectively and realistically the problem of over-indebtedness.

[100] 'Bankruptcy in Comparison', above n 14, at 503.

17

Establishing Financial Literacy Programmes for Consumer Debtors: Complex Issues on the Platter

KAREN GROSS*

I. INTRODUCTION

THIS CHAPTER ADDRESSES a topic with which I have been deeply involved over the past several years: financial literacy education. Many of my specific observations grow out of a pilot project to provide financial literacy education to individuals who have accessed the US bankruptcy system. Through the auspices of a non-profit organisation called the Coalition for Consumer Bankruptcy Debtor Education (the 'Coalition'),[1] this pilot financial literacy project—which has been in place since 2001—has provided more than 90 debtor education classes. As of February 2003, approximately 500 consumers have received the Coalition's educational offering comprising a single three-hour session and 125 individuals have been trained by the Coalition as debtor educators. This chapter deals with two topics that surround and emerge from this 'in the trenches' experience: (1) an exploration of the theoretical underpinnings for providing financial literacy education to individuals within a formalised bankruptcy system, including an accompanying assessment of whether such offerings are replicable for other audiences such as consumers who are over-indebted but have not accessed an insolvency system; and (2) the programmatic issues surrounding the creation

* I am deeply indebted to the Coalition for Consumer Bankruptcy Debtor Education, on whose Board I serve and in respect of which I am President, and those who are working with me at the Coalition to improve the lives of debtors. Special thanks are extended to Professors Susan Block-Lieb and Richard Wiener, Olivia Mellan, a psychotherapist and money coach, and New York Law School students John Vavas and Charles Walsh.

[1] For more information about the Coalition, its activities, and its empirical studies, visit its website at <http://www.debtoreducation.org>. See also C Baron-Donovan, S Block-Lieb, K Gross, R Wiener and S Wright, 'The Coalition for Consumer Bankruptcy Debtor Education: An Overview of its Pilot Project' (2003) Proceedings of the National Conference of Bankruptcy Judges; S Block-Lieb, K Gross, and R Wiener, 'Lessons From the Trenches: Debtor Education in Theory and Practice' (2002) 7 *Fordham Journal of Corporate & Financial Law* 503 ['Lessons From the Trenches']; L Fickenscher, 'Bankruptcy Education Unites Warring Groups' *The American Banker* 11 <http://www.debtoreducation.org> (27 March 2000). The teaching portion of the pilot project terminated in April 2003.

and implementation of financial literacy courses, including an initial assessment of the political, social and psychological impediments to successful programme development. This chapter is thus relevant for those considering establishing financial literacy programmes in their jurisdictions, both by providing an initial road map that can be followed and by exploring the key challenges and pitfalls that accompany implementation.

The issues concerning implementation of financial literacy courses are of particular importance in the United States since, for several years, there has been federal legislation pending that would mandate post-filing financial management education for the more than 1.5 million individuals who access the bankruptcy system annually.[2] Under this proposed mandate, assuming the existence of available programmes, debtors would be denied a discharge in bankruptcy—the essential benefit derived from seeking bankruptcy relief—if they failed to obtain the requisite education. The proposed legislation indicates that the education can be provided in a variety of ways: one-on-one education, live classes, Internet programmes and telephone classes. The pending legislation also requires that individuals obtain 'counselling' before they access the bankruptcy system, a suggestion that then creates an additional hurdle to system entry.

Interestingly, while existing studies demonstrate that most Americans lack financial literacy skills[3] and that we, as a society, have a generalised notion that education is a good thing, debtor education has not been uncontroversial.[4] In the US, there have been limited forays into the field of debtor education apart from the efforts of the Coalition. Some Chapter 13 trustees in select regions of the country have been offering debtor education programmes, and they are seeking to expand these offerings under the rubric of an organisation called TEN (Trustee's Educational Network).[5] VISA has developed a post-filing education programme (including a recent web-based initiative) for Chapter 7 and

[2] See HR 975, § 105–06, 108th US Congress (2003). For a recent discussion of how the proposed US bankruptcy legislation addressing debtor education is problematic, see S Block-Lieb and K Gross, 'Debtor Education: Making Sure A Good Idea Does Not Go Awry' (2000) 1 *Norton Bankruptcy Law Adviser* 6; 'Lessons From the Trenches n 1 at 519–23. For a more general account of the proposed legislation, see MB Jacoby, 'Generosity versus Accessibility: Bankruptcy, Consumer Credit, and Health Care Finance in the US,' this volume.

[3] A recent study documented some disturbing results. Only 3% of adults in the US could effectively identify the differences between two consumer credit card documents and only 4% could figure out the cost of credit from the contracts and disclosure documents. See A White and C Mansfield, 'Literacy and Contract' (2002) 13 *Stanford Law and Policy Review* 233 at 237–38.

[4] See, eg A Dickerson, 'Can Shame, Guilt, or Stigma be Taught, Why Creditor-Focused Debtor Education May Not Work' (1999) 32 *Loyola Law Review* 945. Judge Edith Jones, who served on the National Bankruptcy Review Commission, was not a strong supporter of debtor education. See National Bankruptcy Review Commission, *Recommendations For Reform of Consumer Bankruptcy Law by Four Dissenting Commissioners* <http://govinfo.library.unt.edu./nbrc/report/24commvi06.html (last modified: 26 November 1997).

[5] Professor Jean Braucher has completed a study of selected operative Chapter 13 debtor education programmes with a grant from the American Bankruptcy Institute. See J Braucher, 'An Empirical Study of Debtor Education in Bankruptcy: Impact of Chapter 13 Completion Not Shown' (2001) 9 *American Bankruptcy Institute Law Review* 557. See also J Braucher, 'Debtor Education in Bankruptcy: Adding the Institutional Perspective', in this volume.

13 debtors, which it offers to any trustee interested in implementing the same. Sporadically, Chapter 7 trustees have provided financial management education to their debtors. By way of contrast, Canada has had a system of mandatory financial management education in place for several years.[6] Efforts to implement programmes need to be informed by that which has occurred elsewhere, particularly to the extent that these programmes have been assessed empirically.

II. THE THEORY OF DEBTOR EDUCATION: WHY HELP INDIVIDUAL DEBTORS?

Given the controversy surrounding debtor education and the proposed legislation in the US, it is critical to begin with a theoretical assessment of why providing financial literacy education to individuals within the bankruptcy system is a useful and meaningful effort. If we cannot justify the concept in general, then the efforts to implement programmes will be on a shaky foundation. Moreover, providing such education—even on a pro bono basis to debtors—is not cost-free.

Most people's initial reaction to debtor education concerns its timing rather than its efficacy: isn't post-bankruptcy education too little too late? Isn't the horse already out of the barn? Obviously, these aphorisms suggest that focusing attention on education of *bankrupt debtors* is misguided; we would be better off offering financial literacy education to people before, not after, they have to access the bankruptcy system. My answer to this concern is twofold. First, debtors in a formalised insolvency system are an identifiable subset of the financially troubled population that can benefit from financial literacy education; and second, these debtors need the education now.

Many people create a false dichotomy between pre- and post- bankruptcy education. My desire for post-filing bankruptcy education does not eliminate, nor is it inconsistent with, increased financial literacy training for everyone. There is plenty of room in this country (and elsewhere as well) for providing people with the increased financial literacy skills that are a necessity for successful functioning in our market-based world, particularly where the legal regime focuses on disclosure as the paradigm for consumer protection. In the US, we do a better job in our schools (albeit not a great job) of teaching about sex than we do about money. I am very much in favour of augmenting our knowledge of and teaching about money starting in elementary schools and working our way through high school, college and even into the work

[6] A fascinating study of the Canadian programme has been undertaken although the results are not, as yet, available. See I Ramsay, 'Mandatory Bankruptcy Counseling: The Canadian Experience' (2002) 7 *Fordham Journal of Corporate & Finance Law* 525. For an interesting and sharp critique of the Canadian programme and its philosophical underpinnings see, eg C Curnock, 'Insolvency Counselling—Innovation Based on the Fourteenth Century' (1999) 37 *Osgoode Hall Law Journal* 387.

environment.[7] Indeed, I have recently implemented, initially on a pilot basis, a financial advocacy course for law students, a group that emerge from their graduate education with sizable debt burdens but remarkably little financial sophistication. This particular programme, when assessed empirically, was an enormous success in terms of both knowledge acquisition by, and behavioral changes in, the enrolled law students.[8]

In fact, many of the educative materials employed in courses focused on individual debtors are transferable to other groups (with certain significant but not overwhelming additions and deletions).[9] Financial literacy education can be instituted in a number of non-bankruptcy settings. For example, immigrant groups (a sizable portion of whom are 'unbanked'[10]), the elderly, women in shelters and recipients of micro-loans are all candidates for programmes designed to provide improved financial literacy. Indeed, there is little in the content of the Coalition's programme that is unique to the 'bankrupt' debtor population and many people struggle with how to make ends meet.[11] However, the 'bankrupt' debtor population is an audience that can be easily identified, and it is an audience that has already chosen to address its financial dilemmas through the legal system, two factors that may facilitate implementation of programming.

Recent proposed US bankruptcy legislation[12] would mandate that no individual be permitted to seek bankruptcy relief without first obtaining financial counselling.[13] The target audience for this counselling/education would be self-identified prospective debtors. Quality financial counselling may benefit

7 See L Mandell, *Improving Financial Literacy, What Schools and Parents Can and Cannot Do* (Washington, Jump$tart Coalition for Personal Financial Literacy, 2001);. For information about financial education in the workplace, see W Wood and J Doyle, 'Economic Literacy Among Corporate Employees' (2002) *Journal of Economic Education* 195; T Garman *et al*, 'Workplace Financial Education Improves Personal Financial Wellness' (1999) 10 *Financial Counseling and Planning* 79. See also the following websites addressing this issue (visited: 15 October 2002): *Economic Education Web* <http://www.ecedweb.unomaha.edu, *Jump$tart Coalition for Personal Financial Literacy,* <http://www.jumpstartcoalition.org>, *National Council on Economic Education,* <http://www.economicsamerica.org>, *National Endowment for Financial Education,* <http://www.nefe.org>, *National Institute For Consumer Education,* <http://www.nice.emich.edu>.

8 Materials related to this programme, together with the empirical results therefrom, are available from the author.

9 See, 'Lessons From the Trenches', above n 1, at 523. In addition to teaching mothers, I also ran a parent-child workshop where we read children's books with money themes and did related group exercises.

10 Many immigrant communities in the US choose not to participate in our banking system, often sensing that it is either not friendly to consumers or untrustworthy, commonly based on experiences from their countries of origin.

11 See T Sullivan, E Warren and J Westbrook, *The Fragile Middle Class: Americans In Debt* (New Haven, CT, Yale University Press, 2000).

12 Above n 2.

13 There is a distinction between counselling and education, although some clear overlap exists. To simplify some of these distinctions for our purposes here, suffice it to say that counselling is frequently one-to-one and has something of a therapeutic orientation, while education is more group-oriented and substantive in focus.

individuals, but mandating counselling at the debtor's expense,[14] as a prerequisite to accessing the bankruptcy system, is problematic in that it creates an unnecessary bar to entry into the legal system.

In contrast to the legislation pending in the US, I much prefer a system that encourages all individual debtors who have made the choice to access the bankruptcy system to participate in a high-quality, low-cost course that augments financial literacy skills. One would hope that debtors have made that choice thoughtfully, although that may not always be the case. However, as I see it, debtor education is not meant to assist people in choosing whether or not to seek bankruptcy relief. Informing choice on that issue is best left to lawyers. Instead, debtor education is intended to provide prospective benefits by focusing on substantive skills training, among other topics.[15] Debtors as a group have already recognised the existence of problems that manifest themselves in economic terms. At a minimum, debtors can benefit from learning more about the market-based economy in which we live, recognising that not all debtors end up where they did due to fiscal mismanagement or poor budgetary skills. This latter point is an important one. The value of financial literacy education is not contingent upon a perfect match between a debtor's level of financial literacy and the cause of that debtor's bankruptcy filing. The debtor has landed in financial distress and that fact alone makes learning about the world of money, credit and debt particularly useful and timely. As detailed below, the very filing for bankruptcy creates a learning opportunity.

Moreover, loss of money is a sign of failure in our society. Money, at least in the United States, is the language of exchange. Since the presence of money defines who we are, so does its absence. Indeed, a lack of money creates a type of aphasia.[16] Debtors are, in a very real sense, cut off from the language we speak because they cannot participate meaningfully in our commercial marketplace. The filing of a bankruptcy is an overt recognition of one's failure at life's major game—at least in America. It is also a very public act since bankruptcy filings are a matter of public record and, soon, all bankruptcy filings (and the accompanying plethora of financial data) will be available online.[17] As such, filing for bankruptcy creates, in the parlance of educators and psychologists, a

[14] Questions can also be raised about the quality and cost of the programming to be offered pre-bankruptcy. Since debtors remain remarkably easy targets for abusive schemes (see, eg the experience with bankruptcy preparers and debt consolidators), a massive development of financial counselling for all potential debtors is problematic—in terms of feasibility, quality and cost.

[15] M Toussaint-Comeau and S Rhine, 'Delivery of Financial Literacy Programs', *Policy Studies, Consumer Issues Research Services* (Federal Reserve Bank of Chicago, December, 2000) 3–6.

[16] See M Albert and A Velez, 'Aphasia Therapy Research Update' (1999) 11 *National Aphasia Association Newsletter* <http://www.aphasia.org/newsletter/112aphasiatherapy.html> (visited: 13 October 2002).

[17] See P Alexander, 'Thinking About Private Matters in Public Documents: Bankruptcy Privacy in an Electronic Age' (2001) 75 *American Bankruptcy Journal* 437; 'Privacy and Access to Electronic Case Files in Federal Courts', *Administrative Office, the Judicial Conference of the US Courts* <www.uscourts.gov/privacyn.pdf> (visited: 12 December 2002).

'teachable' moment;[18] debtors are an audience in need. Even if the reasons for debtors filing are vastly different from each other (involving a complex intersection of endogenous and exogenous factors), all debtors can benefit from a well-constructed financial management course. They can all use information on the issues about how our credit economy functions. They can all use information about common schemes and abuses to which they may be subjected following bankruptcy. They can all benefit from hearing the stories of others who are similarly situated. A debtor education programme then would offer both substantive and emotive material. A medical analogy is useful. Consider the disease diabetes. Clearly, education about eating habits and proper medication is important to control the disease. However, if someone with the disease has a disease-related crisis, perhaps additional teaching at that moment (obviously, once the medical emergency has passed) would be particularly productive—even if the crisis was not precipitated by a complete lack of knowledge.

Why we should help consumer debtors also relates to and is rooted in larger issues of a society's interest in and willingness to help those who are less privileged. In recent times, social safety nets have been contracting, and there has been increased emphasis on looking to the private sector for support for those less fortunate.[19] Bankruptcy is a form of social safety net for failures that manifest themselves in economic terms.[20] An educational programme for those who seek that relief is a way of empowering debtors prospectively. Rather than simply moving debtors through the bankruptcy system, enabling them to obtain a legal fresh start, we should focus on giving them a true fresh start.[21] This means enabling debtors to function more effectively. While some want to focus on this issue as a means of curtailing bankruptcy recidivism, I am more interested in rehabilitating debtors so they can function more effectively in society—in their homes, their workplaces, their communities (all of which also have clear economic benefits). Because debtors do not live in isolation, if we can assist debtors, we can probably also assist their families. Moreover, if a debtor starts to feel

[18] See R Tharp and R Galimore, *Rousing Minds To Life: Teaching, Learning, and Schooling in Social Context* (Cambridge, Ohio Press, 1991); S Osteen and T Auberle, 'Homebuyer Education: A Doorway to Financial Literacy' (2002) 94 *Journal of Family & Consumer Sciences* 29.

[19] See A Bullock, 'Taxes, Social Policy and Philanthropy: The Untapped Potential of Middle and Low Income Generosity' (1997) 6 *Cornell Journal of Law and Public Policy* 325; J Wolpert, 'What Charity Can and Cannot Do; The Impact of the Contract With America' (New York, Twentieth Century Fund, 1996). See also R Chami and C Fullenkamp, 'Should Subsidised Private Transfers Replace Social Insurance?' *Social Science Research Networ Working Papers* <http://papers.ssrn.com/sol3/papers.cfm?abstract_id=76028> (visited: 21 October 2002) (arguing that socialised insurance programmes are no longer tenable in the modern economy and advocating a privately-based solution).

[20] See K Gross, *Failure and Forgiveness* (New Haven, CT, Yale University Press, 1997) at 91–103; M Jacoby and T Sullivan, 'Medical Problems and Bankruptcy Filings' *West's Bankruptcy Newsletter* (21 May 2000); T Sullivan and E Warren, 'From Golden Years to Bankrupt Years' (1998) 7 *Norton Bankruptcy Law Advisor* 1; N Martin, 'Fee Shifting in Bankruptcy: Deterring Frivolous, Fraud Based Objections to Discharge' (1997) 76 *North Carolina Law Review* 97 at 113–115.

[21] This is a point that I explore in my book, above n 20, at 115–134.

better about him or herself, he or she will be a more effective parent, co-worker, spouse, neighbour and member of society.[22]

Debtor education can, then, operate at a variety of levels. It can provide debtors with substantive information about financial literacy—information that the general population would benefit from as well. It can provide concrete information specific to the bankruptcy system and how filing will affect the debtor's future. It can also operate at the level of psychology. Psychologists have long observed, in a wide range of contexts, that individuals who have an external locus of control feel less responsible for their lives; they are less in control, less emotionally stable, and less able to handle life's common struggles. To my mind,[23] one of the central goals of debtor education and one that has been shown —at least in a small scale effort—to be achievable,[24] should be to shift the debtor's economic locus of control from external to internal. If debtors feel more in control of their economic futures, then they will behave more responsibly when confronted with financial choices and they will feel differently about themselves and their situation. Stated differently, debtor education has an empowerment capability that should not be ignored.

There are a number of ways in which a debtor education programme can help re-locate the economic locus of control of the debtor. The imparting of specific, concrete knowledge is one such way. Another way is informing debtors of things they can do themselves, such as writing to debt collectors to get them to cease and desist, correcting credit reports, taking steps to improve credit scores, challenging erroneous bills, reporting creditor contact post-discharge and comparing credit offers. Providing psychological support through, for example, live group discussions where debtors can share their experiences (rather than providing videotaped programmes or telephone meetings) are additional avenues to pursue. Moreover, one could then empirically assess—as the Coalition is doing—whether a debtor education programme shifted the locus of economic control, both long -term and short-term.

[22] See S Barsdale, 'The Ripple Effect: Emotional Contagion In <http://papers.ssrn.com/abstract=250894> (visited: 21 October 2002).

[23] I am particularly interested, in terms of my own scholarly interests, in Furnham's observations about how men and women differ in terms of the economic locus of control. As stated, '. . . [F]emales more than males . . . tended to rate the power of chance as determinants of both wealth and poverty more highly . . . The fact that some people . . . believe that both wealth and poverty are uncontrollable . . . may explain aspects of the (somewhat irrational) behavior on the part of certain groups . . . [I]t may explain the low incidence of savings or any form of financial planning on the part of poorer people.' A Furnham, 'Economic Locus of Control' (1986) 39 *Human Relations* 29, citing P Spector, 'Behaviour as a Function of Employees' Locus of Control' (1982) 91 *Psychological Bulletin* 482; K Gross, 'Portraits of Grief; A Focus on Survivors' (2002–2003) 46 *New York Law School Law Review* 631.

[24] See P Stokes and S Polansky, 'Shifting the Economic Locus of Control: Improving Financial Decision-Making in High Risk Populations'(1999) 3 *Academy of Accounting and Financial Studies Journal* 95. The study looked at whether a debtor education programme for Chapter 13 debtors shifted the external locus of control based on Furnham's questionnaire. Even though the course was short in duration (three hours), there was a statistically significant shift from external to internal attribution.

Let me make one final observation. Debtor education, as I conceptualise it and as it has been implemented in the Coalition's pilot project described below, is premised on a belief that debtors are not deviants and that poor credit habits are not a form of social or psychological pathology. Neither is debtor education a form of punishment for those who have failed to fulfil societal norms, like programmes such as drunk-driving school. Instead, debtor education operates from the premise that the playing field of debt and credit is not level; creditors have vastly greater sophistication and knowledge than their consumer counterparts. So, financial literacy education is intended to help level that playing field. As such, it views the participants as individuals fully capable of acquiring knowledge and then using that knowledge to make better financial choices. The Coalition's financial literacy programme endorses the opposite of a deviance or punishment model; it operates from an empowerment model.

At some level, all education has a paternalistic/maternalistic quality. Someone or some organisation is determining what should be learned and how it should be learned. No educational offering is, in truth, value-neutral. That said, the Coalition's debtor education programme is not intended to be doctrinaire, forcing a world -view favouring either consumption or saving onto the participants. Instead, the programme is intended to alert participants to information and ideas that they may not have known or thought about—at least in any systematic way. Phrased differently, all educational offerings are to some extent value-driven, but we are still better off providing some education than providing no education (thereby eliminating the risk of value inculcation).

III. THE SIZE OF THE PLATTER: THE PRAGMATICS OF PROGRAMME DEVELOPMENT

Debtor education, once we move beyond the basic theoretical justifications, raises a plethora of implementation issues. In addition to the normally difficult choices that must be made in structuring any educational offering, the politics of the bankruptcy system and its administration, the sociological profile of consumer debtors, and the psychological dimensions of money and over-indebtedness also play a role. To develop these issues, I have divided the topic of debtor educational programme development into ten categories: Audience, Course Structure, Course Content, Delivery Mechanisms, Teacher Training, Diversity Concerns, Empirical Assessment, Funding and Financing, Follow-up and Rewards and How to Begin Initially. Within each category, I have identified the key questions to be asked and then have provided some of my own answers, observations, and concerns. These latter comments are intended to highlight the political, sociological, and psychological impediments to implementing debtor education programmes, recognising that this discussion is meant only to further, not conclude, debate about education in general and financial literacy education in particular.

A. Audience

The Questions: Who should receive the debtor financial literacy education: all consumer debtors on a mandatory basis or 'only' those debtors who voluntarily participate? If participation is voluntary, how many debtors will receive the proffered education, and what variables will account for differing participation levels? Will a single programme work for debtors in Chapters 7 and 13, or should there be different educational programming for those liquidating and those reorganising?[25] How will programme attendance be 'policed' or promoted? Should family members and significant others be allowed or encouraged to join the debtor in the programme offerings?

Some Answers/Concerns: There are a variety of bases upon which to support voluntary education: it is more consistent with concepts of adult learning, which suggest that voluntary adult learners are more motivated to learn new materials than those required to attend a class;[26] it is less paternalistic; it will be easier to implement as there will be fewer debtors in attendance, at least initially; and it will not be linked to the bankruptcy discharge and thereby lead to forced attendance as the price for the benefits of bankruptcy.

That said, the experience of the Coalition has been that voluntary attendance of debtors in high numbers is difficult to achieve and is an immensely time-consuming effort. A number of unrelated factors may contribute to low enrolments. It worries me that the individuals who can most benefit from the education may not be those who choose to attend the classes.[27] This means that the educational offering, while hopefully helpful to those who receive it, may not benefit an important segment of the population that could use the education. If home pressures, job pressures, social conditioning, fear of unfamiliar settings or unknown education providers, language and educational barriers and absence of time are among the key factors militating in favour of or against debtor attendance at classes,[28] the most vulnerable may not attend, thereby undermining the value of the programming. Attendance may improve (although there will be added administrative costs) if family members (including children) are invited and

[25] A combined programme could also include individual debtors filing under Chapters 11 and 12.

[26] See 'Lessons From the Trenches', above n 1, at 523. In a forthcoming article, Gary Neustader is extremely critical of mandatory education, suggesting that it is unlikely to reduce recidivism, will be difficult to implement and raises vast questions in terms of the need for and implementation difficulties of non-English programming. (contact the author to obtain a copy of this article at kgross@nyls.edu).

[27] See P Stokes, 'Bankruptcy Reform and Education—Research on Debtor Education Programmes' (2000) 46 *Consumer Interests Annual* 2. Stokes suggests that classes should be mandatory because '. . . the reasons for non-attendance are the same ones that [brought about] their financial problems—avoiding 'uncomfortable' topics, blaming 'others' for their situation, procrastination . . . and so forth.'

[28] At present, I am only speculating as to the contributing factors regarding enrolment. Indeed, it is easier to assess why some debtors attend than to capture empirically why others do not attend. For a discussion of relevant factors, see 'Lessons From the Trenches', above n 1, at 517–18; 'Delivery of Financial Literacy Programs', above n 15, at 6.

encouraged to attend. Providing the education in familiar settings with invitations to attend from familiar and trusted providers may improve the situation. It is likely that the Coalition's studies will be able to provide some guidance on these questions. But, it is critical to recognise immediately that the basis of participation affects other choices, like the amount of time and effort that must be extended to market programmes to the intended participants.

B. Course Structure

The Questions: How long should the programme run realistically (as opposed to idealistically)—a few hours, more than one session? How large should the class sizes be, and should the format be interactive work as opposed to 'lecture' material? What materials (type, kind and length) should be made available to debtors before, during and after the course? Should debtors have 'homework' to do at home before, during, or after the course?
The Answers/Comments: One of the keys to the success of a debtor education programme is attention to adult pedagogy.[29] This means that there must be an opportunity for interaction and small group work regardless of the size of the group. A pure lecture for several hours (the proverbial 'talking heads' approach) will not work for debtor education. Moreover, 'experts' speaking to (not with) non-experts is problematic in that it hardens the hierarchy between those who know and those who do not. Instead, active and participatory learning should be encouraged, which is consistent with the empowerment focus of financial literacy education.

Moreover, the debtor educator needs to recognise the difficulty of the material for many people. This difficulty operates at several levels. First, participants need to address topics that are not inherently easy: largely law-based topics that involve numbers and unfamiliar vocabulary and concepts. But, of equal importance, the participants need to be open to the learning, and learning, talking, and dealing with money is difficult for many people. As the money therapist, Olivia Mellan, has pointed out to me, for some over-spenders, just the use of the word 'budget' feels constricting even before one has turned to addressing how to create and maintain a budget.

Although more rather than less classroom time seems better, there are a number of competing concerns. Adults can only learn so much in one sitting. Debtors have little time in many instances, between work and family. Moreover, travel time to and from classes, as well as safety concerns in terms of evening travel, must be taken into account. If the Coalition experience is transportable, then getting debtors to attend more than one class will confound the already difficult problem of getting them to attend just one class. One option to

[29] For a useful summary of adult learning approaches and strategies, see G Hess and S Friedland, *Techniques For Teaching Law* (Durham, NC, Carolina Academic Press, 1999) 3–19.

consider is prospective feedback that does not require physical presence—written materials sent to the debtor's home, interactive websites for those with computer access and telephone dialogues.

C. Course Content

The Questions: What should be the core content of a debtor education curriculum, particularly one that, in its development, would not be beholden to any single interest group? Should a debtor education programme focus on financial literacy skills and information only, and, if so, what particular skills and information? At what reading level should the programme be pitched? Should the course also seek to explore and change a debtor's attitude toward money, spending, savings and finance? Should there be a dissemination of information about the bankruptcy process itself? Should there be a dissemination of information about legal rights and responsibilities following bankruptcy (discharge, anti-discrimination provisions, post-discharge scams and abuses)? In allocating time among these subject areas, how much time should be spent on attitudinal versus substantive issues or can they be addressed together?

Some Answers/Concerns: Interestingly, there is no paucity of materials addressing financial literacy issues; the problem is, rather, in selecting among the various materials given the lack of classroom time for teaching about the world of money. The Coalition selected seven key subject areas to address in its three-hour course, with full knowledge that these topics could not be covered in extensive depth in the time allotted. The topics are: Understanding the Nature of Buying and Spending, Goal Setting (long- and short-term), Developing a Spending Plan (budgeting), Credit and Interest, Common Consumer Scams, Credit Reporting and Credit Scoring and Future Resources. These topics reflect a conscious effort to include attitudinal material together with substantive material, recognising that one without the other can impede the learning process.

The Coalition has, quite rightly in my view, shied away from providing legal advice regarding the bankruptcy system and the bankruptcy process. Other programmes, particularly those offered by Chapter 13 trustees, provide vastly greater information about bankruptcy, in part to respond to the lack of information that debtors receive from their counsel and in recognition of the relatively large number of pro se debtor filings.[30] While I appreciate that all debtors are not well-represented and may lack information about the legal process they have just entered, for me the goal of the provided education should be the acquisition of greater financial acumen. I would rather spend the limited time available understanding why a single point difference in interest rates over the term of a five-year loan can make a huge economic difference rather than focusing on

[30] For a detailed account of these programmes, see the authorities cited above n 5.

what happens at a Section 341 meeting or how to respond to an objection to discharge.[31]

As difficult as issues of curricula are, they should not preoccupy planners because, at least to my mind, almost any choice of quality material is better than nothing. There is enough material to provide a 12 hour course, and, hence, the debtor educators need to pick and choose among the materials. What matters vastly more than content is how the material is taught and delivered—two issues of far greater impact and complexity than coverage. Indeed, while imparting certain information is key, the level of need for information is so great that any information delivered is valuable. The potential curricula is sufficiently rich that it can be used both for bankrupt debtor and non-bankrupt audiences, although in some instances it would need to be simplified and in others it would need to be developed in greater depth. If one were able to divine which particular debtors were attending a particular class session, one could choose to emphasise some material and de-emphasise other material based on the attendees' background and baseline knowledge. However, that type of fine tuning is difficult to manage on a regular basis.

D. Delivery Mechanisms

The Questions: How should whatever programme that is developed be delivered to debtors across the country in a way that insures that a quality, low-cost programme is available to all those who want it? How can certain groups of debtors be reached, and should different marketing approaches and strategies be employed (mailings, community or grass roots efforts or advertisements) for different debtors? When should the course be offered and in what type of setting? What kind of childcare needs to be available? Should there be food, parking and transportation?

The Answers/Comments: This particular category raises the most difficult and challenging issues. Stated most simply, the best programme is useless without an adequate delivery mechanism. As those who have worked on community economic development know, reaching the targeted audience is a hard task,[32] rendered all the more complex with non-homogeneous populations (such as debtors). Indeed, in some geographic environments, simply finding a place to offer debtor education is difficult due to lack of public transportation, distance, terrain and family considerations. By way of example, the Coalition's programme covers a wide geographic area, and individuals living on the tip of Long

[31] 11 USC §§341(a), 727(c). This is not to suggest that the legal issues are unimportant. But, it is to suggest that the handling of these issues is best left to others.

[32] *Economic Development Update, RACE to the Top in Generating Community Support,* (Institute for Decision Making, Spring, 1999). A recent study examined some ways to overcome these obstacles through the use of creative marketing. For instance, a heavily advertised seminar on 'wealth building' had over 2, 500 attendees: 'Delivery of Financial Services', above n 15, at 6.

Island are not going to travel into downtown Brooklyn to take a debtor education course as travel time alone could exceed two hours one way. In addition to just travel time, the new location is also unfamiliar.

My experience with debtors thus far makes one thing clear: debtors need to feel comfortable getting to and being in the place where the course is offered. Familiar locations are vastly better than the unknown where just getting to the right place is a task unto itself. In addition, certain types of space carry baggage. For example, holding the classes in the courthouse or in the rooms designated for formal meetings with creditors is not ideal since too many negative associations are made with the space itself. By way of analogy to the medical arena, a classroom right outside the hospital emergency room may not be the best location to teach kids with diabetes about ways of preventing sudden attacks. It would be vastly better to find a less charged location, a location that does not carry so many messages. To borrow a phrase from Tony Hiss, 'experience of place' matters.[33]

In addition to ease of access and familiarity, the Coalition is studying what actually brings debtors into the class. There is no single easy answer to programm delivery. No one system will work everywhere. However, it has become clear that a programme can and does build momentum and there are multiple variables, which likely work together, that serve to get debtors to attend the voluntary classes that the Coalition offers. Notices from the court or postings on a wall are not enough to get debtors to attend financial management classes. Non-court based mailings are more effective. Incentives such as food, gifts and certificates of completion may help. The trained debtor educators described below can play a central role in improving attendance, as can working with intermediaries (parties who regularly work with debtors in a capacity of trust). In addition, information delivered through the 'official actors' overseeing the bankruptcy process (Chapter 13 trustees or Chapter 7 panel trustees in the US) adds credibility. Importantly, the Coalition's insights into delivery mechanisms have implications beyond debtor education: they can inform others seeking to implement community outreach programmes.

E. Teacher Training

The Questions: What types of individuals should be selected to teach the programme? Can they be drawn from vastly different backgrounds: lawyers, accountants, teachers, community development leaders, financial planners and bankers? Is diversity among teachers a benefit to the programme? Should a debtor's lawyer teach his/her own clients or does that raise a conflicts problem? How will the selected teachers be trained, and how will they be monitored on an ongoing basis? Would the teachers benefit from some type of mentoring

[33] T Hiss, *The Experience of Place* (New York, Knopf, 1990).

programme? How will the educators be paid? How will class scheduling be handled?

The Answers/Concerns: Unlike programmes for the debtors, it is vastly easier to develop and conduct a quality teacher training programme. Although these programmes have numerous components, I want to focus on one aspect here: teaching to a diverse audience of potential debtor educators. Although I believe that qualified debtor educators can be drawn from a wide pool, it is key first to acknowledge such diversity and then to adapt strategies to address it in the teacher training programme. Some attendees will be vastly more comfortable with the substantive material but inexperienced in speaking before large audiences. Other attendees may have experience dealing with students but lack a comfort level with the material to be taught. Stated differently, every new debtor educator is likely to have an area of concern. That is why the Coalition has now developed and has currently implemented a Debtor Education Mentor Programme which pairs new debtor educators with an experienced mentor who can assist them one-on-one with a variety of issues ranging from how to conduct a class to answering questions about the substance of what is taught.[34] The Mentoring Programme also allows ongoing feedback between the debtor educator and the sponsoring organisation, which enables there to be continuous feedback about the debtor education programme itself. The overarching theme here is to establish a training programme that produces a highly qualified group of trained debtor educators.

F. Addressing Diversity Concerns

The Questions: How should the debtor education programme account for regional differences across the US? How should the programme address ethnic, racial and demographic differences among debtors? How should the programme address different languages spoken by debtors? How should the programme address the different educational levels of debtors? Should the programme be targeted and specifically adapted for specific subgroups of debtors such as women, minorities, the elderly and students?

The Answers/Comments: In the US, dealing with diversity is not a choice but a necessity, and this ratchets up the complexity of any debtor education programme. Just take the issue of multiple languages. First, all the written materials need to be translated into the languages in question, recognising that within a given language there are regional differences which means that even the 'best' translation is not going to work perfectly for all recipients. Second, there is the problem of actually holding classes in different languages, ensuring that the teacher speaks the relevant language and that all of the attendees who attend a

[34] A copy of the Mentoring Programme is available upon request to the author at kgross@nyls.edu.

particular session are correctly matched in terms of language. Finally, there is the necessary follow-up, including access to website materials—some of which may not be in the relevant language, at least initially. In sum, in countries with populations with many languages and a need for courses in more than one language, there are significant pragmatic issues to be addressed in the effort to capture as wide an audience as feasible.

Issues of diversity extend well beyond language. Given the complexities of people's backgrounds, they come to the classes with very different experiences with respect to money and finance. For example, for those who are recent immigrants from nations with non-market based economies, there can be a distrust of a formal banking system and an inclination toward using local and informal lending options, some of which are unregulated. For these individuals, cashing a cheque at the corner store in their neighbourhood feels vastly safer than proceeding to an established bank. For some debtors, borrowing money through a pay-day lender or obtaining goods through a rent-to-own store is more comfortable than obtaining a credit card or entering a mainstream bank to request a loan or even a bank account. For some debtors, cash—not credit—is the norm. Sensitivity to these issues is of critical importance and a course must not be judgemental. Pay-day lending (borrowing at high rates using future wages as security) can and should be explained without 'looking down' on those who have used that service.

G. Empirical Assessment

The Questions: How should the 'success' of a debtor education programme be defined and once so defined, evaluated empirically both short and long term? What specific assessment devices should be used to evaluate the programme? What type of ongoing monitoring should be in place to update and modify the programme prospectively? Should debtors be required to consent to ongoing monitoring of their financial lives prospectively?

The Answers/Comments: Without ongoing empirical assessments, it is difficult to determine whether the costs of debtor education offset its benefits. As the Coalition's efforts demonstrate, debtor education is expensive—in person power and dollars—for students and teachers alike. What needs to be determined is whether the effort is justified. The Coalition has conducted two major studies: one looked at the education provided to debtors and whether it changed debtors' knowledge, attitude, beliefs and behaviour with respect to money, while the other looked at the effect and effectiveness of the teacher training programme. The most difficult issue in study design is what, precisely, to measure. If the 'wrong' thing is studied, we will not have good evidence as to whether the education was worthwhile. For example, if one studied whether financial management courses alleviated bankruptcy recidivism and it was demonstrated that education had no identifiable effect on that issue, would one conclude that debtor education is not worth doing? Perhaps, in focusing on recidivism, one missed things that debtor education did accomplish, such as improving the debtor's ability to avoid scams.

H. Funding and Financing

The Questions: How can a debtor education programme be funded and financed over the short and long term? If debtors are required to pay a fee, what dollar amount is acceptable and what sort of *in forma pauperis* assistance will be available? How and how much will the teachers be paid? If a pilot programme is proposed, how would it be funded?
The Answers/Comments: Using the Coalition's efforts in the Eastern District of New York as a gauge, it is clear that, absent considerable funding or a huge outpouring of volunteers and in-kind services, a nationwide educational effort will not succeed. Once the pilot project has been completed, the Coalition plans to release the per debtor costs of the programme, taking into account the numerous in-kind contributions that were made in addition to a significant grant and ongoing corporate and individual fund-raising. When that figure is released, there needs to be some hard discussions regarding who pays for the benefit. One thought on that: if the cost is foisted on the individual debtor (rather than creditors or the government), then there is the clear prospect that some debtors will not be able to afford the same quality or education as other debtors. The goal has to be to provide quality, low cost financial literacy education for all debtors, not superior education for those debtors who can afford it and inferior education for the others.

I. Follow-up and Rewards

The Questions: What type of follow-up can be provided to debtors? What type of legending could be placed on credit reports? What effect could debtor education have on credit scoring? What type of certificate could debtors receive and what type of materials could debtors obtain through the programme (magazine subscriptions, computer programmes, books, credit reports, or gifts)?
The Answers/Comments: If one of the goals of the financial literacy education is to make a debtor more comfortable with and more knowledgeable about money, then some form of reward (in addition to personal satisfaction over course completion) is needed. Possibilities are restricted in many respects by costs. In a world of infinite resources, debtors could receive ongoing follow-up from the debtor educators (either in person or on-line), magazine subscriptions related to money issues, and additional classes on an 'as needed' basis. The Coalition awards each debtor who has completed the course a certificate and a small gift, with the gifts bearing a 'slogan' to tie them into the course.

For example, a slinky bears the motto, 'Spring Back to Financial Success.' A small keychain calculator reminds debtors to consider the costs before spending.

Another possible reward of significance is the possibility that, if it can it be shown that financial literacy education leads to greater consumer knowledge about money and credit, and consumer behaviour can be positively impacted by the education, credit reports and credit scores could reflect positively the completion of such education. Since credit reports and credit scores are the main vehicle for determining both the access to, and price of, credit that an individual receives, this would be an immensely appealing reward. However, it is a reward that is difficult to obtain. One needs to convince both the credit reporting agencies and those who prepare the credit scores to factor in completion of a debtor education course. To date, there has been little willingness to do so. The impetus to do so, unless mandated through the legal system, will probably need to come through the creditors themselves, as they are the entities that economically support the reporting agencies and their scoring models. The credit reporting agencies are unlikely to give weight to financial literacy education if the creditors see no benefit to them arising from it.

So, there is the question of how to convince the creditors that credit reports and credit scoring models should be adjusted to reflect the receipt of financial education. There is a 'chicken and egg' aspect to this problem. If such an adjustment in scoring systems were made, it might well encourage debtors to participate in the educational offering, leading to improved debtor attendance at proffered programmes and perhaps changes in debtor attitudes and behaviour. However, if an adjustment to credit scores must await proof that behaviourial changes result from completion of courses (and the quantum of needed proof is yet another level of complexity), then the key issue is getting debtors to the classes and demonstrating that the learned skills produce debtors who are more likely to repay. If there is resistance to making adjustments, regardless of the outcomes of empirical assessments, then one needs to at least question whether creditors truly want more knowledgeable consumers. In a perverse way, creditors actually benefit from debtor ignorance in that the creditors can charge such consumers vastly more money in the credit marketplace.

J. How to Begin

The Questions: Should a pilot programme be utilised before there is nationwide implementation? If a pilot project is appropriate, what size pilot should be developed and for what duration? Should a new programme, even if mandatory, be ramped-up to facilitate implementation?
The Answers/Comments: The Coalition's pilot project has indicated the value of moving slowly and of proceeding carefully and cautiously. There are far too many issues to launch a nationwide mandatory programme if one is trying to

ensure excellence and low cost.[35] It seems vastly better to think through the issues—curriculum, teacher training and delivery —sooner rather than later. Indeed, what is the rush? We have lived without adequate financial literacy training for decades. Why not pause long enough to give ourselves the best shot at getting it right?

Some of the foregoing issues seemingly involve pure pragmatics—relating to both the content and delivery of a debtor education programme. But, as those in the bankruptcy arena are well aware, the markedly differing perspectives on consumer debtor/creditor issues could lead to markedly different visions of a debtor education programme. Underlying all of these issues are broader, more philosophical questions relating to the degree to which support for those less privileged should be paid for by the government and/or the private sector (including debtors themselves and creditors). Also implicated are questions of how we want to treat those who are less privileged in our society. These are all tough issues and, hence, achieving accord on the general notion of debtor education is just the beginning. The next steps will make us truly wrestle with our vision of debtors, creditors, the bankruptcy system and society.

IV. CONCLUSION

If debtor education programmes are to succeed nationwide, indeed worldwide, we need to look beyond platitudes. We need to look at and then address the myriad of issues raised by such programme development. We also need to think about the commitment we are willing to make, as nations, to those who have lost one of contemporary society's key commodities: money. Debtor education is a very good idea and agreeing with it, at least in concept, is easy. It is the development, implementation, study, and follow-up that are hard, and it is these issues which should now capture our time and attention.

[35] 'Lessons From The Trenches', above n 1, at 523. The currently proposed legislation in the US contemplates—simultaneously—a mandatory programme and a pilot programme. HR 975, § 105–06, 108th US Congress (2003). And, to make matters worse, the pilot does not commence until after the mandatory programme is implemented, a seemingly backward result. See also 'Debtor Education', above n 2, at 6.

Index